Scott Foresman - Addison Wesley MATH

Problem-Solving Masters

Grade 1

Scott Foresman - Addison Wesley

Editorial Offices: Menlo Park, California • Glenview, Illinois
Sales Offices: Reading, Massachusetts • Atlanta, Georgia • Glenview, Illinois
Carrollton, Texas • Menlo Park, California

http://www.sf.aw.com

ISBN 0–201–31268–9

Printed in the United States of America

1 2 3 4 5 6 7 8 9 10 – BW – 02 01 00 99 98 97

Contents

Chapter 1: Numbers to 12 and Graphing

Chapter 2: Addition and Subtraction Readiness

Chapter 3: Addition and Subtraction Concepts

Chapter 4: Facts and Strategies to 12

Chapter 5: Geometry and Fractions

Chapter 6: More Fact Strategies

Chapter 7: Numbers to 60 and Counting Patterns

Chapter 8: Place Value

Chapter 9: Money

Chapter 10: Telling Time

Chapter 11: Measurement

Chapter 12: Facts and Strategies to 18

Chapter 13: Two-Digit Addition and Subtraction

Overview

The ***Problem-Solving Masters*** provide a variety of problem-solving opportunities designed to complement the student lesson.

For Learn lessons, the masters provide additional word problems similar to those on the Student Edition page or apply a problem-solving strategy previously learned. These strategies include the following:

Use Objects/Act It Out	Draw a Picture
Look for a Pattern	Guess and Check
Make a List	Use Logical Reasoning
Make a Table	Choosing Strategies

For Explore lessons, the masters extend the Talk About It questions, or provide a pattern activity related to the content of the Explore lesson.

For Problem-Solving lessons, the masters provide guided problem solving. The *Using the Page* section gives directions on how to use the master. This section also highlights one of the steps from the four-step Problem-Solving Guide: ***Understand, Plan, Solve,*** and ***Look Back.***

The ***Understand*** step asks questions about the *question* in the problem and the *data* provided.

The ***Plan*** step maps out a problem-solving strategy or approach. At times the master suggests a particular strategy or approach. Other times the master offers students choices of strategies, methods, or operations.

The ***Solve*** step prompts students to do the computation and then answer the question.

The ***Look Back*** step allows students to reflect on their answers and the strategy they used to solve the problem. It also encourages the students to consider the reasonableness of their answers.

Name ______________________________

Numbers 1, 2, 3

Put the ⚽ into groups.

Write how many. Then circle the number word.

1. How many  ?

   ______ one

   ______ two

   three

2. How many  ?

   ______ one

   ______ two

   three

3. How many ?

   ______ one

   ______ two

   three

4. How many ?

   ______ one

   ______ two

   three

5. How many ?

   ______ one

   ______ two

   three

6. How many ?

   ______ one

   ______ two

   three

Notes for Home Your child counted to 3, wrote the numbers 1, 2, and 3, and circled the number words to solve a problem. *Home Activity*: Ask your child to count groups of 1, 2, and 3 pennies, nickels, and dimes or other small objects that have been randomly arranged.

Name ______________________

Problem Solving
1-2

Numbers 4, 5, 6

Draw. Write how many in all.
Then circle the number word.

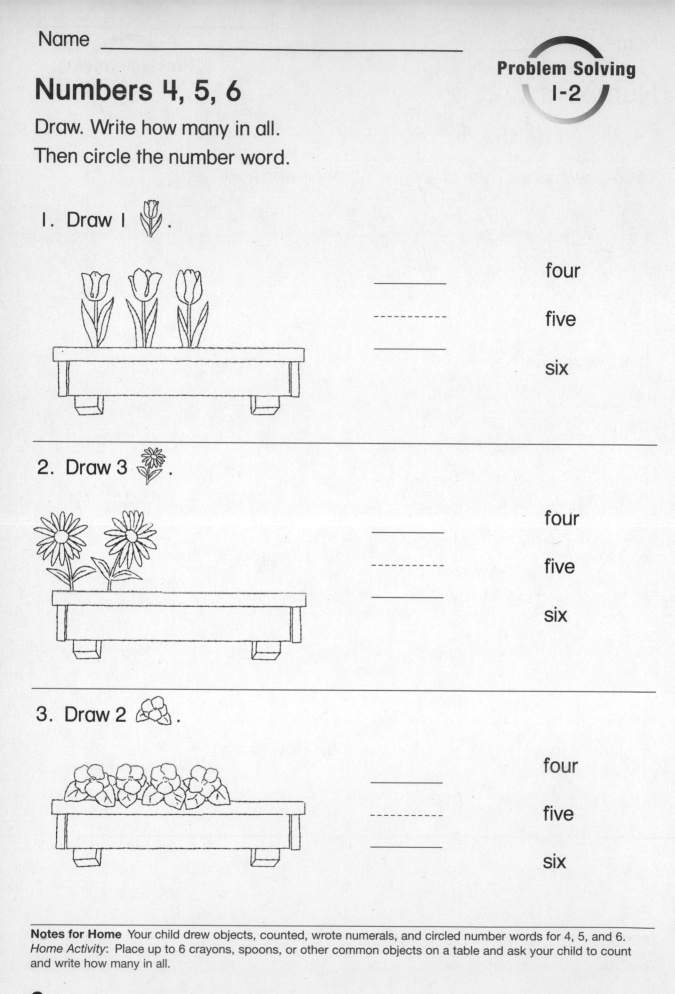

1. Draw 1 .

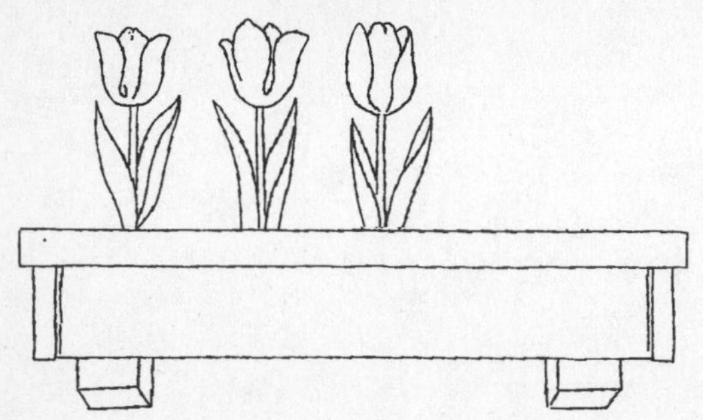

______ four

------ five

______ six

2. Draw 3 .

______ four

------ five

______ six

3. Draw 2 .

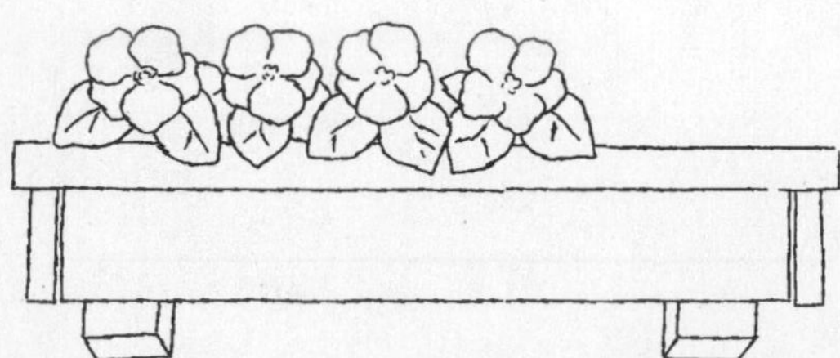

______ four

------ five

______ six

Notes for Home Your child drew objects, counted, wrote numerals, and circled number words for 4, 5, and 6. *Home Activity*: Place up to 6 crayons, spoons, or other common objects on a table and ask your child to count and write how many in all.

 Use with pages 5–6.

Name ______________________________

Numbers 7, 8, 9

Problem Solving
1-3

Solve.

1. How many ☂?

   Write how many. ______ ☂

2. How many children?

   Write how many. ______ children

3. How many 🐦?

   Write how many. ______ 🐦

4. How many 🗑?

   Write how many. ______ 🗑

5. Does each child have a 🪣? yes no

6. Draw a ⚽ for each child.

Notes for Home Your child counted objects in a picture and wrote 7, 8, and 9 to solve problems. *Home Activity:* Ask your child to count how many pails there are and write how many. (4 pails)

Name ______________________

Zero

Problem Solving 1-4

Every basket has apple, grapes, and orange.

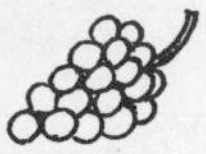

Some have bananas, too. Others have none.

Which have zero bananas? Write 0.

Which have bananas? Write how many.

1. ______ bananas	2. ______ bananas
3. ______ bananas	4. ______ bananas
5. ______ bananas	6. ______ bananas
7. ______ bananas	8. ______ bananas

9. How many baskets need bananas? ______

Notes for Home Your child recognized when to write 0. *Home Activity:* Ask your child what *zero* means. Then have him or her draw 1, 2, or 3 bananas in each basket with 0 bananas, and write the numeral to show how many.

Name ______________________________

Problem Solving
1-5

Numbers to Ten

Which groups show 10 △?

Write 10.

Then draw △ so each group has 10.

1.

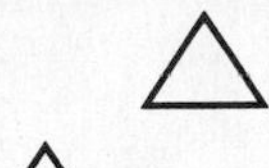

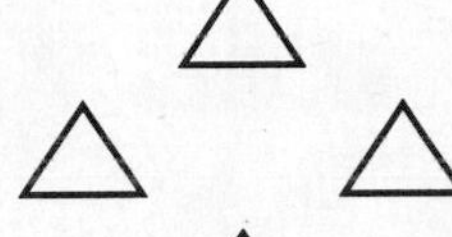

2.

3.

4.

5.

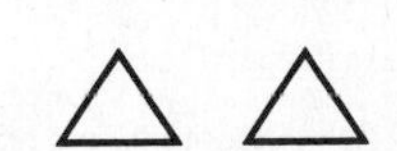

6.

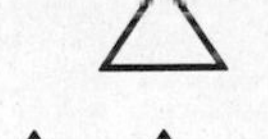

Notes for Home Your child counted up to 10. *Home Activity:* Ask your child to create a pattern by drawing 10 triangles.

Name ______________________________

Use Data from a Picture

Problem Solving
1-6

1. How many? Write the number.

2. How old is the birthday  ?

Using the Page Have children count the items in the picture and write the number below the respective picture. Have children explain how they determined the age of the birthday girl. Ask children to ***look back*** and color each group of items the same color and then count again. **Notes for Home** Your child counted objects in a picture to gather data. *Home Activity:* Ask your child to count the cups on the table. (9)

Name ______________________

Problem Solving
1-7

Explore More and Fewer

Draw some ♡.

Draw more △ than ♡.

Draw fewer ○ than ♡.

1. Look at the shapes. How many of each did you draw? Write the number.

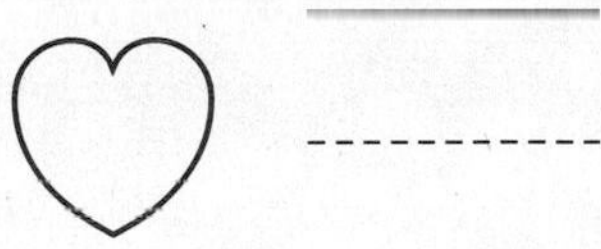

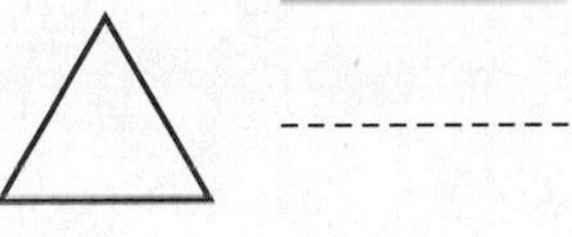

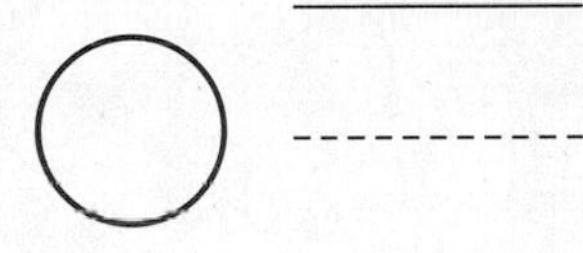

2. Complete each sentence. Write more or fewer.

There are ______ ♡ than ○.

There are ______ ○ than △.

There are ______ △ than ♡.

Notes for Home Your child drew groups of objects, recorded how many in each group, and then compared one group to another to determine which had more or fewer than the other. *Home Activity:* Have your child count to determine how many hearts and circles he or she drew in all. Then ask if he or she has more than, fewer than, or the same number of triangles as hearts and circles.

Name ______________________

Problem Solving
I-8

Order Numbers to 10

How many dots are in each circle?
Write the number.
Then draw a path in order from 0 to 10.

Count from 0 to 10 in your head.

Hint: There is more than one path.

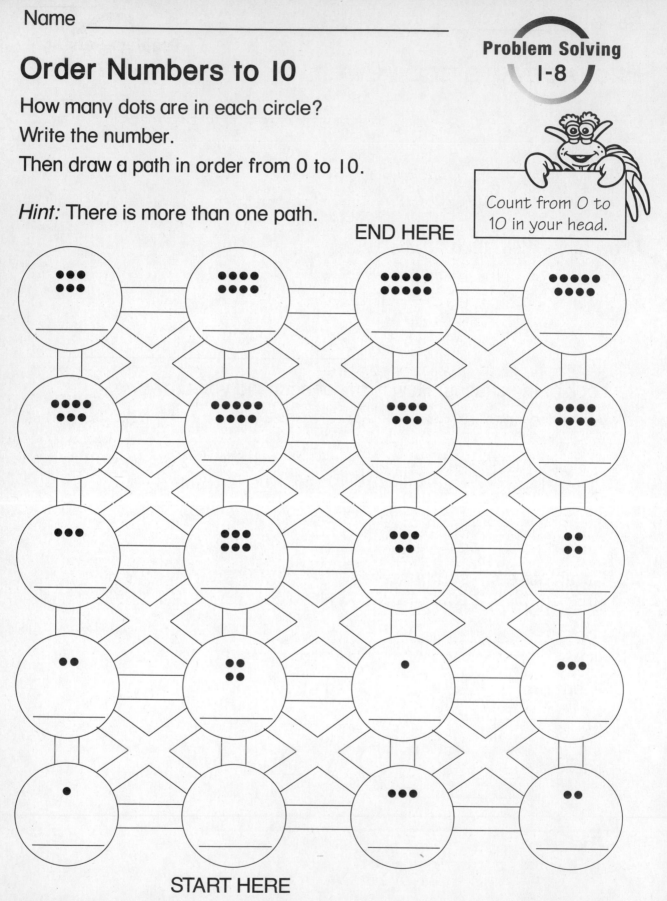

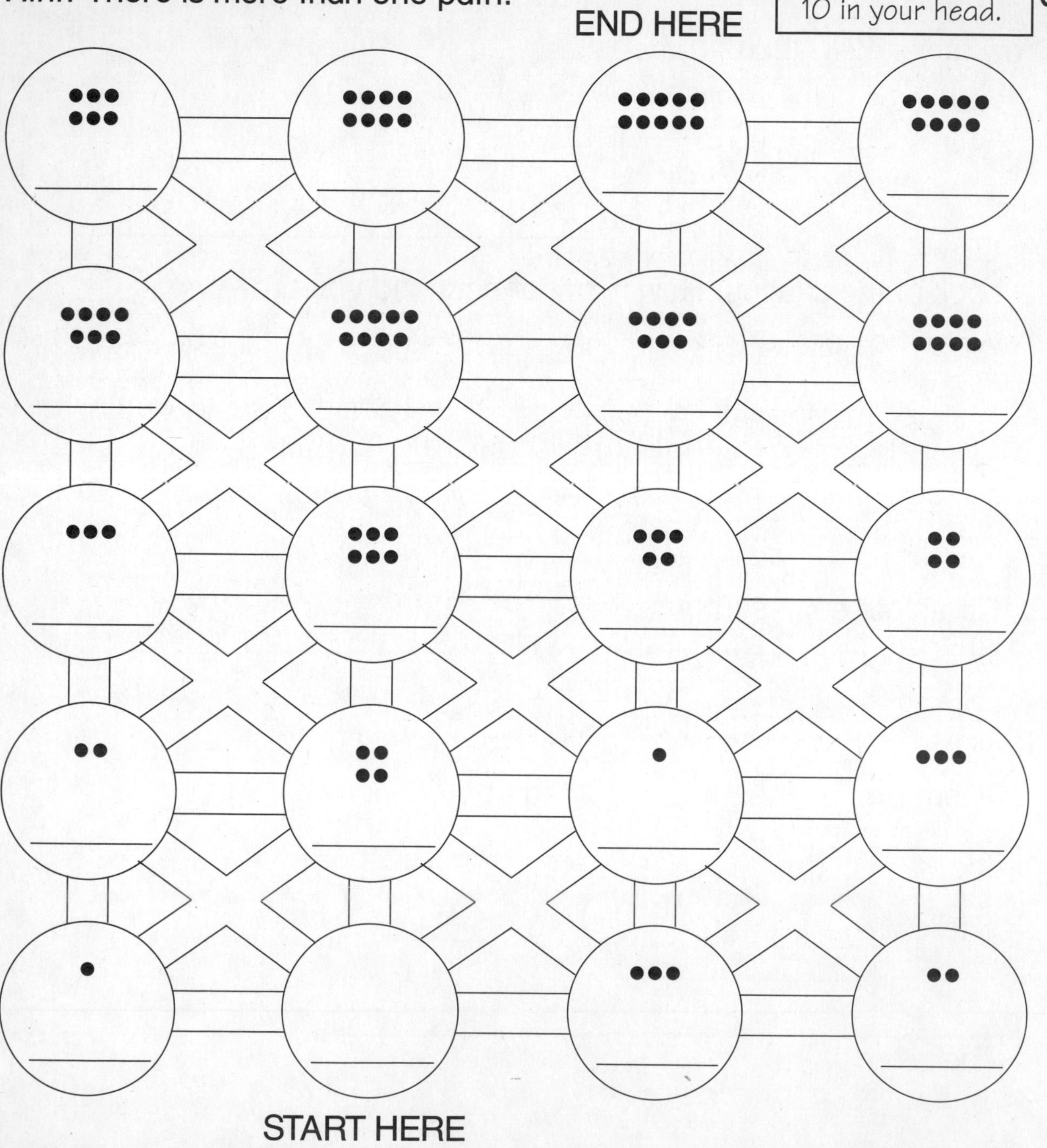

Notes for Home Your child ordered numbers through 10 to find a path. *Home Activity:* Ask your child to find and draw another path from 0 to 10.

Name ______________________

Understand 11 and 12

How many more ◯ must draw to show each number?

Help  draw ◯. Write each number.

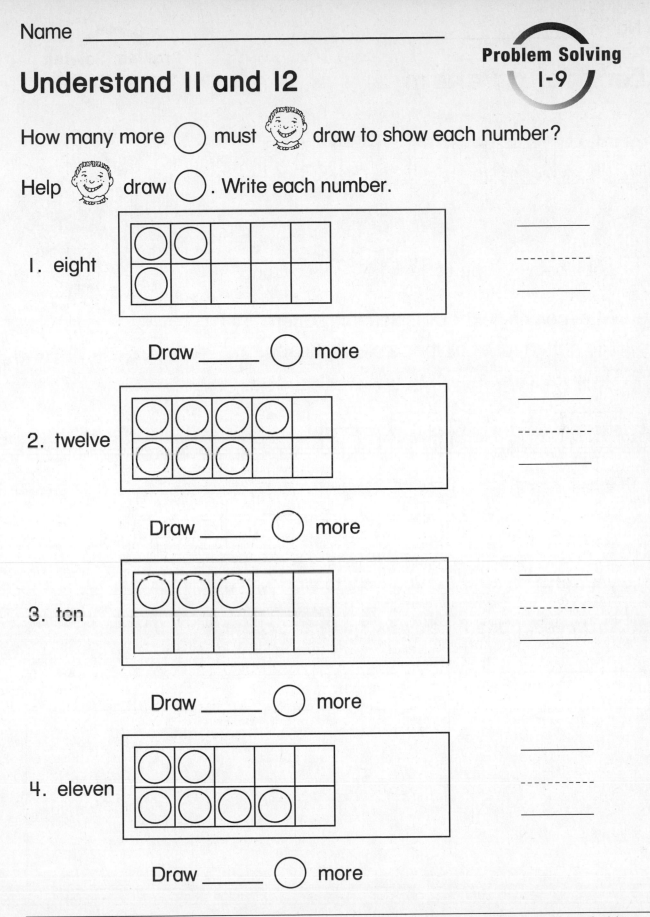

1. eight

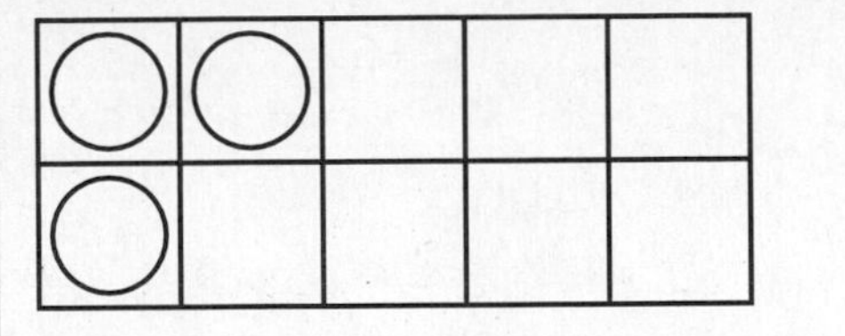

Draw ______ ◯ more

2. twelve

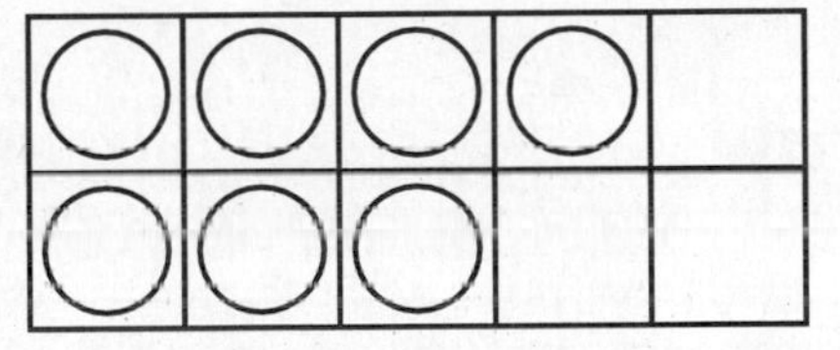

Draw ______ ◯ more

3. ten

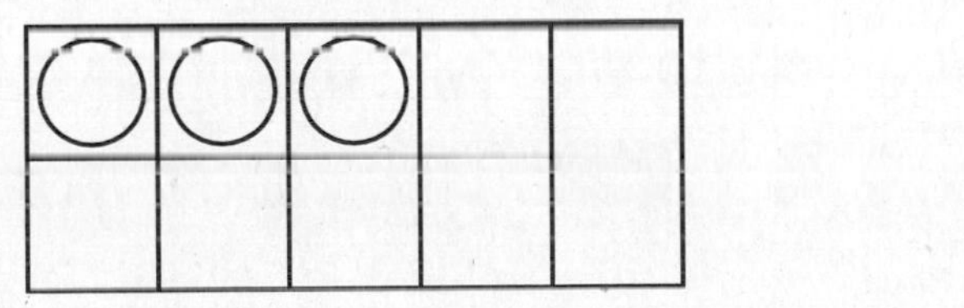

Draw ______ ◯ more

4. eleven

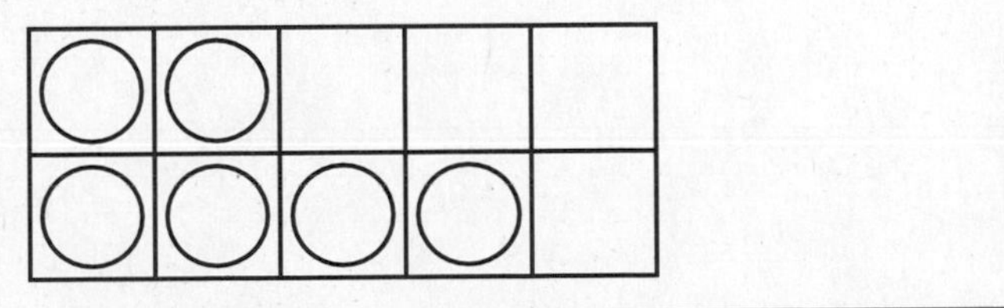

Draw ______ ◯ more

Notes for Home Your child counted to 12 and recognized and wrote the symbols for 11 and 12. *Home Activity:* Ask your child to show 11 and 12 another way. (10 and 1; 10 and 2)

Name ___________________________

Problem Solving
1-10

Look for a Pattern

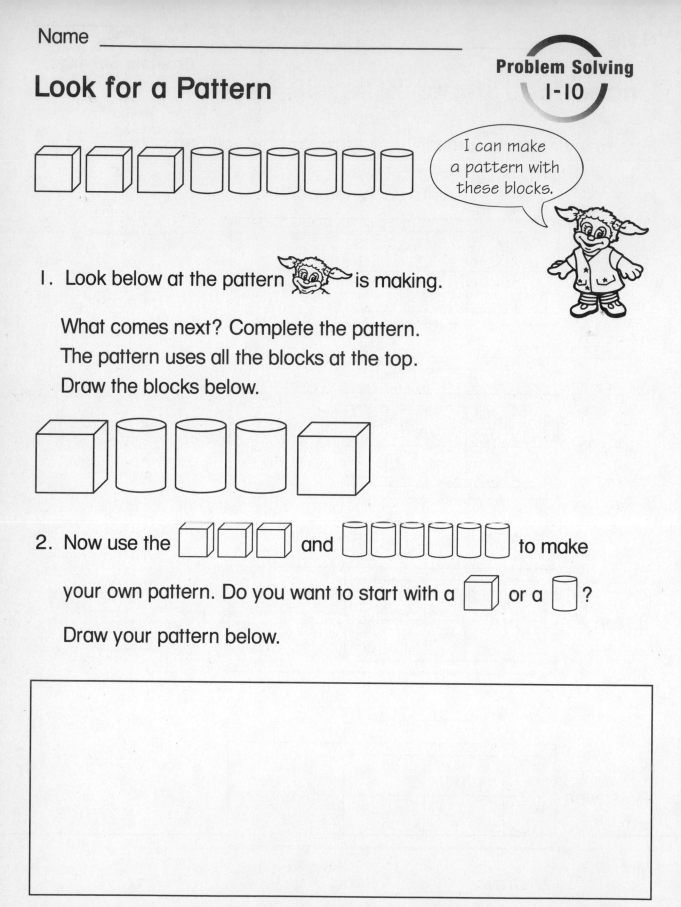

I can make a pattern with these blocks.

1. Look below at the pattern is making.

What comes next? Complete the pattern.
The pattern uses all the blocks at the top.
Draw the blocks below.

2. Now use the and to make your own pattern. Do you want to start with a or a ?

Draw your pattern below.

Using the Page Have children complete the pattern using all the remaining blocks. Help children to ***solve*** by asking them to describe the partially completed pattern, including the number of blocks that remain.
Notes for Home Your child discovered and completed a pattern and then created a different pattern, using the same blocks. *Home Activity:* Ask your child to tell how the patterns are the same and how they are different.

 Use with pages 27–28.

Name ______________________

Problem Solving
1-11

Explore Sorting and Classifying

Find the animal that belongs in each group. Draw a line to make a match. Then write the letter that tells about each group.

a. Kittens   b. Big Cats and Kittens   c. Big Cats with Stripes

1. ______

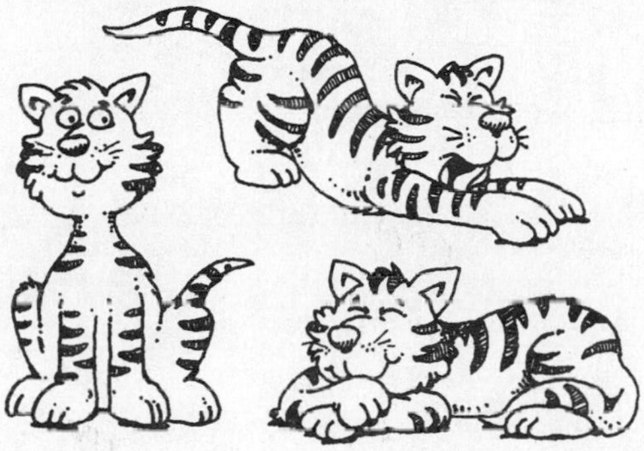

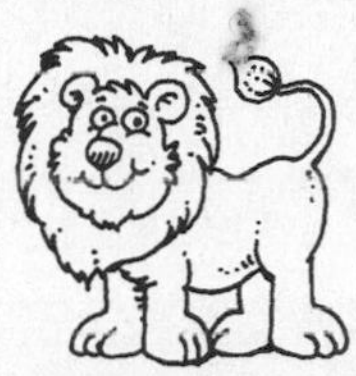

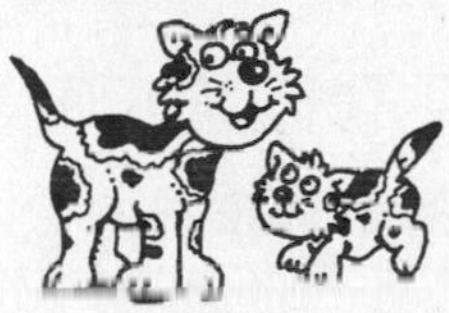

2. ______

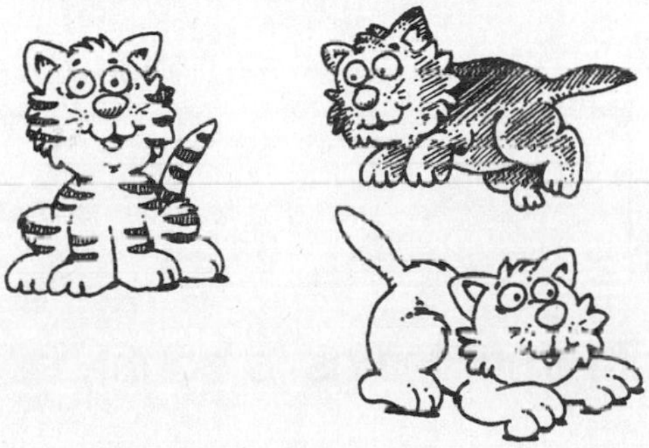

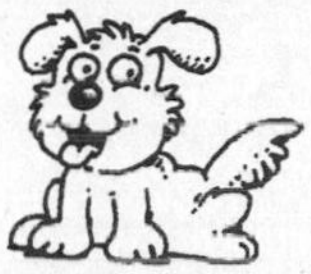

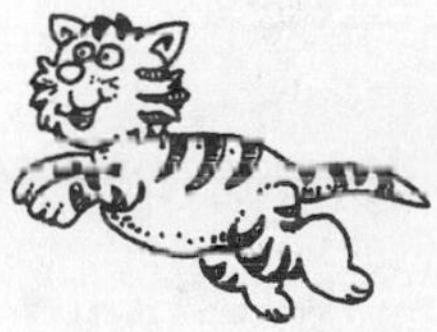

3. ______

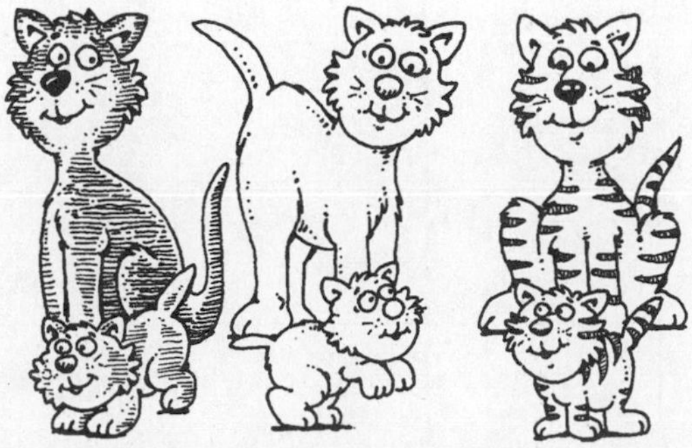

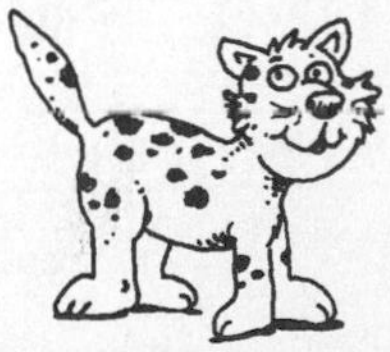

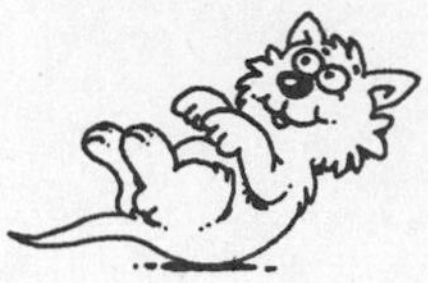

Notes for Home Your child determined which animals belong in each group and the rule for each group.
Home Activity: Ask your child to sort all the cats a different way. (all black, all white, all striped, all calico)

Name ______________________________

Create a Graph

Problem Solving
1-12

Look at the picture.
Make a graph.
Then use the graph.
Which group has more?

Things in the Picture

1.  

2. 

3. Draw a picture. Choose 3 different things to count.
Then make a graph.
Ask a friend which group has more.

Notes for Home Your child used items in a picture to make a graph and compared amounts. *Home Activity*: Ask your child to explain how he or she created the graph. Have him or her create another graph with other small objects, such as buttons and paper clips.

Name ______________________

Problem Solving
I-13

Create a Pictograph

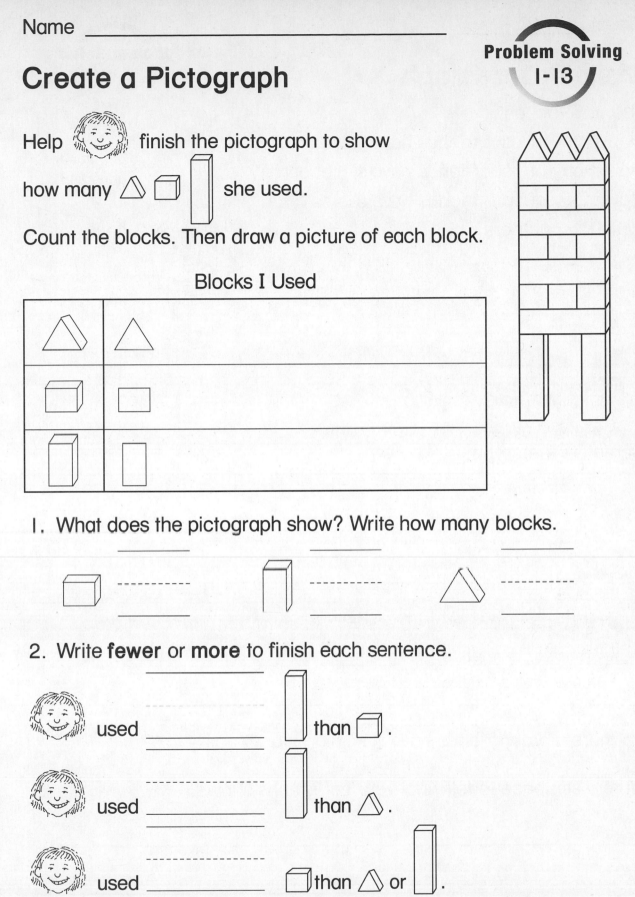

Help finish the pictograph to show

how many she used.

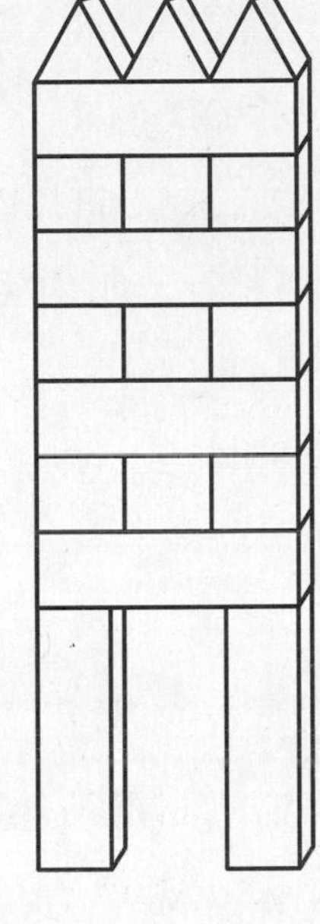

Count the blocks. Then draw a picture of each block.

Blocks I Used

1. What does the pictograph show? Write how many blocks.

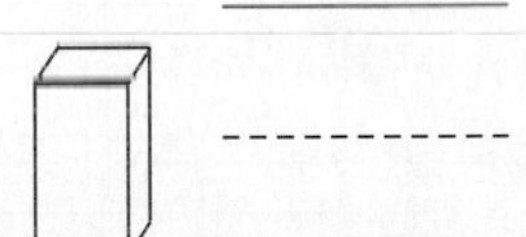

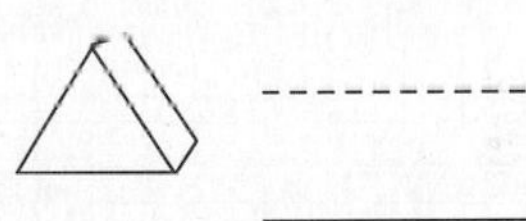

2. Write **fewer** or **more** to finish each sentence.

used ______ than .

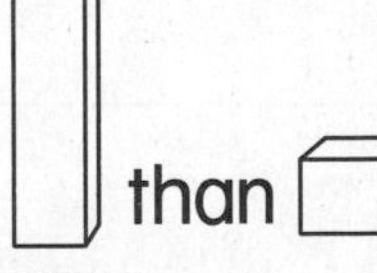

used ______ than .

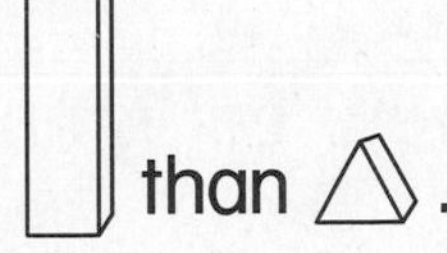

used ______ than or .

Notes for Home Your child completed a pictograph. *Home Activity:* Ask your child to explain how he or she completed the graph. Then have your child count the blocks in the top and bottom rows of the graph and compare that total with the number of blocks in the middle row. (The totals are the same; 9.)

Name ______________________________

Problem Solving
1-14

Make a Bar Graph

Talk to 5 friends.
How many of your friends have bikes?
How many of your friends have skateboards?
How many of your friends have skates?
Write the numbers.

Color 1 box for each child.

______  ______  ______ 

Complete the graph.

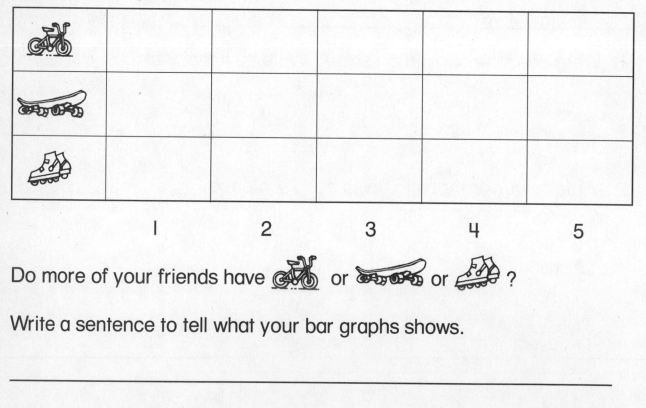

	1	2	3	4	5

Do more of your friends have  or or  ?

Write a sentence to tell what your bar graphs shows.

____

____

Using the Page Have children ask five friends if they have bikes, skateboards, or skates, record the data, and then use the data to complete a bar graph to solve a problem. Ask children how they can ***solve*** the problem. (By looking at the graph to see which row has more shaded blocks.) **Notes for Home** Your child gathered information and completed a bar graph. *Home Activity*: Ask your child to explain how he or she completed and used the graph.

 Use with pages 37–38.

Name ______________________________

Problem Solving
2-1

Explore Ways to Make 4 and 5

How can you show 4 and 5?

Write how many you have.

Write how many you draw.

1\.

_____ and _____ is 4.

2\.

_____ and _____ is 5.

3\. 

_____ and _____ is 4.

4\. 

_____ and _____ is 5.

5\. 

_____ and _____ is 5.

Notes for Home Your child explored different ways to make 4 and 5 by counting and drawing flowers and writing the numerals to show how many. *Home Activity*: Draw 2 flowers. Then ask your child to draw more flowers to show 5. Repeat by drawing 3 flowers and having your child draw more flowers to show 4.

Name ______________________________

Problem Solving
2-2

Ways to Make 6 and 7

What is hiding?

Color the ways to make 6 brown.

Color the ways to make 7 black.

1 and 5 is one way to make 6.

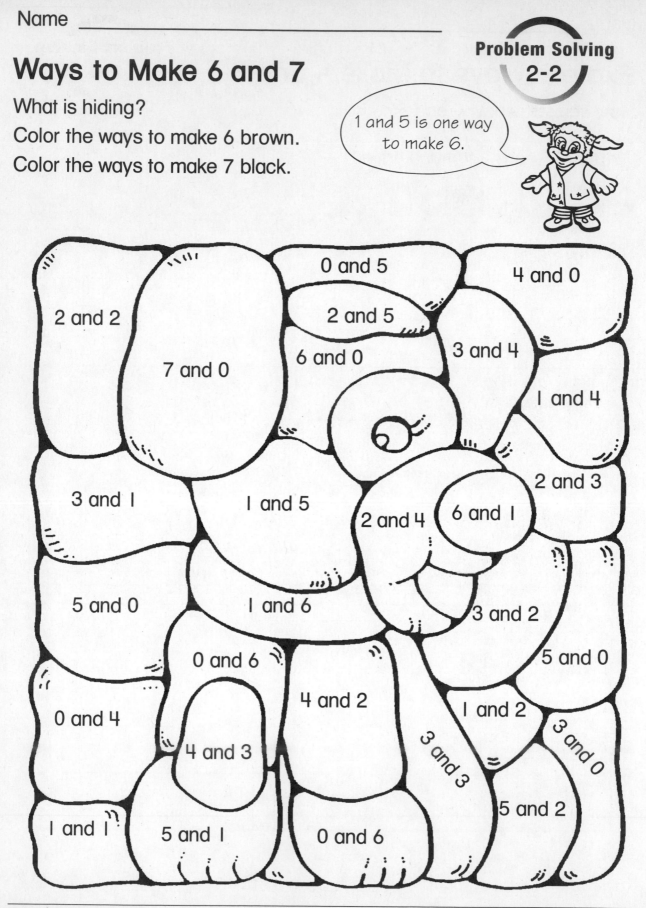

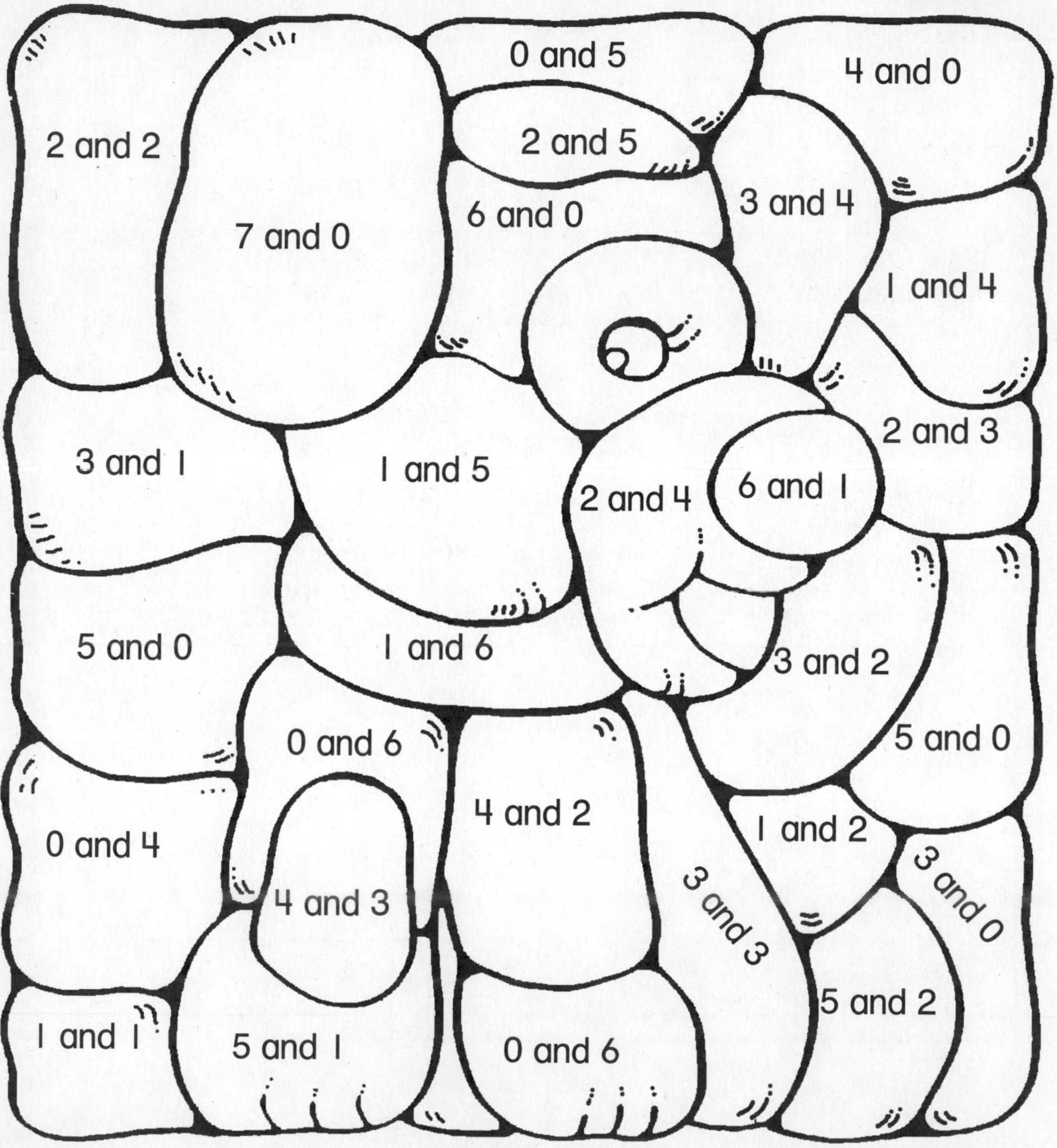

2 and 2

7 and 0

0 and 5

2 and 5

4 and 0

6 and 0

3 and 4

1 and 4

3 and 1

1 and 5

2 and 4

6 and 1

2 and 3

5 and 0

1 and 6

3 and 2

0 and 6

5 and 0

4 and 2

0 and 4

4 and 3

1 and 2

3 and 3

3 and 0

1 and 1

5 and 1

0 and 6

5 and 2

Notes for Home Your child colored ways to make 6 and 7 to solve a problem. *Home Activity:* Ask your child to show one way to make 7 using small objects such as dried beans, coins, or buttons.

Name ___________________________

Problem Solving
2-3

Ways to Make 8 and 9

Draw a picture to solve each problem.

1. 3 △

5 more △

How many in all? _____ △

2. 6 □

3 more □

How many in all? _____ □

3. 2 ○

6 more ○

How many in all? _____ ○

4. 5 ☆

4 more ☆

How many in all? _____ ☆

5. 4 ⏢

4 more ⏢

How many in all? _____ ⏢

Notes for Home Your child drew pictures for the names of 8 and 9 to solve problems. *Home Activity:* Ask your child to make up a problem for 8 and a problem for 9 for you to solve.

Name ______________________________

Ways to Make 10

Problem Solving 2-4

Help the [cat].

Color the ways to make 10 to find the way home.

Notes for Home Your child colored ways to make 10 to solve a problem. *Home Activity*: Ask your child to use two kinds of objects, such as dried beans and coins, to demonstrate the different ways to make 10.

Name ______________________________

Problem Solving 2-5

Make a Table

1. How many ways can you put 4 

on 2  ?

Make a table to find out.

plate	plate	muffins in all
4		4
3		4

Step 1: If you put 4  on one 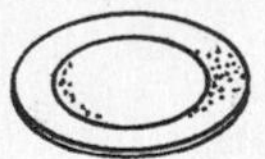,

how many are on the other 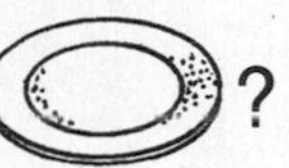 ?

Write how many on each 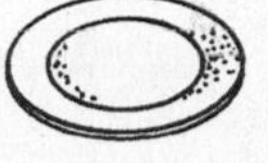.

Write how many in all.

Step 2: If you put 3  on one 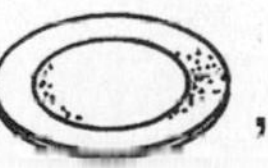,

how many are on the other 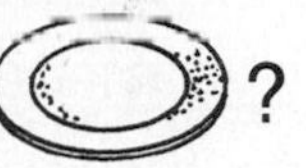 ?

Write how many on each 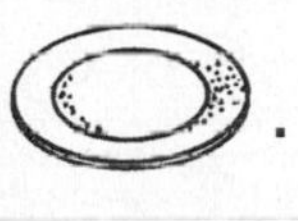.

Write how many in all.

Step 3: Finish the table.

Step 4: How many ways can you put 4 

on 2  ?

______ways

2. How many ways can you put 5 

in 2 baskets ? Make a table to find out.

basket	basket	yarn in all

______ways

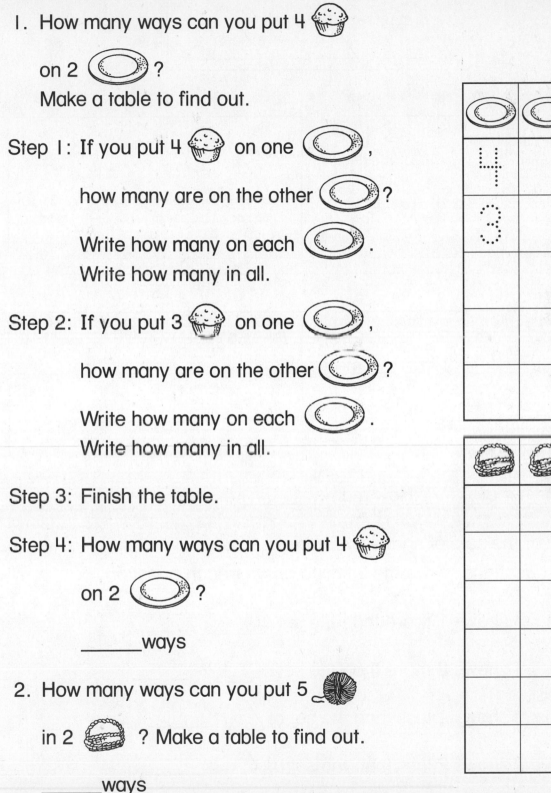

Using the Page To help children ***understand*** how to make a table, have them read the problem without answering the question. Then ask them to go back to solve the problems. **Notes for Home** Your child completed a table to solve problems. *Home Activity*: Ask your child to explain to you how to read a table.

Name ______________________________

Problem Solving 2-6

More and Fewer

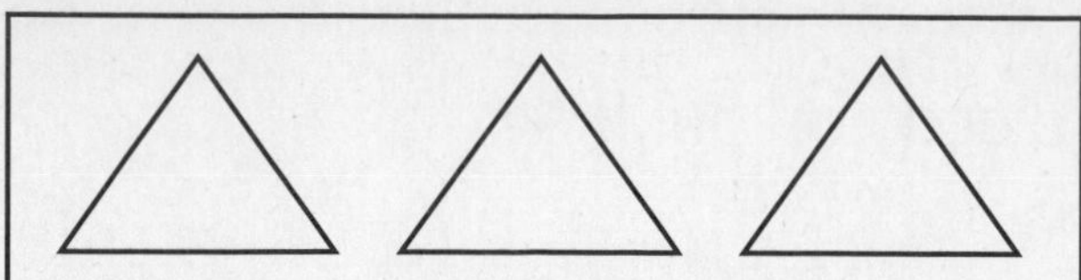

A.

Draw 5 □.

B.

Draw 1 ☆.

C.

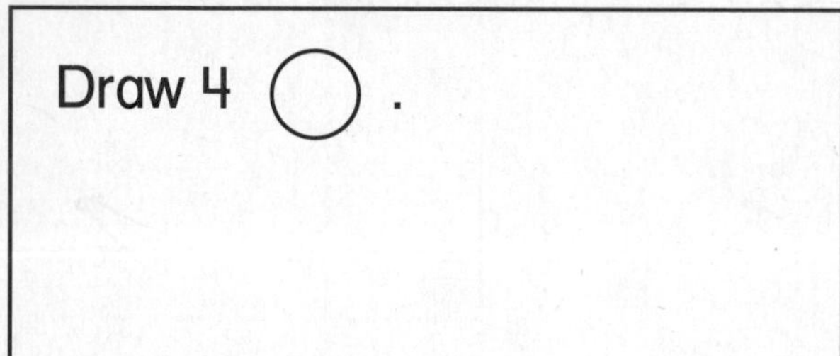

Draw 4 ○.

D.

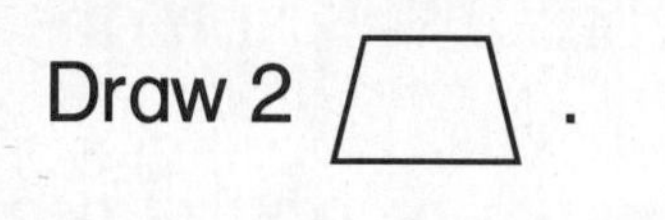

Draw 2 ⏢.

Look at the set of △. How many? _____

Then look at the sets of shapes you drew.
Read the questions. Write the letter to answer each question.

1. Which set shows 1 more than the set of △? _____
2. Which set shows 2 more than the set of △? _____
3. Which set shows 1 less than the set of △? _____
4. Which set shows 2 less than the set of △? _____

Notes for Home Your child drew sets of shapes and compared each with a set of given shapes to determine which are 1 more and less, and 2 more and less. *Home Activity*: Show your child 6 objects and ask him or her to tell you the numbers that are 1 more and 1 less, and the numbers that are 2 more and 2 less.

Name ______________________________

Odd and Even Numbers

Problem Solving 2-7

How many pairs can Jason make?

Circle each pair.

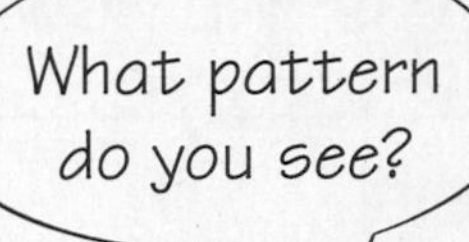

	Number of Pairs	Number of Left Over
1.	1	0
2.	____	____
3.	____	____
4.	____	____
5.	____	____
6.	____	____
7.	____	____
8.	____	____
9.	____	____

Notes for Home Your child circled pairs to determine if a number is odd or even. *Home Activity*: Ask your child to name numbers that are even. (2, 4, 6, 8,...)

Name ______________________________

Problem Solving
2-8

Ways to Make 11 and 12

1. How many ways can you find to make 11?
Look across and down. Circle the ways.

11	and	0	and	8	and	3
and	5	and	7	and	0	and
2	and	9	and	2	and	8
and	6	and	4	and	7	and
10	and	1	and	9	and	0
and	7	and	6	and	5	and
2	and	10	and	3	and	11

2. How many ways can you find to make 12?
Look across and down. Circle the ways.

12	and	0	and	8	and	4
and	6	and	7	and	6	and
3	and	9	and	3	and	8
and	6	and	5	and	7	and
10	and	2	and	11	and	0
and	7	and	1	and	11	and
1	and	10	and	1	and	12

Notes for Home Your child found and circled ways to make 11 and 12. *Home Activity*: Have your child use two kinds of small objects to show different ways to make 11 and 12.

 Use with pages 69–70.

Name ______________________________

Find Missing Parts Through 7

Solve the problems.

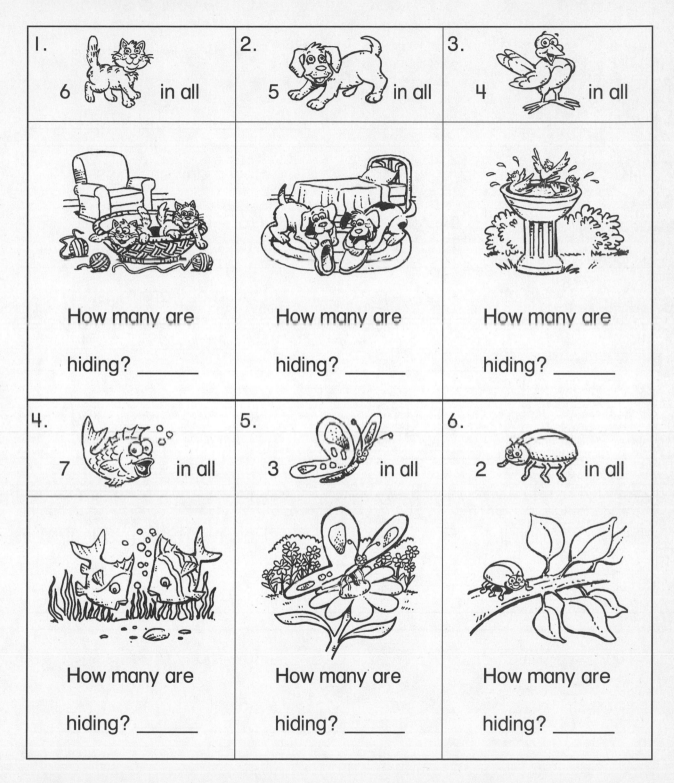

1. 6 in all	2. 5 in all	3. 4 in all
How many are hiding? ______	How many are hiding? ______	How many are hiding? ______
4. 7 in all	5. 3 in all	6. 2 in all
How many are hiding? ______	How many are hiding? ______	How many are hiding? ______

Notes for Home Your child determined how many animals are hiding to solve problems. *Home Activity*: Use the problems as a model to create new problems for your child to solve.

Name ______________________________

Problem Solving 2-10

Find Missing Parts Through 10

Read. Look. Circle your answers.

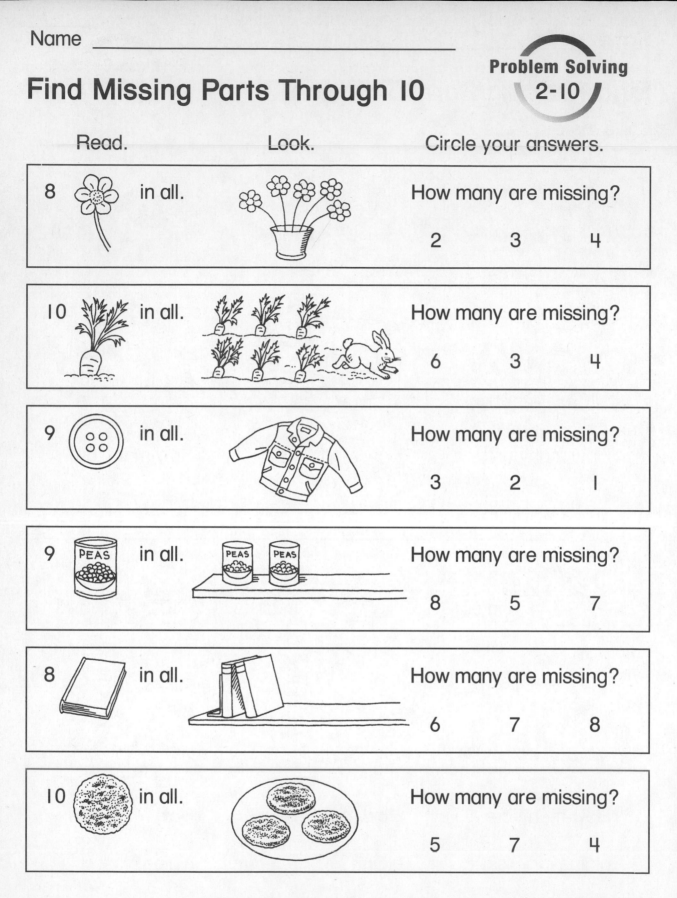

8  in all. 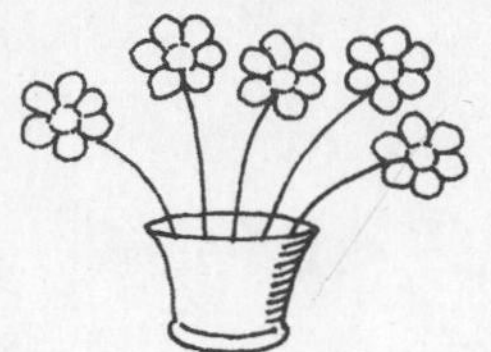

How many are missing?

2 3 4

10 in all. 

How many are missing?

6 3 4

9 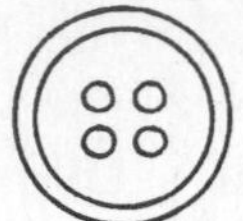 in all. 

How many are missing?

3 2 1

9 

in all. 

How many are missing?

8 5 7

8 in all. 

How many are missing?

6 7 8

10 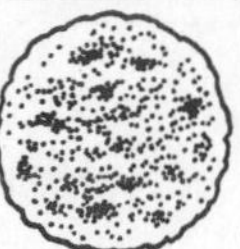 in all. 

How many are missing?

5 7 4

Notes for Home Your child determined how many objects are missing to solve problems. *Home Activity*: Ask your child to explain his or her answers.

Name ______________________________

Draw a Picture

1. There are 5  in the .

There are 4  in the .

How many  in all?

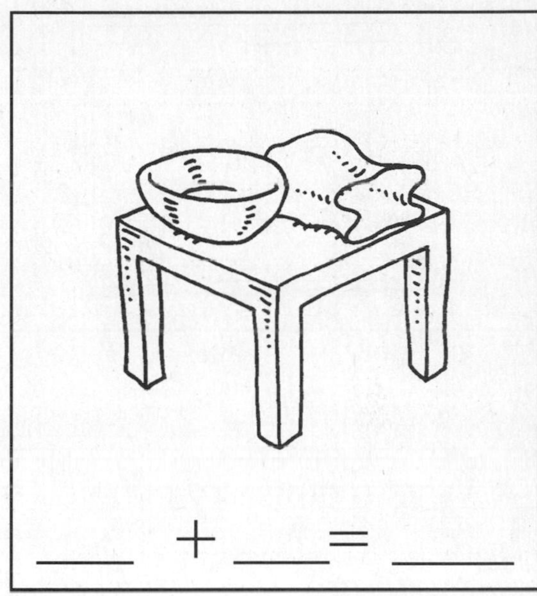

Step 1: How many  are in the ? Draw them.

Step 2: How many  are in the ? Draw them.

Step 3: Look at your picture. Write how many  in all.

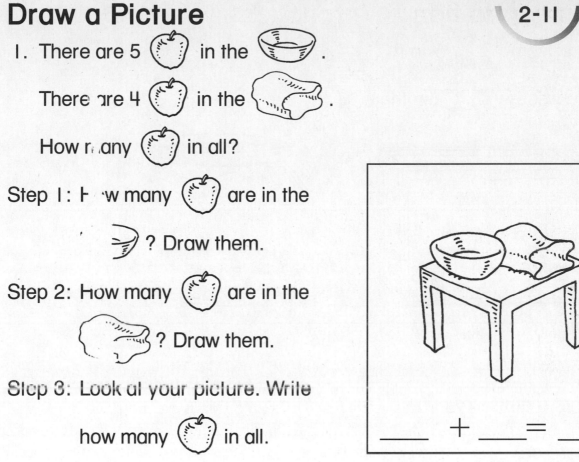

2. There are 3 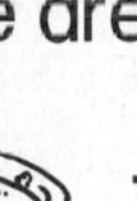 in the . There are 2  on the grass. How many  in all? Draw a picture.

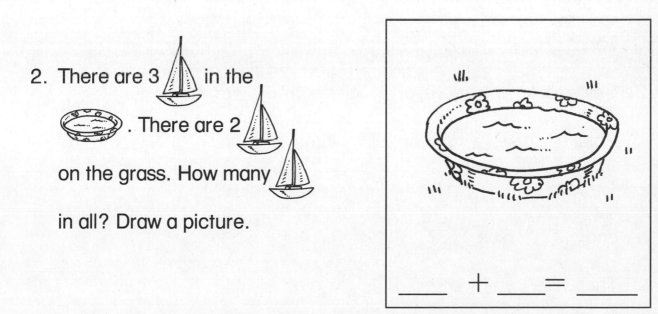

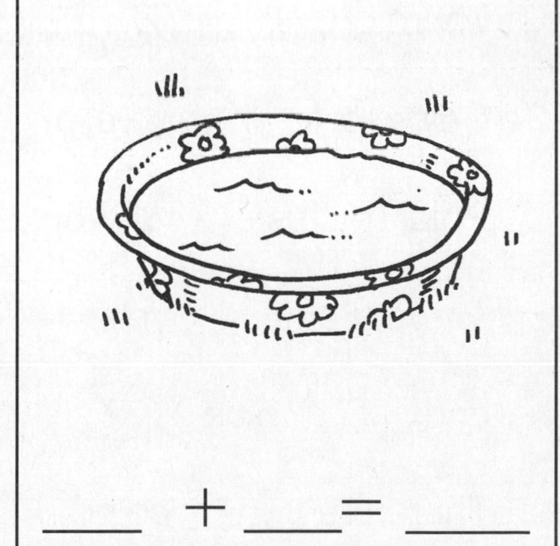

Using the Page To help children ***plan***, have them read through the problem, and identify what they know and need to find out. Then have children follow the steps to solve the problem. **Notes for Home** Your child drew pictures to solve problems. *Home Activity*: Ask your child to explain how he or she solved Exercise 2.

Name ____________________________

Problem Solving 3-1

Explore Addition

1. Draw some 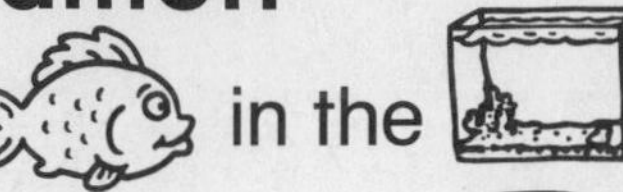.

Draw some  in the .

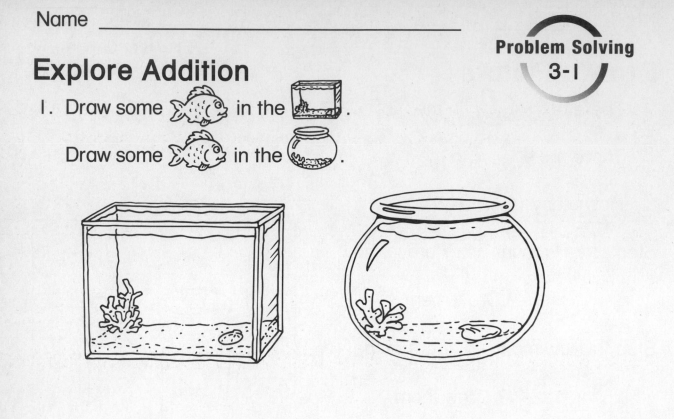

What math story can you tell? Write how many.

There are _____  in the 

and _____  in the .

There are _____ in all.

2. Color some  yellow. Color some  blue.

What math story can you tell? Write how many.

There are _____ yellow 

and _____ blue .

There are _____ colorful  in all.

Notes for Home Your child explored addition by drawing pictures and telling math stories. *Home Activity:* Have your child draw some more fish on a separate sheet of paper and tell another math story.

Name ________________________________

Problem Solving
3-2

Show Addition

Draw some 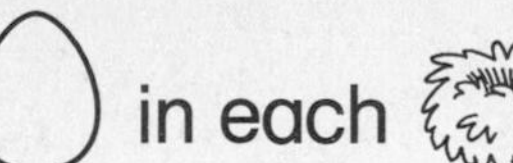 in each .

Then tell about each picture.

Write how many  in each .

Write + or = in each □.

1.

2.

3.

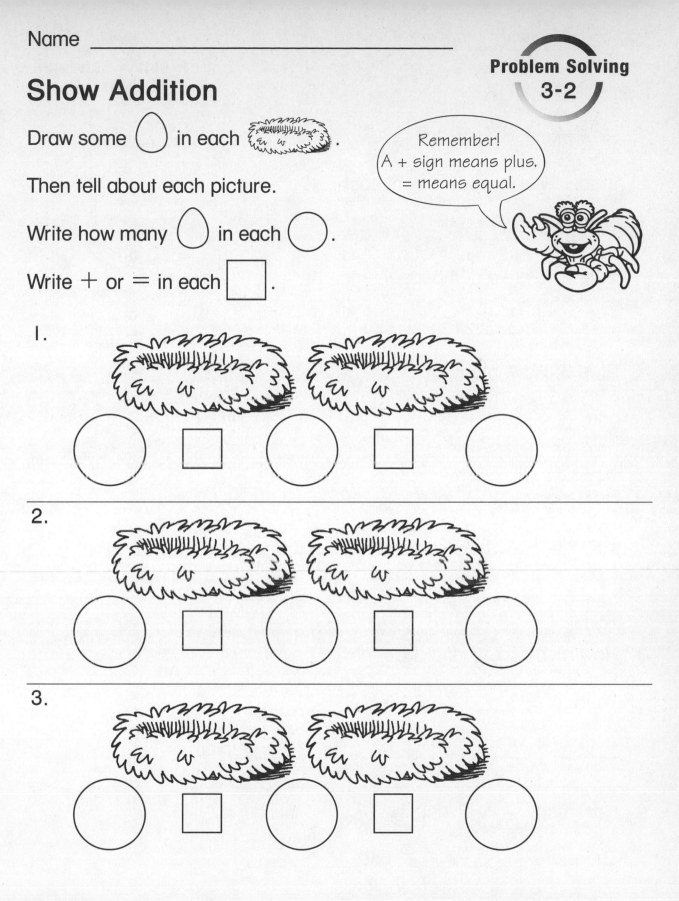

Notes for Home Your child wrote number sentences using the plus sign and the equal sign to tell about the pictures. *Home Activity:* Ask your child to tell about each problem another way.

Name ______________________________

Use Addition

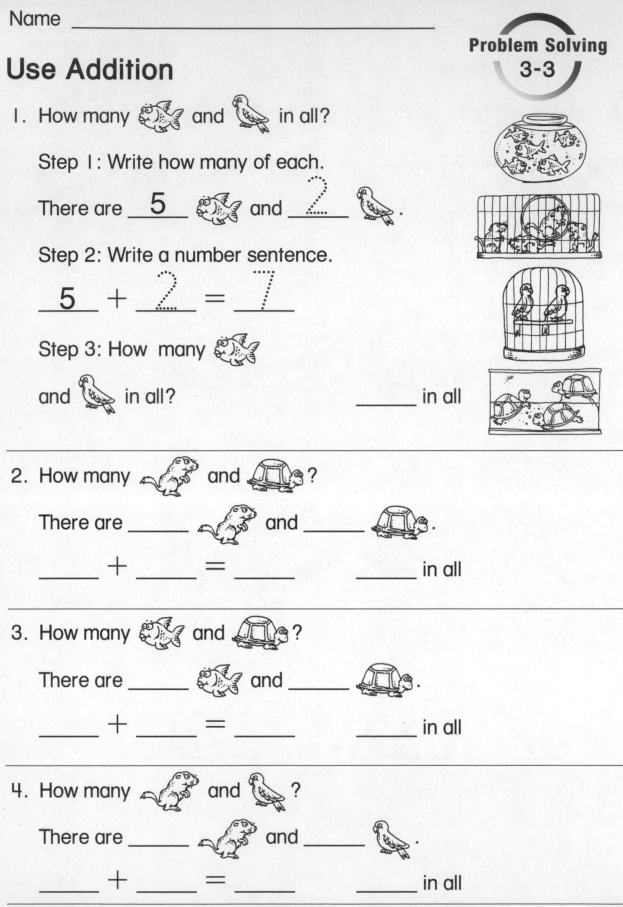

Problem Solving 3-3

1. How many fish and parrot in all?

Step 1: Write how many of each.

There are __5__ fish and __2__ parrot.

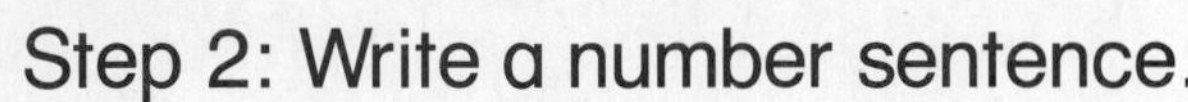

Step 2: Write a number sentence.

__5__ + __2__ = __7__

Step 3: How many fish

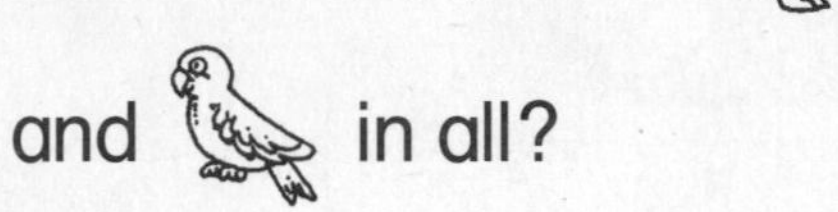

and parrot in all? ______ in all

2. How many gerbil and turtle?

There are ______ gerbil and ______ turtle.

______ + ______ = ______ ______ in all

3. How many fish and turtle?

There are ______ fish and ______ turtle.

______ + ______ = ______ ______ in all

4. How many gerbil and parrot?

There are ______ gerbil and ______ parrot.

______ + ______ = ______ ______ in all

Using the Page To **solve** each problem, have children use the pictures at the top of the page to record how many of each animal and then use addition to find each sum. **Notes for Home** Your child read math stories and wrote the number sentences to answer the questions. *Home Activity:* Ask your child to write a number sentence to tell how many fish and gerbils there are in all. (5 + 4 = 9 in all.)

Name ______________________________

Problem Solving
3-4

Addition Sentences to 12

Make 2 addition sentences with the numbers in each box.
You can use counters.

1. 9, 6, 3

____ + ____ = ____

____ + ____ = ____

2. 0, 7, 7

____ + ____ = ____

____ + ____ = ____

3. 4, 11, 7

____ + ____ = ____

____ + ____ = ____

4. 2, 5, 3

____ + ____ = ____

____ + ____ = ____

5. 1, 8, 7

____ + ____ = ____

____ + ____ = ____

6. 8, 12, 4

____ + ____ = ____

____ + ____ = ____

7. 4, 10, 6

____ + ____ = ____

____ + ____ = ____

8. 1, 4, 3

____ + ____ = ____

____ + ____ = ____

Notes for Home Your child wrote two number sentences for each set of numbers. *Home Activity:* Ask your child to choose a number from 6 to 12 and then write all the possible number sentences for that number. (Example: 0 + 6 = 6; 1 + 5 = 6; 2 + 4 = 6; 3 + 3 = 6; 4 + 2 = 6; 5 + 1 = 6; 6 + 0 = 6)

Name ______________________________

Add in Vertical Form

Find the missing numbers.

Write the numbers in each ◯.

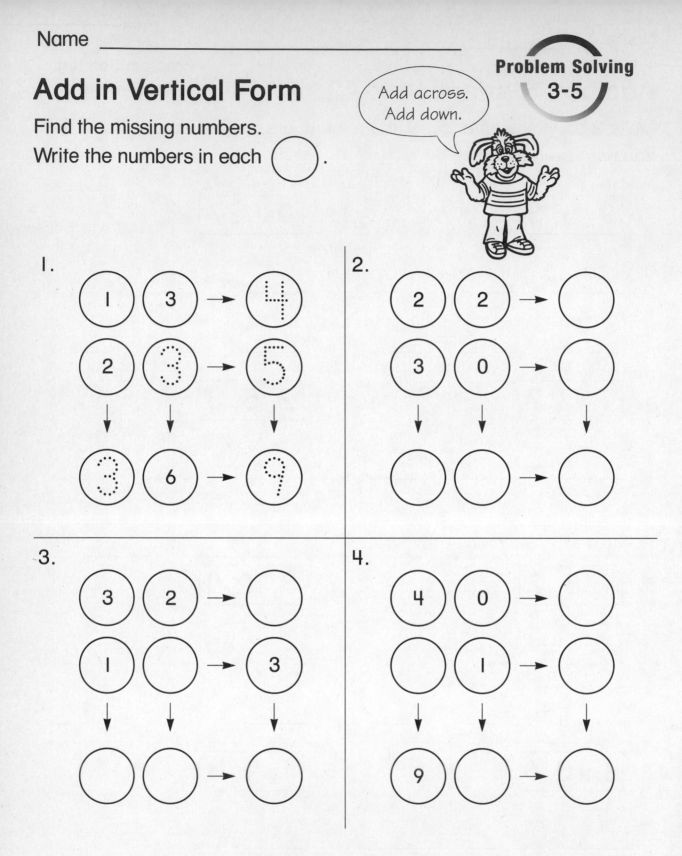

1.

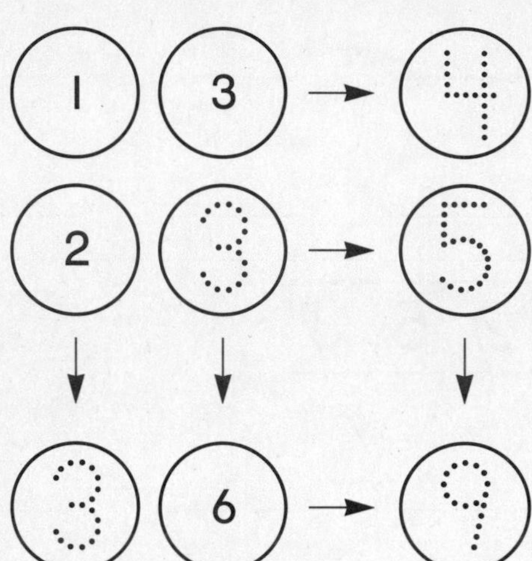

2.

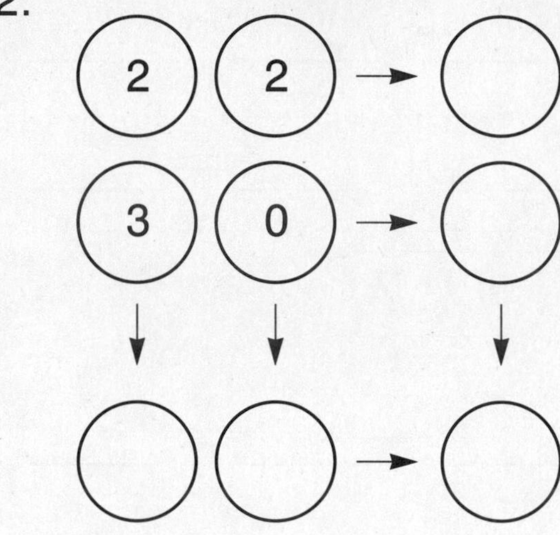

3.

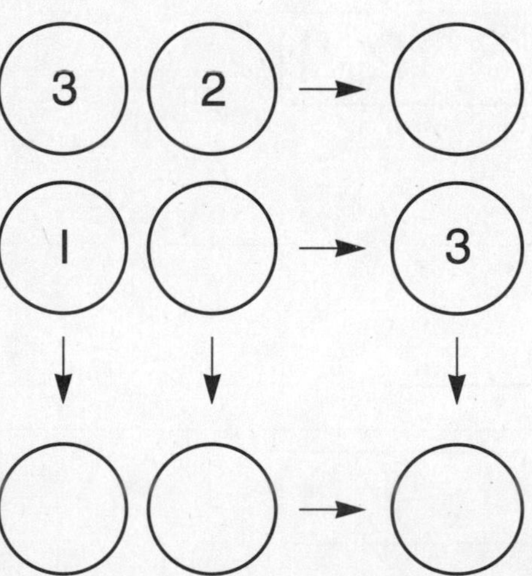

4.

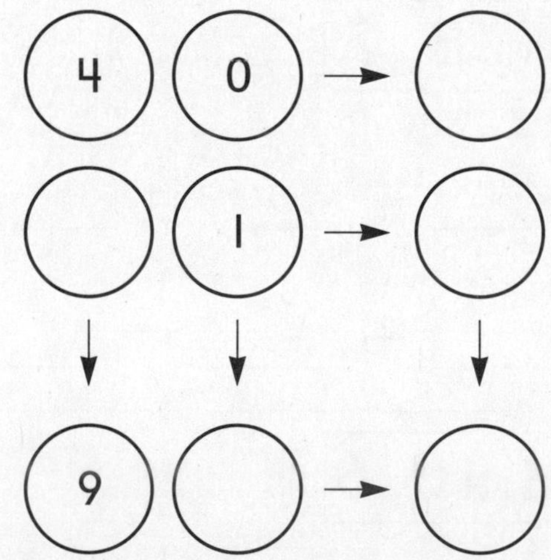

Notes for Home Your child added horizontally and vertically. *Home Activity:* Using Exercise 2 as a model, create additional addition problems for your child to solve.

Name ______________________________

Problem Solving
3-6

Draw a Picture

1. Mia saw 6 in the

and 4 more on the .

How many did Mia see in all?

Step 1: Draw how many

Mia saw in the .

Step 2: Draw how many

Mia saw on the .

Step 3: Write a number sentence.

_____ + _____ = _____

Step 4: How many 

did Mia see in all? _____

2. Max has 5 . Tina

has 3 .

They found 3 .

How many

do they have now? _____

____ + ____ + ____ = ____

Draw a picture. Write a number sentence.

Using the Page After reading through Exercise 1 help children to ***understand*** by asking them to tell what they know and what they must find out before solving the problem. **Notes for Home** Your child read math stories, drew pictures to show the stories, and wrote number sentences. *Home Activity:* Ask your child to draw one more bird in the tree and one more bird on the fence, and then write a new number sentence to tell how many in all. (7 + 5 = 12 in all)

Name ______________________________

Explore Subtraction

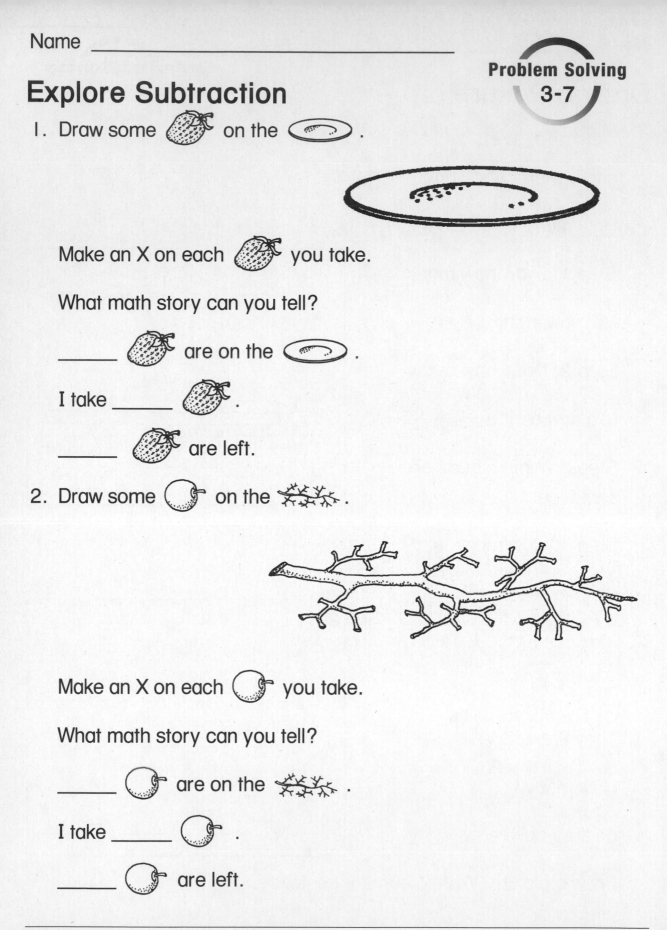

1. Draw some  on the .

Make an X on each  you take.

What math story can you tell?

_____  are on the .

I take _____ .

_____  are left.

2. Draw some on the.

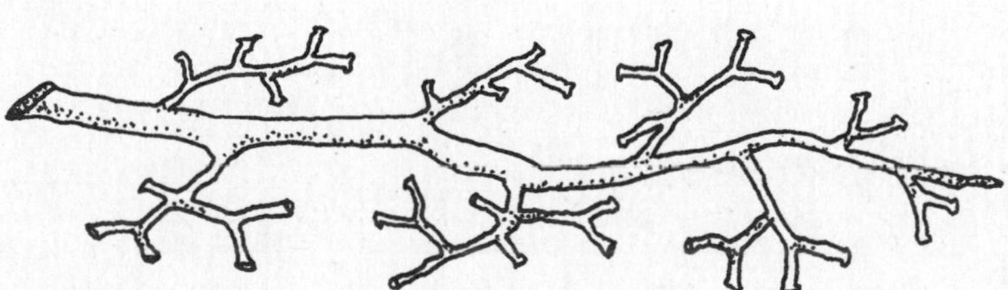

Make an X on each 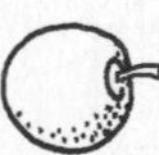 you take.

What math story can you tell?

_____  are on the .

I take _____ .

_____  are left.

Notes for Home Your child explored subtraction by drawing pictures and telling math stories. *Home Activity:* Ask your child to explain how he or she solved each subtraction problem.

Name ________________________________

Show Subtraction

Problem Solving 3-8

The first number in a subtraction sentence is greater than the number you subtract. 4 − 3 = 1

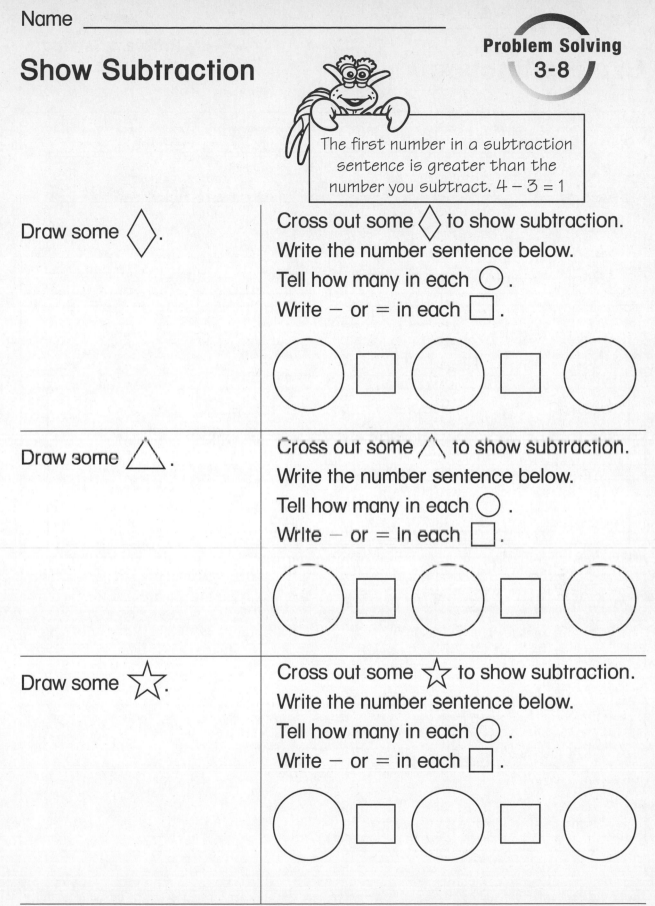

Draw some ◇.	Cross out some ◇ to show subtraction. Write the number sentence below. Tell how many in each ○. Write − or = in each □.
Draw some △.	Cross out some △ to show subtraction. Write the number sentence below. Tell how many in each ○. Write − or = in each □.
Draw some ☆.	Cross out some ☆ to show subtraction. Write the number sentence below. Tell how many in each ○. Write − or = in each □.

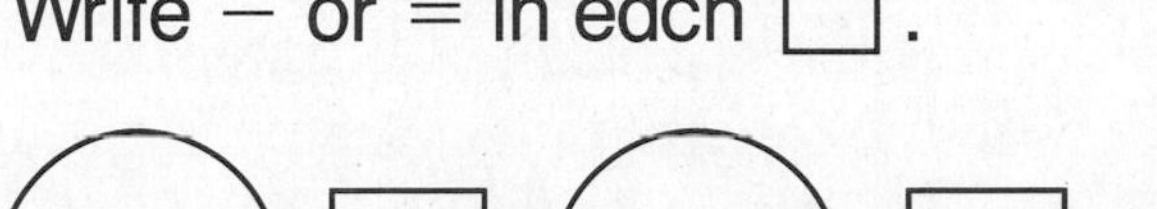

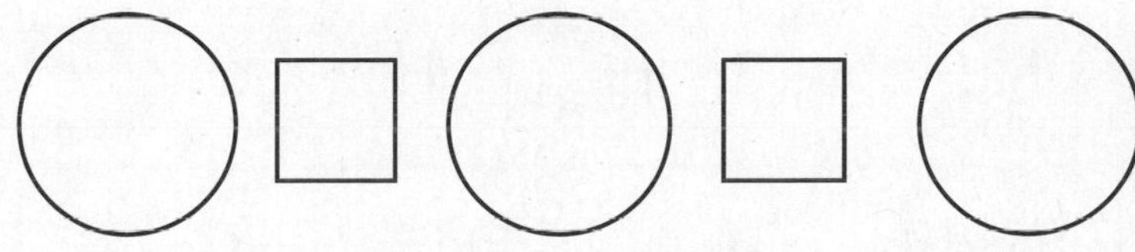

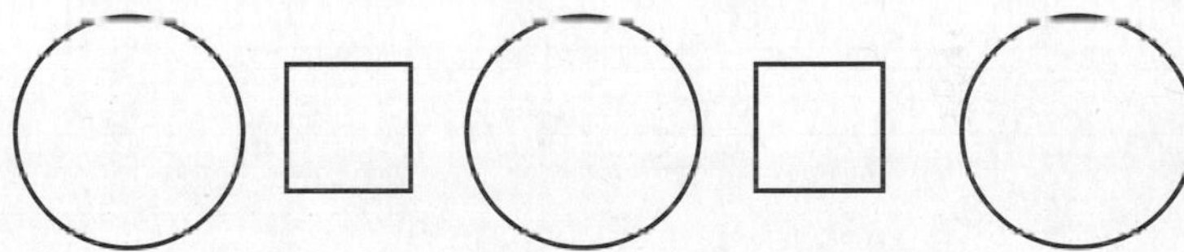

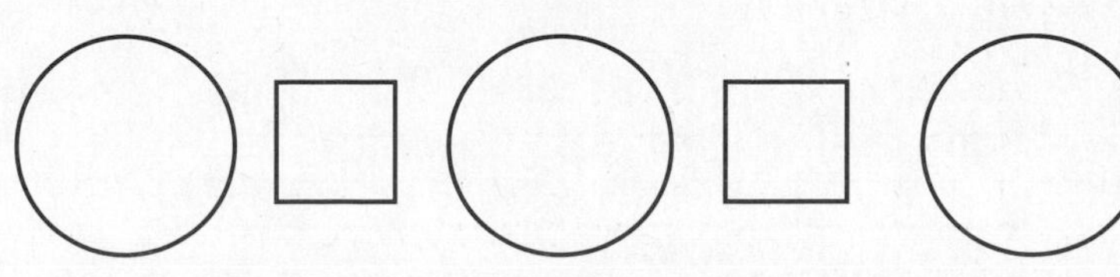

Notes for Home Your child drew pictures to show subtraction and then wrote number sentences. *Home Activity:* Ask your child to tell a number story about each problem.

Name ______________________________

Use Subtraction

Problem Solving 3-9

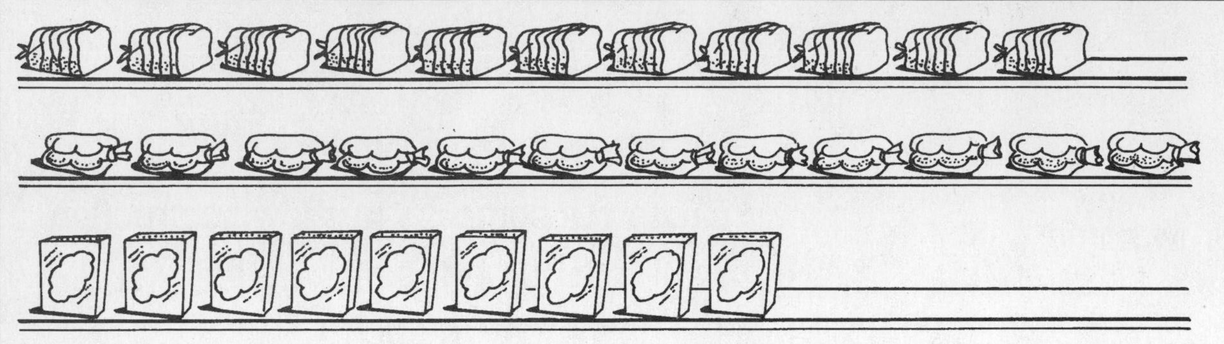

1. Max buys 3 . How many are left?

Step 1:	Step 2:	Step 3:
Write how many in all.	Write how many Max buys.	Subtract to find how many are left.

_____ – __3__ = _____

2. Max buys 1 . How many are left?

_____ – _____ = _____

3. Max buys 2 . How many are left?

_____ – _____ = _____

Using the Page After solving the problems, have children **look back** to check their answers by crossing out the items that Max buys and then counting to see if the number of remaining items on each shelf is the same as each answer. **Notes for Home** Your child read subtraction math stories and wrote number sentences to answer the questions. *Home Activity:* Have your child use the remaining items on the shelves to solve problems such as the following: If you buy 3 boxes of cereal, how many are left? (7 – 3 = 4)

Name ______________________________

Subtract in Vertical Form

Problem Solving 3-10

What numbers are missing?

Write the numbers in each ◯.

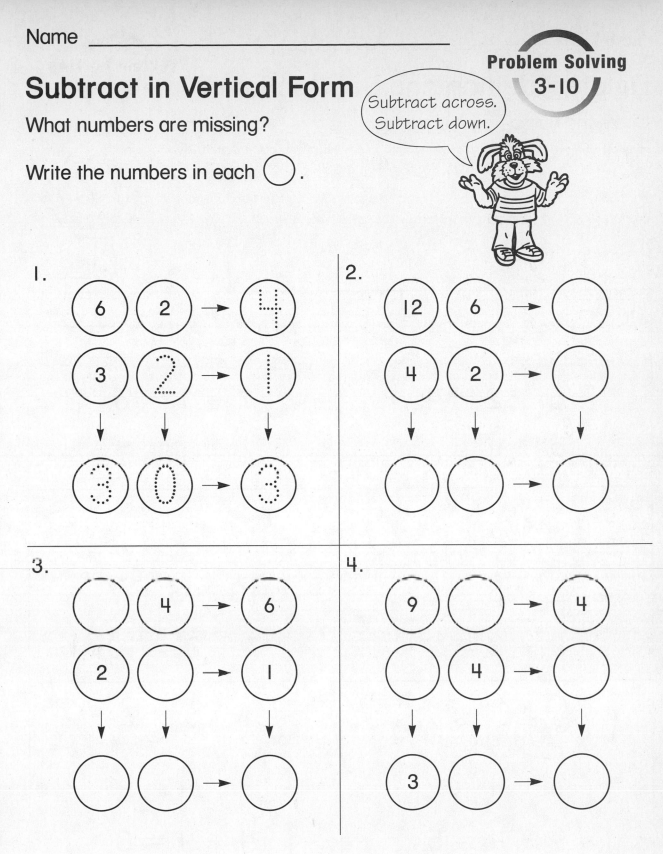

1.

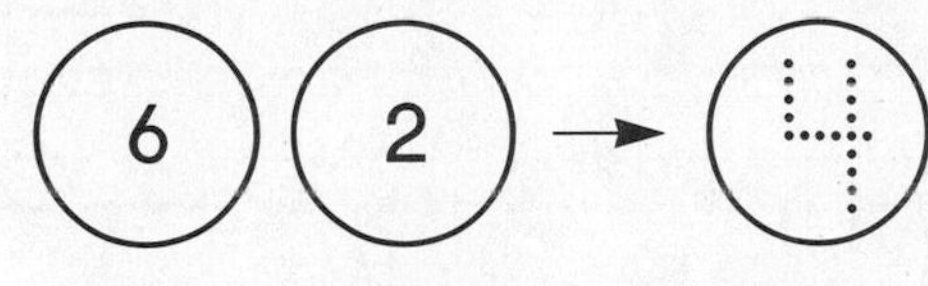

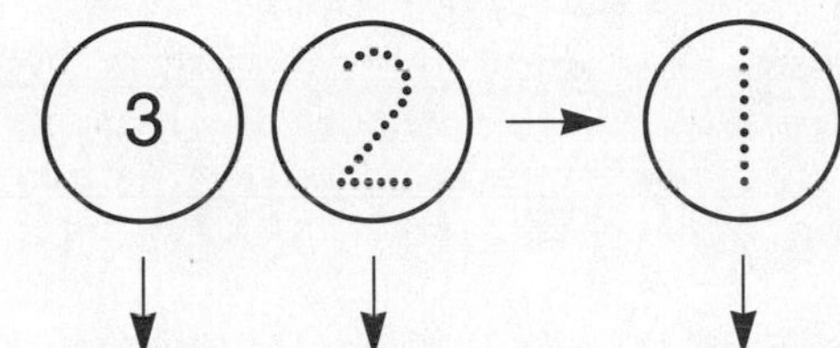

3 0 → 3

2.

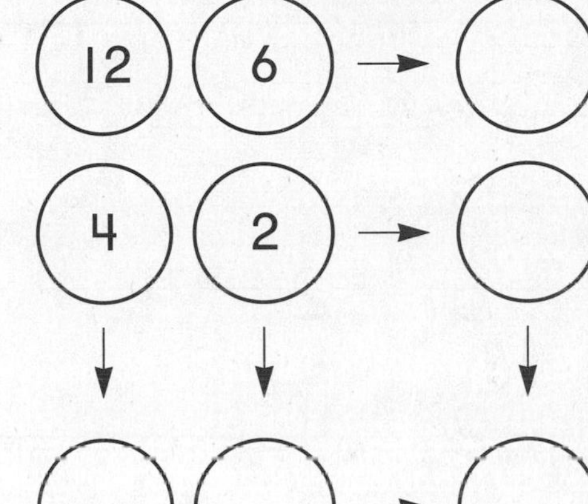

3.

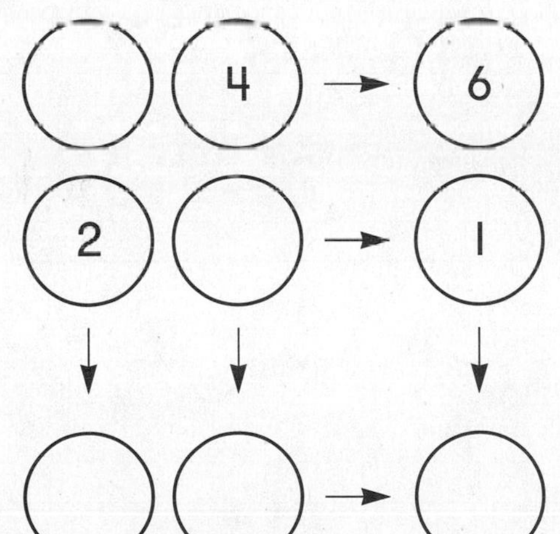

4.

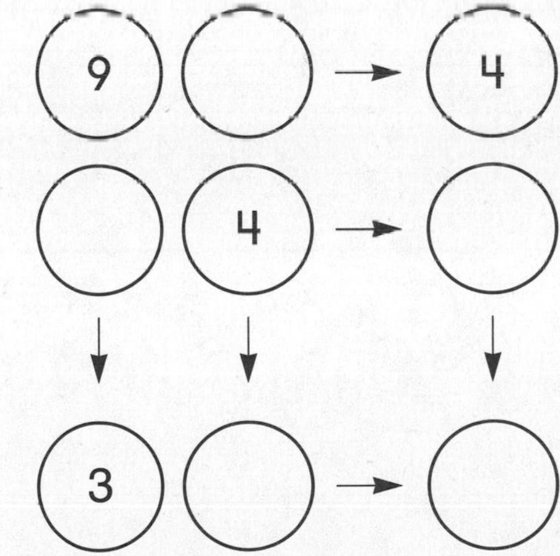

Notes for Home Your child subtracted horizontally and vertically. *Home Activity:* Using Exercise 2 as a model, create additional subtraction problems for your child to solve.

Name ______________________________

Problem Solving
3-11

Relate Addition and Subtraction

Circle the number sentence that tells about each picture.

Look carefully at the signs!

1.

6 − 2 = 4

2 + 4 = 6

2.

7 − 1 = 6

6 + 1 = 7

3.

2 + 3 = 5

5 − 3 = 2

4.

10 − 3 = 7

7 + 3 = 10

5.

5 + 4 = 9

9 − 4 = 5

6.

8 − 4 = 4

4 + 4 = 8

Notes for Home Your child chose between pairs of related addition and subtraction sentences to solve problems. *Home Activity:* Using the numbers 2, 4, and 6, challenge your child to write two addition and two subtraction sentences. (4 + 2 = 6; 2 + 4 = 6; 6 − 4 = 2; 6 − 2 = 4.)

Name ______________________________

Choose an Operation

1. There are 5 kittens.
   1 kitten runs off.
   How many are left?

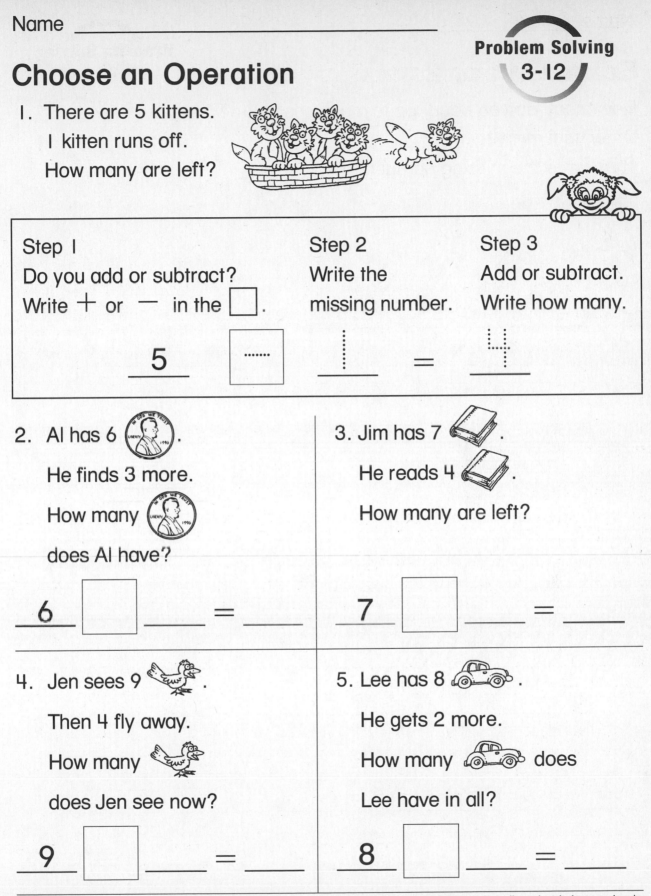

Step 1	Step 2	Step 3
Do you add or subtract? Write + or − in the □.	Write the missing number.	Add or subtract. Write how many.

5 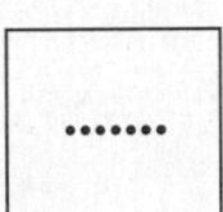  = 

2. Al has 6 .
   He finds 3 more.
   How many  
   does Al have?

   6 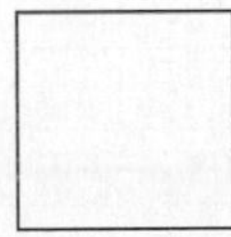 ____ = ____

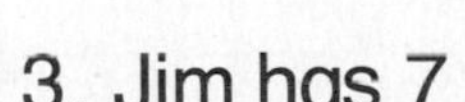

3. Jim has 7 .
   He reads 4.
   How many are left?

   7 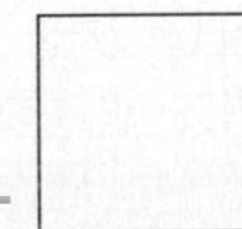 ____ = ____

4. Jen sees 9 .
   Then 4 fly away.
   How many 
   does Jen see now?

   9 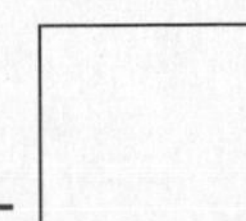 ____ = ____

5. Lee has 8 .
   He gets 2 more.
   How many  does
   Lee have in all?

   8 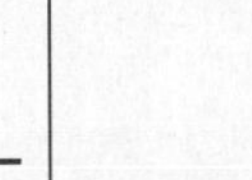 ____ = ____

Using the Page To help children ***plan*** solutions to the problems, encourage them to describe what is happening in each picture and then read through the problems. **Notes for Home** Your child read math stories, decided whether to add or subtract, and then solved the problems. *Home Activity:* Continue the story about Al in Exercise 2. Tell your child that Al spends 5 pennies. Then his mother gives him 2 pennies. Ask how many pennies he has now. (9 – 5 = 4; 4 + 2 = 6)

Name ______________________

Problem Solving
4-1

Count On 1 or 2

How many do you count on to make each sum?
Draw how many.
Then write the missing number.

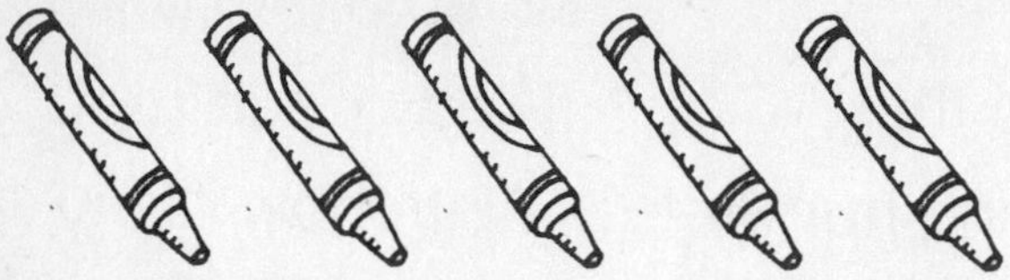	5 + ____ = 6
	7 + ____ = 9
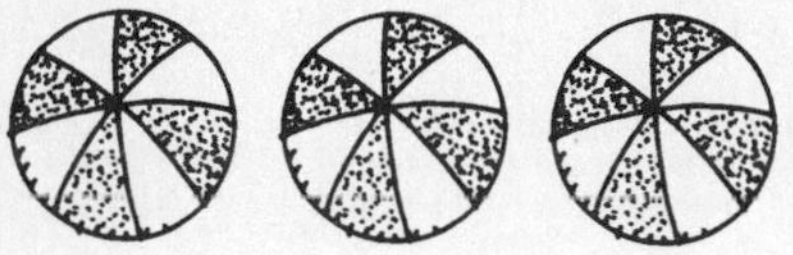	3 + ____ = 5
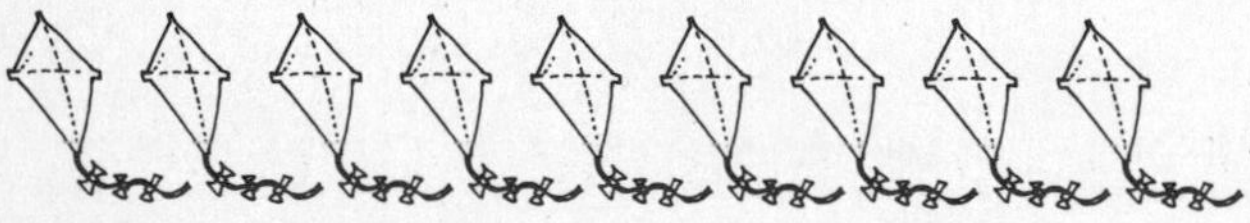	9 + ____ = 10
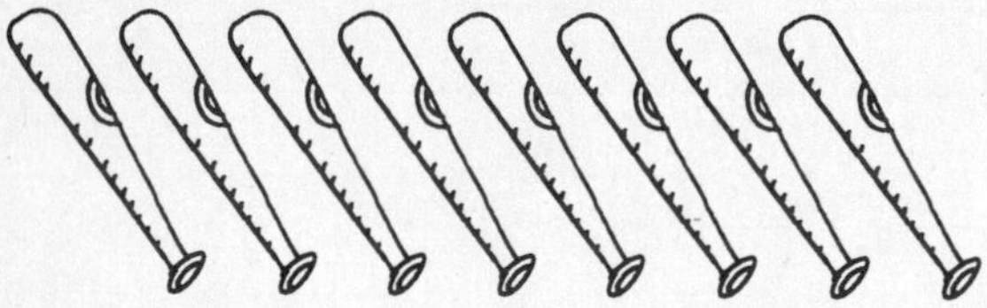	8 + ____ = 10
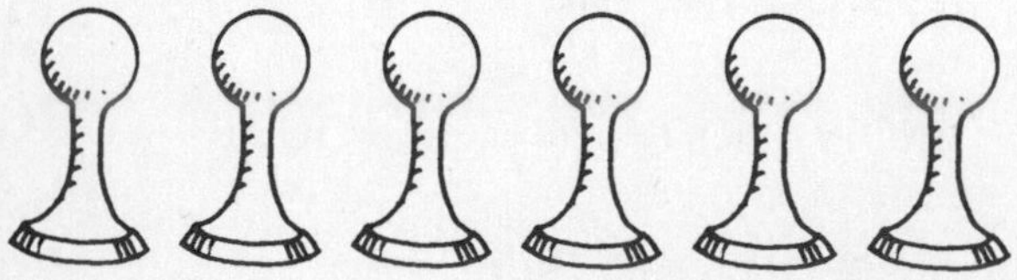	6 + ____ = 7
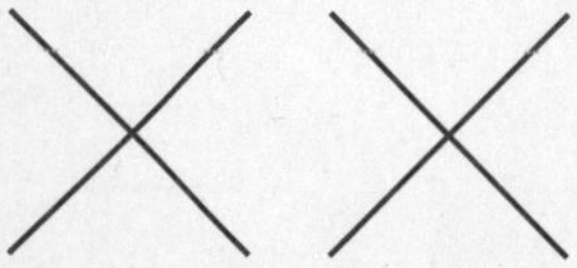	2 + ____ = 4

Notes for Home Your child counted on 1 or 2 to find how many in all. *Home Activity:* Ask your child to explain how he or she determined the missing numbers.

Name ______________________

Problem Solving
4-2

Explore Turnaround Facts

Find 5 hidden facts for 10.

Look across and down. Circle each fact you find.

0	+	10	+	8	+	4		
+	2	+	7	+	5	+		
1	+	3	+	7	+	6		
+	8	+	4	+	4	+		
9	+	5	+	5	+	0		

Write an addition sentence for each fact.

Then write the fact another way.

____ + ____ = ____

____ + ____ = ____

____ + ____ = ____

____ + ____ = ____

____ + ____ = ____

____ + ____ = ____

Notes for Home Your child learned that facts like 1 + 9 and 9 + 1 always have the same sum. *Home Activity:* Ask your child to explain what a **turnaround** fact is.

Name ________________________

Problem Solving 4-3

Count On from Any Number

Which number is greater? Circle that number.
Then count on. Write the numbers.
Then write the sum.

Remember to count on from the greater number.

1. Count on. 7, 8
$2 + 6 = 8$

2. Count on. ________
$3 + 7 =$ ____

3. Count on. ________
$7 + 2 =$ ____

4. Count on. ________
$1 + 9 =$ ____

5. Count on. ________
$3 + 8 =$ ____

6. Count on. ________
$9 + 2 =$ ____

7. Count on. ________
$1 + 7 =$ ____

8. $5 + 3 =$ ____

____

9. Count on. ________
$9 + 3 =$ ____

10. Count on. ________
$8 + 2 =$ ____

Notes for Home Your child counted on from the greater number to find sums. *Home Activity:* Ask your child to explain how he or she found the missing number for Exercise 8.

Name ______________________

Problem Solving
4-4

Use a Number Line to Count On

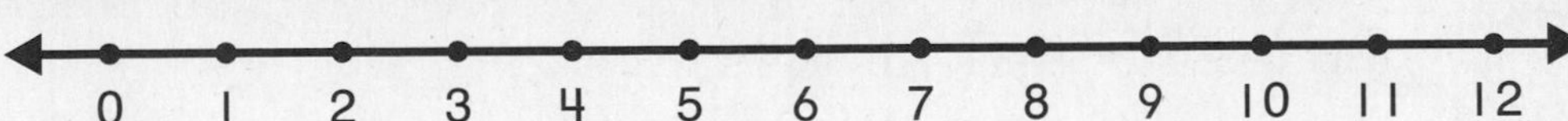

What number comes between each sum? Write each sum.
Then write the number in between. You can use the number line.

1. $2 + 8 =$ ____ $\quad \begin{array}{r} 7 \\ +5 \\ \hline \end{array}$ The number between is ____.

2. $2 + 7 =$ ____ $\quad \begin{array}{r} 3 \\ +8 \\ \hline \end{array}$ The number between is ____.

3. $2 + 5 =$ ____ $\quad \begin{array}{r} 2 \\ +3 \\ \hline \end{array}$ The number between is ____.

4. $0 + 5 =$ ____ $\quad \begin{array}{r} 1 \\ +2 \\ \hline \end{array}$ The number between is ____.

5. $3 + 7 =$ ____ $\quad \begin{array}{r} 6 \\ +2 \\ \hline \end{array}$ The number between is ____.

6. $2 + 4 =$ ____ $\quad \begin{array}{r} 1 \\ +3 \\ \hline \end{array}$ The number between is ____.

Notes for Home Your child used a number line to add 1, 2, or 3 to numbers. *Home Activity:* Ask your child to choose one exercise and draw the jumps to show how to use a number line to count on.

Name ______________________________

Problem Solving
4-5

Add Zero

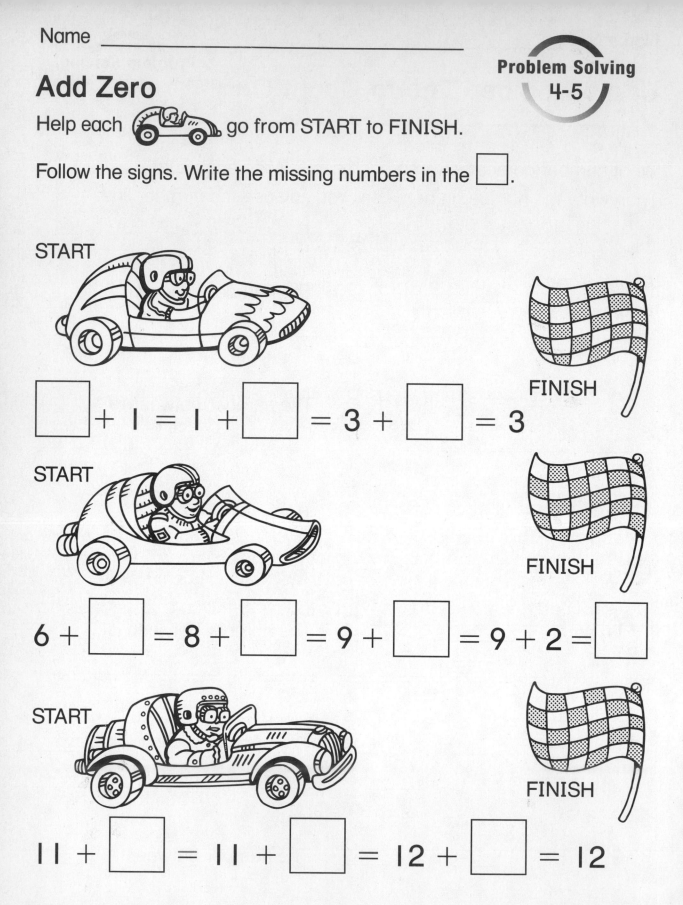

Help each car go from START to FINISH.

Follow the signs. Write the missing numbers in the □.

START

FINISH

□ + 1 = 1 + □ = 3 + □ = 3

START

FINISH

6 + □ = 8 + □ = 9 + □ = 9 + 2 = □

START

FINISH

11 + □ = 11 + □ = 12 + □ = 12

Notes for Home Your child added 0 to solve an addition problem. *Home Activity:* Ask your child to explain how he or she found each missing number.

Name ______________________________

Problem Solving
4-6

Add with 5

What can each child buy?
Write an addition sentence.
Write the letter.

1. What can Al buy with 1  and 6  ?

_____ + _____ = _____

Al can buy _____.

2. What can Meg buy with 1  and 7  ?

_____ + _____ = _____

Meg can buy _____.

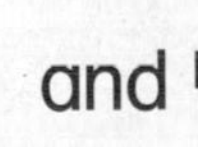

3. What can Ed buy with 1  and 4  ?

_____ + _____ = _____

Ed can buy _____.

4. What can Li buy with 1 and 3  ?

_____ + _____ = _____

Li can buy _____.

5. What can Ana buy with 1  and 5  ?

_____ + _____ = _____

Ana can buy _____.

6. What can Ty buy with 1  and 2  ?

_____ + _____ = _____

Ty can buy _____.

Notes for Home Your child added 5 to numbers. *Home Activity:* Ask your child to add 5 to 0, 1, 2, 3, 4, 5, 6, and 7 and then tell about the pattern. (5,6,7,8,9,10,11,12; The pattern is +1.)

Name ________________________________

Make a List

Problem Solving 4-7

How many ways can Mina buy 9 shells?

Step 1: Start a list. I bag of __6__ shells and I bag of __3__ shells

Step 2: Look at the bags of shells. Find names for 9. Add each to the list.

I bag of ______ shells and I bag of ______ shells

I bag of ______ shells and I bag of ______ shells

I bag of ______ shells and I bag of ______ shells

Step 3: Answer the question.

______ ways to buy 9 shells

Try adding 3 bags together, too!

How many ways can you buy exactly 11 shells? Make a list.

Using the Page Ask children to ***look back*** at their lists by drawing pictures or using connecting cubes of two different colors to make sure each totals 9. **Notes for Home** Your child made a list to solve problems. *Home Activity:* Challenge your child to find and list two ways to combine three bags of shells to make 12. (6 + 3 + 2 = 11; 5 + 4 + 2 = 11; 7 + 1 + 3 = 11; 8 + 1+ 2 = 11)

Name ______________________________

Use a Number Line to Count Back

Problem Solving 4-8

What does each number line show?

Write a number sentence for each.

Write + or − and = in the □.

1.

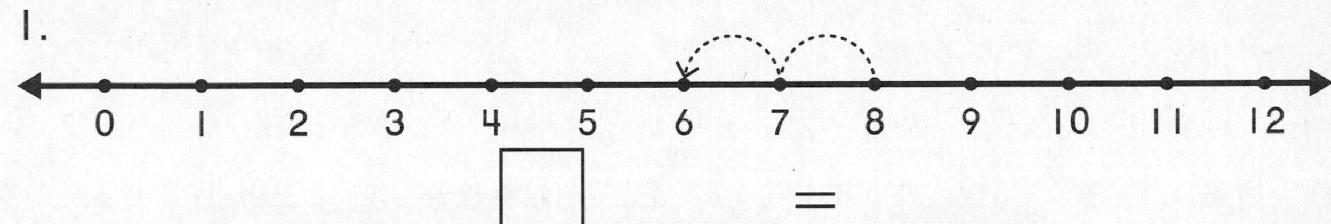

_____ □ _____ = _____

2.

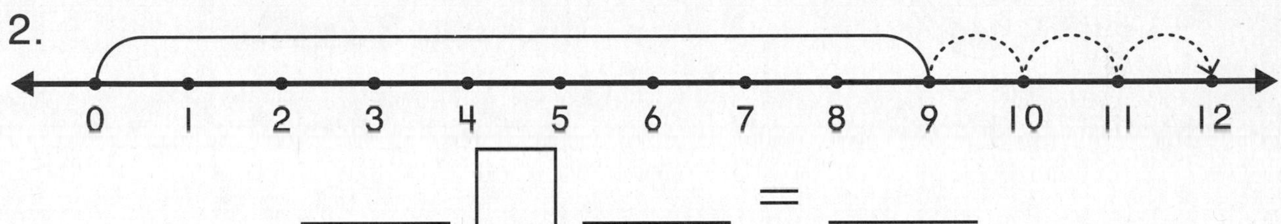

_____ □ _____ = _____

3.

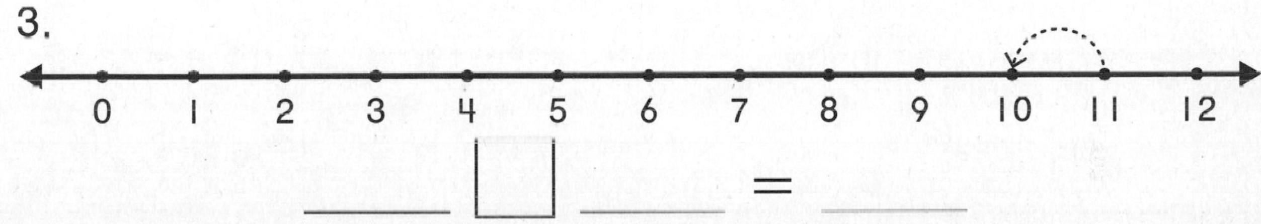

_____ □ _____ = _____

4.

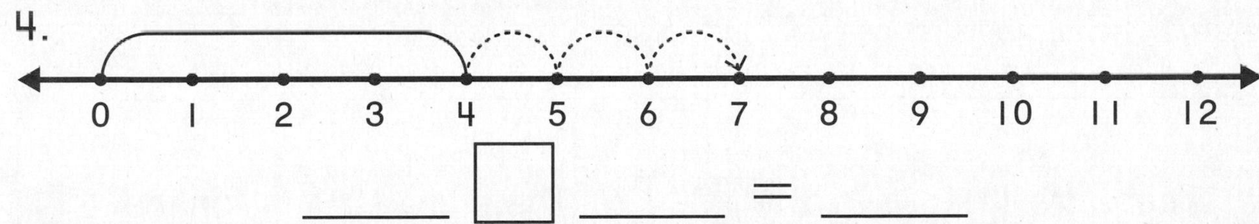

_____ □ _____ = _____

5.

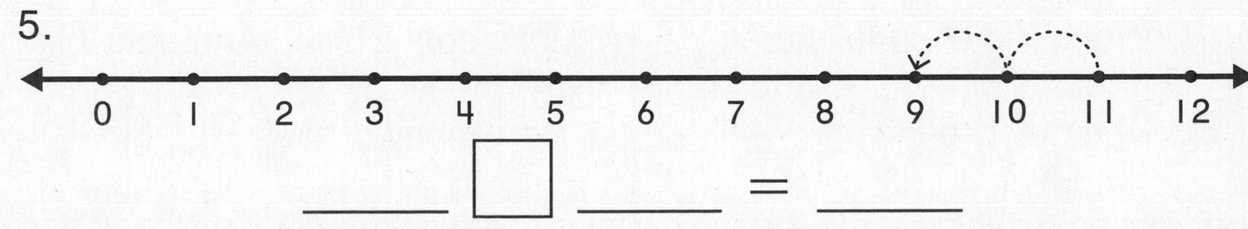

_____ □ _____ = _____

Notes for Home Your child used a number line to add and to subtract 1, 2 or 3. *Home Activity:* Ask your child to draw a number line to solve other problems such as 11 – 2.

Name ______________________________

Count Back 1 or 2

Problem Solving 4-9

Remember to count back. Start with how many there are.

0 1 2 3 4 5 6 7 8 9 10 11 12

Subtract.

1. There are 7 in the . Tim eats 1 . How many are left _____?

2. There are 12 in the . Max eats 2 . How many are left _____?

3. There are 9 in the . Lee eats 2 . How many are left _____?

4. There are 8 in the . Meg eats 1 . Al eats 1 . How many are left _____?

5. There are 11 in a . Dan and Tia each take an . How many are left _____?

6. There are 10 on the . Jake eats 2 . Ana eats 1 . How many are left _____?

Notes for Home Your child counted back 1 or 2 from a number. *Home Activity:* Ask your child to explain his or her answers.

Name ________________________________

Subtract All and Subtract Zero

Finish each number sentence to find the difference.

1. There are 7 in the . All fly away. How many are left?

   6 – ____ = ____

2. There are 8 on a . No hop away. How many are left?

   8 – ____ = ____

3. There are 5 at the . All run off. How many are left?

   5 – ____ = ____

4. There are 8 in the for . None are eaten. How many are left?

   7 – ____ = ____

5. There are 9 and 9 . Not one eats an . How many are left?

   9 – ____ = ____

6. There are 4 in the . Bob, Ed, Ana, and Lea each go for a ride. How many are left?

   4 – ____ = ____

Notes for Home Your child subtracted all and 0 from numbers. *Home Activity:* Have your child use small objects to model each subtraction.

Name ______________________________

Subtract with 5

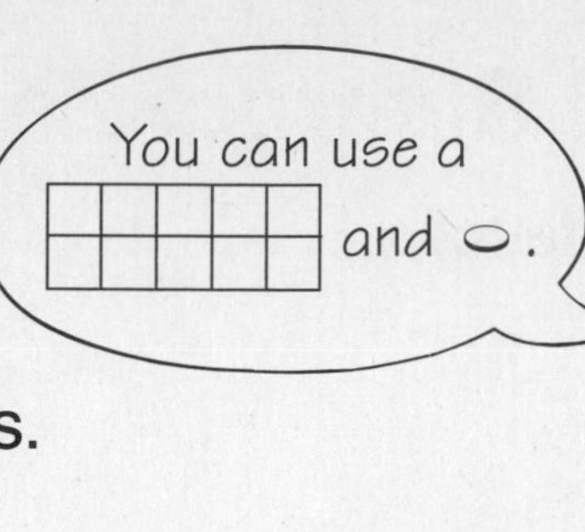

Read the problems.
Look at the pictures.
Finish the number sentences.

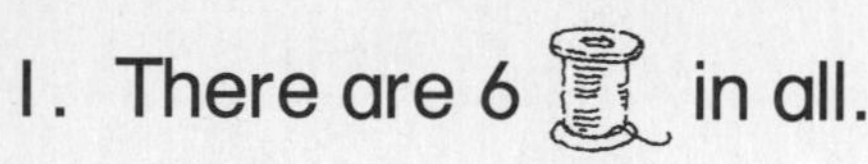

1. There are 6 in all.

   How many are in the  ?

   6 − ____ = ____

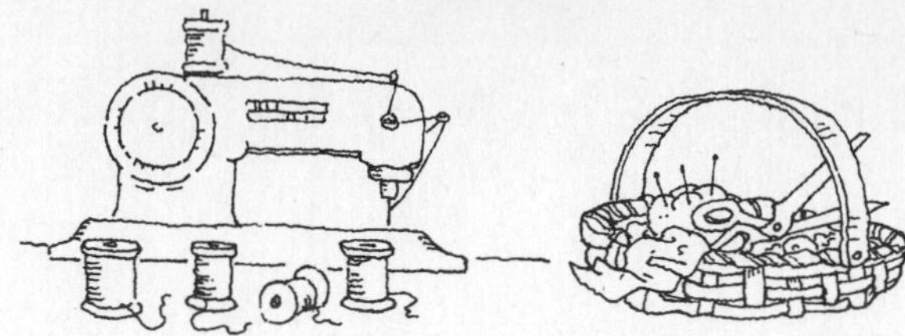

2. There were 9 in all.

   How many are in the ?

   6 − ____ = ____

3. There are 10 in all.

   How many are in the ?

   10 − ____ = ____

4. There are 8 in all.

   How many are in the  ?

   8 − ____ = ____

5. There are 7 in all.

   How many are in the ?

   7 − ____ = ____

Notes for Home Your child subtracted 5 from numbers. *Home Activity:* Ask your child to make up a math story with 12 and 5.

Name ______________________________

Problem Solving 4-12

Write a Number Sentence

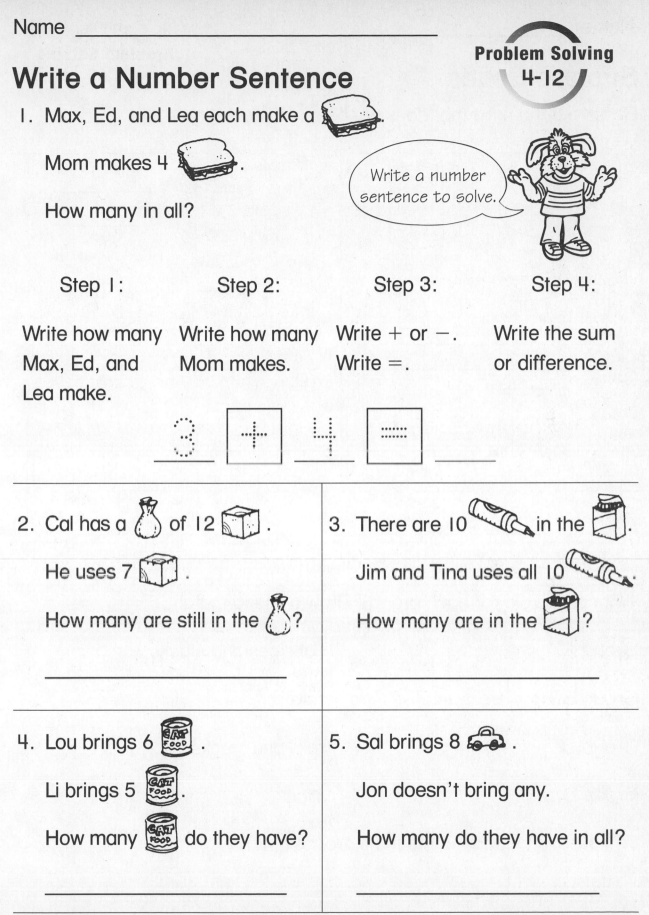

1. Max, Ed, and Lea each make a .

Mom makes 4 .

How many in all?

Step 1:	Step 2:	Step 3:	Step 4:
Write how many Max, Ed, and Lea make.	Write how many Mom makes.	Write + or −. Write =.	Write the sum or difference.

   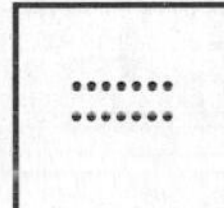 ______

2. Cal has a  of 12 .

He uses 7 .

How many are still in the ?

____

3. There are 10  in the .

Jim and Tina uses all 10 .

How many are in the ?

____

4. Lou brings 6 .

Li brings 5 .

How many  do they have?

____

5. Sal brings 8 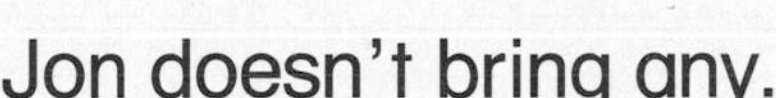.

Jon doesn't bring any.

How many do they have in all?

____

Using the Page Ask children to ***plan*** by reading the problems and then telling whether they will add or subtract to solve each problem and how they know. **Notes for Home** Your child wrote number sentences to solve problems. *Home Activity:* Ask your child to use small objects to show each story.

Name ______________________________

Problem Solving
5-1

Explore Solids

Cross out the solid that does not belong in each group.

A.

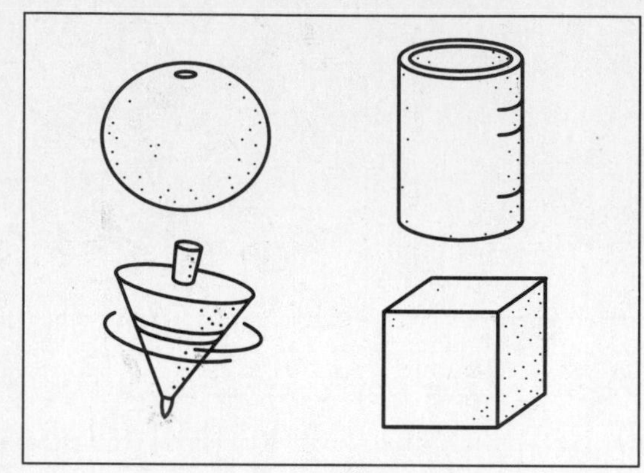

B.

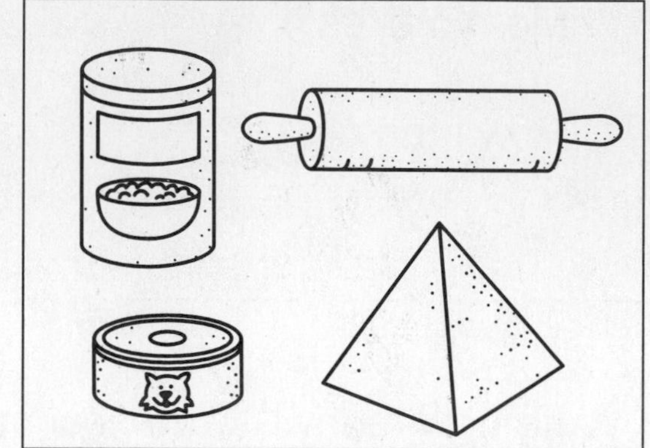

C.

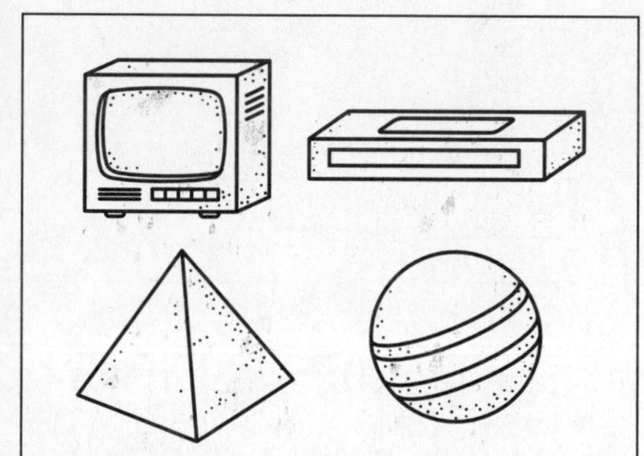

D.

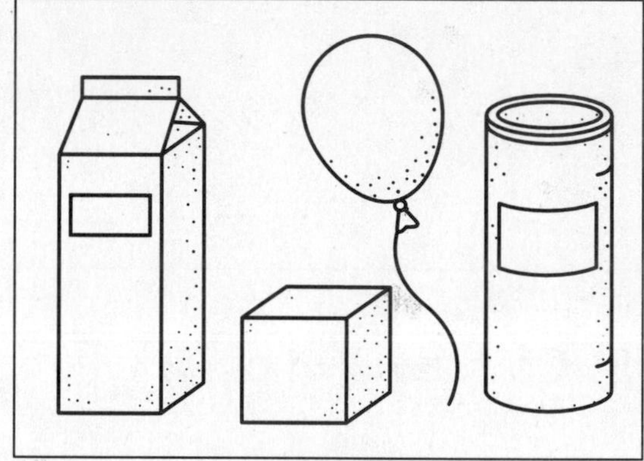

What's the rule for each group? Draw a line to match.

Group A.	flat sides and stacks
Group B.	rolls
Group C.	rolls and stacks
Group D.	slides

Which solid belongs to the most groups? Why?

Notes for Home Your child identified how each group of solids are alike and crossed out the solid that does not belong in each. *Home Activity:* Ask your child to explain his or her reasoning.

Name ____________________

Faces of Solids

Draw the missing face in the pattern for each solid.

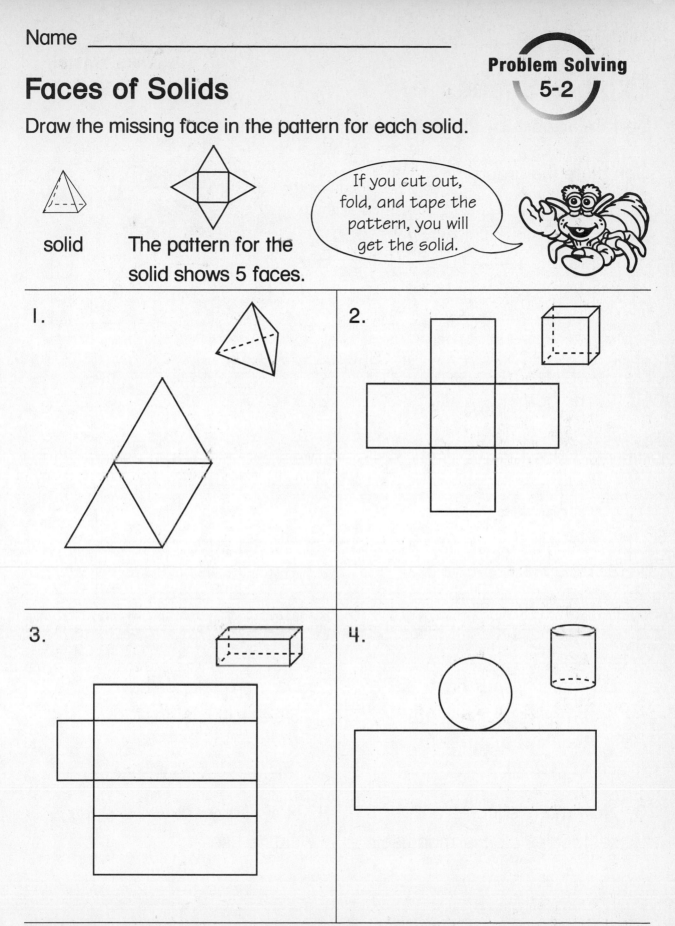

solid

The pattern for the solid shows 5 faces.

If you cut out, fold, and tape the pattern, you will get the solid.

1.

2.

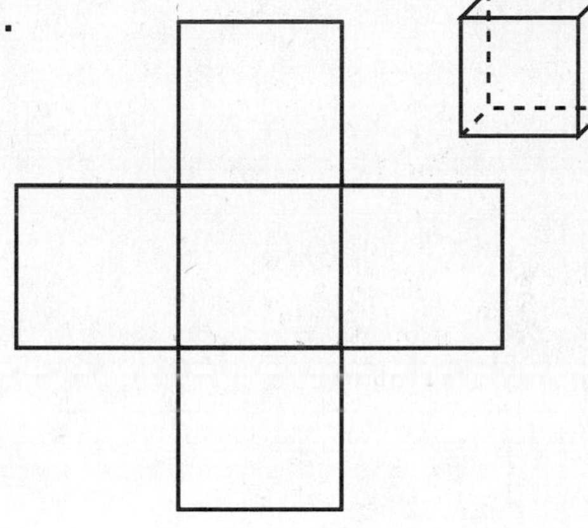

3.

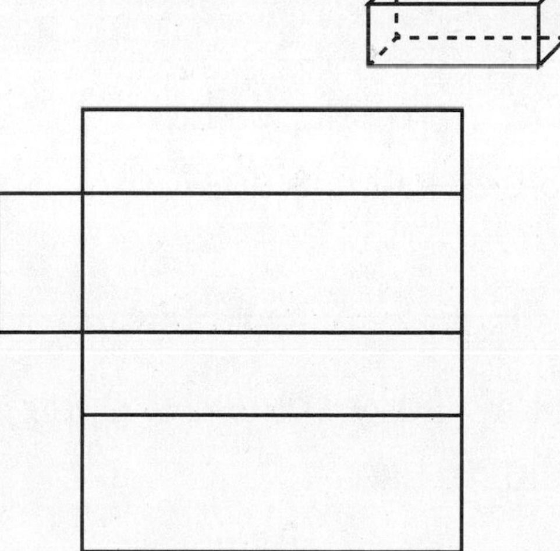

4.

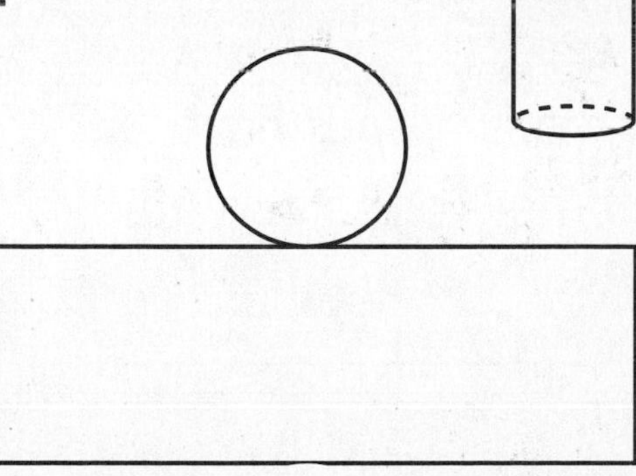

Notes for Home Your child used a picture of a solid to decide which face (side) of a pattern is missing. Then he or she drew the missing face, or side. *Home Activity:* Invite your child to use a box or carton and trace all the faces on a piece of paper.

Name ____________________

Explore Shapes

Sort the shapes by the number of sides and corners.

Complete the graph.

Color 1 box for each shape.

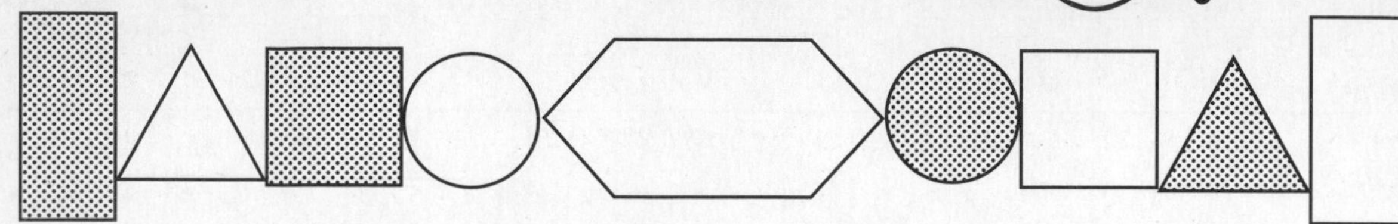

Shapes

no corners					
3 sides					
4 corners					
6 sides					
	1	2	3	4	5

1. Do more shapes have 4 corners or no corners?

   ____

2. Do more shapes have 3 sides or 6 sides?

   ____

3. How many squares and rectangles did Herman use?

   ______

4. How many shaded shapes did he use?

   ______

Notes for Home Your child sorted the picture of plane figures by the number of sides and corners and used the data to complete a bar graph. *Home Activity:* Ask your child to draw two more shapes on the border design and tell you how to count the sides and corners.

 Use with pages 179–180.

Name ______________________________

Problem Solving
5-4

Same Size and Shape

Draw a house the same size and shape.

Help me build the same house.

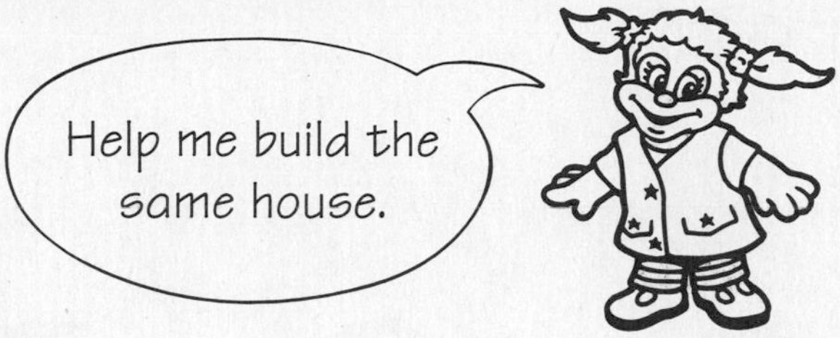

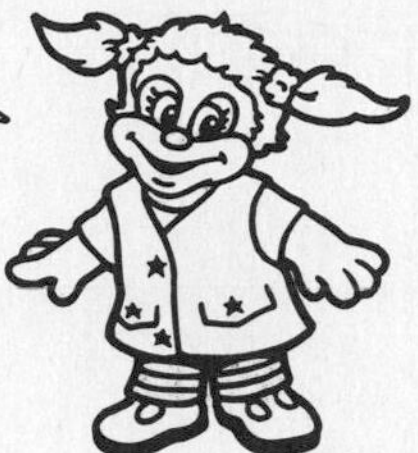

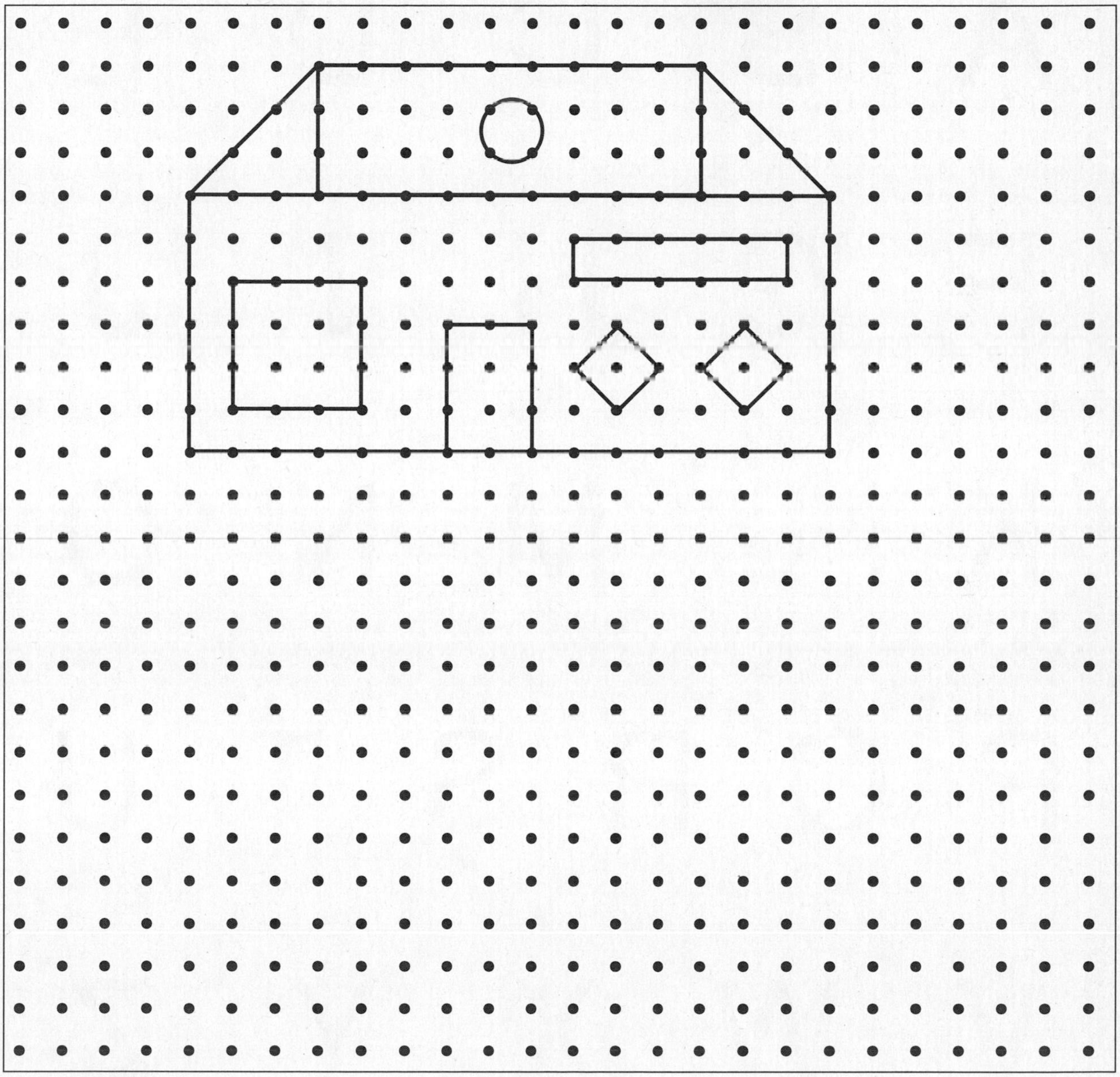

Notes for Home Your child used a dot grid to draw a house that is the same size and shape as the given house. *Home Activity:* Draw another window on the house that is given, and ask your child to draw the same size and shape on his or her house.

Name ______________________________

Problem Solving 5-5

Symmetry

Which letters can be folded so that both sides match? Draw the fold lines.

A B C D E

F G H I J

K L M N O

P Q R S T U

V W X Y Z

Notes for Home Your child drew lines of symmetry for the letters of the alphabet. *Home Activity:* Give your child a square piece of paper and ask him or her to show you several different ways to fold it so that the parts match.

Name ______________________________

Problem Solving
5-6

Make a Table

How many ways can you make this shape?
Use pattern blocks.
Make a table to record the ways.

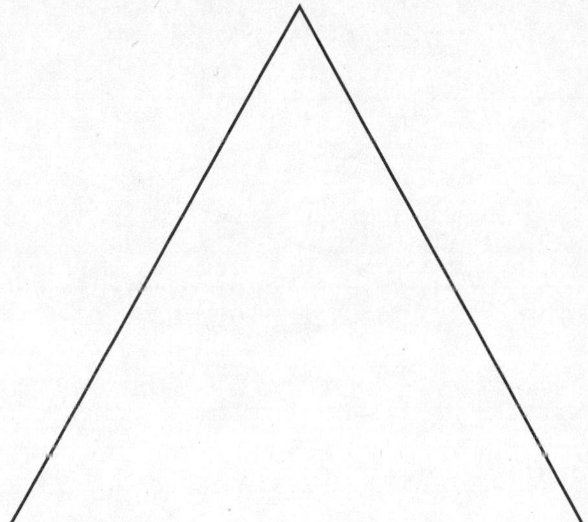

Shapes I Used				
1st	1	3	0	0
2nd				
3rd				
4th				
5th				
6th				
7th				

Step 1
Decide which blocks you can use.

Step 2
Write how many of each block you need to make the shape.

Step 3
Try other shapes. Finish the table.

There are ______ ways to make the triangle.

Using the Page To help children ***solve*** the problem, have them place the pattern blocks on the triangle.
Notes for Home Your child used pattern blocks to find ways to make a triangle. *Home Activity:* Make a 5-inch cardboard square. Cut the square into a variety of shapes including a trapezoid, parallelogram, and triangles. Have your child use the shapes to create new shapes.

Name ______________________

Problem Solving
5-7

Fair Shares

Solve.

1. Jamal and Ann want to share some pens.
   There are 6 pens.
   How can they make fair shares?

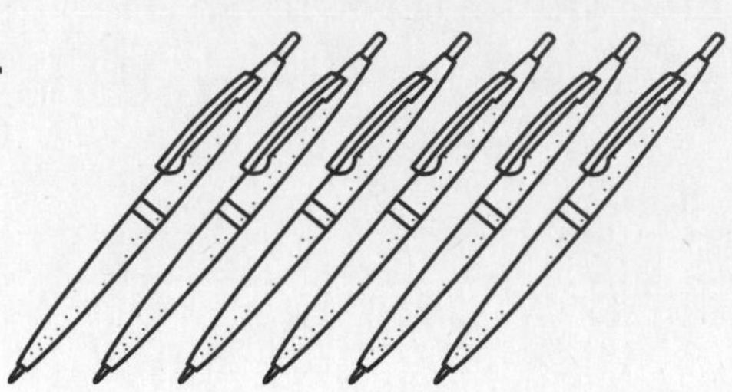

____

2. Four girls will share a berry pie.
   There are 4 slices of pie.
   How can they make fair shares?

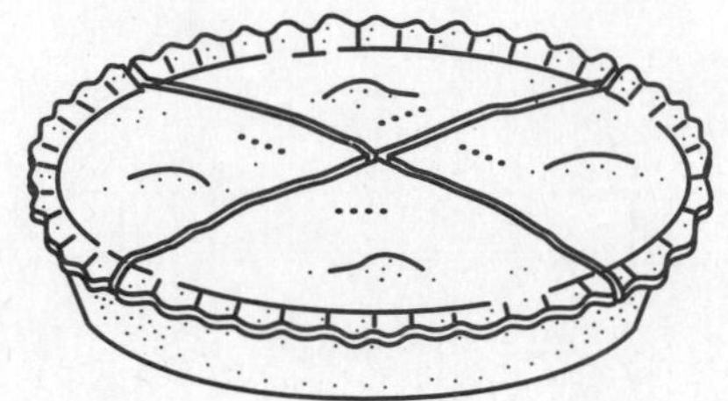

____

3. Three boys want to share some balloons.
   There are 6 balloons.
   How can they make fair shares?

____

4. Bill and Amber will share a banana.
   There is 1 banana.
   How can they make fair shares?

____

5. Kira and Ben want to share some popcorn.
   There are 8 bags of popcorn.
   How can they make fair shares?

____

Notes for Home Your child solved word problems about how to make fair shares. *Home Activity:* Draw a circle and pretend it is a pizza. Ask your child to tell you some different ways that you and he or she could share a pizza to make fair shares.

Name ______________________________

Halves

Problem Solving 5-8

Draw a line and color to show what Kira ate each day.

1. On Monday, Kira drank half a glass of milk.

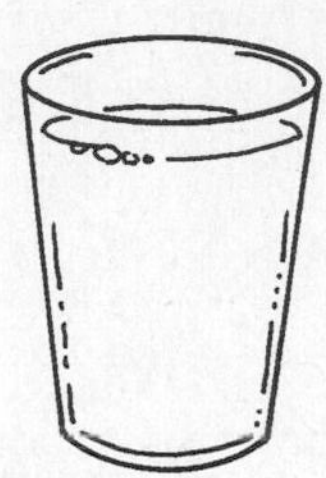

2. On Tuesday, she ate half a sandwich.

3. On Wednesday, she ate half a slice of pizza.

4. Kira ate half an apple on Thursday.

5. She ate half a muffin on Friday.

Notes for Home Your child drew a line and colored to show one half on each pictured item. *Home Activity:* Give your child an apple or orange, and ask him or her to show how to divide it into halves.

Name ______________________________

Fourths

Jim and Jan want to show fourths in different ways.
Show what Jim and Jan could do.

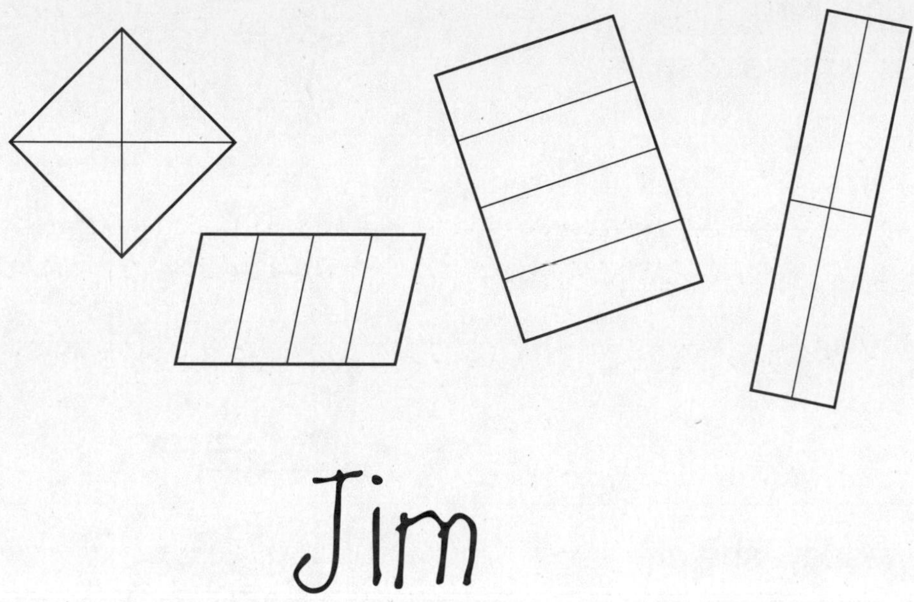

Jim

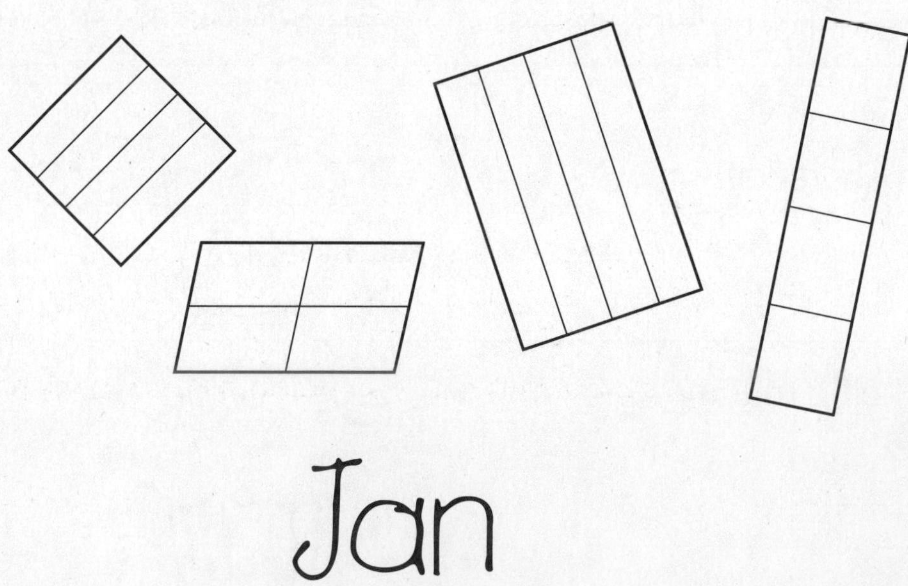

Jan

Notes for Home Your child found different ways to divide shapes into fourths. *Home Activity:* Draw a circle and ask your child to show how to divide it into fourths. Then ask him or her to explain why there is only one way to divide the shape into fourths.

Name ______________________________

Thirds

Problem Solving
5-10

Look at the picture.
Circle the correct word. Solve.

1. About $\frac{1}{3}$ of the children are girls. boys.

   Are there more boys or girls? girls boys

2. 1 boy and 2 girls go home.
   About $\frac{1}{3}$ of the children are girls. boys.

   Are there more boys or girls? girls boys

3. Draw a picture with many things. Circle about $\frac{1}{3}$ of your things.

Notes for Home Your child used a picture to estimate the fraction 1/3. *Home Activity:* Ask your child to fold a piece of paper into thirds.

Name ______________________

Explore Probability

Problem Solving
5-11

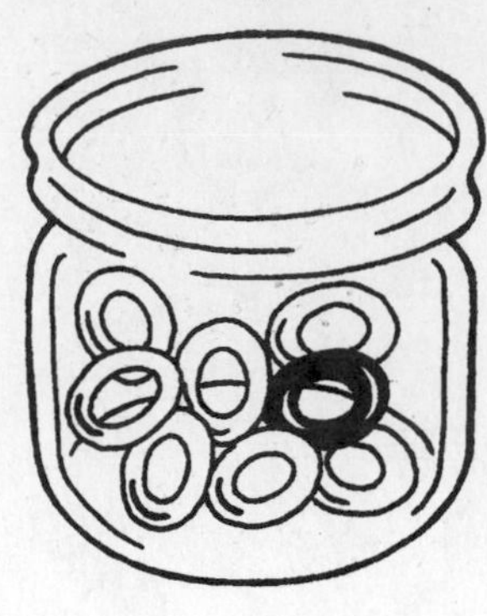

1. This jar has 8 rings in it.
   7 rings are white and 1 ring is black.
   Which color ring are you more likely to pick each time? Why?

   ____

   ____

2. Color some apples red and some apples green. Color more of the apples red. If you covered your eyes and picked an apple, are you more likely to pick a red apple or a green apple? Why?

   ____

   ____

3. Color some balls brown and some blue.
   Have a friend cover his or her eyes and point to a ball.
   Which color is the ball?

   ____

   ____

Notes for Home Your child decided how likely it was to pick an object of a certain color. *Home Activity:* Ask your child to describe events that always happen, sometimes happen, and never happen.

Name ______________________

Problem Solving 5-12

Fractions and Probability

Solve.

We're spinning on different colored spinners.

1. Pedro got 8 yellow and 2 blue. How many times did he spin? ____

2. Sara got 1 yellow, 4 green and 3 red. How many times did she spin? ____

3. Ming got 4 purple. He got the same number of yellow. How many times did he spin? ____

4. Mia had 6 spins. She got 2 red. How many blue did she get? ____

5. Katlin had 12 spins. She got 4 black and 3 red. How many yellow did she get? ____

6. Jay had 6 spins. He got 3 red and 3 yellow. How many green did he get? ____

Notes for Home Your child solved problems about the results of probability activities. *Home Activity:* Ask your child if he or she would be likely to get more red when using a red and yellow fair spinner, or when using a red, yellow, and blue fair spinner. (red and yellow spinner)

Name ______________________________

Use Data from a Picture

Come fly a kite.

Find the fractions in the picture.

Solve the riddles.

1. I show fourths.
   One fourth is a triangle.
   Color $\frac{1}{4}$ of me blue.

2. I show thirds.
   One third is yellow.
   Color $\frac{1}{3}$ of me yellow.

3. I show halves.
   One half is red.
   Color $\frac{1}{2}$ of me red.

4. I show fourths.
   One fourth of me is orange.
   Color $\frac{1}{4}$ of me orange.

What shape can you color to show $\frac{1}{2}$ blue and $\frac{1}{2}$ green? ____________
Color the shape.

Using the Page To help children ***understand*** the riddles, first have them look for fractions in the kites. Then have them solve each riddle. **Notes for Home** Your child used a picture to answer riddles about fractions. *Home Activity:* Ask your child to make up some riddles about the picture for you to answer.

Name ______________________________

Problem Solving
6-1

Add with Doubles

What animals does Lee see at the zoo?

Find the sums.

Then connect the dots to show the sums in order.

0	1	2	3	4	5	6
+ 0	+ 1	+ 2	+ 3	+ 4	+ 5	+ 6

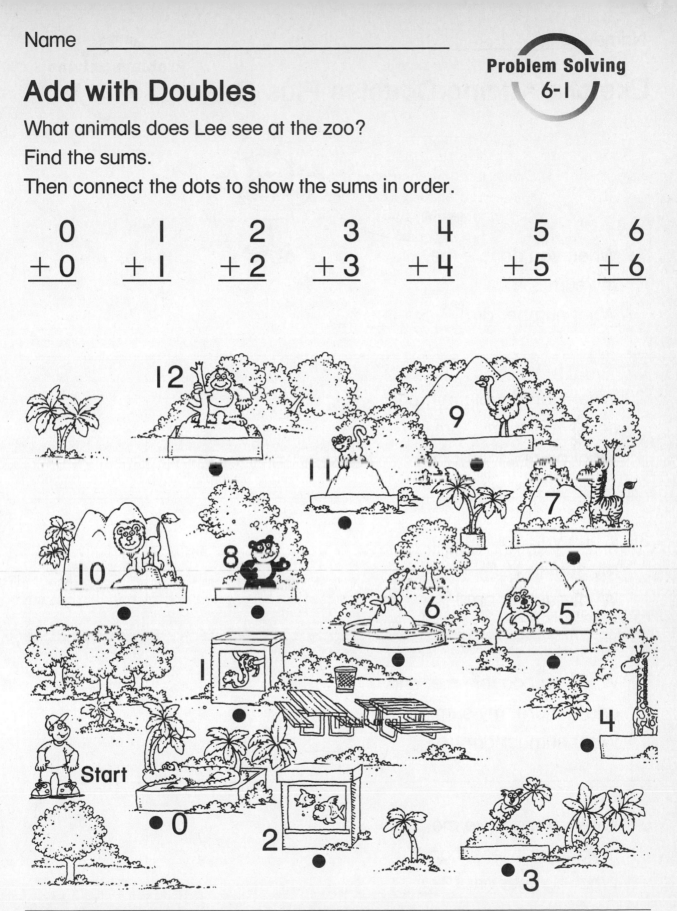

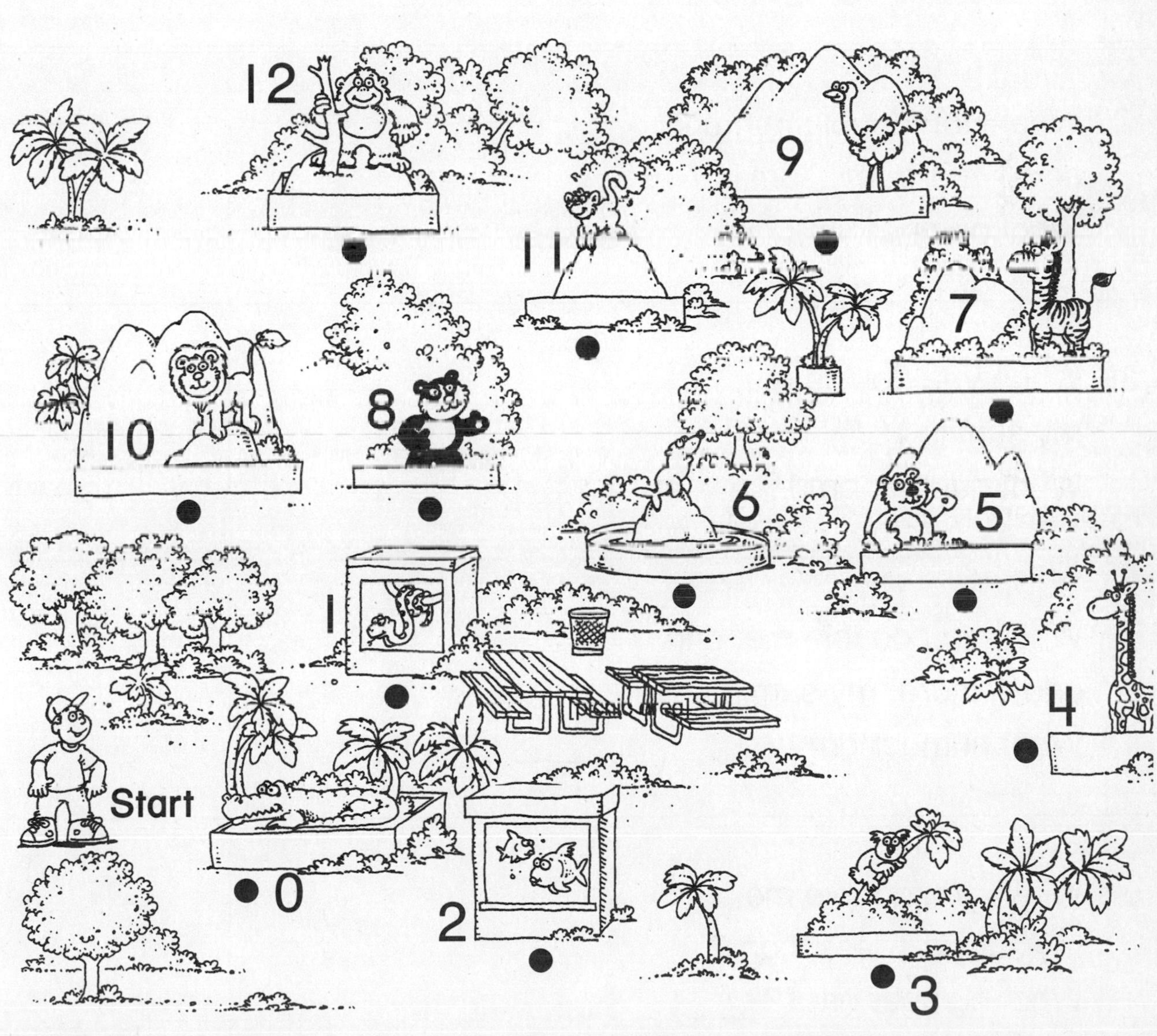

Notes for Home Your child added doubles and used the sums to solve a problem. *Home Activity:* Provide your child with 6 buttons, paper clips, or other small objects. Ask how many more like objects must be added to make a sum of 12. (6)

Name ________________________________

Explore Adding Doubles Plus One

Problem Solving 6-2

Solve the riddles.
Draw dots on each side of the line to show doubles or doubles plus one.

1. When you double me,
   my sum is 4.
   What number am I? _____

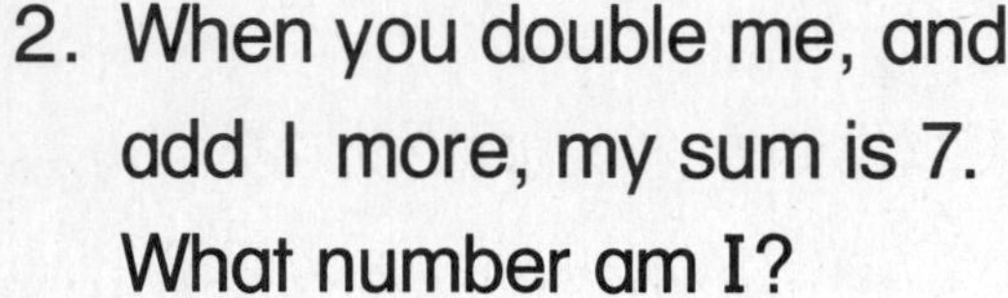

2. When you double me, and
   add 1 more, my sum is 7.
   What number am I? _____

---

3. When you double me,
   my sum is 12.
   What number am I? _____

---

4. When you double me, and
   add 1 more, my sum is 11.
   What number am I? _____

---

5. When you double me,
   my sum is 1 less than 9.
   What number am I? _____

Notes for Home Your child explored adding one more to a double to solve riddles. *Home Activity:* Ask your child to make up a riddle for a sum of 9. (When you double me, and add 1 more, my sum is 9. What number am I? 4.)

Name ______________________________

Problem Solving 6-3

Add with Doubles Plus One

What is the hidden picture?

Find each sum. Next, add 1 to each number in your head.

Then color the shape with the new sum.

0	1	2	3	4	5
+ 0	+ 1	+ 2	+ 3	+ 4	+ 5

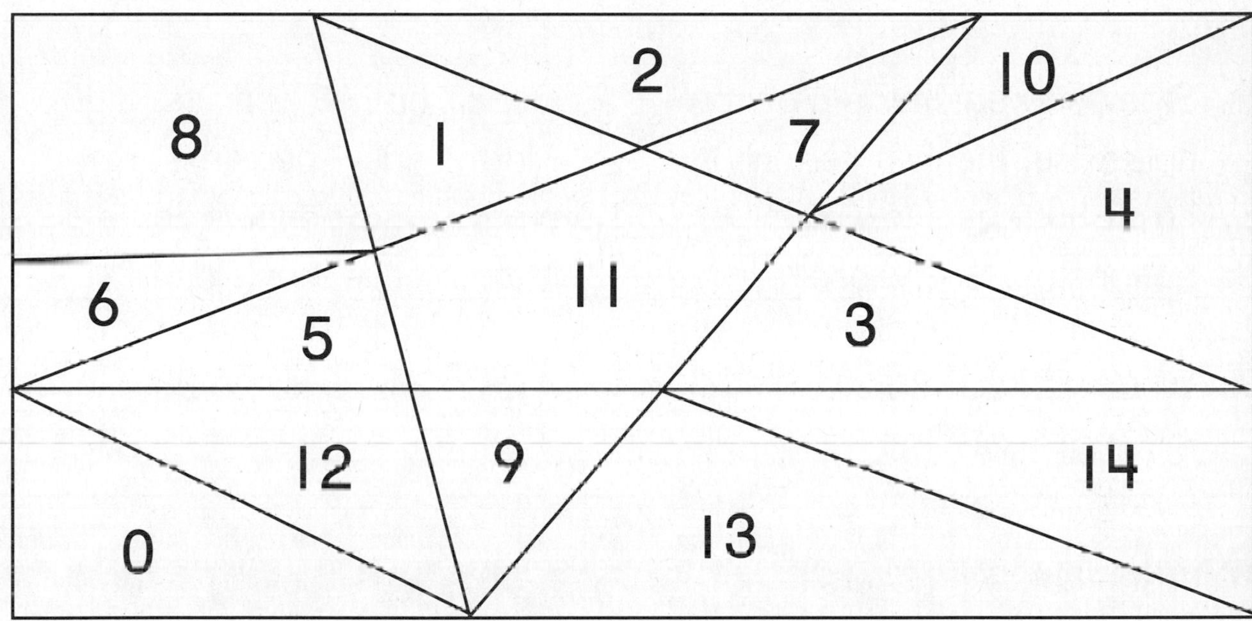

Write a double plus one fact for the sum in each shape you colored.

____ + ____ = ____ ____ + ____ = ____

____ + ____ = ____ ____ + ____ = ____

____ + ____ = ____ ____ + ____ = ____

Notes for Home Your child used double facts to find sums, added 1 to each sum, and then wrote doubles plus one facts for each shape. *Home Activity:* Ask your child to give you a turnaround fact for each addition sentence he or she wrote. (1 + 0 = 1; 4 + 3 = 7; 2 + 1 = 3; 5 + 4 = 9; 3 + 2 = 5; 6 + 5 = 11)

Name ______________________________

Problem Solving
6-4

Use Doubles to Subtract

Solve the problems. Write the number sentences.

1. Marita collected 12 shells on the beach. Sam collected 6 shells. How many more shells did Marita collect?

   ____ – ____ = ____ shells

2. Betty's Bakery baked 8 apple pies. 4 pies were sold on Friday. How many were left?

   ____ – ____ = ____ pies

3. Stacy's sweater has 6 button holes. But the sweater only has 3 buttons. How many buttons did Stacy lose?

   ____ – ____ = ____ buttons

4. Robert has 10 pennies. Martha has 5 pennies. How many fewer pennies does Martha have than Robert?

   ____ – ____ = ____ pennies

5. Jason had 4 crackers to eat with his soup. He gave 2 crackers to his sister. How many crackers does Jason have left?

   ____ – ____ = ____ crackers

6. 2 dogs were playing in the park. 1 went home. How many dogs were left in the park?

   ____ – ____ = ____ dog

Notes for Home Your child solved word problems by subtracting. *Home Activity:* Say each subtraction fact. Ask your child to say the corresponding addition fact. (Example: 10 – 5 = 5; 5 + 5 = 10)

Name ______________________________

Collect and Use Data

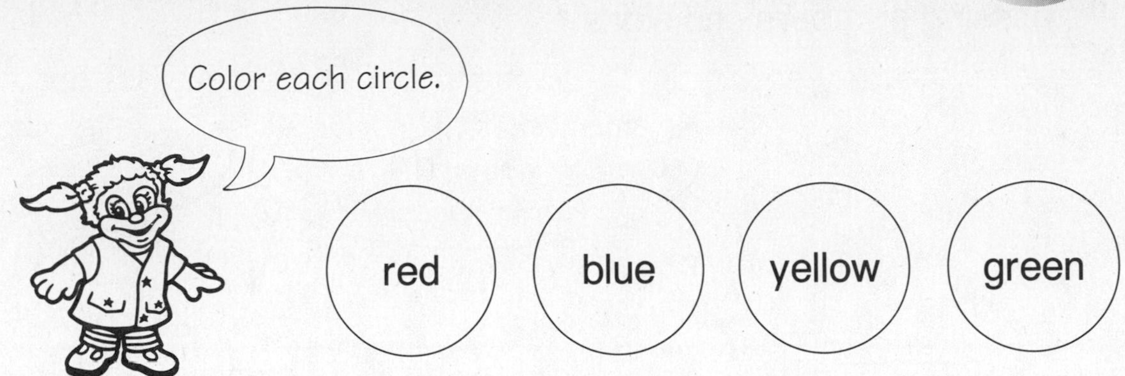

Which color do 12 of your friends like the most?
Take a vote. Make a tally.

Step 1: Write each color on the chart.

Step 2: Ask 12 friends which color they like most. Make a tally mark to show what each friend says.

Step 3: Write each total.

Color	Tally	Total
red		
blue		
yellow		

Step 4: Use the chart to solve.

1. How many friends picked yellow? ______
2. Which color did most friends pick? ______________
3. Which color did they pick least? ______________
4. What else does the chart tell you? ______________

Using the Page Have children ***look back*** at their charts to make sure there is a tally mark for each friend who responded. **Notes for Home** Your child made tally marks in a chart to record their classmates' responses to a question. *Home Activity:* Have your child repeat the activity by asking family members to name the color each prefers.

Name ______________________________

Problem Solving
6-6

Relate Addition and Subtraction

Fill in the missing numbers and signs.

Remember, if the numbers are the same, the facts are related.

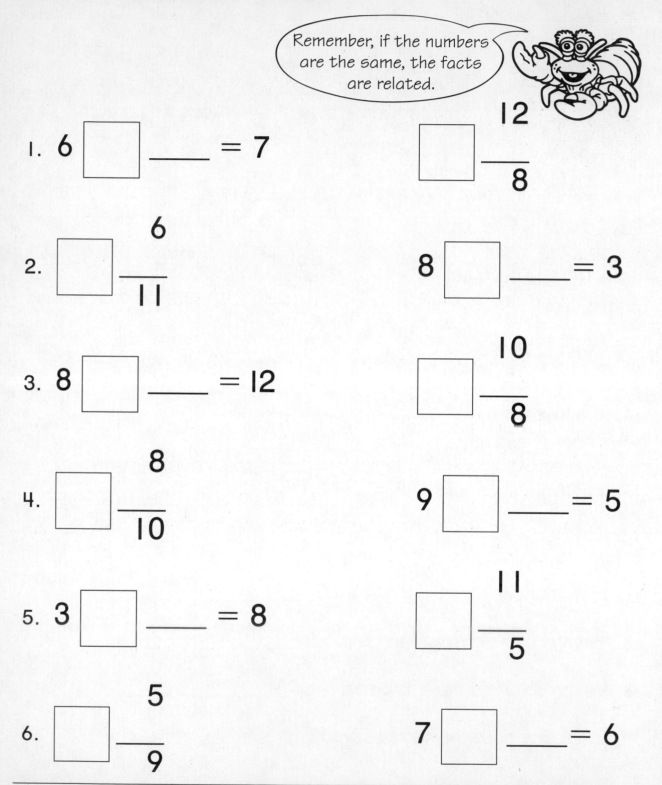

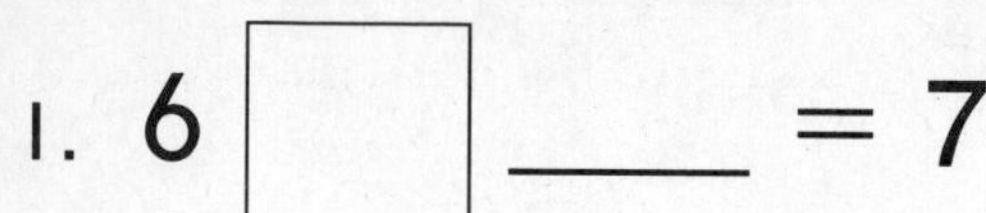
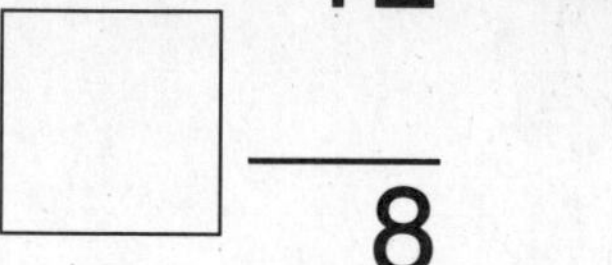

1. 6 ☐ ____ = 7   12
☐ ____
8

2. 6
☐ ____
11   8 ☐ ____ = 3

3. 8 ☐ ____ = 12   10
☐ ____
8

4. 8
☐ ____
10   9 ☐ ____ = 5

5. 3 ☐ ____ = 8   11
☐ ____
5

6. 5
☐ ____
9   7 ☐ ____ = 6

Notes for Home Your child completed related addition and subtraction facts. *Home Activity:* Give your child two numbers which are less than 10, such as 6 and 7. Challenge your child to use the numbers in a pair of related addition and subtraction facts. (1 + 6 = 7; 7 – 6 = 1)

Name ______________________

Fact Families

What numbers are missing?

What sign belongs in each ◯ ?

Write the missing numbers and signs to show two fact families.

The sum is 8.	The sum is 9.
3 ◯ ____ = ____	4 ◯ ____ = ____
____ ◯ ____ = ____	____ ◯ ____ = ____
____ ◯ ____ = ____	____ ◯ ____ = ____
____ ◯ ____ = ____	____ ◯ ____ = ____

Now write the missing numbers in each story.

1. Sam, Max, Jen, and Lea are at the playground. Here come 5 more children. Now there are ______ children at the playground. At noon, Sam, Max, Jen, and Lea go home for lunch. Now ______ children are at the playground.

2. Luis, Ty, and Gina want to play a game, but they need 5 more players. It takes ______ players in all for their game.

3. Meg, Jon, Sal, Lew, and Ali are playing tag. Then 3 more friends come. Now ______ children are playing tag. John, Sal, and Lew leave, but 4 more friends come. Now ______ friends are playing.

Notes for Home Your child completed related addition and subtraction facts and then used those numbers to complete a story. *Home Activity:* Ask your child to identify the number sentences he or she wrote for each problem. (Problem 1. 4 + 5 = 9; 9 - 4 = 5; Problem 2. 3 + 5 = 8; Problem 3. 5 + 3 = 8; 8 - 3 = 5; 5 + 4 = 9)

Name ______________________________

Problem Solving 6-8

Think Addition to Subtract

Use addition facts you know to find the missing numbers. Then make up a problem of your own.

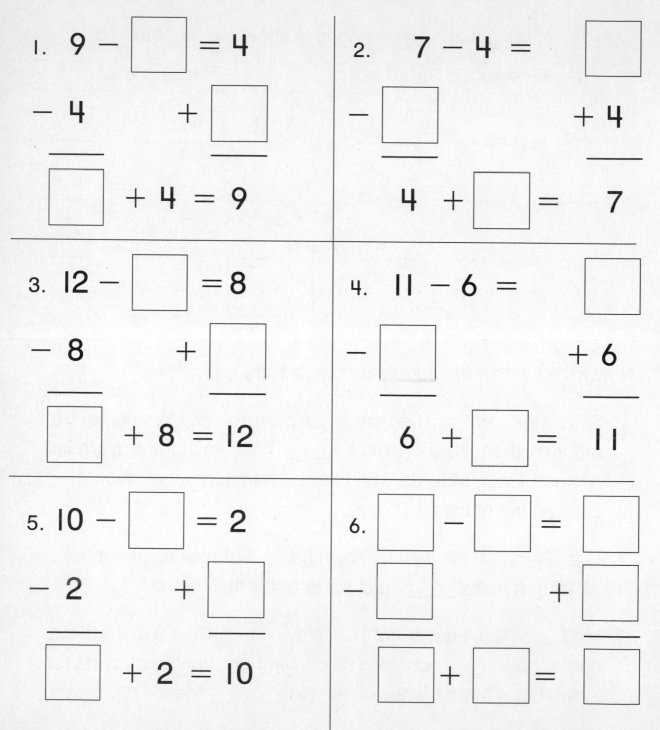

1. 9 − □ = 4

   − 4   + □

   □ + 4 = 9

2. 7 − 4 = □

   − □   + 4

   4 + □ = 7

3. 12 − □ = 8

   − 8   + □

   □ + 8 = 12

4. 11 − 6 = □

   − □   + 6

   6 + □ = 11

5. 10 − □ = 2

   − 2   + □

   □ + 2 = 10

6. □ − □ = □

   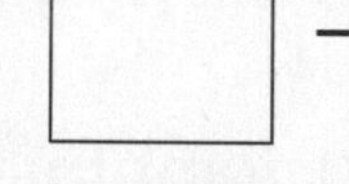
   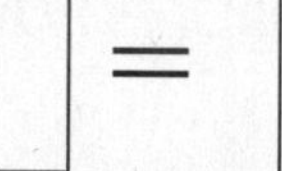

   − □   + □

   □ + □ = □

Notes for Home Your child used addition facts to help solve subtraction facts. *Home Activity:* Challenge your child to identify addition facts to solve these problems: 9 − 3, 12 − 5, and 8 − 1. (6 + 3 = 9 or 3 + 6 = 9; 7 + 5 = 12 or 5 + 7 = 12; 7 + 1 = 8 or 1 + 7 = 8)

Name ____________________

Problem Solving 6-9

Fact Families for 10

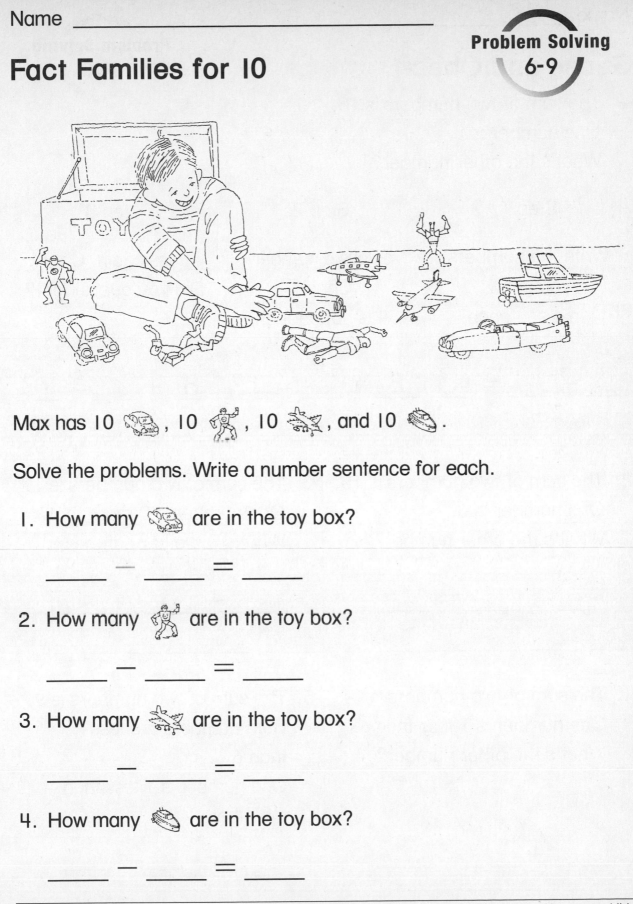

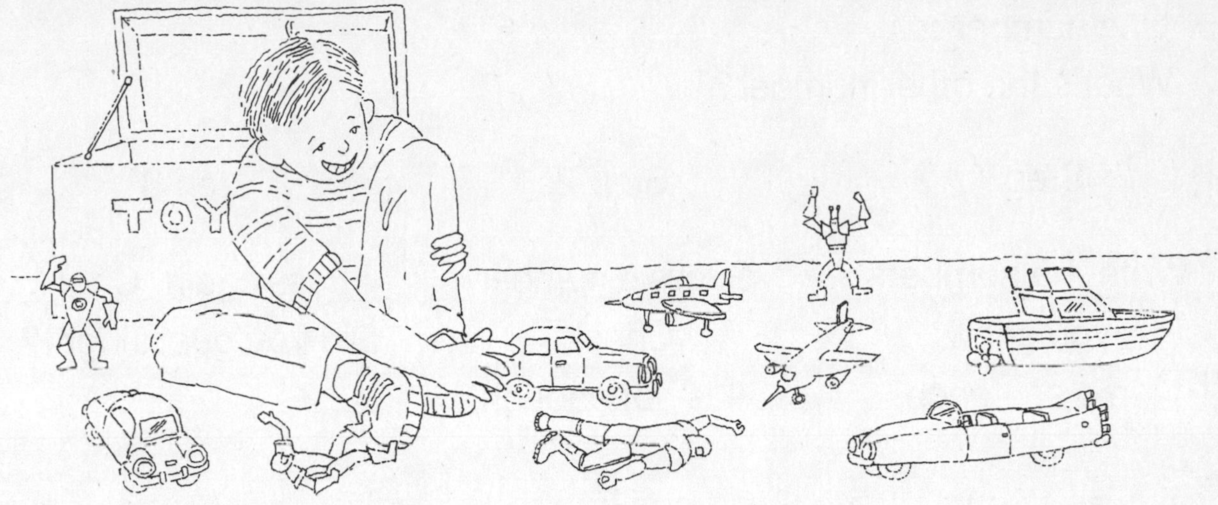

Max has 10 cars, 10 robots, 10 airplanes, and 10 boats.

Solve the problems. Write a number sentence for each.

1. How many cars are in the toy box?

   ____ – ____ = ____

2. How many robots are in the toy box?

   ____ – ____ = ____

3. How many airplanes are in the toy box?

   ____ – ____ = ____

4. How many boats are in the toy box?

   ____ – ____ = ____

Notes for Home Your child solved problems by writing number sentences for 10. *Home Activity:* Have your child use small objects to demonstrate how to solve each problem.

Name ______________________________

Problem Solving 6-10

Guess and Check

1. The sum of two numbers is 13.
   One number is 8.
   What's the other number?

Step 1	Step 2	Step 3
Write the numbers you know in a sentence.	Guess a number. Check. 4 is not enough.	Guess again. Check. Did you guess right?
8 + ___ = 13	8 + 4 = 13	8 + ___ = 13

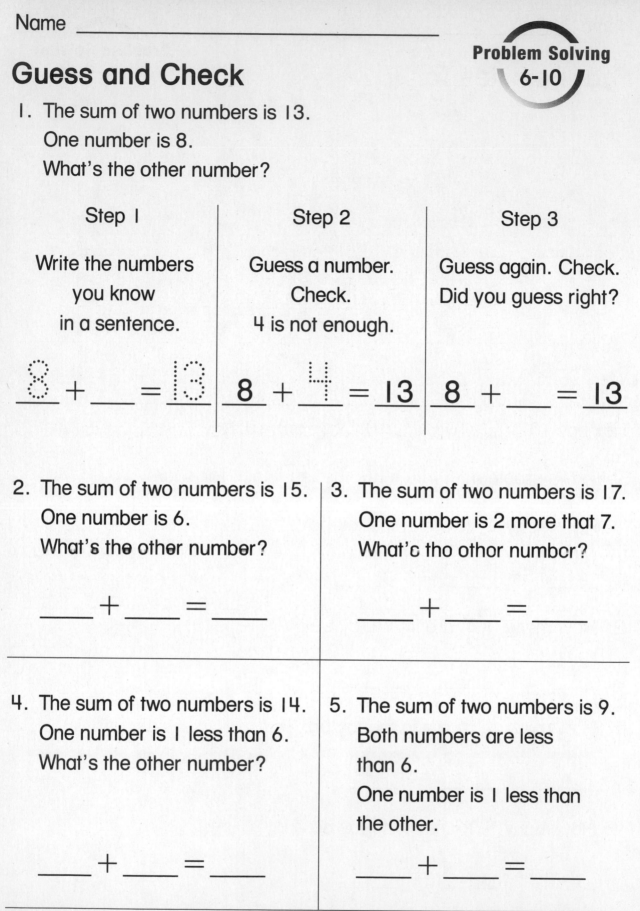

2. The sum of two numbers is 15.
   One number is 6.
   What's the other number?

   ___ + ___ = ___

3. The sum of two numbers is 17.
   One number is 2 more that 7.
   What's the other number?

   ___ + ___ = ___

4. The sum of two numbers is 14.
   One number is 1 less than 6.
   What's the other number?

   ___ + ___ = ___

5. The sum of two numbers is 9.
   Both numbers are less than 6.
   One number is 1 less than the other.

   ___ + ___ = ___

Using the Page Have children read through the first problem and suggest possible ways to ***solve*** it before following the suggested steps. **Notes for Home** Your child used the guess-and-check method to solve problems. *Home Activity:* Use the problems as models to create other problems for your child to solve.

Name ______________________

Numbers to 19

Problem Solving 7-1

1. Which row has 16 books? Make a ✓
   Then color the books red.

2. Which row has nineteen books? Make an X.
   Color the books blue.

3. Which row has 10 and 3 books? Make ✓✓.
   Color the books green.

4. How many books are in the bottom row?

   ______ and ______ is ______.

5. Make X X next to the third row.
   Are there eighteen, fifteen, or sixteen books?

   ____

Notes for Home Your child identified amounts to 19 to solve problems. *Home Activity:* Ask your child to use small objects such as buttons, coins, or paper clips to show 13 to 19.

Name ______________________________

Tens

Problem Solving 7-2

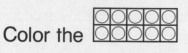

Color the [ten-frame] to show each number.

Circle the number word that tells how many in all.

20		ten thirty twenty
50		fifty forty sixty
40		sixty thirty forty
60		twenty sixty ten
30		ten twenty thirty

Notes for Home Your child identified tens to 60, demonstrated each amount, and circled the number word for each one. *Home Activity:* Write 10, 20, 30, 40, 50, 60, and the number words for each on separate index cards. Mix the cards. Have your child match the cards and then use small objects to show each amount.

Name ____________________

Numbers to 60

How many more shapes must you draw to show each number? Draw the shapes.

Circle the groups of 10.

35 △△△△△△△△△△ △△△△△△△△△△ △△△△△△△△

59 ○○○○○○○○○○ ○○○○○○○○○○ ○○○○○○○○○○ ○○○○○○○○○○ ○○○○○○○○○

27 ☆☆☆☆☆☆☆☆☆☆ ☆☆☆☆☆☆

48 □□□□□□□□□□ □□ □□□□□□□□□□ □□□□□□□□□□ □□□□□□□□□□

Notes for Home Your child circled groups of 10 and drew additional shapes to show each amount. *Home Activity:* Draw 21 dots on a sheet of paper. Write 30. Ask your child how many more dots he or she has to draw.

Name ______________________

Explore Estimation

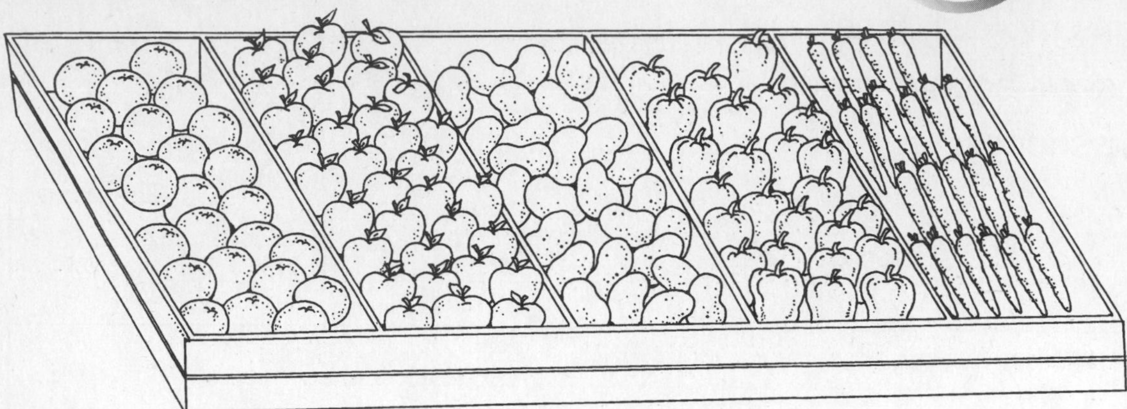

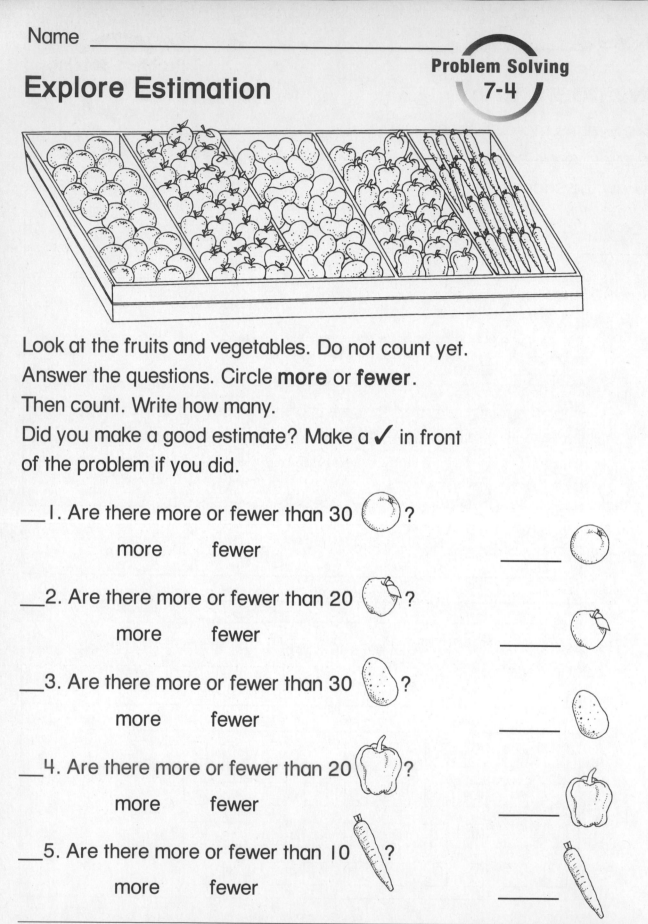

Look at the fruits and vegetables. Do not count yet.
Answer the questions. Circle **more** or **fewer**.
Then count. Write how many.
Did you make a good estimate? Make a ✓ in front of the problem if you did.

__1. Are there more or fewer than 30 ?

more fewer ______

__2. Are there more or fewer than 20 ?

more fewer ______

__3. Are there more or fewer than 30 ?

more fewer ______

__4. Are there more or fewer than 20 ?

more fewer ______

__5. Are there more or fewer than 10 ?

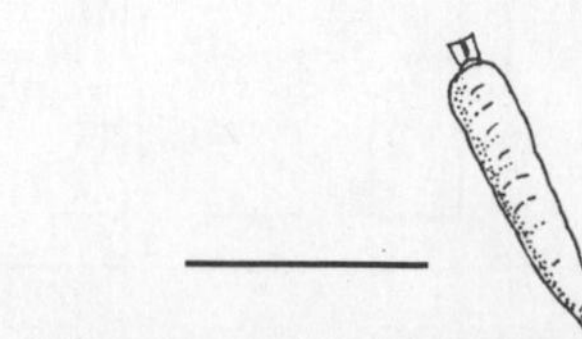

more fewer ______

Notes for Home Your child explored estimation by deciding if there were more or fewer fruits and vegetables, and then counted to determine if estimates were accurate. *Home Activity:* Count the number of canned goods on a shelf, and ask your child if there are more or fewer than 10, 20, 30. Then ask your child to count the objects.

Name ______________________________

Problem Solving
7-5

Estimation

1. Here are some □. Draw some more.

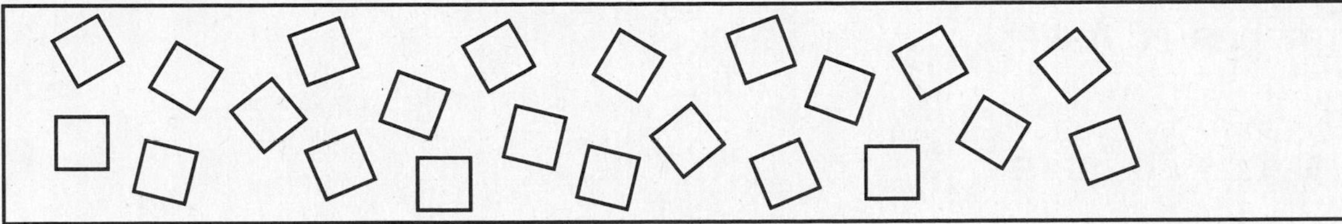

About how many □ are there in all? about _____

Count and see. Did you make a good estimate? Yes No

2. Here are some ☆. Draw some more.

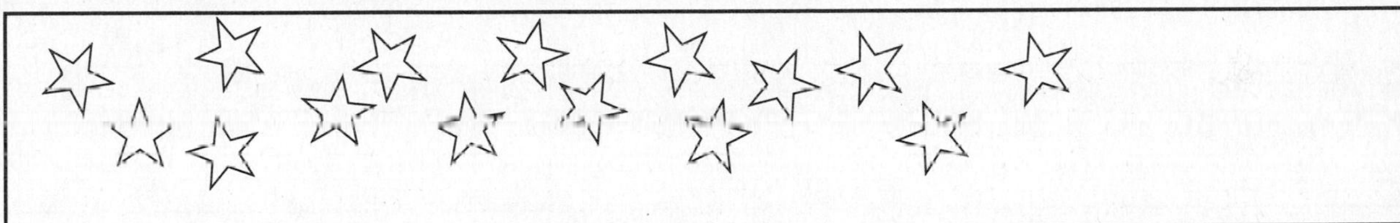

About how many ☆ are there in all? about _____

Count and see. Did you make a good estimate? Yes No

3. Here are some ⊖. Draw some more.

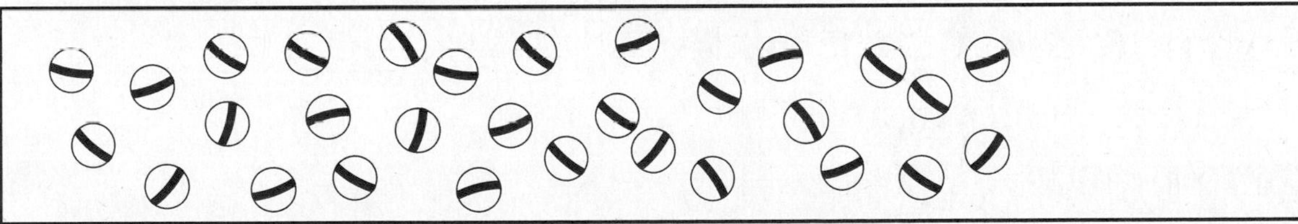

About how many ⊖ are there in all? about _____

Count and see. Did you make a good estimate? Yes No

Notes for Home Your child drew additional shapes, estimated how many in all, and then counted to verify estimates. *Home Activity:* Ask your child to explain how he or she estimated.

Name ______________________________

Use Data from a Graph

Problem Solving 7-6

1. Use the clues to finish the graph.

Amy has 10 fewer  than Mel.

Alex has 20 more  than Amy.

Make groups of 10 . Draw a ○ for each .

Mel	○○○○○○○○○○ ○○○○○○○○○○ ○○○○○○○○○○
Amy	
Alex	

Complete.

1. Mel has 30 . Amy has  20 .

Alex has ______ .

2. Who has 10 fewer  than Alex? ____________

3. How many more 

does Amy need to have 30? ____________

4. Do Mel and Amy together have

more or fewer  than Alex? ____________

Using the Page To help children ***understand,*** have them read the problem and tell what they know. Discuss how to complete the graph and then use the information to answer the questions. **Notes for Home** Your child completed data on a graph to solve problems. *Home Activity:* Ask your child to use the graph to tell who has the fewest pennies and how many more pennies that child would need to have the same number of pennies as Alex. (Amy; 20 pennies more)

Name ______________________________

Problem Solving 7-7

Count by 2s and 10s

How many in your class?
Count by 2s or 10s to find out.

1. boys' ______	2. girls' ______
3. on boys and girls ______	4. of boys toes ______
5. of girls' fingers ______	6. of boys and girls fingers toes ______
7. with ______	8. boys' with elbows ______

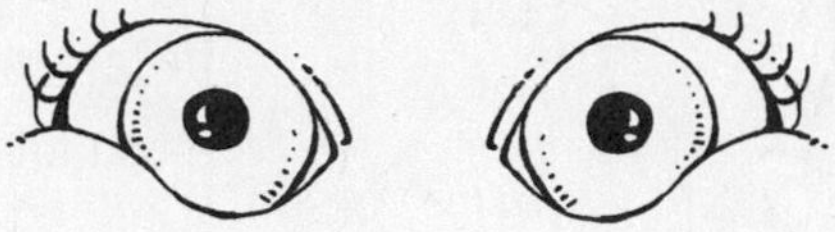

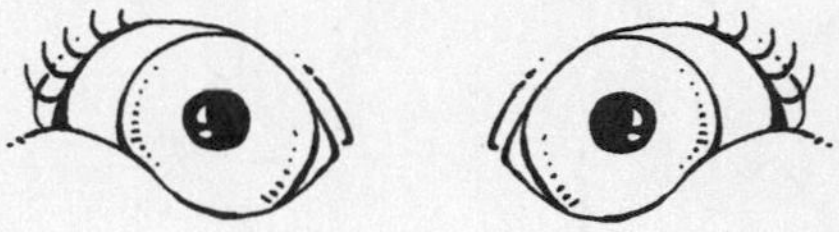

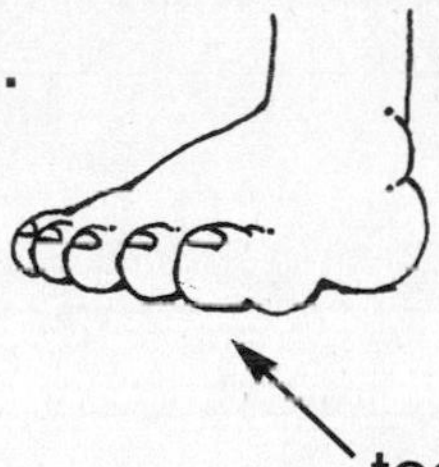

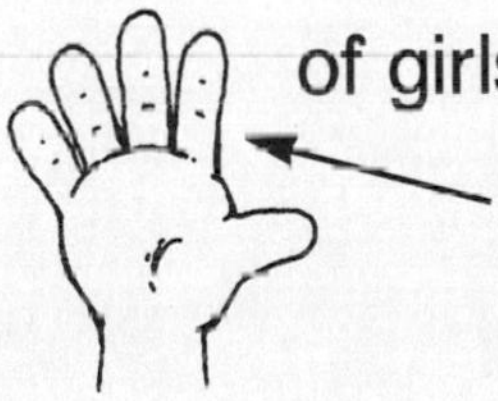

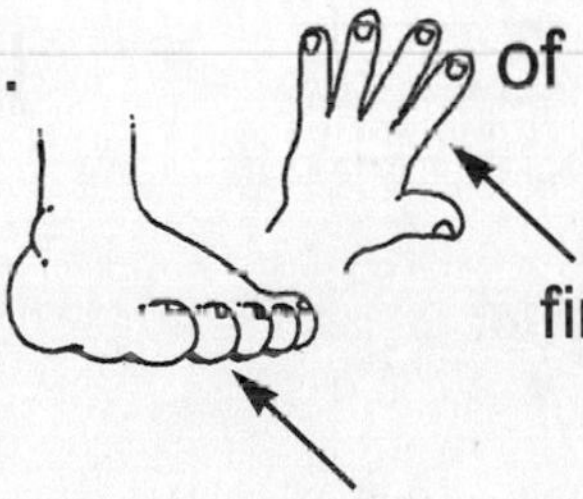

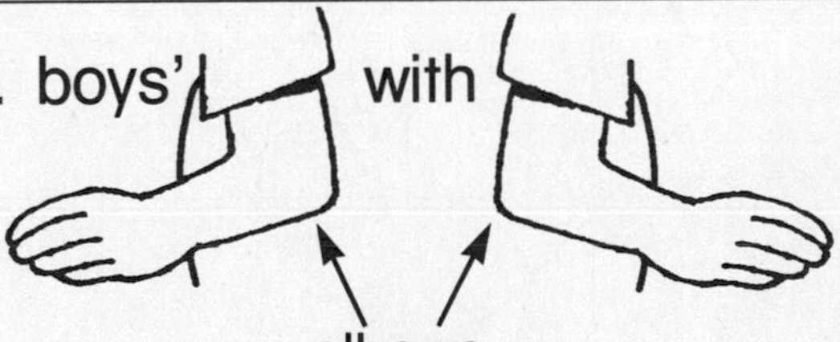

Notes for Home Your child counted by 2s and 10s to solve problems. *Home Activity:* Have your child count by 2s and 10s to determine the number of eyes, fingers, toes, ears, arms, and feet of family members.

Name ____________________________

Problem Solving
7-8

Count by 2s, 5s, and 10s

What numbers are missing on each spinner?
Write the numbers.

To see if you should count by 2s, 5s, or 10s, find the difference between 2 numbers that follow each other.

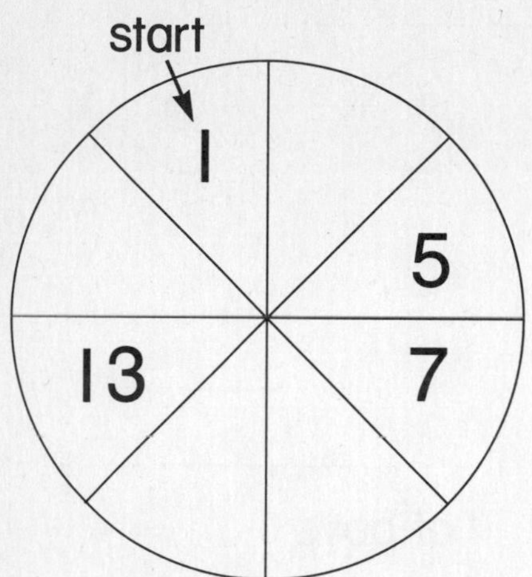

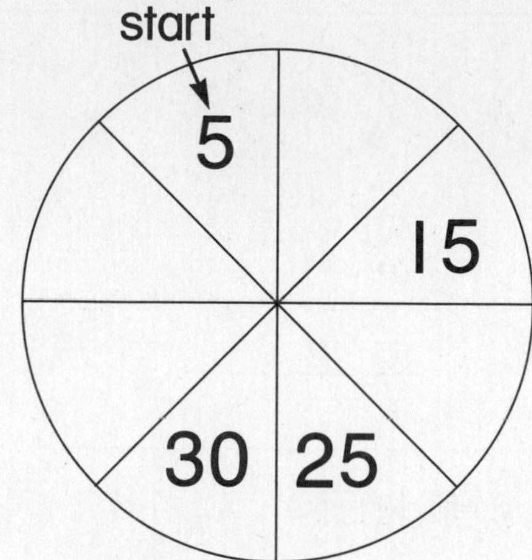

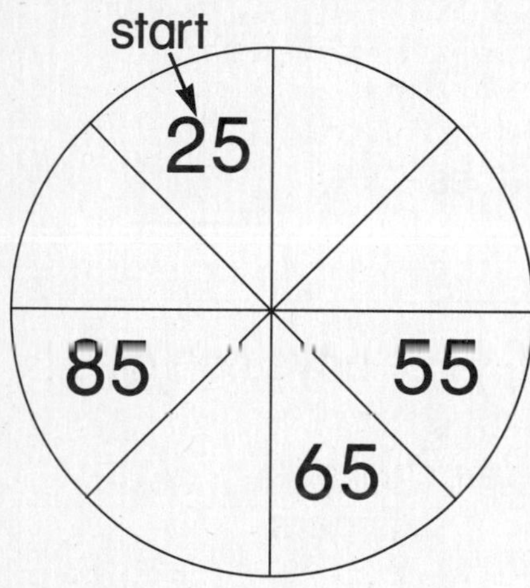

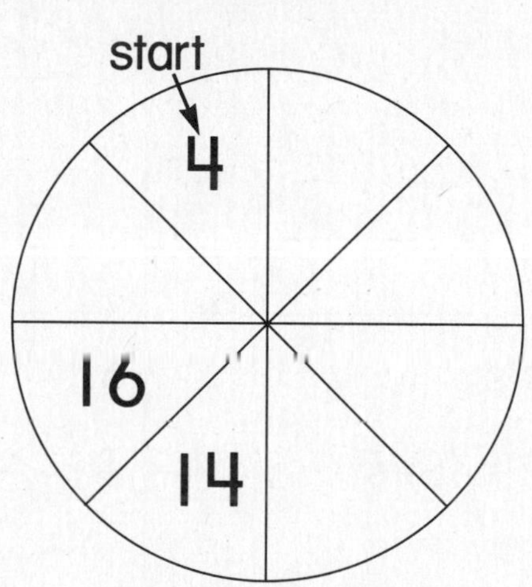

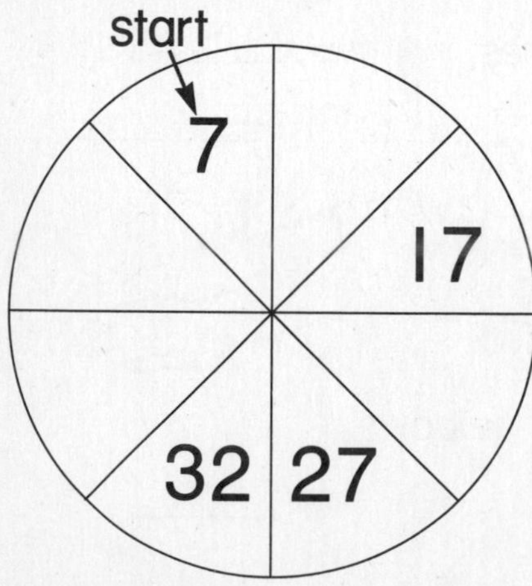

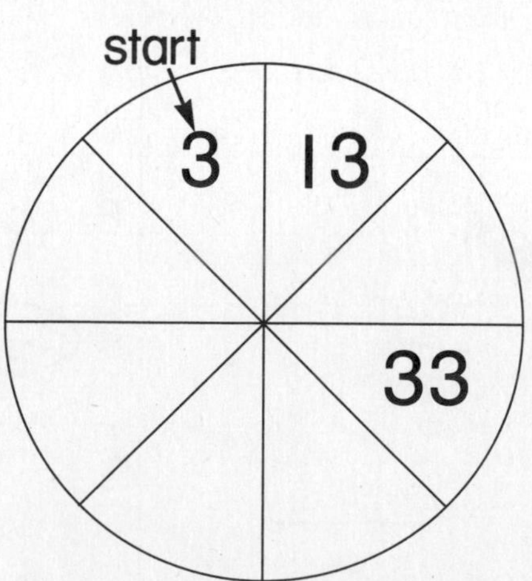

Notes for Home Your child counted by 2s, 5s, and 10s to solve problems. *Home Activity:* Ask your child to explain how he or she determined the missing numbers.

Name ______________________________

Problem Solving 7-9

Ordinals

Solve the problems.

1. Max is second in line.
   James is fourth.
   Lori is in between.
   In which place is Lori?

   ____

2. There are 8 cars in line. Miss Lee's car is last. Mr. Smith is next to last. In which place is Mr. Smith's car?

   ____

3. Al was first in line. He left.
   Kate was tenth in line.
   In which place is she now?

   ____

4. Meg has 9 teddy bears on a shelf. The big brown bear is in the middle. The little yellow bear is just before the big brown bear. In which place is the little yellow bear?

   ____

Notes for Home Your child identified ordinal positions to solve problems. *Home Activity:* Arrange ten objects in a line. Ask your child to identify the sixth object. Then remove the first and last objects from the line and have your child identify the position of what was originally in fifth place. (It now is in fourth place.)

Name ______________________

Problem Solving
7-10

Look for a Pattern

1. How can you continue the pattern?

1	2	3
4	5	6
7	8	9
10	11	12
13	14	15
16	17	18
19	20	21
22	23	24
25	26	27
28	29	30

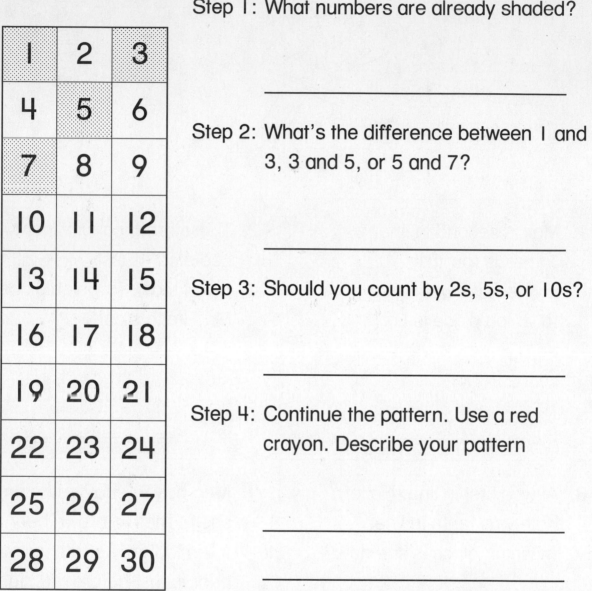

Step 1: What numbers are already shaded?

____

Step 2: What's the difference between 1 and 3, 3 and 5, or 5 and 7?

____

Step 3: Should you count by 2s, 5s, or 10s?

____

Step 4: Continue the pattern. Use a red crayon. Describe your pattern

____

____

____

2. Start another pattern.
Make an X on the numbers 2, 4, and 6.
Now continue the pattern.

Using the Page After completing the first pattern, have children ***look back*** at rows 1, 3, 5, 7, and 9 to make sure the first and third squares are shaded, and rows 2, 4, 6, 8, and 10 to make sure the middle square is shaded.
Notes for Home Your child determined and then completed a pattern by counting by 2s. *Home Activity:* Provide your child with a page from an old calendar and then count by 3s to create a pattern.

 Use with pages 281–282.

Name ______________________________

Explore Tens and Ones

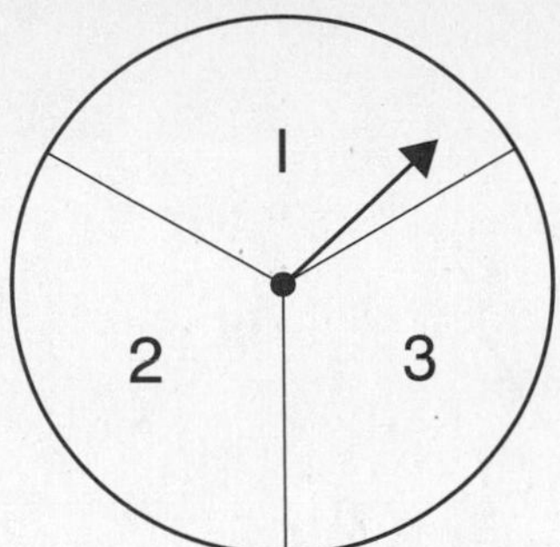

Spin a number. Show that many tens.
Toss a number cube that has the numbers 1 through 6 on it. Show that many ones.
Record how many tens and ones.

1.

tens	ones

2.

tens	ones

3.

tens	ones

4.

tens	ones

5.

tens	ones

6.

tens	ones

7. What is the smallest number you could get?

_____

8. What is the greatest number you could get?

_____

Notes for Home Your child used a spinner and a number cube to record tens and ones. *Home Activity:* Give your child a pile of pennies and ask her or him to make groups of tens and ones, and then tell you the number of pennies.

Name ________________________________

Problem Solving
8-2

Tens and Ones to 60

Solve.

1. Jena has 12 jacks.
   She gets 10 more.
   How many does she have now? ______ 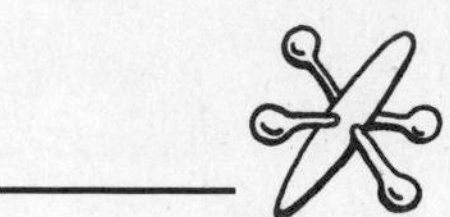

2. Ben finds 10 balls in the grass.
   He finds 20 more.
   How many does he find in all? ______ 

3. Zeke has 47 stamps.
   He buys 10 more.
   How many does he have now? ______ 

4. Luisa makes 33 necklaces.
   She makes 20 more.
   How many does she have now? ______ 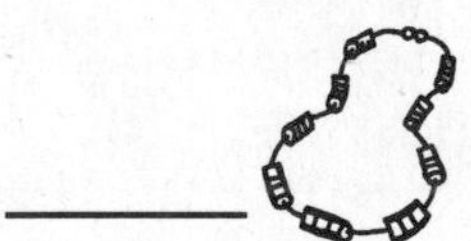

5. The Cubs get 25 points.
   Then they get 10 more.
   How many points do they have now? ______ points 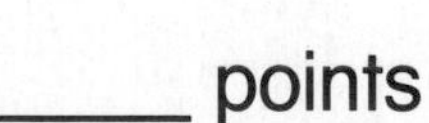

6. Lee wins 18 points.
   He wins 30 more.
   How many points does he win? ______ points

Notes for Home Your child solved word problems using numbers to 60. *Home Activity:* Ask your child how many points Lee would have if he won 10 more points. (58)

Name ______________________________

Numbers More than Ten

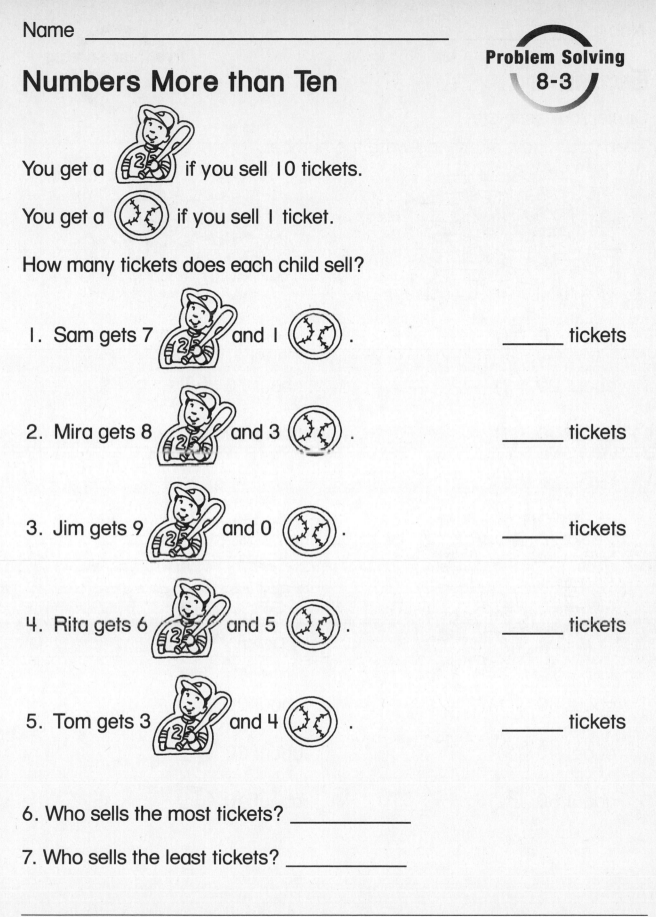

Problem Solving 8-3

You get a 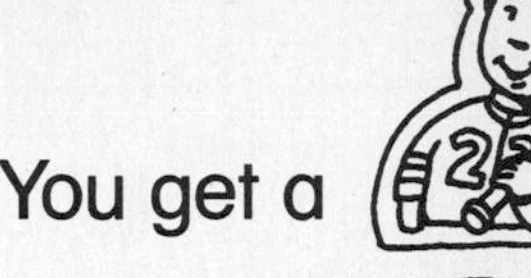  if you sell 10 tickets.

You get a  if you sell 1 ticket.

How many tickets does each child sell?

1. Sam gets 7  and 1 . ______ tickets

2. Mira gets 8  and 3 . ______ tickets

3. Jim gets 9  and 0 . ______ tickets

4. Rita gets 6  and 5 . ______ tickets

5. Tom gets 3  and 4 . ______ tickets

6. Who sells the most tickets? ____________

7. Who sells the least tickets? ____________

Notes for Home Your child solved word problems about place value. *Home Activity:* Ask, "If Lee sold 10 tickets more than Rita, how many did she sell?" (75)

Name ______________________________

Estimation

Circle your estimate.

Then count how many and write the number.

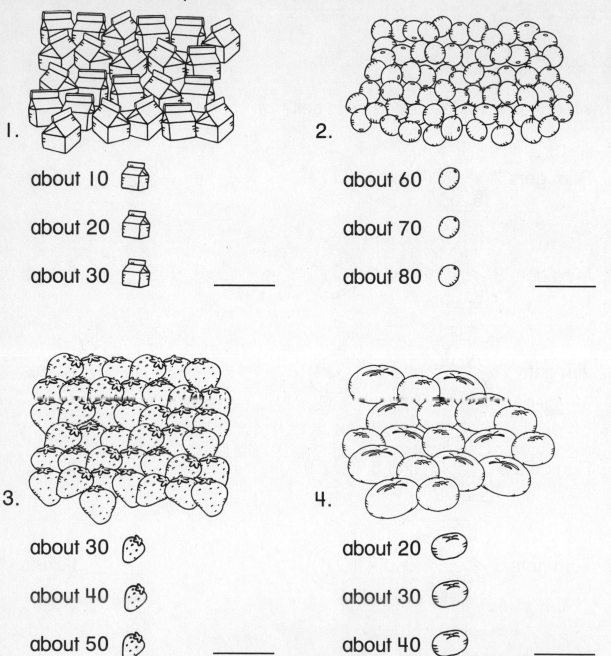

1. 

about 10

about 20

about 30 ______

2. 

about 60

about 70

about 80 ______

3. 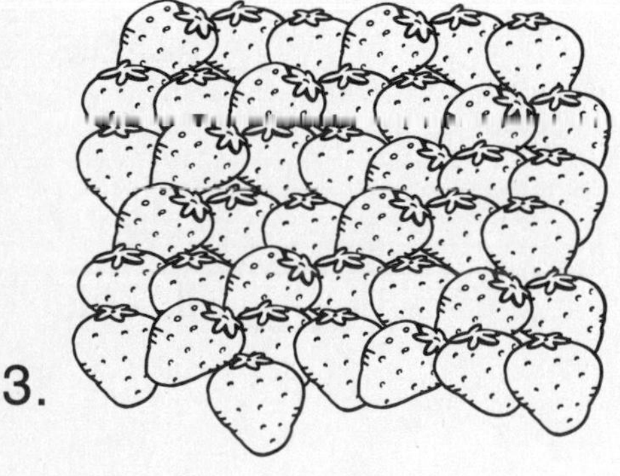

about 30

about 40

about 50 ______

4. 

about 20

about 30

about 40 ______

Notes for Home Your child estimated the number of objects in each group. Then he or she counted to check the estimate. *Home Activity:* Have your child estimate how many pairs of socks are in a drawer, and then count to check.

Name ____________________

Problem Solving 8-5

10 Ones Make 1 Ten

Lyn used the ones under the hat.
How many ones did she add to get the number?
Write the number on the hat. Circle to show if she exchanged 10 ones for 1 ten.

Exchange 10 ones for 1 ten?

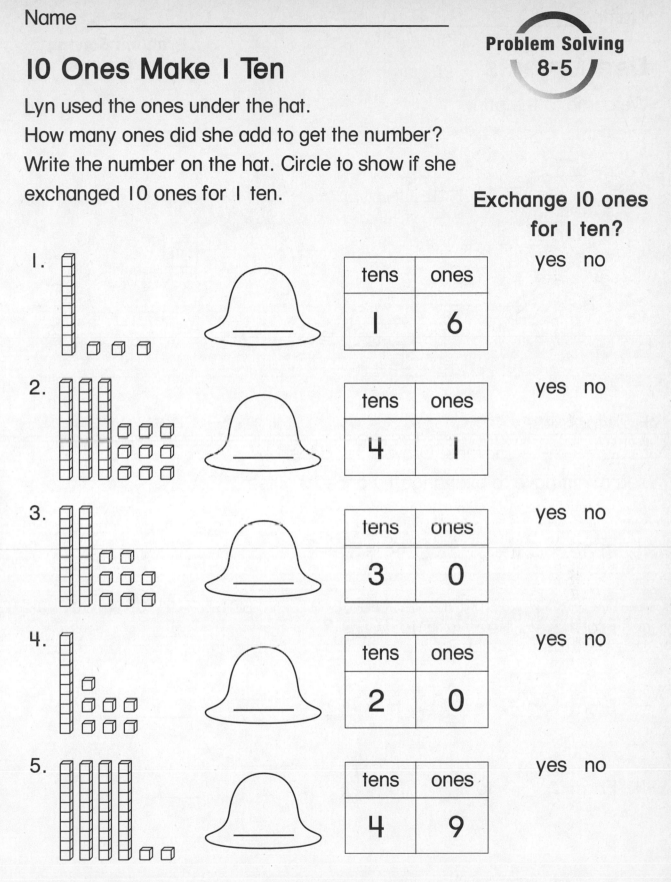

1. 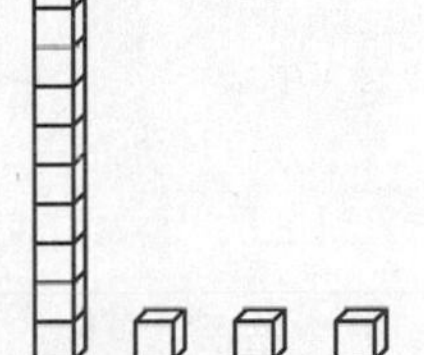 

tens	ones
1	6

yes no

2. 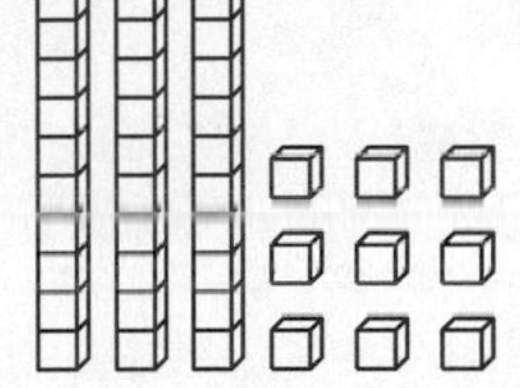 

tens	ones
4	1

yes no

3. 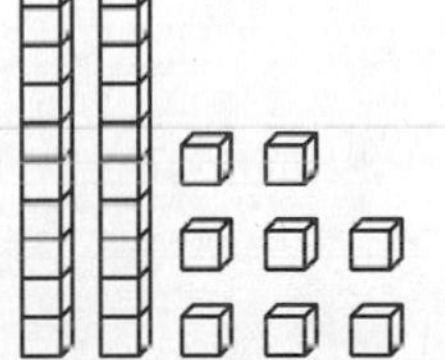 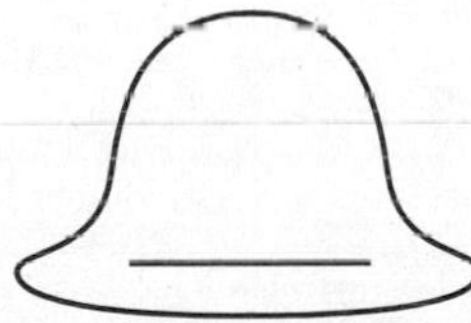

tens	ones
3	0

yes no

4. 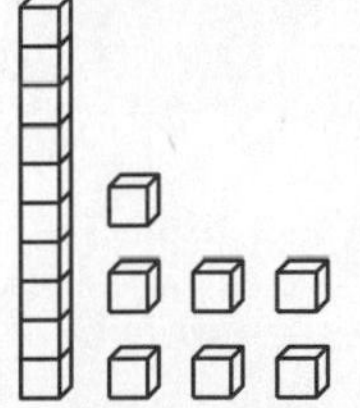 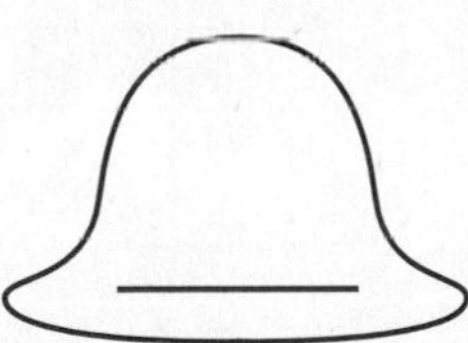

tens	ones
2	0

yes no

5. 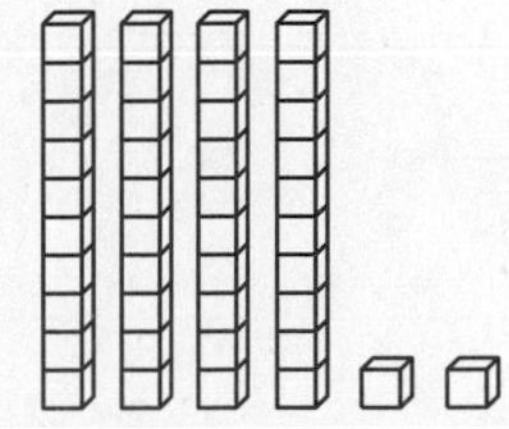 

tens	ones
4	9

yes no

Notes for Home Your child solved problems to find sums and then decided if 10 ones were exchanged for 1 ten. *Home Activity:* Gather a group of pennies and 2 dimes. Give your child a group of pennies, have him or her make groups of ten, and say that you will trade 1 dime for 10 pennies.

Name ______________________________

Problem Solving
8-6

Use Objects

Welcome to the park.

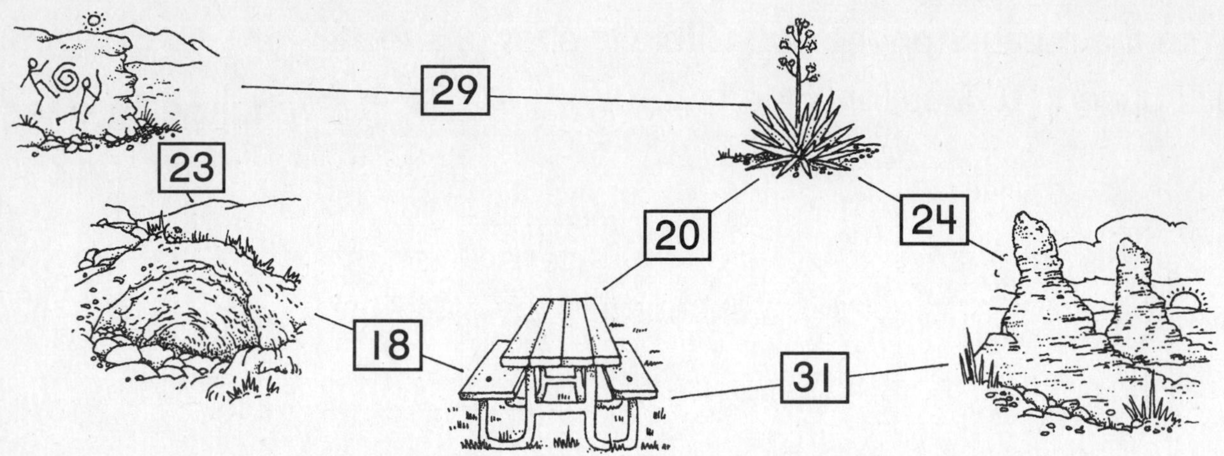

How far is it?

Draw ——— for tens. Draw ● for ones.

You might have to exchange 10 ones for 1 ten.

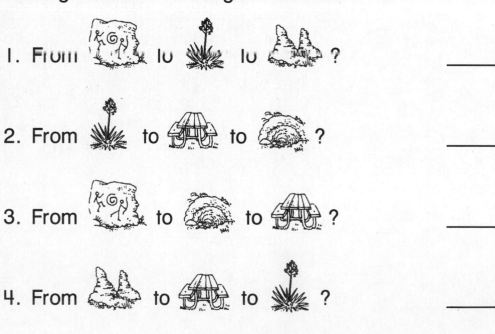

1. From to to ? ______

2. From to to ? ______

3. From to to ? ______

4. From to to ? ______

Using the Page To help children ***solve*** the problem, have them decide what they have to do first. Discuss the steps they need to complete to find the answers. **Notes for Home** Your child drew tens and ones, and exchanged 10 ones for 1 ten to solve problems about distances on a map. *Home Activity:* Ask your child to trace the map, write different two-digit numbers, and then solve.

Name ___________________________

Compare Numbers

Problem Solving
8-7

You need a 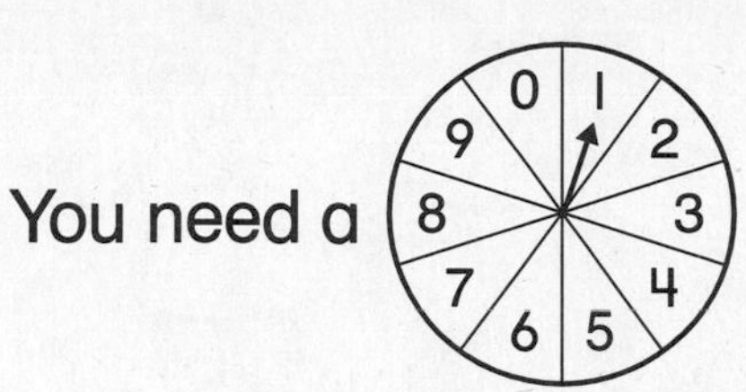

. Play with a friend.

1. Spin twice and write the numbers in the first chart.
2. Have a friend spin twice and write the numbers in the second chart.
3. Compare. The greatest number scores 1 point.
4. The most points wins the game. Circle the winner in each game.

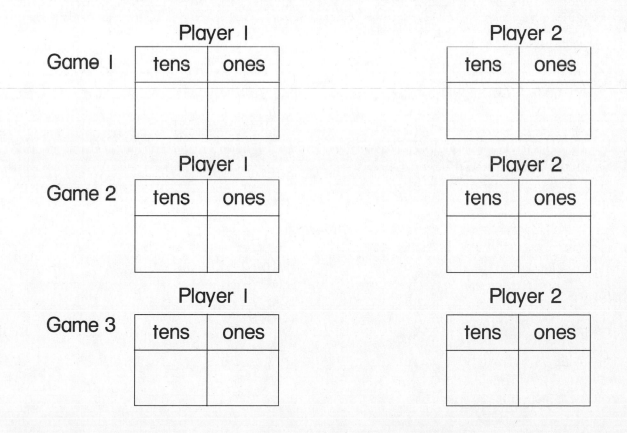

Game 1

Player 1

tens	ones

Player 2

tens	ones

Game 2

Player 1

tens	ones

Player 2

tens	ones

Game 3

Player 1

tens	ones

Player 2

tens	ones

Notes for Home Your child compared 2 numbers to tell which is greater. *Home Activity:* Play a similar game with your child.

Name ______________________________

Order Numbers to 100

Problem Solving 8-8

Annie makes number patterns.
Write the numbers that are missing from each pattern.

I'm thinking of numbers before, after, and between.

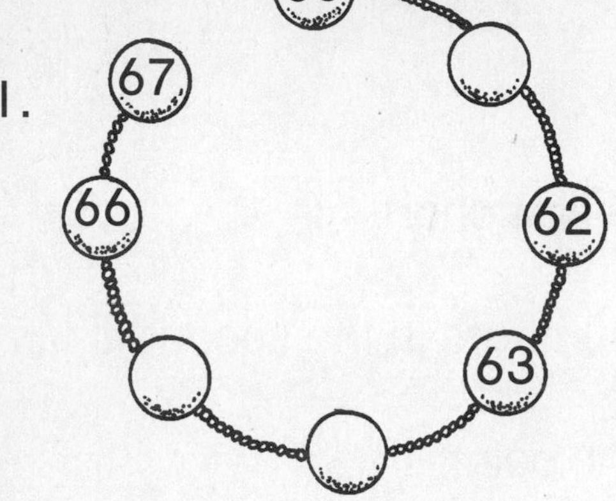

2.

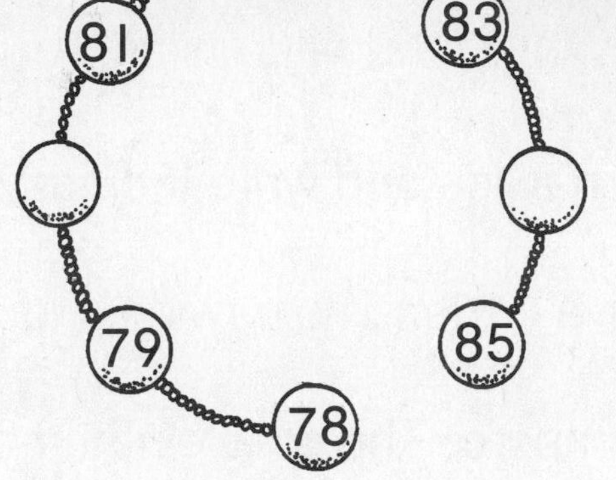

3.

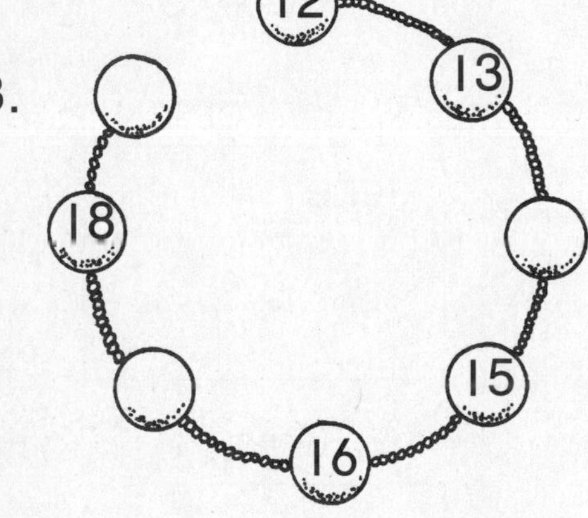

4.

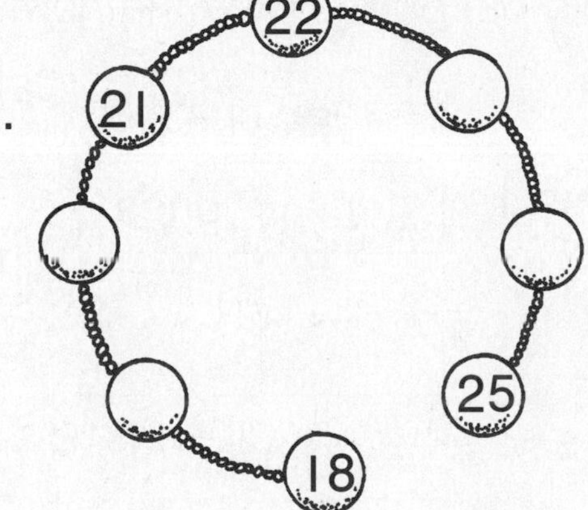

5.

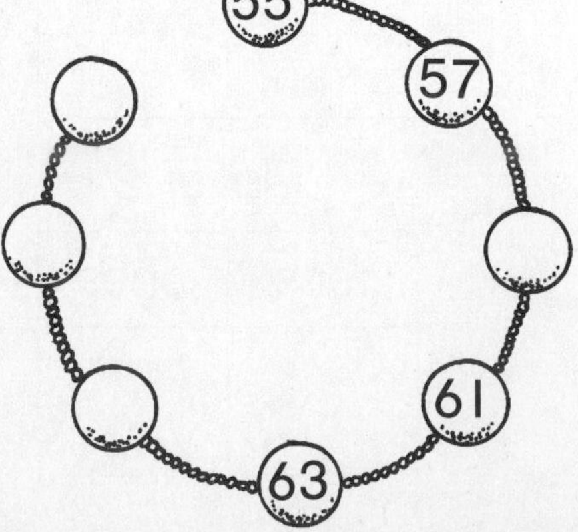

6.

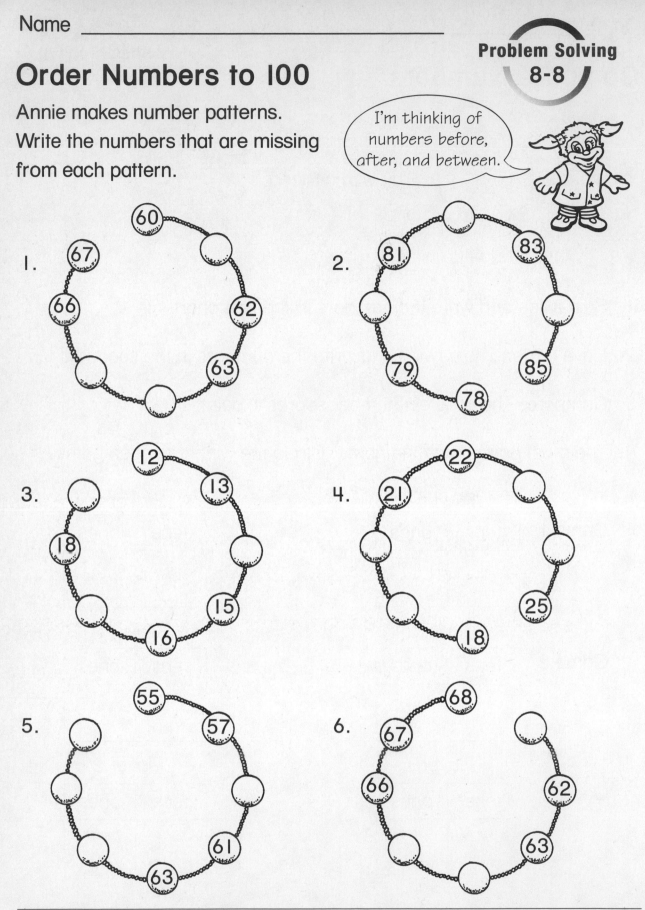

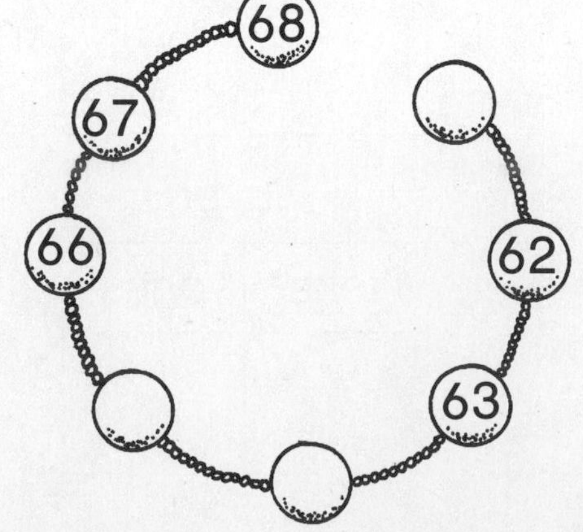

Notes for Home You child solved number patterns by writing numbers that come before, after, or between other numbers. *Home Activity:* Show your child a page number in a magazine or book. Ask him or her to tell the number that comes before and after.

Name ______________________________

Problem Solving
8-9

Patterns on the 100 Chart

Color the patterns to solve the problems.

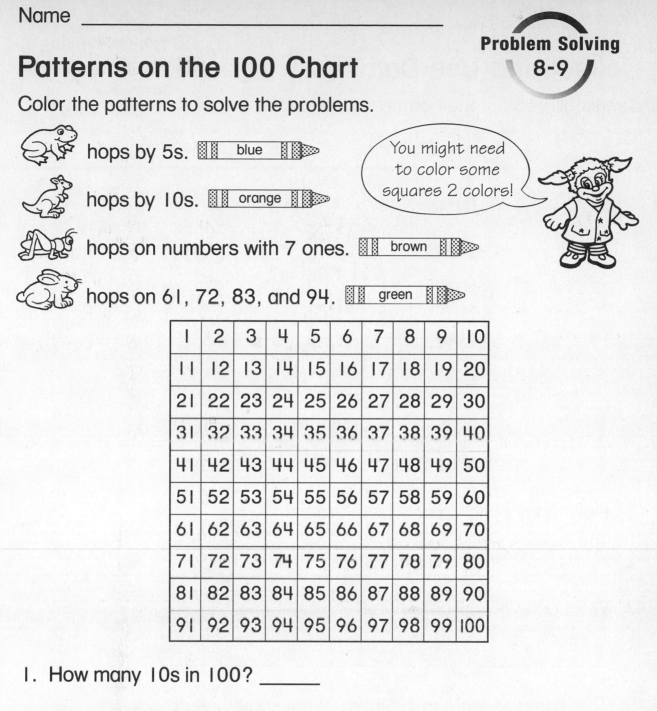

 hops by 5s. blue

 hops by 10s. orange

You might need to color some squares 2 colors!

 hops on numbers with 7 ones. 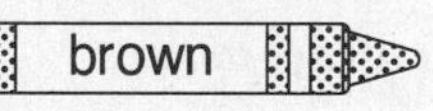

 hops on 61, 72, 83, and 94. green

1	2	3	4	5	6	7	8	9	10
11	12	13	14	15	16	17	18	19	20
21	22	23	24	25	26	27	28	29	30
31	32	33	34	35	36	37	38	39	40
41	42	43	44	45	46	47	48	49	50
51	52	53	54	55	56	57	58	59	60
61	62	63	64	65	66	67	68	69	70
71	72	73	74	75	76	77	78	79	80
81	82	83	84	85	86	87	88	89	90
91	92	93	94	95	96	97	98	99	100

1. How many 10s in 100? ______

2. How many 5s in 100? ______

3. Which two are counting by 10s? Circle.    

4. What happens to the 10s and 1s when the rabbit hops?

____

Notes for Home Your child found number patterns and used them to solve problems. *Home Activity:* Have your child color the numbers 1, 12, 23, 34 and continue the pattern to 100. Ask him or her to explain the pattern.

Name ______________________________

Problem Solving 8-10

Collect and Use Data

Some children put their names in the circles.

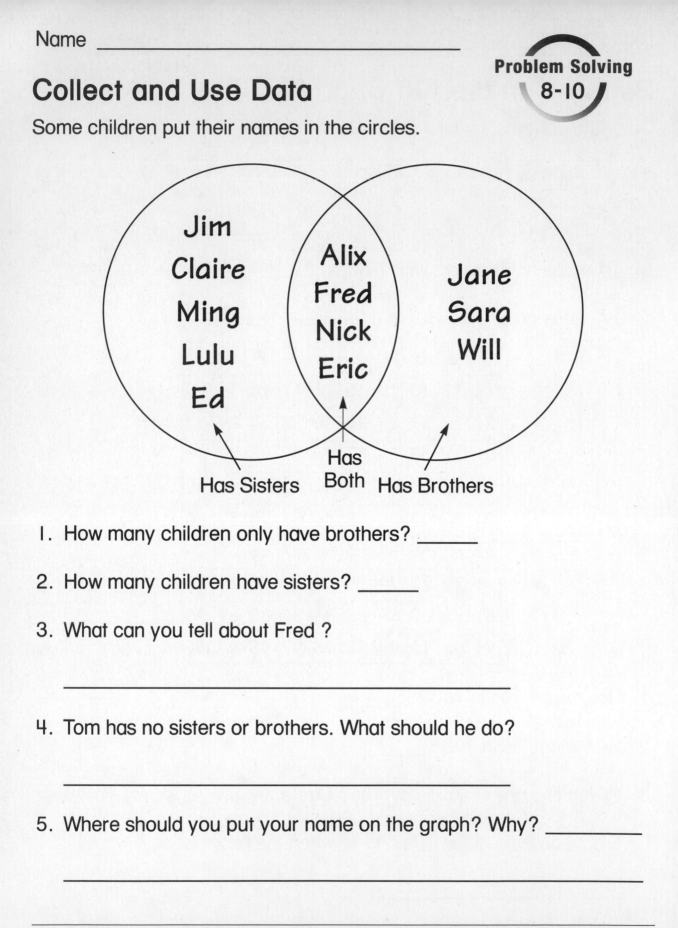

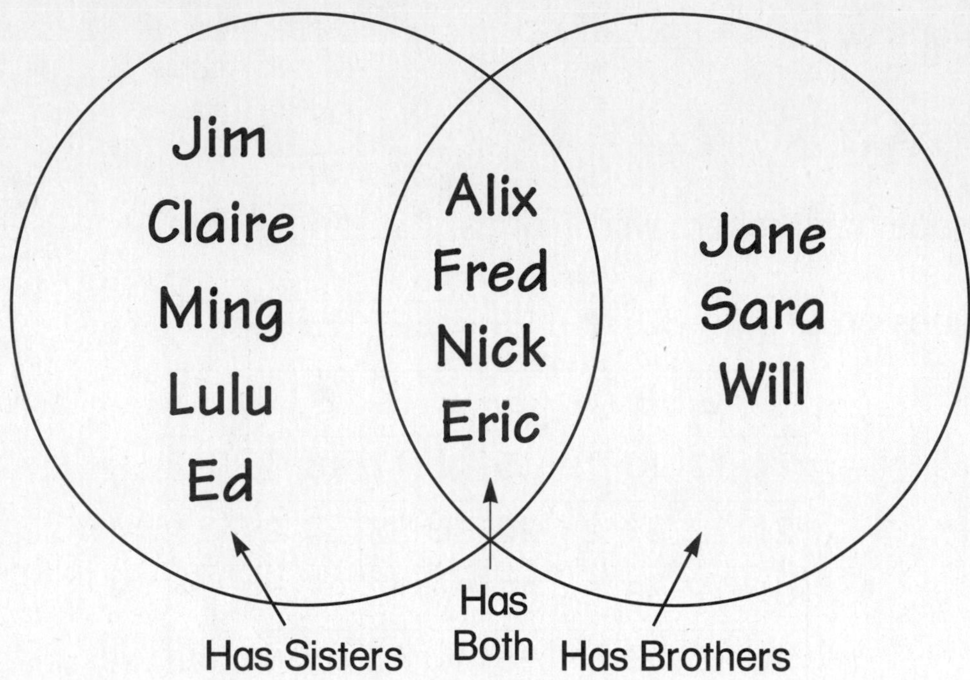

1. How many children only have brothers? ______

2. How many children have sisters? ______

3. What can you tell about Fred ?

____

4. Tom has no sisters or brothers. What should he do?

____

5. Where should you put your name on the graph? Why? __________

____

Using the Page Help children ***understand*** the diagram by asking them to explain what group is represented in the part where the circles intersect. Then have them count to answer questions 1–2, and explain their answers to questions 3–5. **Notes for Home** Your child interpreted a diagram. *Home Activity:* Ask your child to copy the names in the diagram in three lists: sisters, sisters and brothers, and brothers, and to compare the lists and the diagram.

Name ______________________________

Nickels and Pennies

How can you show each amount 2 ways?

Color the coins. Use a red crayon to show 1 way.

Use a blue crayon to show another way.

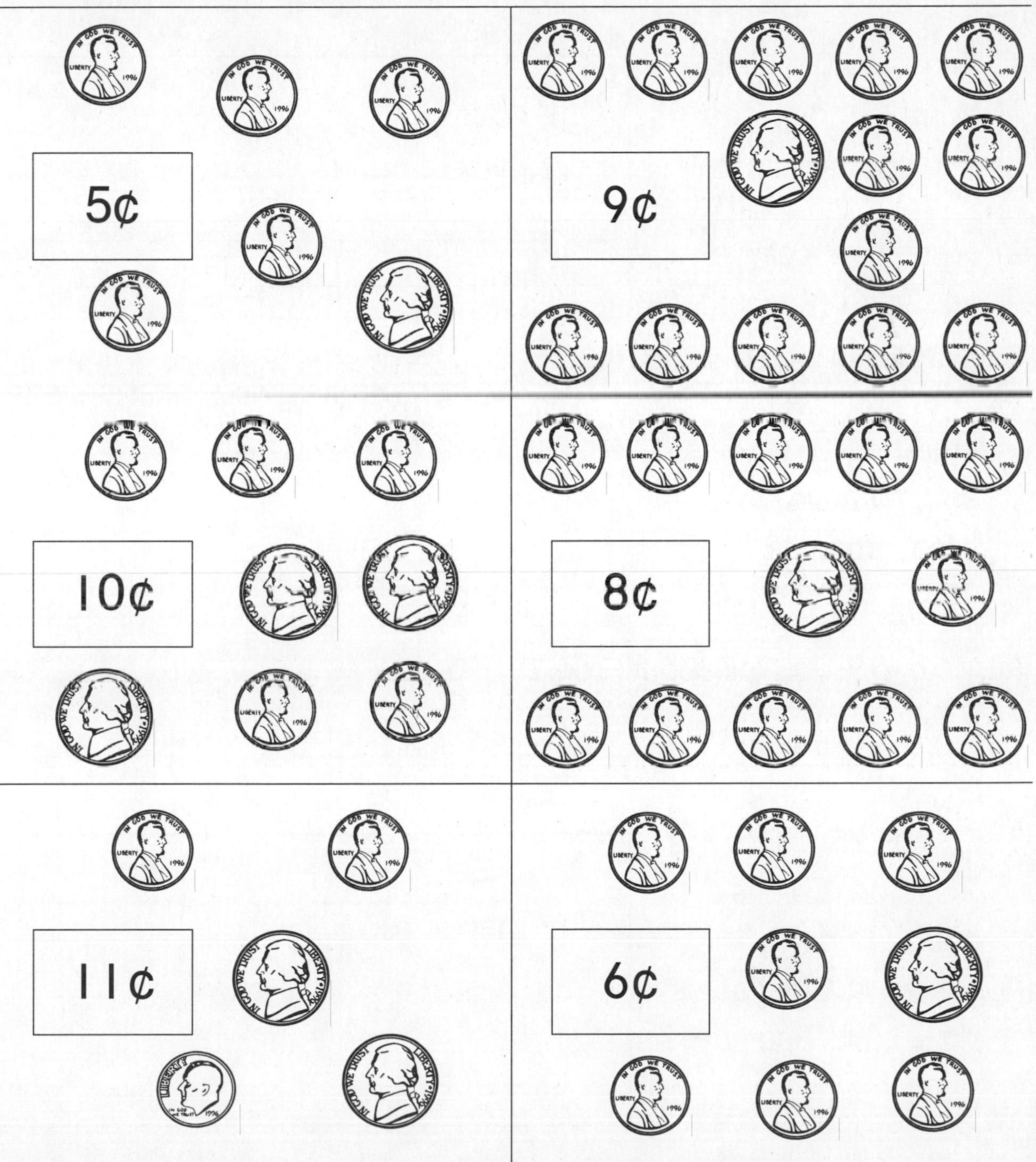

Notes for Home Your child counted and colored nickels and pennies to show amounts of the same value.
Home Activity: Ask your child to show you another way to make 10 cents. (10 pennies or 1 dime)

Name ________________________

Dimes and Pennies

Problem Solving 9-2

Show the coins.
Write D or P
inside the coins.

Remember. A dime is worth 10¢.
A penny is worth 1¢.

1. Ted has 20¢ in all. What 11 coins does Ted have?

○○○○○○○○○○○

2. Mira has 2 coins. Lou has 11 coins. Les has 20 coins. They all have the same amount. What coins do they have? What amount?

Mira	Lou	Les
○○	○○○○○○○○○○○	○○○○○○○○○○○○○○○○○○○○
____¢	____¢	____¢

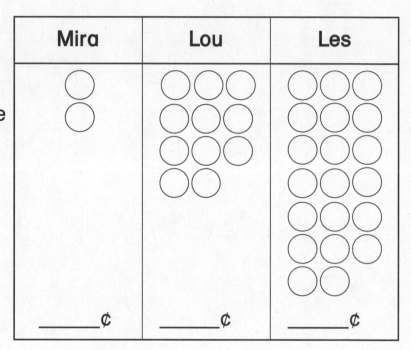

3. Ed has 25¢. Tina has 25¢, too. Ed has 7 coins. Tina has 16 coins. What coins do Ed and Tina have?

Ed	Tina
○○ ○○○○○	○ ○○○○○ ○○○○○

Notes for Home Your child worked with dimes and pennies to show equivalent amounts. *Home Activity:* Tell your child that he or she has 3 coins worth 21¢. Ask your child to determine the 3 coins. (2 dimes and 1 penny)

Name ______________________

Dimes, Nickels, and Pennies

Solve the problems.

Circle your answer.

Use coins if you need to.
Count by 10s or 5s first.
Then count by 1s.

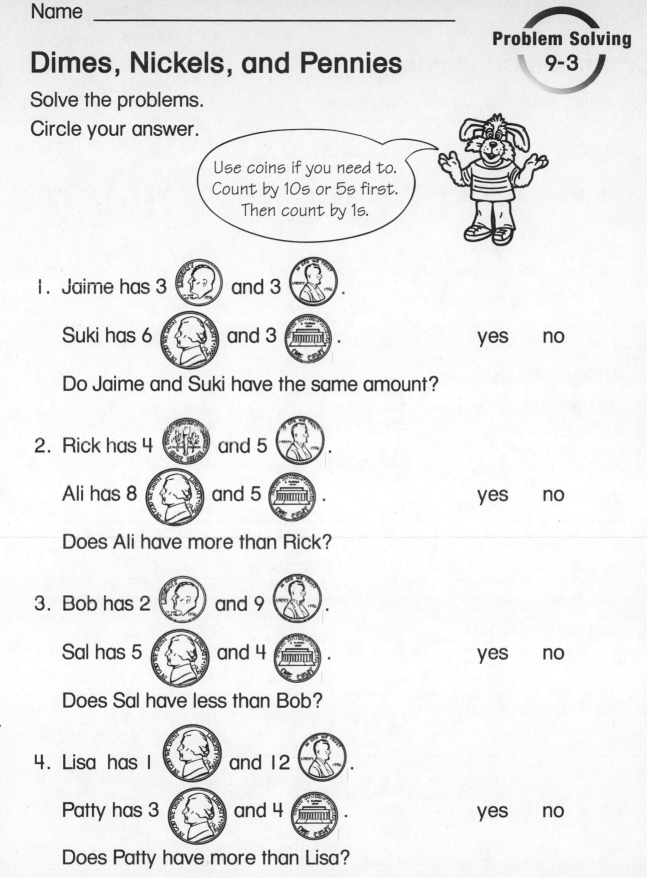

1. Jaime has 3  and 3 .

   Suki has 6  and 3 . yes no

   Do Jaime and Suki have the same amount?

2. Rick has 4  and 5 .

   Ali has 8  and 5 . yes no

   Does Ali have more than Rick?

3. Bob has 2  and 9 .

   Sal has 5  and 4 . yes no

   Does Sal have less than Bob?

4. Lisa has 1  and 12 .

   Patty has 3  and 4 . yes no

   Does Patty have more than Lisa?

Notes for Home Your child counted dimes, nickels, and pennies to solve problems. *Home Activity:* Ask your child how many more pennies Lisa would need to have 1¢ more than Patty. (3 more pennies) Then have your child find how many pennies Lisa would have in all and what coins other than pennies that she can use to show that amount. (15 pennies in all; 1 dime and 1 nickel or 3 nickels)

Name ______________________________

Problem Solving 9-4

Count Mixed Coins

Solve the problems. Circle your answer.

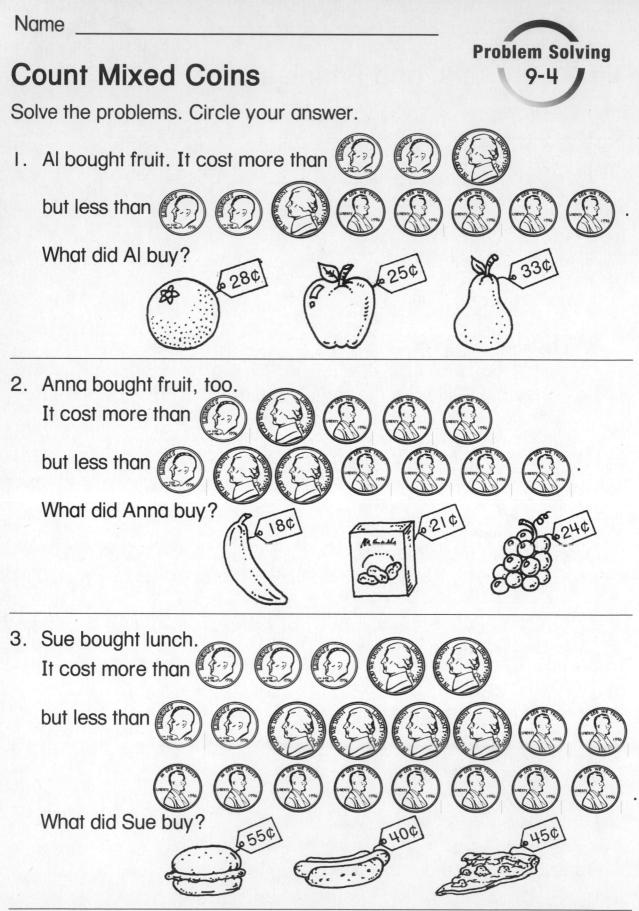

1. Al bought fruit. It cost more than  

but less than       .

What did Al buy?

---

2. Anna bought fruit, too.
It cost more than   

but less than 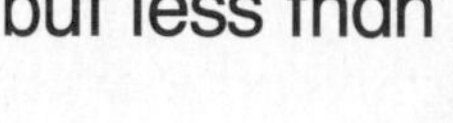     .

What did Anna buy?

---

3. Sue bought lunch.
It cost more than    

but less than   .

What did Sue buy?

Notes for Home Your child counted groups of dimes, nickels, and pennies by 10s, 5s, and 1s to solve problems. *Home Activity:* Using the first problem, explain that Al spent 2 dimes, 1 nickel, and 8 pennies on another piece of fruit. Ask your child how much Al spent and what he bought. (33¢; pear)

Name ______________________________

Problem Solving 9-5

Use Data from a Picture

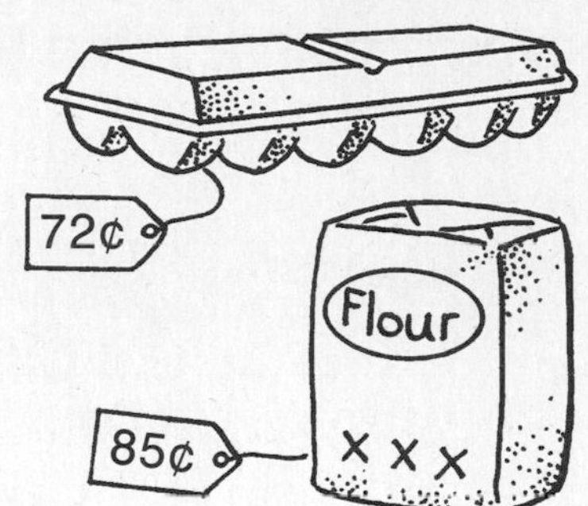

1. Ann has 2 , 3 , and 5 .

Which thing can't Ann buy?

 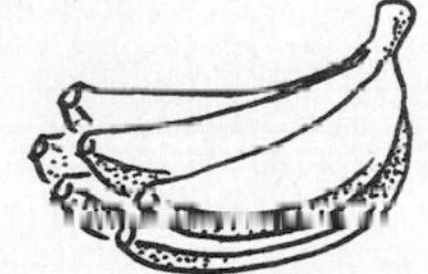 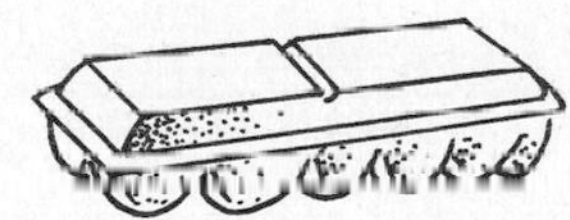

Step 1:	Step 2:	Step 3:
Count Ann's money. Write the amount. 40 ¢	Look at the 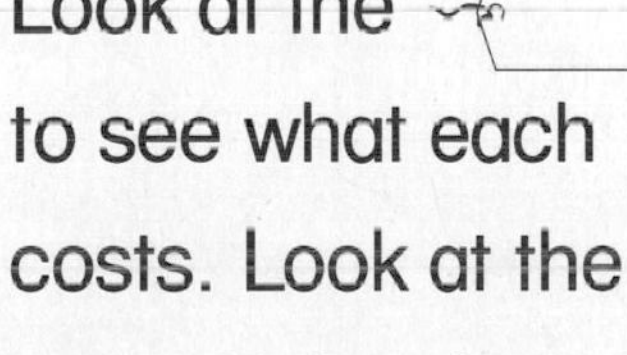 to see what each costs. Look at the amount Ann has.	Answer the question. Circle what Ann can't buy.

2. Walt has 4 , 5 , and 4 .

Which one can Walt buy?

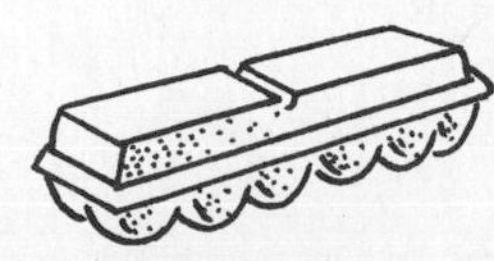  

3. Jan has 3 , 2 , and 5 . Which 2 things can Jan buy together?

  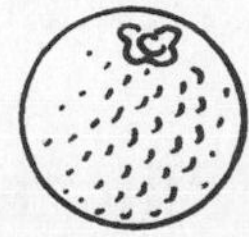

Using the Page To help children ***solve***, have them read through the problem and use coins to count each amount.
Notes for Home Your child used data from a picture to solve problems. *Home Activity:* Provide your child with 3 dimes, 5 nickels, and 10 pennies. Then ask your child which items at the top of the page he or she can buy. (gum, bread, orange, bananas, yogurt)

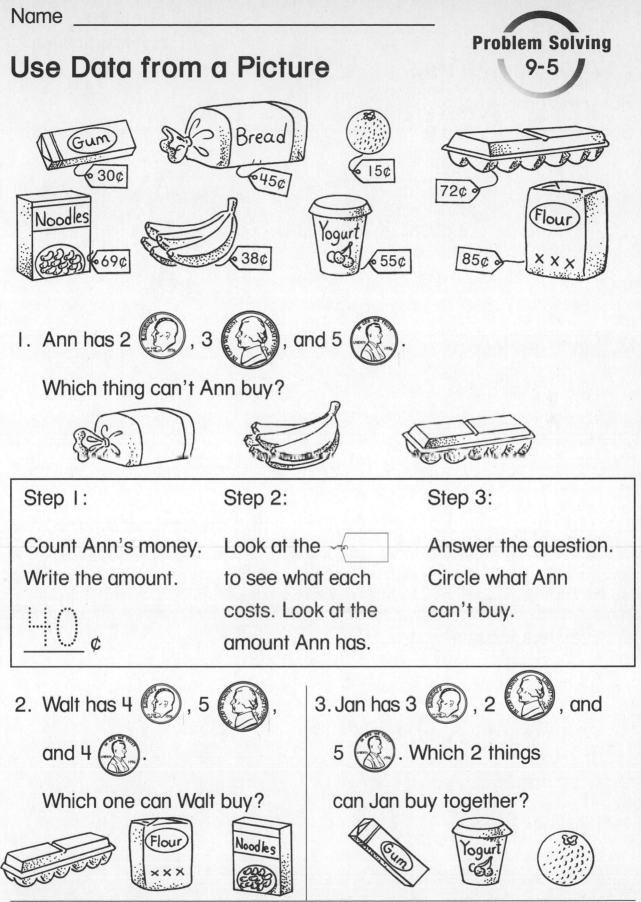

Name ___________________________

Explore Quarters

Solve the problems.

Show the coins. Write P, N, D, or Q in each ◯.

Remember! A quarter is worth 25¢. A dime is worth 10¢. A nickel is worth 5¢. A penny is worth 1¢.

1. Marta has 4 coins worth 25¢.

   One coin is a .

   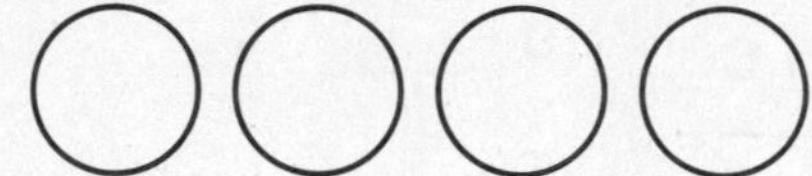

   What are the other 3 coins.

2. Jarod has 7 coins worth 25¢.

   None of the coins are .

   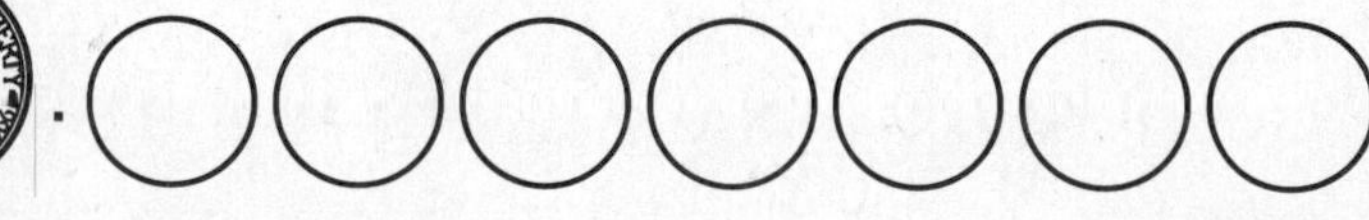

   What are the coins?

3. Jody has 5 coins worth 25¢.

   All the coins are the same.

   What coins does Jody have?

4. Greg has 25¢.

   One coin is a .

   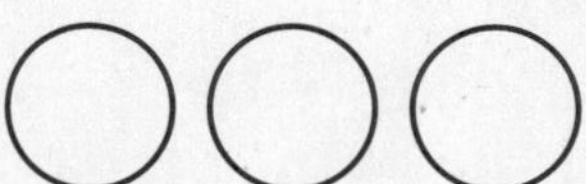

   What are the other 2 coins?

Notes for Home Your child read clues to determine combinations that equal 25¢. *Home Activity:* Ask your child to create clues for different coin combinations that equal 25¢.

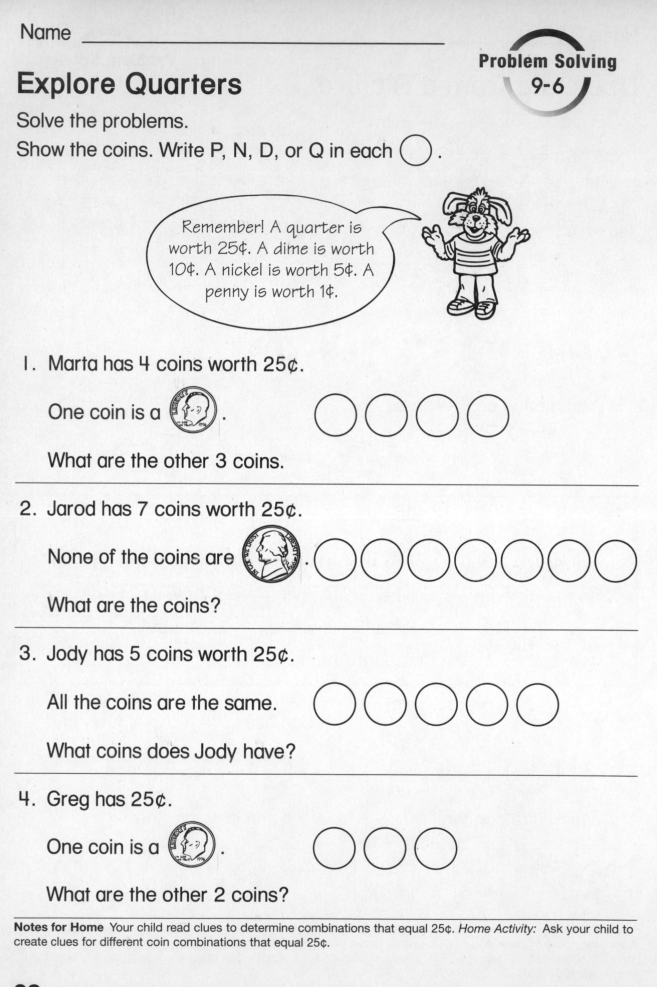

Name ______________________________

Quarters, Dimes, Nickels, and Pennies

Problem Solving 9-7

What are the fewest number of coins that Herman can use to pay for each thing?

Q means Quarters.
D means Dimes.
N means Nickels.
P means Pennies.

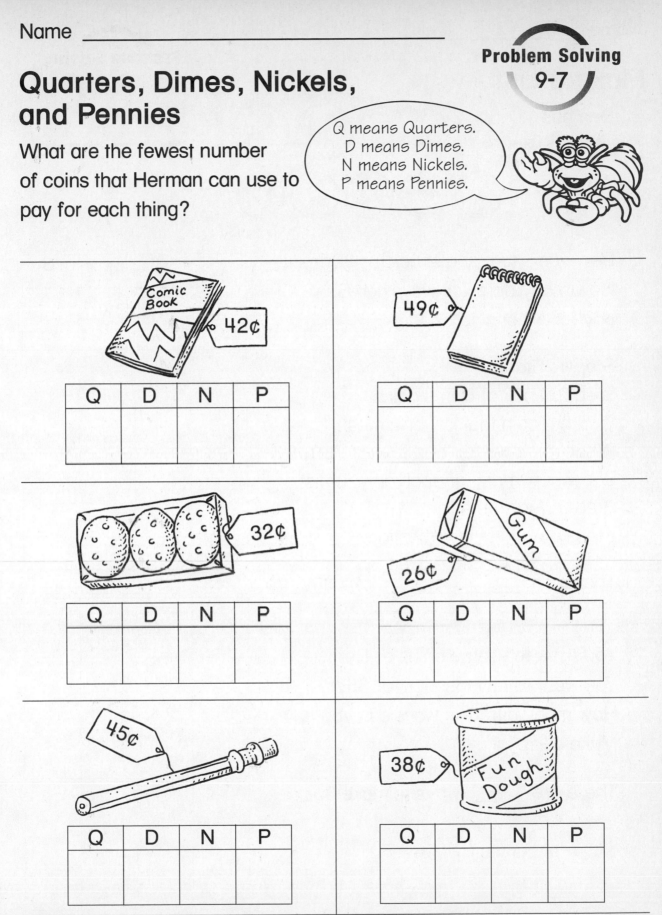

Comic Book 42¢

Q	D	N	P

49¢

Q	D	N	P

32¢

Q	D	N	P

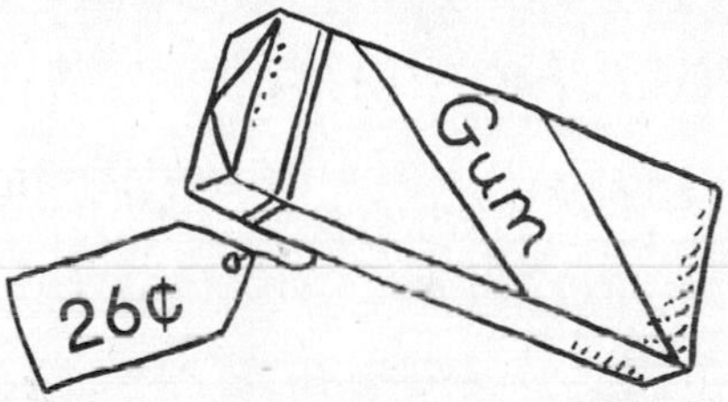

Gum 26¢

Q	D	N	P

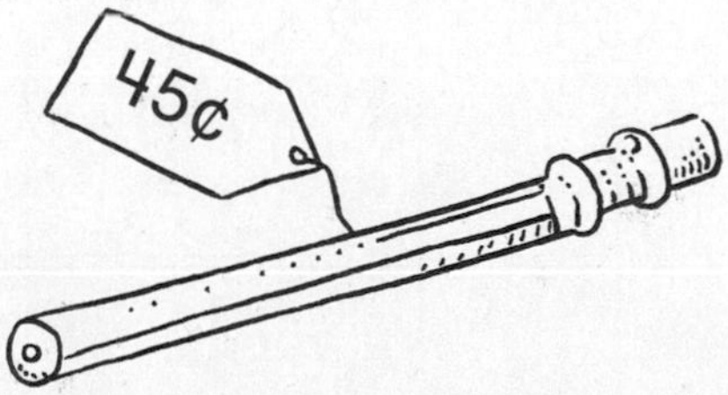

45¢

Q	D	N	P

Fun Dough 38¢

Q	D	N	P

Notes for Home Your child determined the fewest coins it would take to purchase each item. *Home Activity:* Ask your child to choose an item on the page and find another combination of coins to pay for it.

Name ______________________________

Problem Solving
9-8

Make a List

1. Ben has

Ben wants to buy a snack for 30¢.
How many different ways can Ben pay for his snack?

Step 1: Start a list.
Step 2: Look at Ben's coins.
Find the coin that is worth most.
What coin can you add to make 30¢?
Show how many of each on your list.
Step 3: Finish the list.
Step 4: Answer the question.

There are ______ ways to make 30¢.

Q	D	N	P
1	0	1	0

2. You have the same coins as Ben.
You want to buy a snack for 35¢.
How many different ways can you pay?
Make a list.

There are ______ ways to make 35¢.

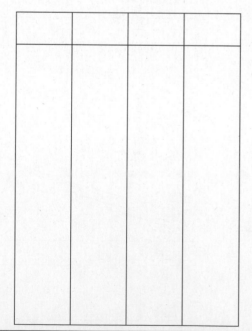

Using the Page To help children make a ***plan*** for solving a problem, have them read through the problem, tell what they know, what they must find out, and how they might go about solving the problem. Then have children follow the steps to solve. **Notes for Home** Your child made a list of different ways to make 30¢ and 35¢ using a specific group of coins. *Home Activity:* Ask your child to find different ways to make 40¢ with the same coins as Ben.

Name ______________________________

Explore Time

Look at each picture.

Circle about how long you think it would take to do each thing.

minute

less than a minute

more than a minute

minute

less than a minute

more than a minute

minute

less than a minute

more than a minute

minute

less than a minute

more than a minute

minute

less than a minute

more than a minute

minute

less than a minute

more than a minute

Notes for Home Your child connected pictures of events to measurements of time. *Home Activity:* Ask your child to do two of the pictured activities, and then tell how long he or she spent doing each.

Name ______________________________

Problem Solving 10-2

Clocks

Jose feeds a different zoo animal every hour.
He starts at 2 o'clock. Complete his schedule. Show the times.

Feeding Times	
bear	2 o'clock clock
lion	clock
tiger	clock
seal	clock
elephant	clock

Draw the hands on each clock.

How many hours after feeding the bear did Jose feed the tiger? ______ hours

How many hours after feeding the bear did Jose feed the seal? ______ hours

Notes for Home Your child drew hands on clocks to complete a schedule. *Home Activity:* Ask your child to write a schedule telling what he or she will do this Saturday.

Name ______________________________

Problem Solving
10-3

Write Time to the Hour

Choose the time you would do each thing.
Then color the times that match in the same color.

Go to sleep. 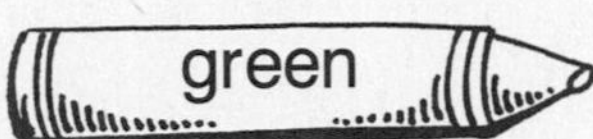

Have lunch. 

Leave school. 

8 o'clock

6:00

8:00

3 o'clock

12:00

3:00

12 o'clock

Notes for Home Your child determined the times that routine activities take place, and colored to show the same time expressed three ways. *Home Activity:* Move the hands of an analog clock to show times to the hour, and ask your child to write the time using numbers, as on a digital clock.

Name ______________________________

Problem Solving
10-4

Write Time to the Half Hour

Start at 2:00.

Draw a path showing the times in order in half hours to 9:30.

Notes for Home Your child ordered times to the half hour from 2:00 to 9:30 by drawing a path. *Home Activity:* Ask your child to start at 9:30 and trace the path backwards to find the time one half hour before.

Name ______________________________

Problem Solving
10-5

Tell Time

Solve.

Look at the clock to help solve each problem.

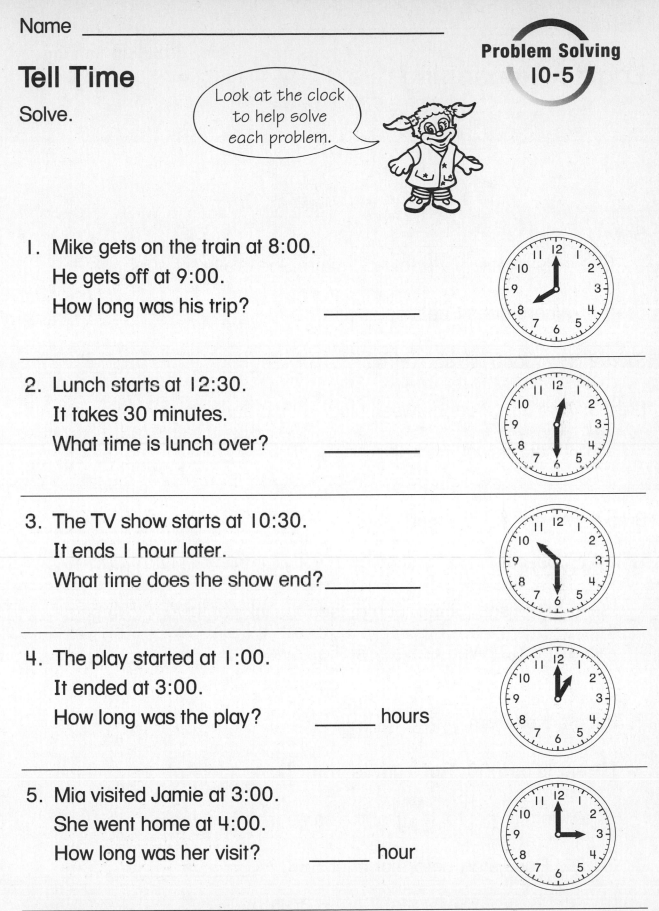

1. Mike gets on the train at 8:00.
He gets off at 9:00.
How long was his trip? __________

2. Lunch starts at 12:30.
It takes 30 minutes.
What time is lunch over? __________

3. The TV show starts at 10:30.
It ends 1 hour later.
What time does the show end? __________

4. The play started at 1:00.
It ended at 3:00.
How long was the play? ______ hours

5. Mia visited Jamie at 3:00.
She went home at 4:00.
How long was her visit? ______ hour

Notes for Home Your child solved problems about time. *Home Activity:* With your child, note the times at which you begin activities such as eating dinner or watching a special television program. When you have finished the activity, note how much time has passed to the nearest hour or half hour.

Name ______________________________

Logical Reasoning

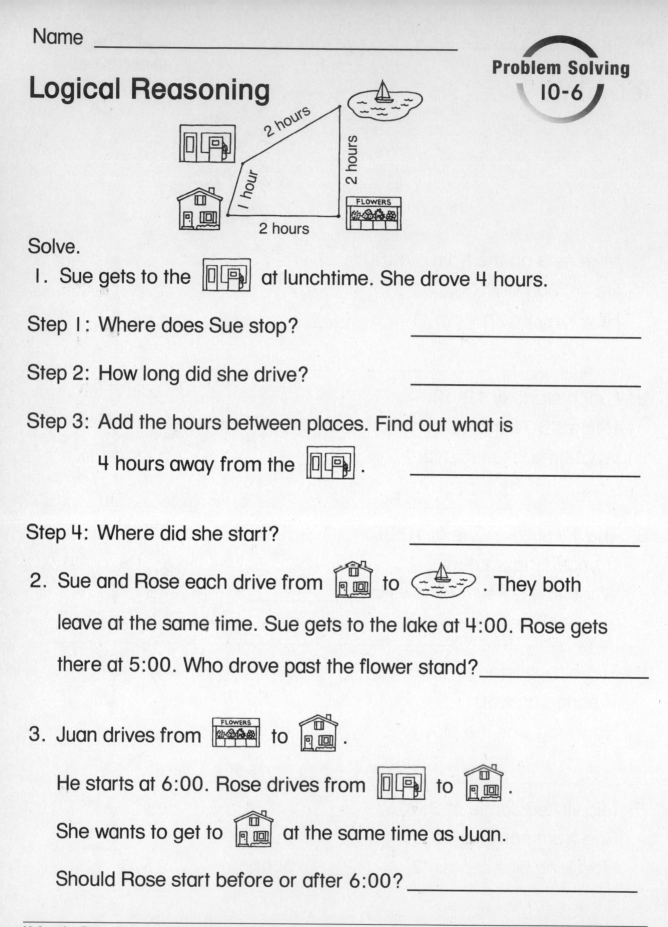

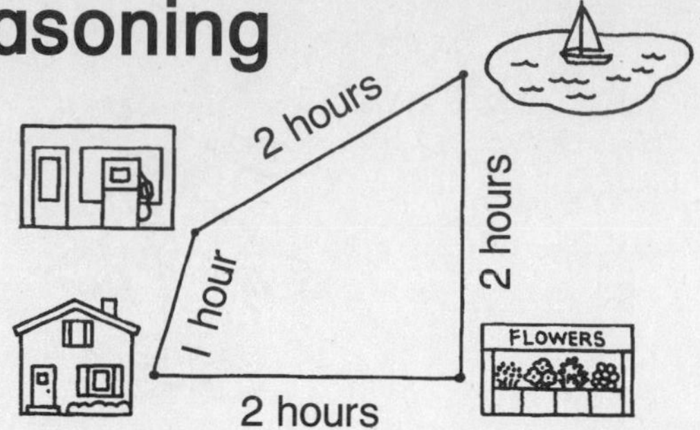

Solve.

1. Sue gets to the gas station at lunchtime. She drove 4 hours.

Step 1: Where does Sue stop? ______________

Step 2: How long did she drive? ______________

Step 3: Add the hours between places. Find out what is 4 hours away from the gas station. ______________

Step 4: Where did she start? ______________

2. Sue and Rose each drive from the house to the lake. They both leave at the same time. Sue gets to the lake at 4:00. Rose gets there at 5:00. Who drove past the flower stand? ______________

3. Juan drives from the flower stand to the house. He starts at 6:00. Rose drives from the gas station to the house. She wants to get to the house at the same time as Juan. Should Rose start before or after 6:00? ______________

Using the Page To help children ***learn***, present the problem another way, such as, "Sue starts somewhere on the map and drives 4 hours to the gas station. I need to find the place that is 4 hours from the gas station. No one place is 4 hours away, so I need to add the hours between two places." **Notes for Home** Your child used a map and logical reasoning to solve problems. *Home Activity:* Talk about the time it takes to get to different places.

Name ______________________________

Order Events

There are 3 stories.
Color each row that tells
a story in order from left to right.

Think about what happens first, next, and last.

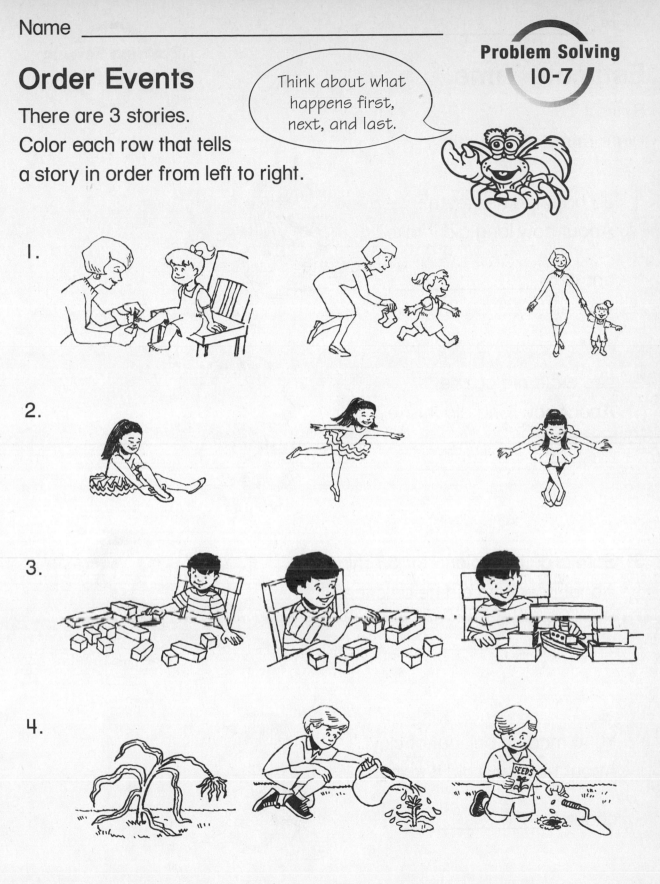

1.

2.

3.

4.

Notes for Home Your child identified pictures that show a story in correct order. *Home Activity:* Ask your child to tell about his or her school day and to tell the events in the order in which they happened.

Name ______________________

Estimate Time

Solve.

Write **minutes** or **hour**.

1. Jill brushed her teeth.
   About how long did it take?

   about 5 ____________

2. Lee did a big puzzle.
   About how long did it take?

   about 1 ____________

3. Sam practiced piano for 55 minutes.
   About how long did he practice?

   about 1 ____________

4. Yung made a ball out of clay.
   About how long did it take?

   about 1 ____________

Notes for Home Your child solved problems about estimating time. *Home Activity:* Ask your child how long he or she spends eating dinner.

Name ____________________

Problem Solving 10-9

Calendar

This is Al's calendar.

May						
S	M	T	W	T	F	S
			1	2	3	4
5	6	7	8	9	10	11
12	13	14	15	16	17	18
19	20	21	22	23	24	25
26	27	28	29	30	31	

Use the calendar.

Solve.

1. Al swims every Saturday.
   How many times will he swim this month? ______ times

2. Al goes on a trip May 15th.
   On what day of the week is May 15th? ____________

3. Al's birthday is the last Thursday in May.
   What is the date of his birthday? ____________

4. Al gets a star each day he cleans his room.
   How many stars can he get in May? ______ stars

Notes for Home Your child used a calendar to solve problems. *Home Activity:* Have your child use a calendar to find the month, date, and day of the week on which his or her birthday falls this year. Then look together for the birthdays of friends and family members.

Name ____________________

Problem Solving
10-10

Too Much Information

Cross out what you do not need. Solve.

1. Ned will go the movies at 1:00. The movie lasts 2 hours. Ned takes a bus for 30 minutes. At what time is the movie over?

Step 1: Read the problem.
Step 2: Find what you do not need to solve the problem.

____

Step 3: Cross out the information you do not need.
Step 4: At what time is the movie over?

____

2. Mira missed 3 days of school. She went to school on Monday. How many days did she go to school that week?

_____ days

3. Story hour begins at 10:00. Math is after story hour. Art time is after math. What comes last?

____

4. Ray eats lunch at 1:30. Alix eats lunch at 12:30. Pam eats dinner at 5:00. Sam eats lunch at 1:00. Who eats lunch second?

____

Using the page To help children ***understand*** how to identify unnecessary information, ask them to read through the first problem to find the question being asked. Then have them read each sentence to see if they need the information to answer the question. **Notes for Home** Your child identified unnecessary information in order to solve problems. *Home Activity:* Ask your child to explain his or her answers.

 Use with pages 391–392.

Name ______________________________

Problem Solving 11-1

Explore Measuring with Nonstandard Units

Look at the snake.

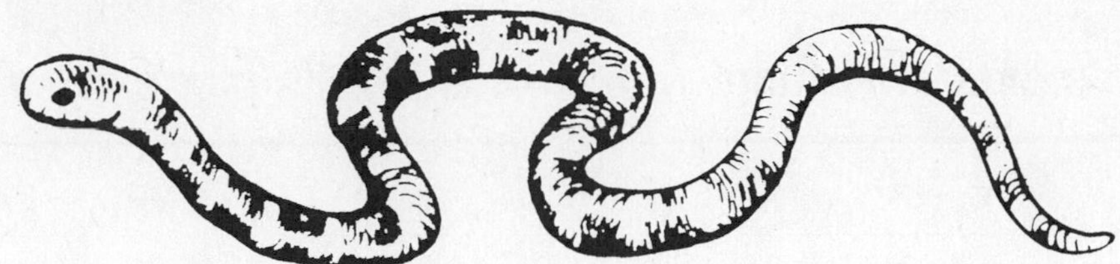

1. About how many
   long do you think the snake is? about ______ long

2. About how many
   long do you think the snake is? about ______ long

3. About how many
   long do you think the snake is? about ______ long

Now, use a string to measure. Then check your estimates.

4. How many , , and
   long is the snake?

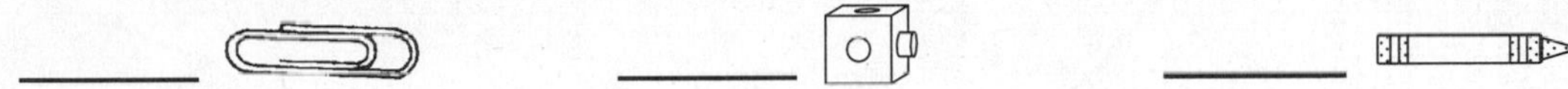

Circle more or fewer.

5. Did you use more or fewer than
   to measure the snake? more fewer

6. Did you use more or fewer than
   to measure the snake? more fewer

Notes for Home Your child explored measurement using crayons, snap cubes, and paper clips. *Home Activity:* On a sheet of paper, draw a line to show the distance from your wrist to your elbow. Ask your child to estimate the length in pennies placed end to end and then measure to check.

Name ______________________________

Problem Solving
11-2

Estimate, Measure, and Compare Lengths

Circle your estimates.

1. This is Lou's piece of string. This is Ali's piece of string.

Ali's string is 3 long.

About how long is Lou's string? 3 7 9 12

---

2. This is Jim's piece of string. This is Meg's piece of string.

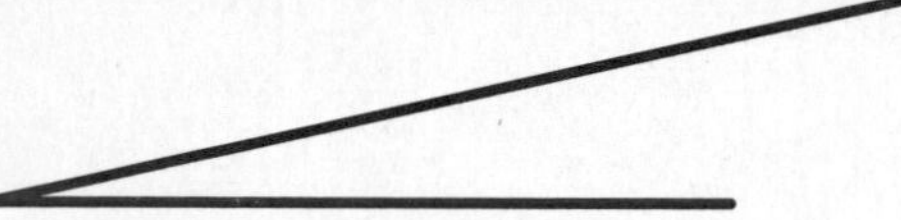

Jim's string is about 6 long.

About how long is Meg's piece of string? 2 4 10 12

---

3. This is Jen's piece of string. This is Mark's piece of string.

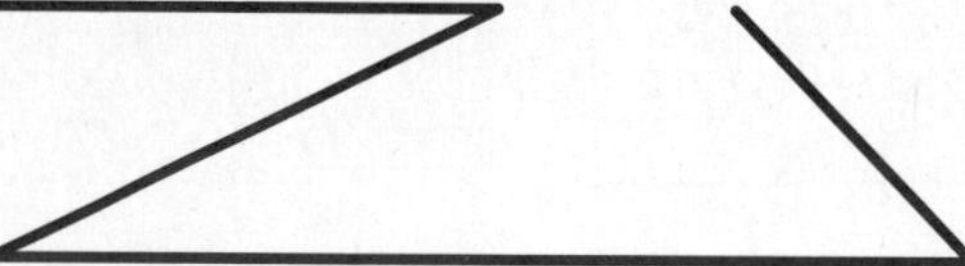

Mark's string is about 4 long.

About how long is Jen's string? 2 5 8 10

Now use a to measure and check your estimates.

Draw a line under each correct length.

Notes for Home Your child estimated and measured lengths of string. *Home Activity:* Cut two pieces of string into varying lengths. Have your child use a paper clip to measure the length of one piece of string and then estimate the length of the other before measuring to check.

Name ______________________________

Problem Solving
11-3

Estimate and Measure with Inches

1. Look at line A.

A

About how many inches long is it?
Estimate. Then measure it to check. Use an inch ruler.

about _____ inches _____ inches

2. Look at line B. Then look at line A.

B

About how many inches longer is line B than line A?
Estimate. Then measure to check.

about _____ inches longer _____ inches longer

3. Look at line C. Then look at line B.

C

About how many inches shorter is line C than line B?
Estimate. Then measure to check.

about _____ inches shorter _____ inches shorter

4. Look at line C. Then look at line A.
About how many inches shorter is line C than line A?
Estimate. Then measure to check.

about _____ inches shorter _____ inches shorter

Notes for Home Your child estimated, compared, and then measured line lengths with an inch ruler.
Home Activity: Draw a 5-inch line. Have your child measure it. Then draw a 3-inch line and an 8-inch line. Ask your child to estimate how much longer and shorter each line is before measuring to check.

Name ______________________________

Compare to One Foot

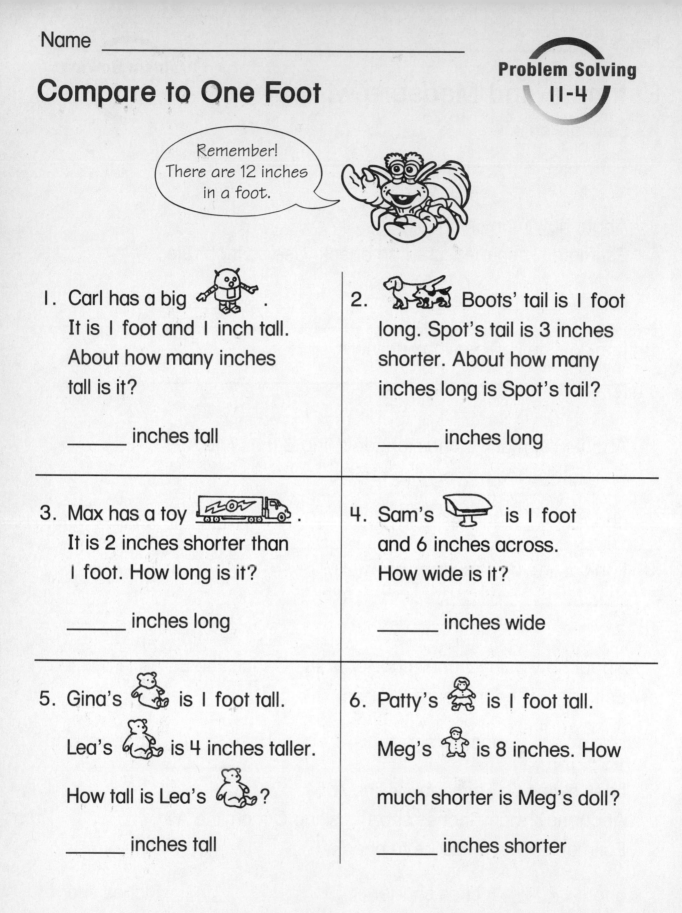

1. Carl has a big [robot]. It is 1 foot and 1 inch tall. About how many inches tall is it?

   ______ inches tall

2. [dog and cat] Boots' tail is 1 foot long. Spot's tail is 3 inches shorter. About how many inches long is Spot's tail?

   ______ inches long

3. Max has a toy [truck]. It is 2 inches shorter than 1 foot. How long is it?

   ______ inches long

4. Sam's [stool] is 1 foot and 6 inches across. How wide is it?

   ______ inches wide

5. Gina's [bear] is 1 foot tall. Lea's [bear] is 4 inches taller. How tall is Lea's [bear]?

   ______ inches tall

6. Patty's [doll] is 1 foot tall. Meg's [doll] is 8 inches. How much shorter is Meg's doll?

   ______ inches shorter

Notes for Home Your child solved problems involving measurements of 1 foot. *Home Activity:* Have your child measure household items that are longer and shorter than 1 foot, and then find the difference.

Name ______________________________

Problem Solving
11-5

Estimate and Measure with Centimeters

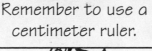

Remember to use a centimeter ruler.

Write the answer. Check.
Then circle yes or no.

H •

C •

A •

E •

F •

D •

B •

G •

★

1. Which dot is about 10 centimeters from the star? ______
   Measure to check. Were you right? yes no
   Draw a line from the star to the correct dot.

2. Which dot is about 3 centimeters from the star? ______
   Measure to check. Were you right? yes no
   Draw a line from the star to the correct dot.

3. Which dot is about 6 centimeters from the star? ______
   Measure to check. Were you right? yes no
   Draw a line from the star to the correct dot.

4. Which dot is about 4 centimeters from the star? ______
   Measure to check. Were you right? yes no
   Draw a line from the star to the correct dot.

Notes for Home Your child estimated and then measured distances with a centimeter ruler. *Home Activity:* Ask your child to draw a dot that is 1 centimter from the star.

Name ___________________________

Problem Solving
11-6

Group Decision Making

Work in a small group.

1. Ed, Ted, and Fred want to measure something.
   Choose an object for them. Then follow the steps below.

Step 1 Decide what to measure. Draw it.	Step 2 Decide what tools to use to measure. Draw what to do.	Step 3 Estimate how big it is.	Step 4 Measure to find how big it is.
		about _____ inches	_____ inches

2. As a group, choose something else to measure.
   Follow the steps. Find how big around it is.

		about _____ inches	_____ inches

Using the Page To help children ***plan***, have them suggest the most effective way to measure the rim of the wastebasket and to explain the reason for their choices. **Notes for Home** Your child worked with a group to solve measurement problems. *Home Activity:* Have your child use a tape measure, a string and ruler, or a string and a yardstick to measure around an object in your home.

Name ______________________________

Explore Weight

Problem Solving
11-7

Read the questions. Circle your answers.

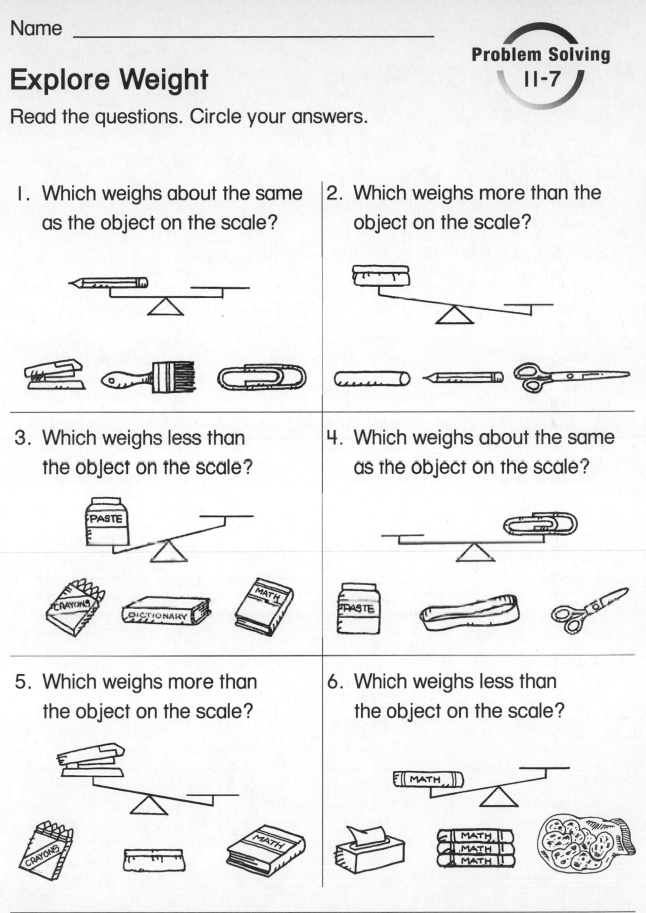

1. Which weighs about the same as the object on the scale?

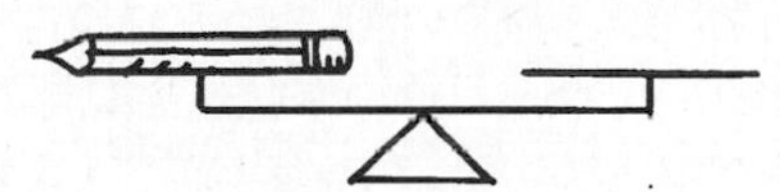

2. Which weighs more than the object on the scale?

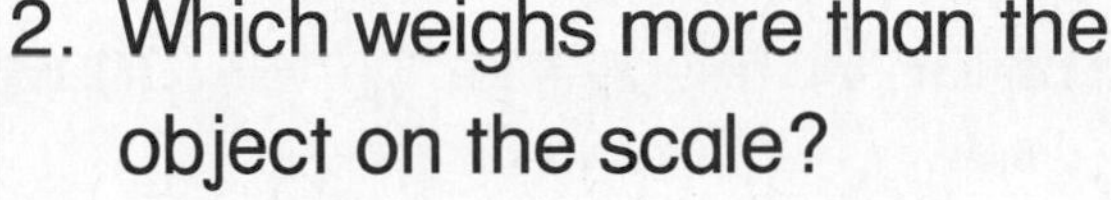

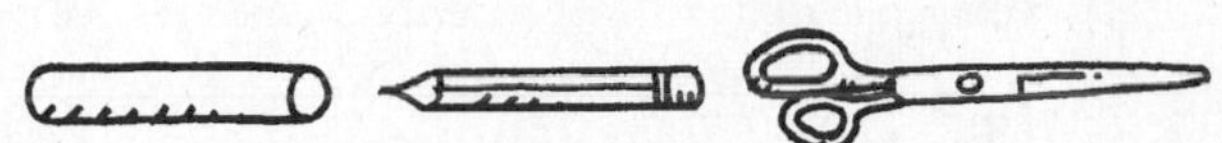

3. Which weighs less than the object on the scale?

4. Which weighs about the same as the object on the scale?

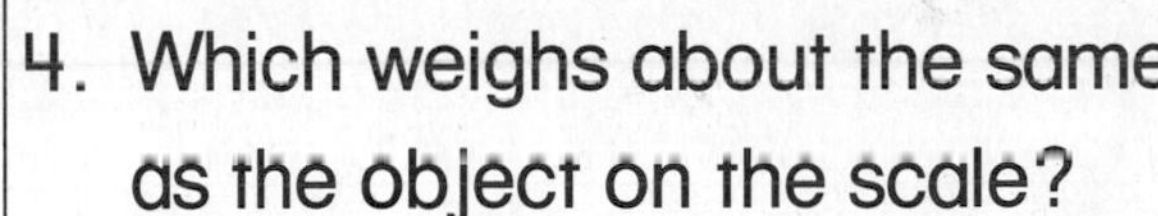

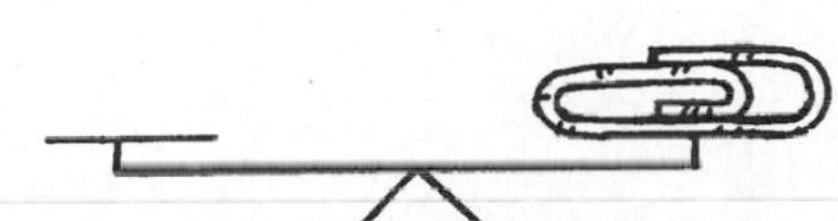

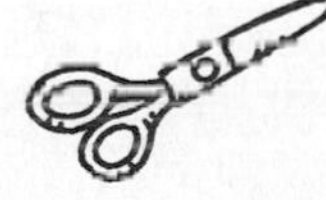

5. Which weighs more than the object on the scale?

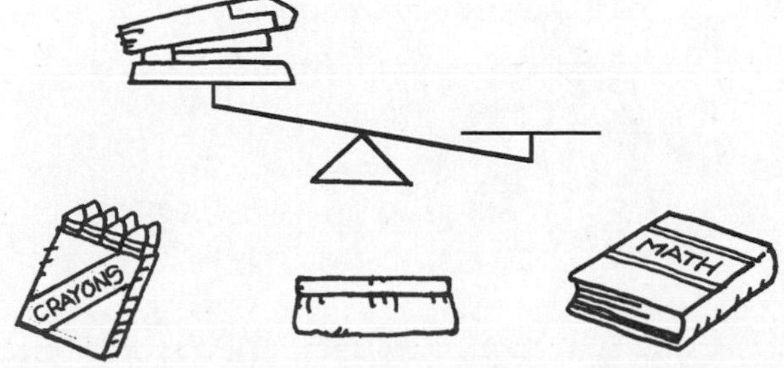

6. Which weighs less than the object on the scale?

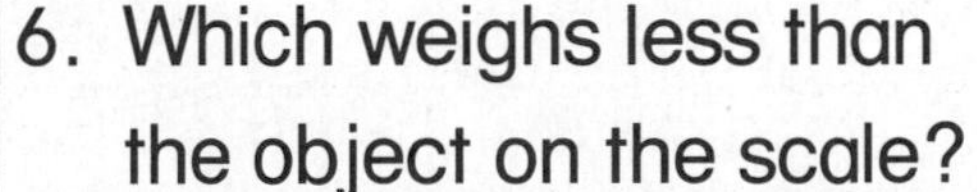

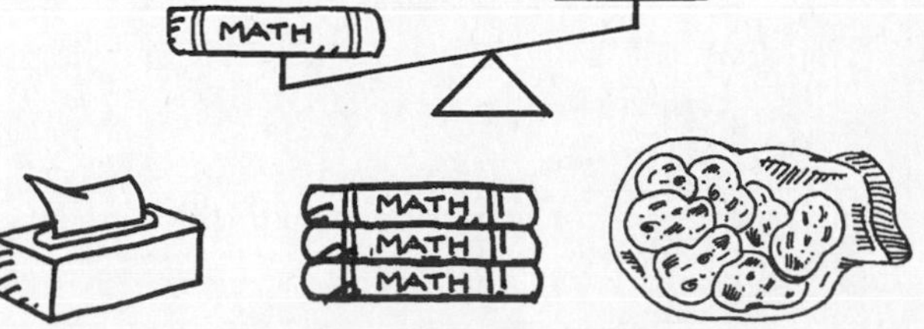

Notes for Home Your child compared the weights of objects. *Home Activity:* Challenge your child to find two objects that weigh about the same and have him or her check the estimate by weighing the objects on a bathroom scale.

Name ______________________________

Compare to One Pound

Mike, Mel, and Matt go to the store.
Each thing Mike buys is about 1 pound.
Each thing Mel buys is heavier than 1 pound.
Each that Matt buys is lighter than 1 pound.

Draw a line to each thing Mike, Mel, and Matt buy.

Notes for Home Your child identified items that weigh more than, less than, and about one pound. *Home Activity:* Have your child sort 10 packaged food items into 3 groups: more than 1 pound, less than 1 pound, about 1 pound.

Name ______________________________

Compare to One Kilogram

Problem Solving 11-9

How many kilograms does each thing weigh?

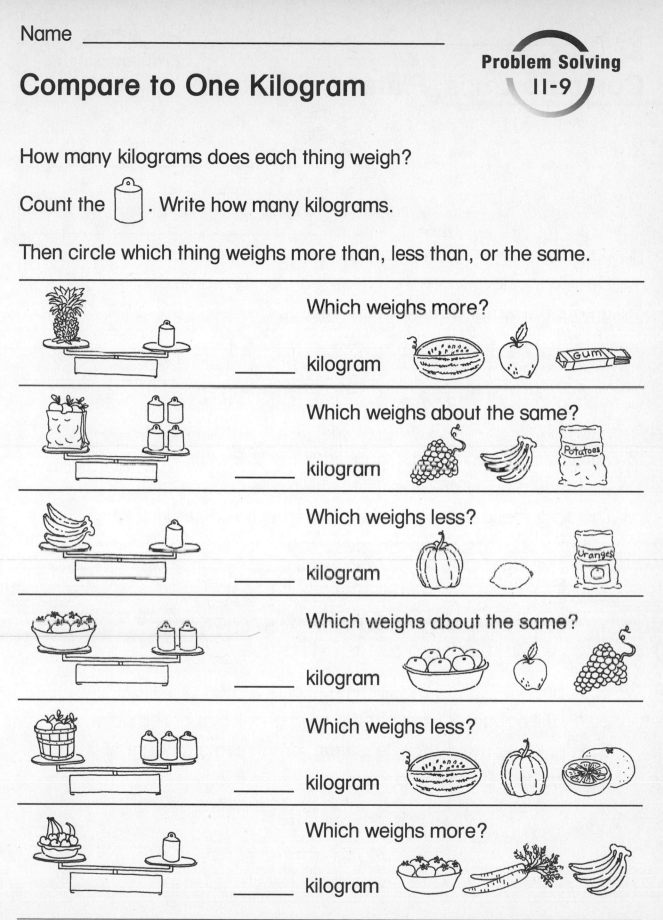

Count the . Write how many kilograms.

Then circle which thing weighs more than, less than, or the same.

Which weighs more?

______ kilogram

Which weighs about the same?

______ kilogram

Which weighs less?

______ kilogram

Which weighs about the same?

______ kilogram

Which weighs less?

______ kilogram

Which weighs more?

______ kilogram

Notes for Home Your child recorded the weights of various items in kilograms and then identified items that weigh more than, less than, and about the same. *Home Activity:* Have your child identify items in your home that are less than one kilogram.

Name ______________________________

Compare Cups, Pints, and Quarts

Problem Solving 11-10

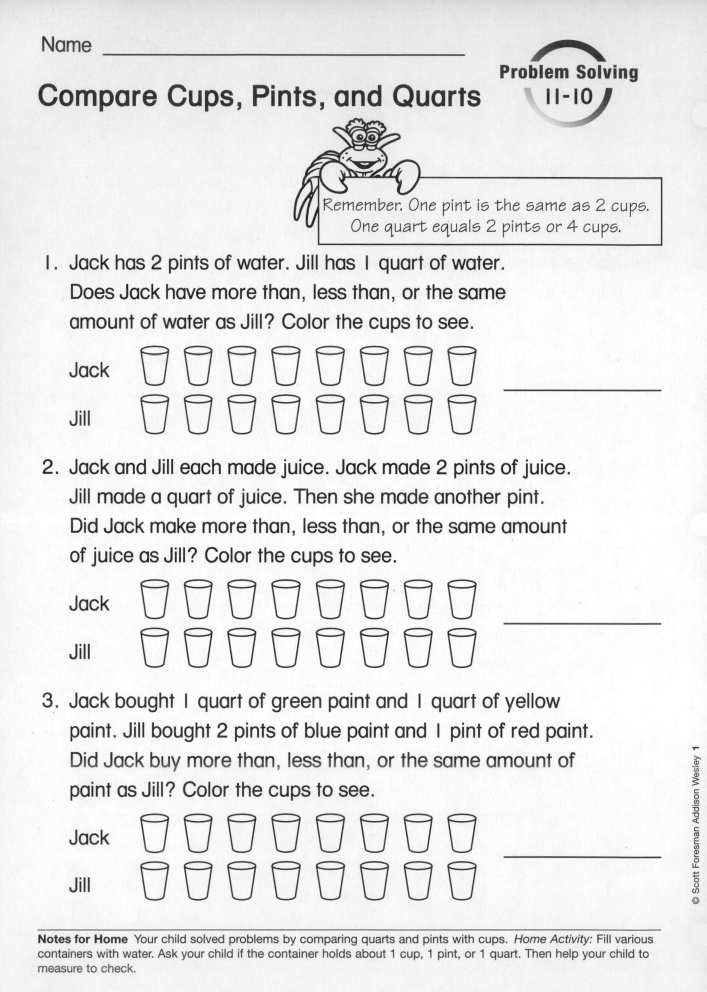

Remember. One pint is the same as 2 cups.
One quart equals 2 pints or 4 cups.

1. Jack has 2 pints of water. Jill has 1 quart of water. Does Jack have more than, less than, or the same amount of water as Jill? Color the cups to see.

Jack

Jill

____

2. Jack and Jill each made juice. Jack made 2 pints of juice. Jill made a quart of juice. Then she made another pint. Did Jack make more than, less than, or the same amount of juice as Jill? Color the cups to see.

Jack

Jill

____

3. Jack bought 1 quart of green paint and 1 quart of yellow paint. Jill bought 2 pints of blue paint and 1 pint of red paint. Did Jack buy more than, less than, or the same amount of paint as Jill? Color the cups to see.

Jack

Jill

____

Notes for Home Your child solved problems by comparing quarts and pints with cups. *Home Activity:* Fill various containers with water. Ask your child if the container holds about 1 cup, 1 pint, or 1 quart. Then help your child to measure to check.

Name ______________________________

Problem Solving
11-11

Compare to One Liter

Draw a picture to solve each problem.

1. Ben went to the store. He bought 1 bottle of apple juice, 2 bottles of grape juice, and 3 bottles of orange juice. Each bottle holds 1 liter. How many liters of juice did he buy?

   ______ liters

2. Mrs. Lee made 1 pot of vegetable soup and 1 pot of chicken soup. Each pot holds 2 liters. How many liters of soup did she make?

   ______ liters

3. Mr. James' class made 3 bowls of punch for the party. Each bowl holds 5 liters. How many liters of punch did the class make?

   ______ liters

4. There are 4 first grade classes. Each class drank 10 liters of juice in 1 week. How many liters did the first grade classes drink in all?

   ______ liters

Notes for Home Your child determined how many liters in all by drawing pictures and counting by ones, twos, fives, and tens to solve problems. *Home Activity:* Ask your child to use one of the problems as a model to create his or her own problem.

Name ______________________

Problem Solving 11-12

Use a Thermometer

Read each story.
Circle the thermometer that shows what the temperature is.

1. The red, brown, and gold leaves are falling from the trees. Jim puts on his jacket and gets the rake. He likes to help his father in the yard.

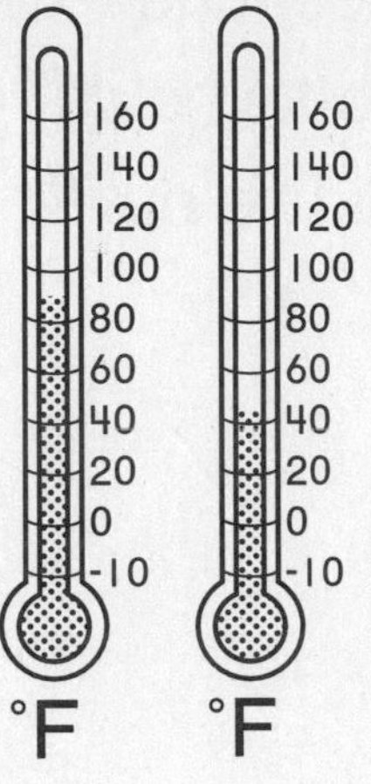

2. The sun is shining. Meg and her friends are down by the water. Meg is looking for shells. Jen is digging in the sand. Lee says, "Let's swim."

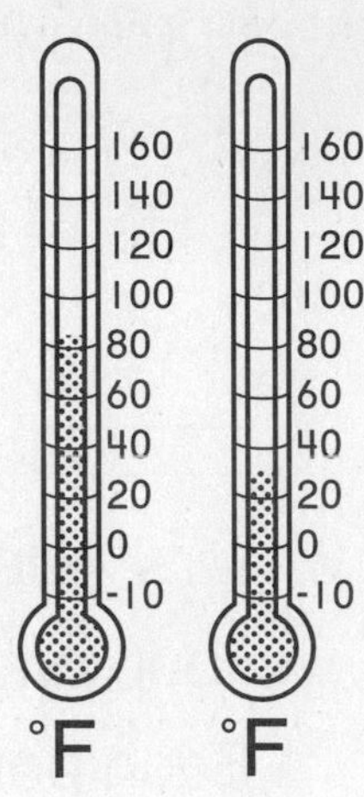

3. It snowed last night. Wes and his friends are having fun outside. First they make a great big snowman. Then they go ice skating.

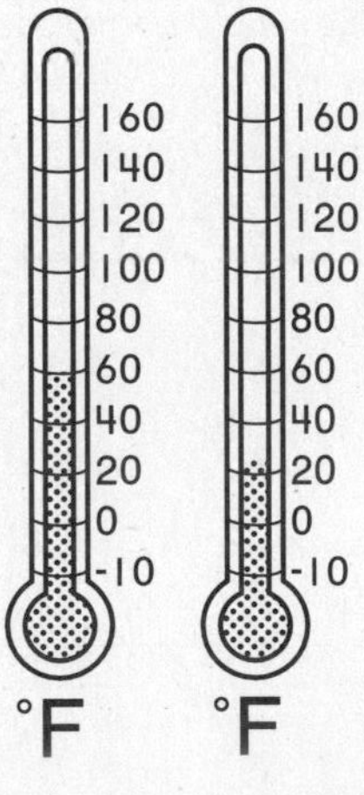

4. The birds are building nests. Jeb and his sister are busy, too. They are working in the garden. Soon it will be ready so they can plant seeds.

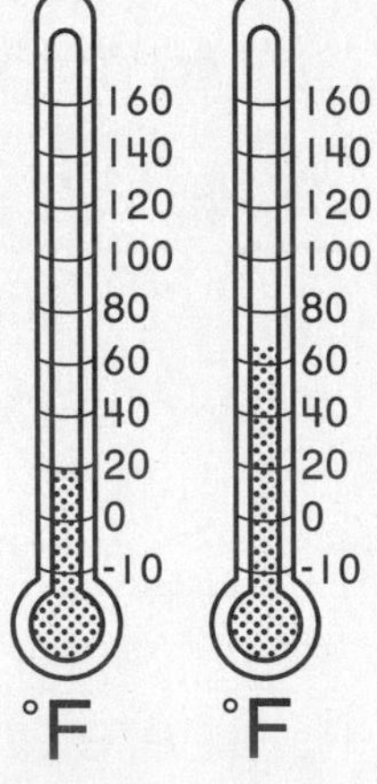

Notes for Home Your child looked for weather and temperature clues in stories and then indicated the appropriate thermometer reading. *Home Activity:* As your child reads a favorite story or comic strip, suggest that he or she look for clues about the weather and temperature and then suggest what the temperature might be.

Name ______________________________

Logical Reasoning

Write the letter for the correct tool to answer each question.

a b c d e

1. Meg has some , , 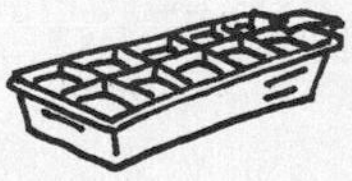 and 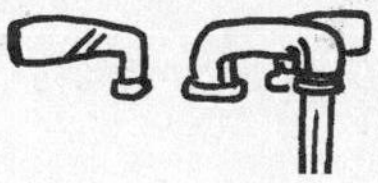.

She wants to make lemonade in the big . Meg wants to know how much lemonade the  will hold.

Which tool can she use? ______

Step 1	Step 2	Step 3
Think about what Meg wants to know.	Look at the tools. Think about what each one measures.	Decide which tool measures what Meg wants to know. Answer the question.

2. Meg wants to know how many pounds of  she has.
Which tool can she use to find out? ______

3. Meg wants to know how tall the  is.
Which tool can she use to find out? ______

4. Meg puts  in the lemonade to make it cold.
Which tool can she use to find out if it is cold? ______

5. Meg wants to know how much  she has.
Which tool can she use to find out? ______

Using the Page Have children ***look back*** by explaining the reasons for their choices. **Notes for Home** Your child solved problems by choosing the appropriate measuring tool. *Home Activity:* Point out objects in your home such as the oven, the freezer, a food storage bag, a picture frame, and a bag of fruit or vegetables. Then ask your child to identify the measuring tool he or she would use to find out how hot or cold the oven or freezer is, how much the bag holds, the perimeter of the frame, and the weight of the fruit or vegetables.

Name ______________________________

Problem Solving
12-1

Add Doubles to 18

Solve.

1. Guy lives 6 blocks from school. He walks to and from school. How far does Guy walk each day?

   ______ blocks

2. Guy's father works in the city. It is 9 miles away. How far does he drive to and from work each day?

   ______ miles

3. Guy's mother has a book store. It is 3 blocks away. She opens the store at 9 a.m. and closes it at 5 p.m. She goes home for lunch. How far does she walk in all?

   ______ blocks

4. Guy's sister is in high school. She walks a total of 16 blocks to and from school each day. How many blocks does Guy's sister walk each day?

   ______ blocks

Notes for Home Your child added doubles to 18. *Home Activity:* Help your child determine how many blocks, steps, or miles it is one way from your home to another location, and then add doubles to find how blocks, steps, or miles a round trip would be.

Name ______________________________

Add Doubles Plus One

Solve. Write a number sentence.

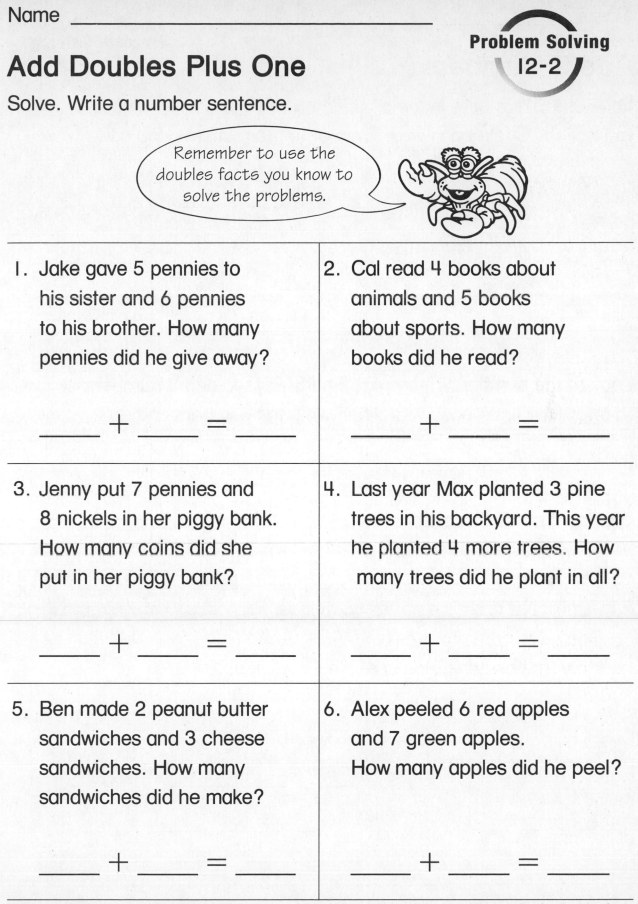

Remember to use the doubles facts you know to solve the problems.

1. Jake gave 5 pennies to his sister and 6 pennies to his brother. How many pennies did he give away?

____ + ____ = ____

2. Cal read 4 books about animals and 5 books about sports. How many books did he read?

____ + ____ = ____

3. Jenny put 7 pennies and 8 nickels in her piggy bank. How many coins did she put in her piggy bank?

____ + ____ = ____

4. Last year Max planted 3 pine trees in his backyard. This year he planted 4 more trees. How many trees did he plant in all?

____ + ____ = ____

5. Ben made 2 peanut butter sandwiches and 3 cheese sandwiches. How many sandwiches did he make?

____ + ____ = ____

6. Alex peeled 6 red apples and 7 green apples. How many apples did he peel?

____ + ____ = ____

Notes for Home Your child added doubles plus one facts. *Home Activity:* Ask your child to write the doubles fact for each problem. (1. 5 + 5 = 10, 2. 4 + 4 = 8, 3. 7 + 7 = 14, 4. 3 + 3 = 6, 5. 2 + 2 = 4, 6. 6 + 6 = 12).

Name ______________________________

Add 3 Numbers

Look at the numbers in the box. Find 5 ways to add 3 numbers to total 14. Circle each way. Then write the numbers and add.

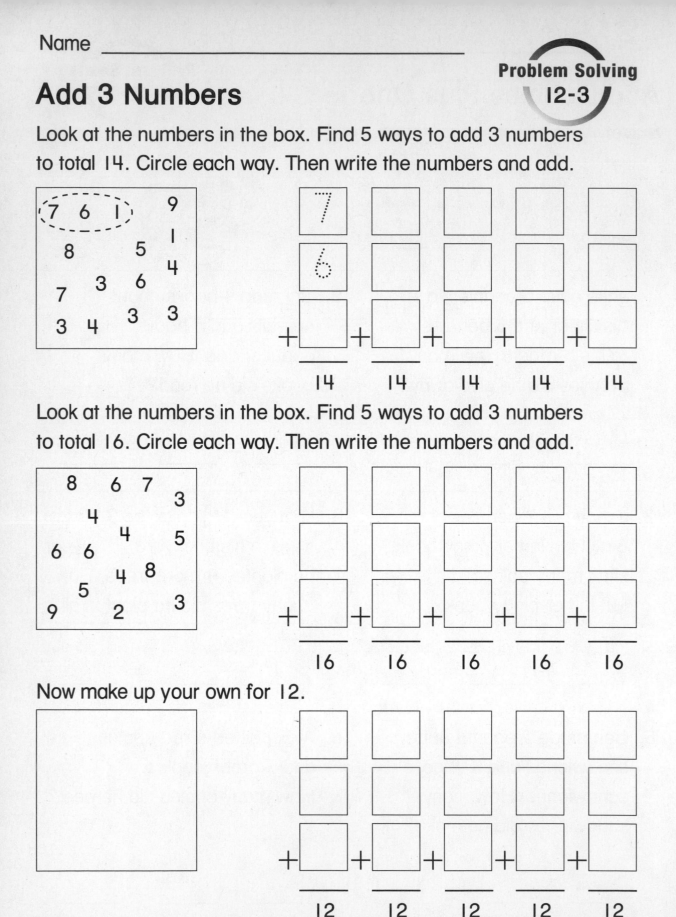

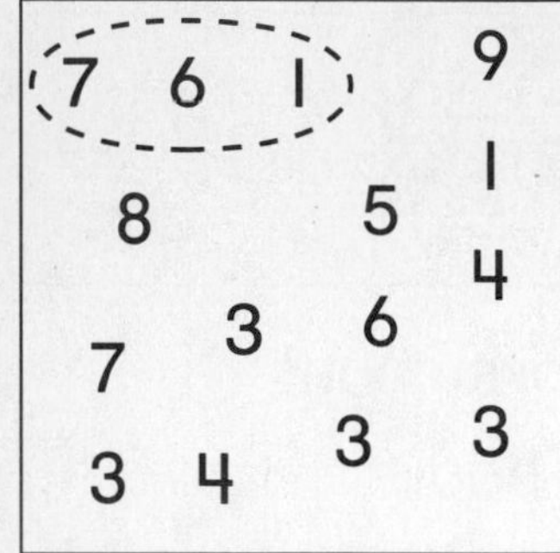

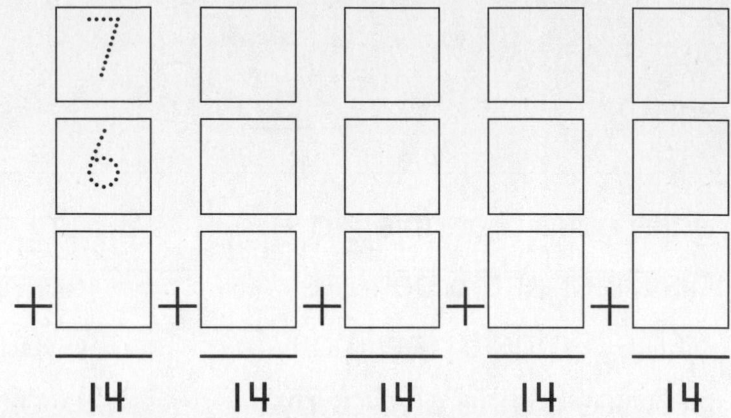

Look at the numbers in the box. Find 5 ways to add 3 numbers to total 16. Circle each way. Then write the numbers and add.

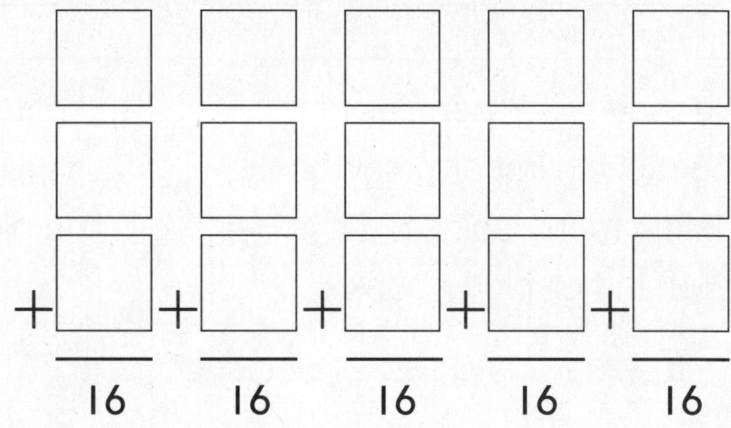

Now make up your own for 12.

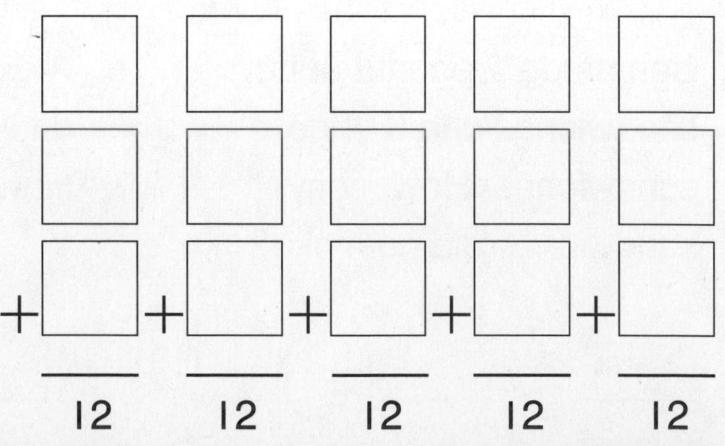

Notes for Home Your child used different strategies to add three numbers . *Home Activity:* Ask your child to explain the order in which he or she added the numbers.

Name ____________________

Explore Making 10 to Add 7, 8, or 9

Problem Solving 12-4

Solve. Write the numbers.

1. Max has 9 cars. His friends gave him 4 more cars for his birthday. How many cars does Max have?

_____ + _____ = 10 + _____ = _____

Max has _____ cars.

2. Cindy has 8 dolls. Her mother gave her 6 more dolls. How many dolls does Cindy have now?

_____ + _____ = 10 + _____ = _____

Cindy has _____ dolls.

3. Meg has 7 toy horses. Her brother Al has 8 toy horses. How many horses do Meg and Al have?

_____ + _____ = 10 + _____ = _____

Meg and Al have _____ horses.

Notes for Home Your child explored making a 10 to add 7, 8, and 9. *Home Activity:* Ask your child how many dolls Cindy would have if she had 8 and she was given 9 more dolls. (8 + 9 = 10 + 7 = 17)

Name ______________________

Problem Solving
12-5

Make 10 When Adding 7, 8, or 9

Lisa is having a party. There will be 14 children in all.
Use the picture to answer the questions.

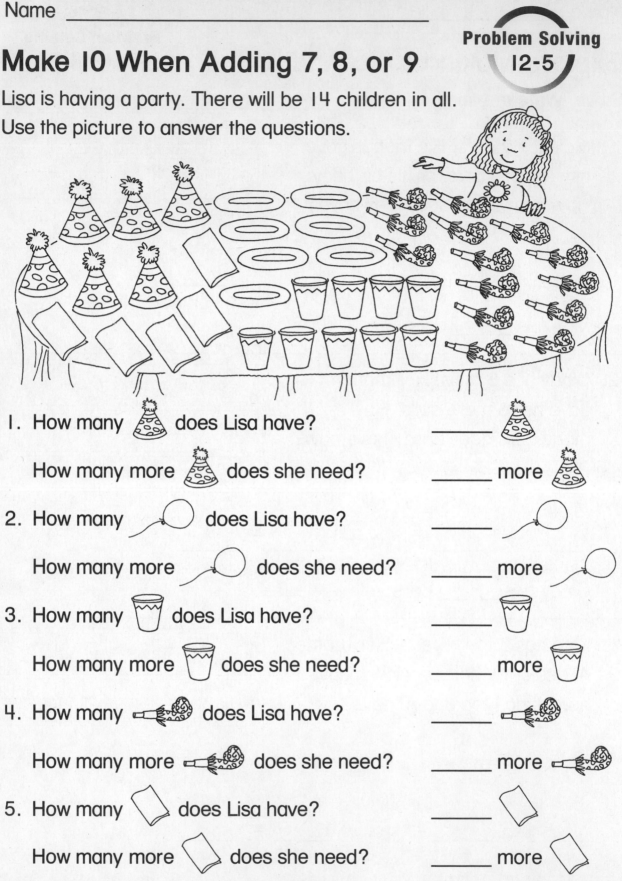

1. How many does Lisa have? ______ 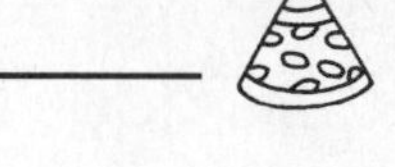

   How many more does she need? ______ more

2. How many does Lisa have? ______

   How many more does she need? ______ more

3. How many does Lisa have? ______ 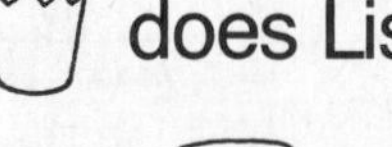

   How many more does she need? ______ more 

4. How many does Lisa have? ______

   How many more does she need? ______ more

5. How many does Lisa have? ______ 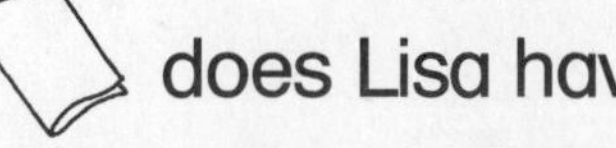

   How many more does she need? ______ more

Notes for Home Your child added numbers including 7, 8, 9. *Home Activity:* Ask your child how many more balloons Lisa would need if she had only 10. (4 more balloons)

Name ______________________________

Choose a Strategy

You can use ⬭ or draw a picture to solve each problem.

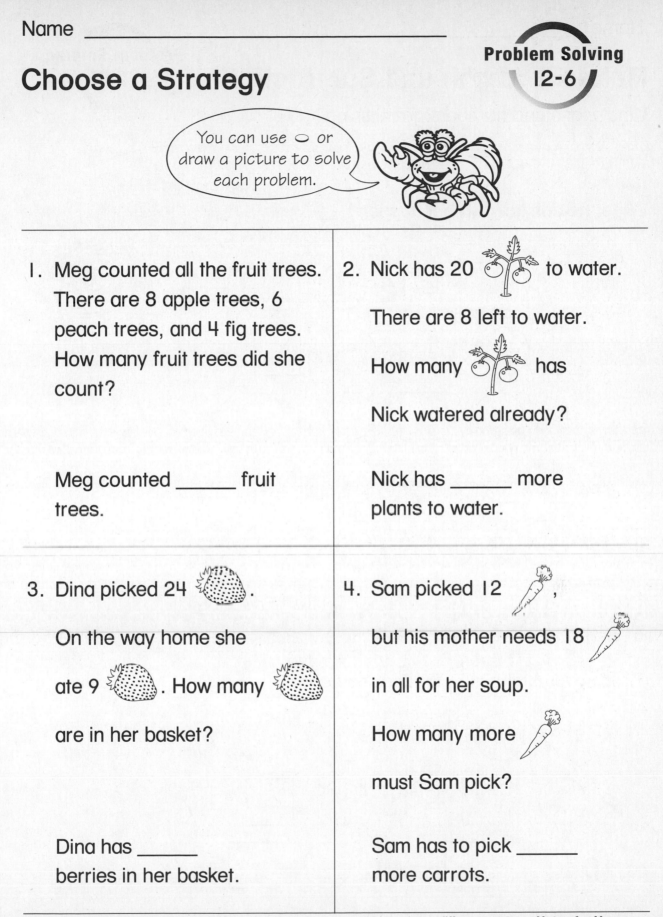

1. Meg counted all the fruit trees. There are 8 apple trees, 6 peach trees, and 4 fig trees. How many fruit trees did she count?

   Meg counted ______ fruit trees.

2. Nick has 20  to water.

   There are 8 left to water.

   How many  has Nick watered already?

   Nick has ______ more plants to water.

3. Dina picked 24 .

   On the way home she ate 9 . How many  are in her basket?

   Dina has ______ berries in her basket.

4. Sam picked 12 , but his mother needs 18  in all for her soup.

   How many more  must Sam pick?

   Sam has to pick ______ more carrots.

Using the Page Have children ***look back*** to check their answers by using a different strategy. **Notes for Home** Your child solved problems by drawing a picture or by using counters and ten frames. *Home Activity:* Ask your child to demonstrate how drawing a picture or using counters and ten frames can help to solve one of the problems.

Name ______________________________

Relate Addition and Subtraction

What signs and numbers are missing?

Write +, −, or = in each ◯.

Write the correct number in each ☐.

Here's a hint. These numbers are related.

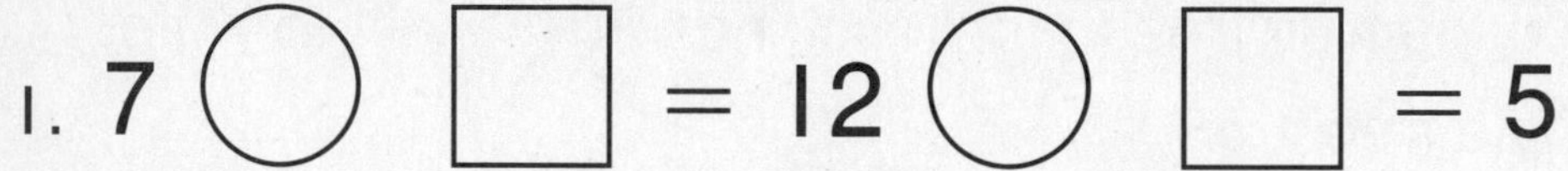

1. 7 ◯ ☐ = 12 ◯ ☐ = 5

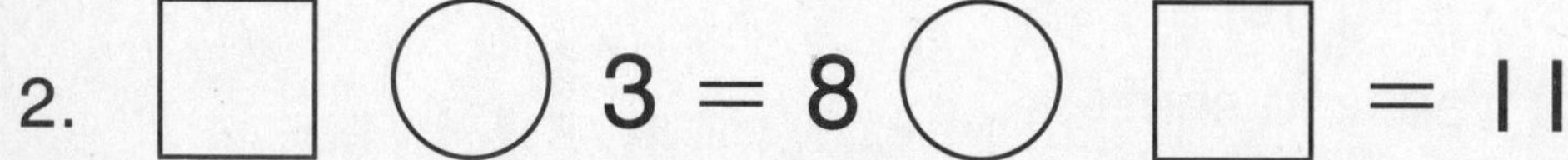

2. ☐ ◯ 3 = 8 ◯ ☐ = 11

3. 3 + 7 ◯ ☐ ◯ 3 ◯ 7

4. ☐ ◯ 7 = 4 ◯ ☐ = 11

5. 12 ◯ 3 ◯ 9 ◯ 3 ◯ 12

6. ☐ ◯ 4 ◯ 5 + ☐ = 9

7. 2 ◯ ☐ = 8 ◯ ☐ = 6

8. 6 + 7 ◯ ☐ ◯ 6 ◯ 7

9. 8 ◯ ☐ = 15 ◯ ☐ = 7

10. 10 ◯ ☐ = 10 ◯ ☐ = 0

Notes for Home Your child completed related addition and subtraction facts. *Home Activity:* Ask your child how he or she identified the missing signs and numbers.

Name ______________________________

Use Doubles to Subtract

Find and color the 4 things hidden in the picture.
To find what color crayon to use, double each number.

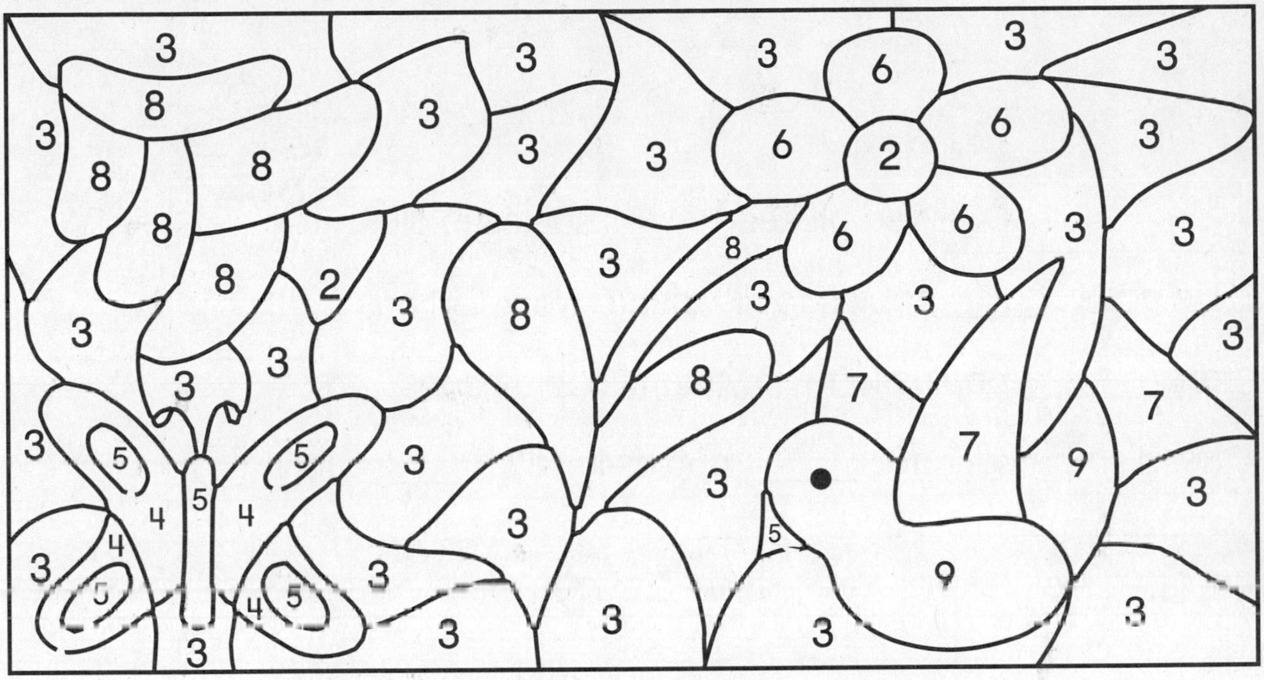

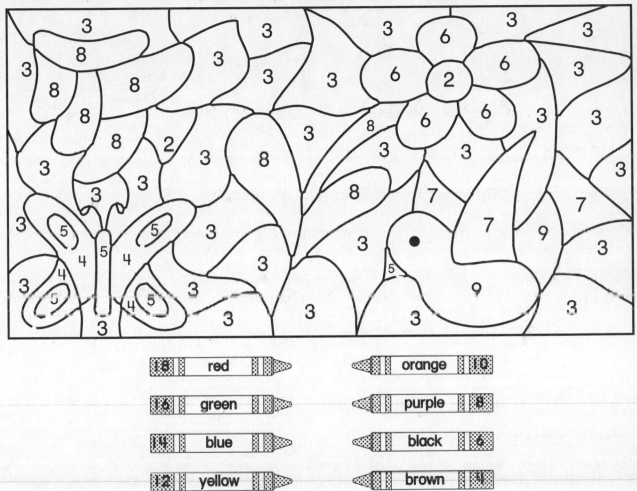

- 18 red
- 16 green
- 14 blue
- 12 yellow
- 10 orange
- 8 purple
- 6 black
- 4 brown

Write a subtraction fact for the number in each crayon and the numbers you doubled.

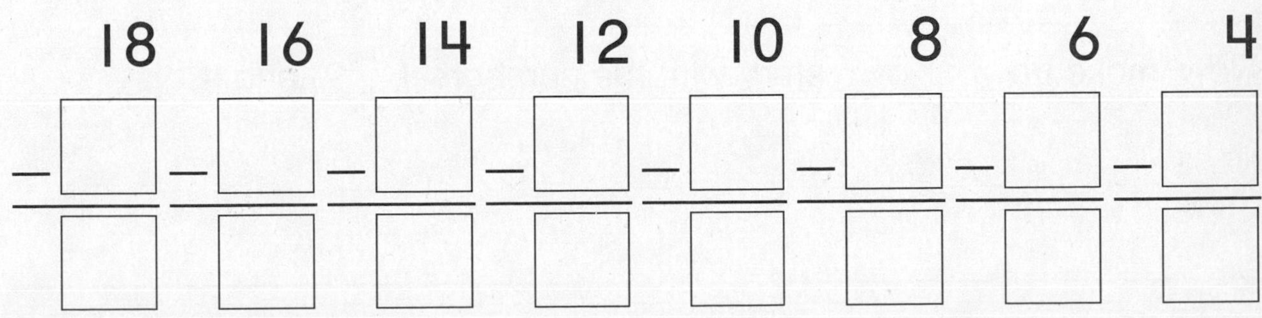

Notes for Home Your child used addition doubles to find a related subtraction fact. *Home Activity:* Ask your child to write a related subtraction fact for 5 + 5 = 10. (10 − 5 = 5)

Use with pages 467–468.

Name ______________________________

Problem Solving 12-9

Subtraction Facts for 13 and 14

Use the numbers in each box to tell the story.
Then write a number sentence to solve.

14 8 6

Ted picked _____ apples in all.

He gave _____ apples to his friend. Now Ted has only _____ apples left. How many apples does Ted need so he will have _____ apples in all? _____ more

_____ ○ _____

15 8 7

Beth and Jenny went for a walk. _____ ○ _____

On the way, they each picked some daisies.

Beth picked _____ daisies and Jenny picked _____ daisies.

Together, the girls have _____ daisies. On the way home, they gave some daisies to Becky. Now they have only _____ left.

How many daisies did they give Becky? _____

Now, make up your own story with the numbers 13, 9, and 4.

____

____

Notes for Home Your child used addition facts to solve subtraction. *Home Activity:* Ask your child to write two related subtraction facts for 9 + 5 = 14. (14 – 9 = 5; 14 – 5 = 9)

Name ______________________________

Problem Solving
12-10

Subtraction Facts for 15 to 18

Solve.

Remember this. A dime is worth 10 cents. A nickel is worth 5 cents. A penny is worth 1 cent.

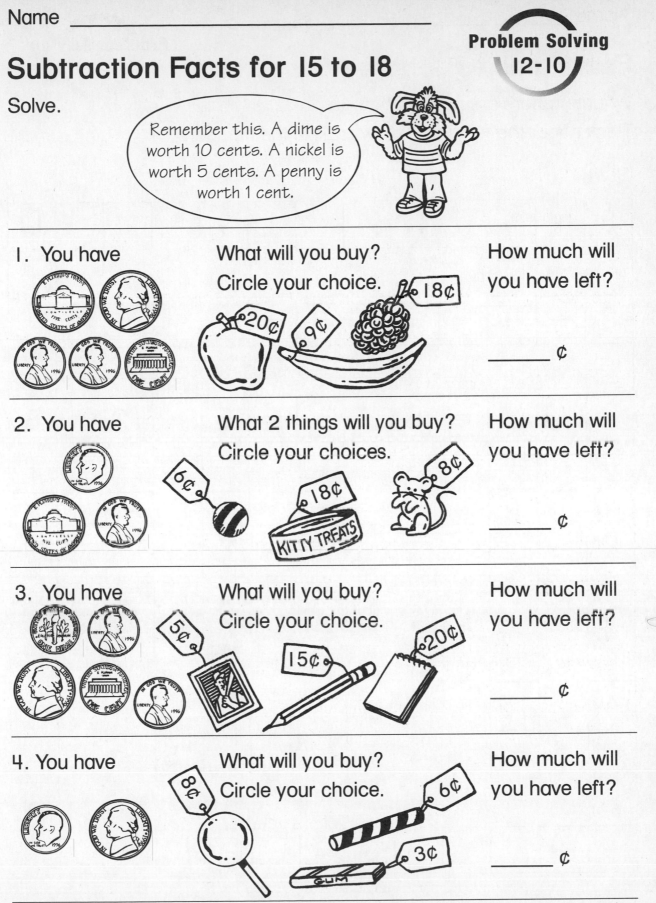

1. You have

What will you buy?
Circle your choice.

How much will you have left?

_____ ¢

2. You have

What 2 things will you buy?
Circle your choices.

How much will you have left?

_____ ¢

3. You have

What will you buy?
Circle your choice.

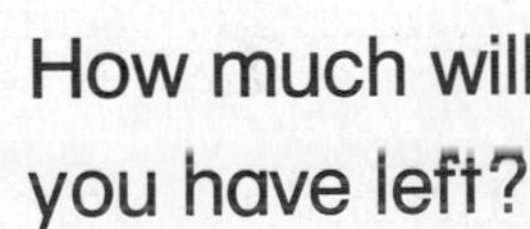

How much will you have left?

_____ ¢

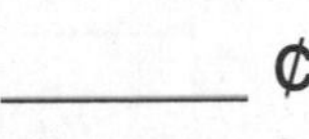

4. You have

What will you buy?
Circle your choice.

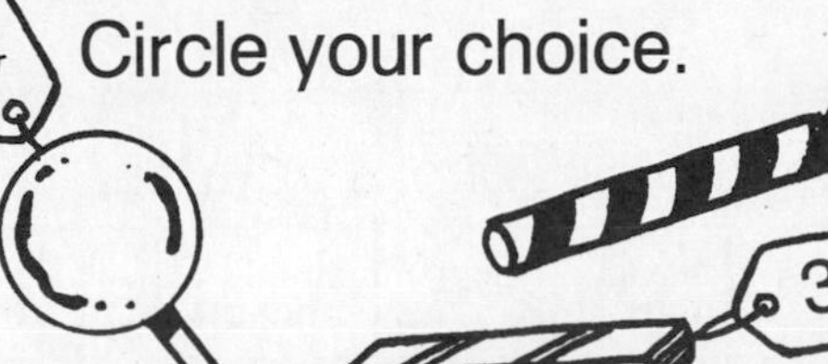

How much will you have left?

_____ ¢

Notes for Home Your child subtracted facts to 18. *Home Activity:* Give your child 1 dime, 1 nickel, and 5 pennies. Ask which items he or she would buy in the above problems and how much would be left each time.

Name ______________________________

Problem Solving
12-11

Fact Families

What numbers are missing?

Think about the facts you know to fill in the numbers.

Start

8	+		=	17	−		=	9	+		=	17
												−
8	+	4	=		−	8	=		+			
=										=		=
			=	8	−		=	8		12		8
−		+						−		−		+
14		8										5
=		=						=		=		=
								0		8		
+		−						End		+		−
6		15										8
=		=		+	7	=		−	15	=		=
												5
−	14	=		+	8	=		−	13	=		+

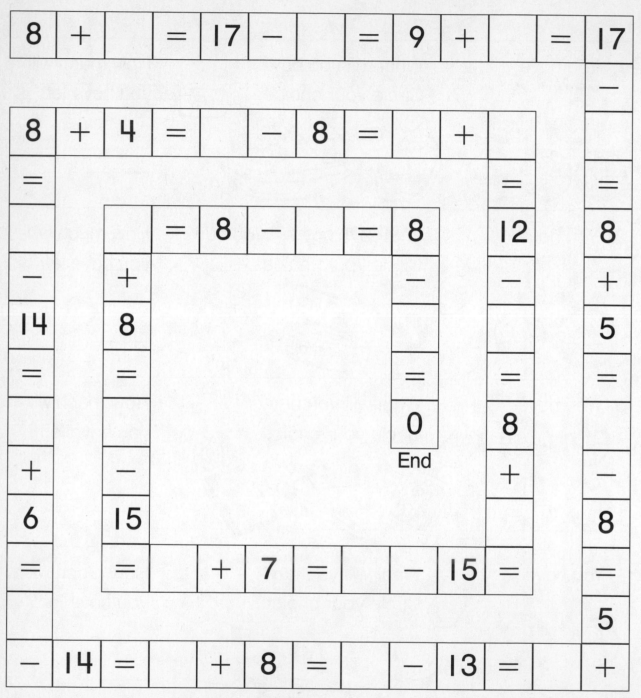

Notes for Home Your child added and subtracted using fact families. *Home Activity:* Have your child write the fact family for the numbers 9, 7, and 16. (9 + 7 = 16, 7 + 9 = 16, 16 − 9 = 7, 16 − 7 = 9)

Name ______________________________

Choose an Operation

Add or subtract. Show your work.

1. Last week Mother Hubbard went to the butcher. She bought 15 bones for her dog. Now there are only 6 bones left. How many bones did Mother Hubbard's dog eat?

   Mother Hubbard's dog ate ______ bones.

2. Simple Simon met a pieman on the way to the fair. Simon bought 6 apple pies and 7 cherry pies. How many pies did Simon buy?

   Simon bought ______ pies.

3. Little Boy Blue had 18 cows. If 9 cows were in the meadow, how many were in the corn fields?

   There were ______ cows in the corn fields.

4. Jack and Jill went up the hill to get water. Jack carried 8 pails and Jill carried 6 pails. How many pails did they carry in all?

   Jack and Jil carried ______ pails of water.

Using the Page Encourage children to suggest different strategies they can use to ***solve*** each problem.
Notes for Home Your child decided whether to add or subtract to solve problems. *Home Activity:* Choose one of the problems and then substitute other numbers. Ask your child to solve the problem.

Use with pages 477–478.

Name ______________________________

Problem Solving
13-1

Explore Adding Tens

Solve.

1. Jeb has .

How much does he have?

______ cents

If his dad gives him a dime today, tomorrow, and the day after, how much will he have?

______ cents

2. Holly has

.

How much does she have?

______ cents

How many more dimes does she need to have 83 cents?

______ more dimes

3. Hal has

.

How much does he have?

______ cents

Hal's mom gave him 6 dimes for his lunch. How much does he have now?

______ cents

4. Pam has

.

How much does she have?

______ cents

Pam found 2 more dimes in her pocket. How many more dimes does she need to buy something for 95 cents?

______ more

Notes for Home Your child used dimes and pennies to explore adding tens. *Home Activity:* Provide your child with a group of dimes and pennies. Name an amount such as 53 cents. Then have your child count out 5 dimes and 3 pennies. Have your child take 2 more dimes. Ask: *How much do you have now?* (73¢)

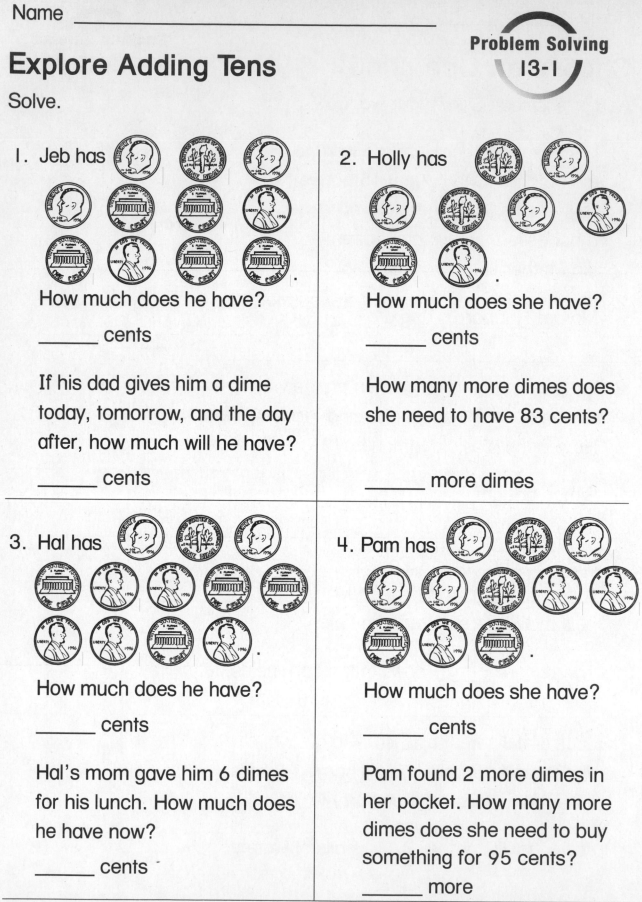

Name ______________________________

Problem Solving
13-2

Add Tens

1. Here are two ways to make the sum of 60.
How many more ways can you make a sum of 60?

$$\begin{array}{r} 10 \\ +\,50 \\ \hline 60 \end{array} \qquad \begin{array}{r} 30 \\ +\,30 \\ \hline 60 \end{array}$$

2. Here are two ways to make the sum of 90.
How many more ways can you make a sum of 90?

$$\begin{array}{r} 10 \\ +\,80 \\ \hline 90 \end{array} \qquad \begin{array}{r} 20 \\ +\,70 \\ \hline 90 \end{array}$$

3. Here are two ways to make a sum of 56.
How many more ways can you make a sum of 56?

$$\begin{array}{r} 16 \\ +\,40 \\ \hline 56 \end{array} \qquad \begin{array}{r} 36 \\ +\,20 \\ \hline 56 \end{array}$$

4. Here are two ways to make a sum of 71.
How many more ways can you make the sum of 71?

$$\begin{array}{r} 11 \\ +\,60 \\ \hline 71 \end{array} \qquad \begin{array}{r} 41 \\ +\,30 \\ \hline 71 \end{array}$$

Notes for Home Your child added tens to two-digit numbers. *Home Activity:* Ask your child to count by tens from 19 to 99 and then backwards by tens from 87 to 17.

Name ______________________

Problem Solving
13-3

Add Tens and Ones

Solve.

1. I am a number between 50 and 65. If you add 3 tens and 2 ones, and 2 tens and 7 ones, you'll find out what I am.

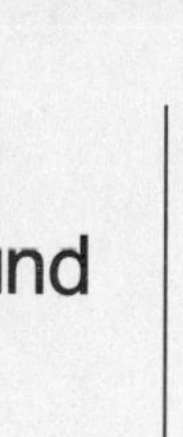

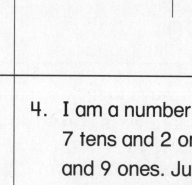

2. I am an even number. I am less than 68 but greater than 51. Just add 4 tens and 3 ones and 23 to see what I am.

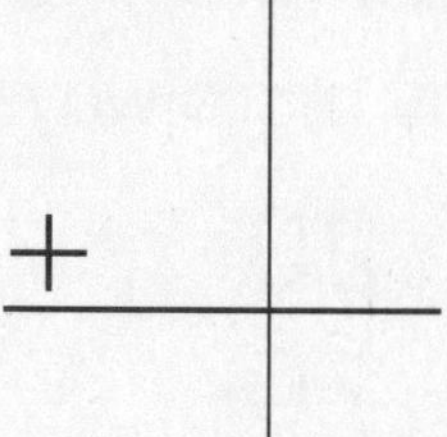

3. I am an odd number. I am greater than the double of 3 tens but less than 7 tens. Add 5 tens and 3 ones, and 1 ten and 4 ones, to find out what I am.

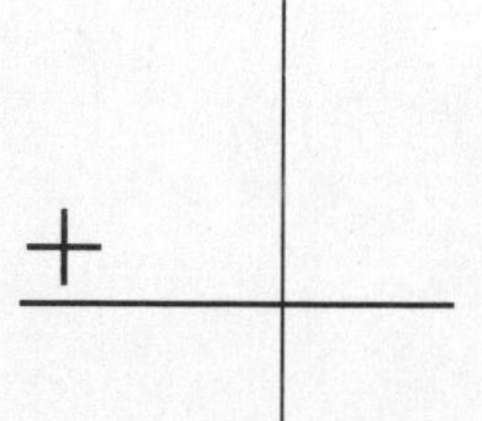

4. I am a number between 7 tens and 2 ones, and 9 tens and 9 ones. Just add 2 tens and 5 ones, and 5 tens and 2 ones, to find out what I am.

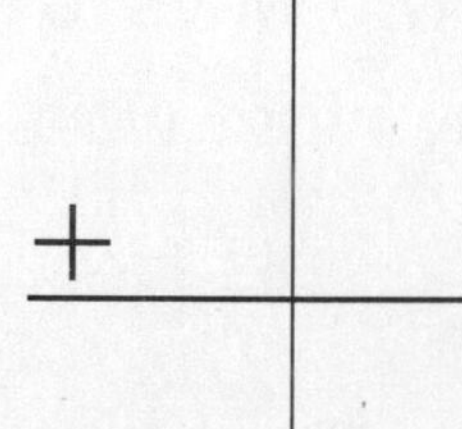

Notes for Home Your child solved riddles by adding two-digit numbers. *Home Activity:* Have your child use one of the riddles as a model to create a new riddle for you to solve.

Name ______________________________

Problem Solving 13-4

Regroup with Addition

What has fifty heads and fifty tails?

To solve this riddle, first write the missing number to solve each problem.

t $79 + \square = 81$	e $87 + \square = 95$	n $89 + \square = 90$	f $29 + \square = 29$
p $60 + \square = 70$	i $11 + \square = 22$	s $56 + \square = 60$	i $28 + \square = 33$
e $48 + \square = 51$	n $56 + \square = 62$	f $29 + \square = 36$	y $43 + \square = 52$

Now write the letter for each problem above its answer.

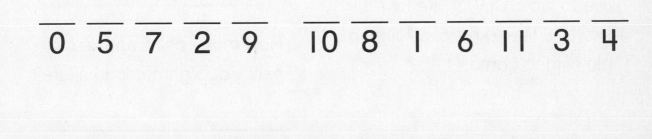

___ ___ ___ ___ ___   ___ ___ ___ ___ ___ ___ ___

0 5 7 2 9   10 8 1 6 11 3 4

Notes for Home Your child found the missing addend and used regrouping to solve problems. *Home Activity:* Ask your child to explain how he or she determined the missing numbers.

Name ______________________________

Use Objects

Problem Solving 13-5

1. Beth and Jeff played ring toss.
Beth scored 18 points in Game 1 and 7 points in Game 2.
Jeff scored 16 points in Game 1 and 8 points in Game 2.
How many points did Beth score?
How many points did Jeff score?
Who had more points?

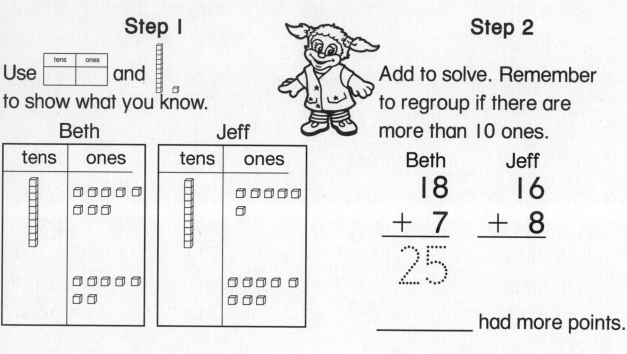

Step 1

Use [tens | ones] and [tens and ones blocks] to show what you know.

Beth

tens	ones
1 ten	8 ones
	7 ones

Jeff

tens	ones
1 ten	6 ones
	8 ones

Step 2

Add to solve. Remember to regroup if there are more than 10 ones.

	Beth	Jeff
	18	16
+	7	8
	25	

__________ had more points.

2. Miss Lee asked 50 first graders what they like to do most after school. 15 children like to watch TV. 9 like to skate. 8 like to read. 17 like to play video games.

How many children in all like to watch TV and read?

____

How many children like to play video games and skate?

____

Using the Page As children read through each problem, help them to ***plan*** by asking how they know whether to add or subtract. **Notes for Home** Your child solved problems involving addition by using objects. *Home Activity:* Ask your child to use pennies or dry beans to demonstrate how he or she solved one of the problems.

Name ____________________

Problem Solving 13-6

Subtract Tens

Solve.

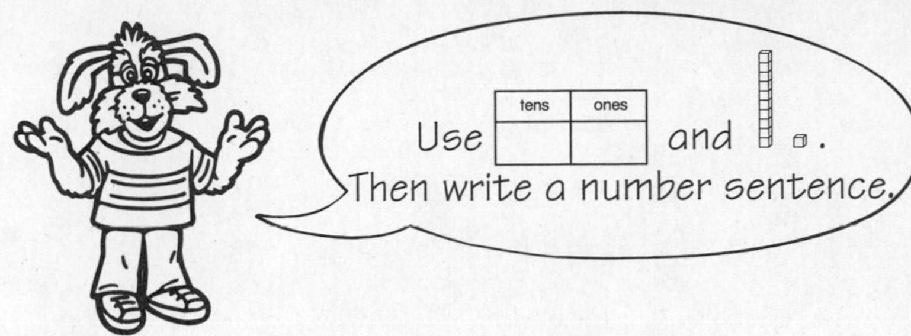

tens
ones
Use and .
Then write a number sentence.

1. Max went to the store to buy a snack. He had 80 cents. He bought some fruit. Now he has only 30 cents. How much did he spend?

____

2. Max counted 30 carts inside the store and 54 carts outside. How many more carts were outside the store than inside ?

____

3. Max counted 36 loaves of bread on the top shelf and 20 loaves on the middle shelf. How many more loaves were on the top shelf?

____

4. Max counted 32 pieces of bubble gum in the big bag and 20 pieces of bubble gum in the smaller bag. How many more pieces are in the big bag?

____

5. Last week, 6 oranges cost 98 cents. This week, they cost 80 cents. How much less are the oranges this week than last week?

____

6. This week lemons are 5 for 60 cents. Last week they cost 5 for 75 cents. How much more were lemons last week than this week?

____

Notes for Home Your child subtracted tens. *Home Activity:* Help your child calculate the number of slices of bread there are in a loaf of bread. Then ask how many would be left if he or she made 5 sandwiches.

Name ______________________________

Problem Solving 13-7

Subtract Tens and Ones

Solve. Write a number sentence.

1. Rosie made

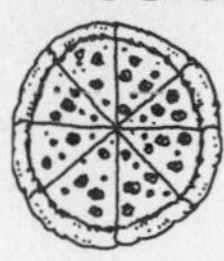   .

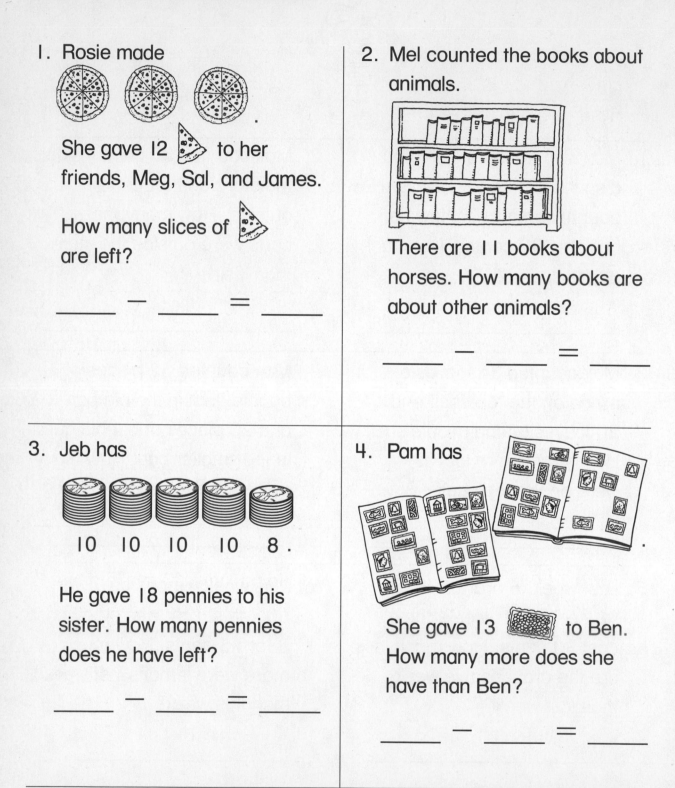

She gave 12 to her friends, Meg, Sal, and James.

How many slices of are left?

_____ − _____ = _____

2. Mel counted the books about animals.

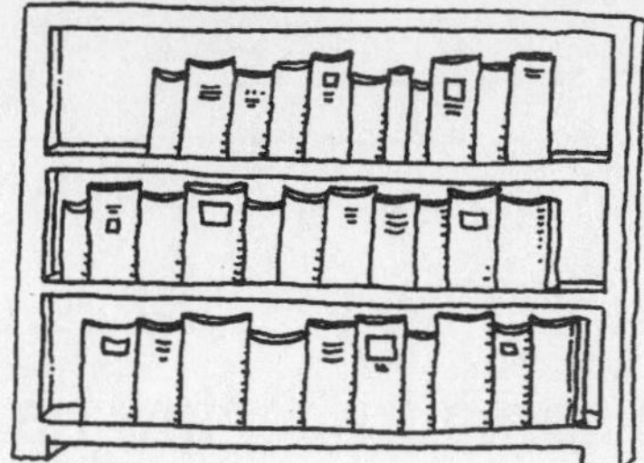

There are 11 books about horses. How many books are about other animals?

_____ − _____ = _____

3. Jeb has

10 10 10 10 8 .

He gave 18 pennies to his sister. How many pennies does he have left?

_____ − _____ = _____

4. Pam has

 .

She gave 13 to Ben. How many more does she have than Ben?

_____ − _____ = _____

Notes for Home Your child subtracted tens from two-digit numbers. *Home Activity:* Have your child count the number of books on several shelves. Then remove 10 books from the shelves. Ask your child to write a subtraction sentence to illustrate the action, then check the subtraction sentence by counting the books.

Name ______________________________

Problem Solving
13-8

Regroup with Subtraction

Solve. Write a number sentence.

1. Maggie has 35 cents. She gave 8 cents to her friend. How much does she have left?

   _____ − _____ = _____

   _____ cents

2. Annie is putting together a puzzle with 98 pieces. She has 9 pieces left. How many pieces has she put together?

   _____ − _____ = _____

   _____ pieces

3. Yesterday Cal and Jeb picked 56 apples. Today they have 47 left. How many did they give to a friend?

   _____ − _____ = _____

   _____ apples

4. Simon is reading a book. It has 92 pages. He has 9 pages left to read. How many pages has he read already?

   _____ − _____ = _____

   _____ pages

5. Mike has saved 42 baseball cards. He gave 7 cards to a friend. How many cards does he have left?

   _____ − _____ = _____

   _____ baseball cards

6. Carlos went to the pet store. He counted 63 fish in a big tank. He bought 6 fish. How many are in the big tank now?

   _____ − _____ = _____

   _____ fish

Notes for Home Your child solved problems involving subtraction with regrouping. *Home Activity:* Using the problems above as a model, ask your child to write a story problem and then explain how to solve it.

Name ______________________________

Choose an Operation

Problem Solving 13-9

1. Ben counted 45 books about sports on the top shelf and 38 books on the middle shelf. How many books are there about sports?

Think about what is happening in each problem.

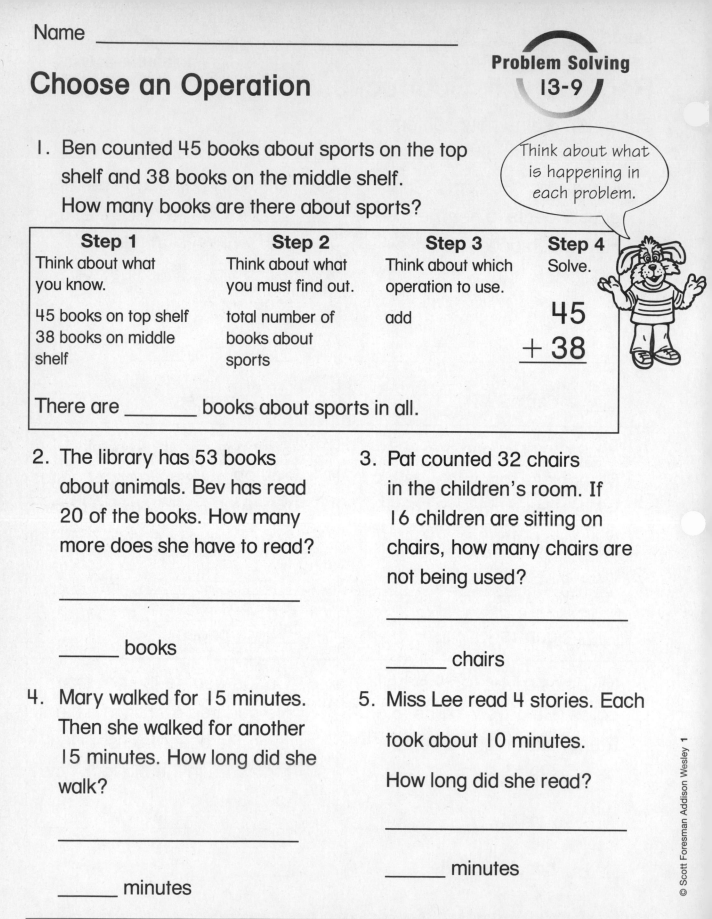

Step 1	Step 2	Step 3	Step 4
Think about what you know.	Think about what you must find out.	Think about which operation to use.	Solve.
45 books on top shelf 38 books on middle shelf	total number of books about sports	add	$45 + 38$

There are ______ books about sports in all.

2. The library has 53 books about animals. Bev has read 20 of the books. How many more does she have to read?

____

_____ books

3. Pat counted 32 chairs in the children's room. If 16 children are sitting on chairs, how many chairs are not being used?

____

_____ chairs

4. Mary walked for 15 minutes. Then she walked for another 15 minutes. How long did she walk?

____

_____ minutes

5. Miss Lee read 4 stories. Each took about 10 minutes. How long did she read?

____

_____ minutes

Using the Page To help children ***solve*** these problems, suggest they think about what they know, what they are asked to find, and what operation defines the action. **Notes for Home** Your child solved problems involving addition and subtraction. *Home Activity:* Ask your child to explain how he or she chose the correct operation to solve the problems.

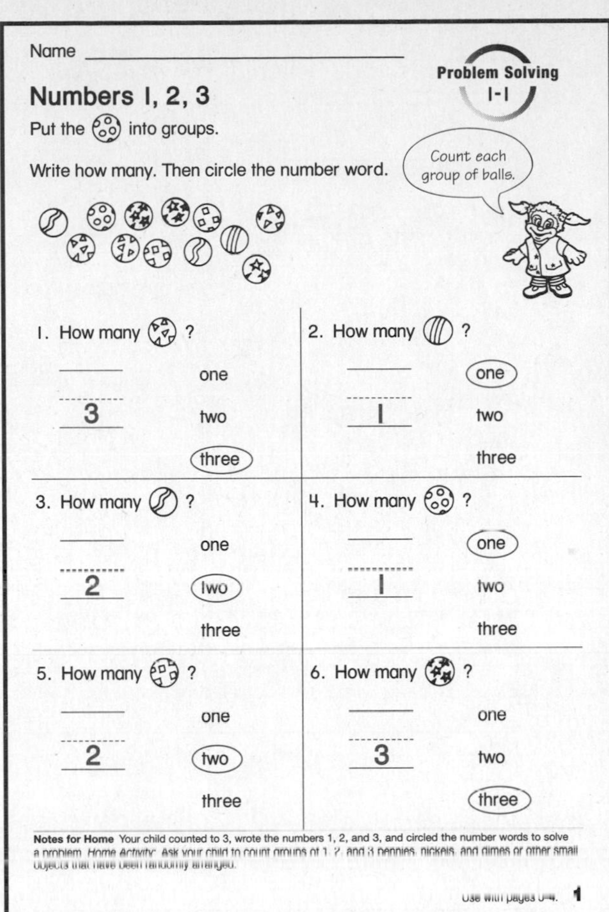

Name ______________________

Problem Solving 1-1

Numbers 1, 2, 3

Put the ( ) into groups.

Write how many. Then circle the number word.

Count each group of balls.

1. How many ( )? 3 — one, two, (three)
2. How many ( )? 1 — (one), two, three
3. How many ( )? 2 — one, (two), three
4. How many ( )? 1 — (one), two, three
5. How many ( )? 2 — one, (two), three
6. How many ( )? 3 — one, two, (three)

Notes for Home Your child counted to 3, wrote the numbers 1, 2, and 3, and circled the number words to solve a problem. *Home Activity:* Ask your child to count groups of 1, 2, and 3 pennies, nickels, and dimes or other small objects that have been randomly arranged.

Use with pages 3–4. 1

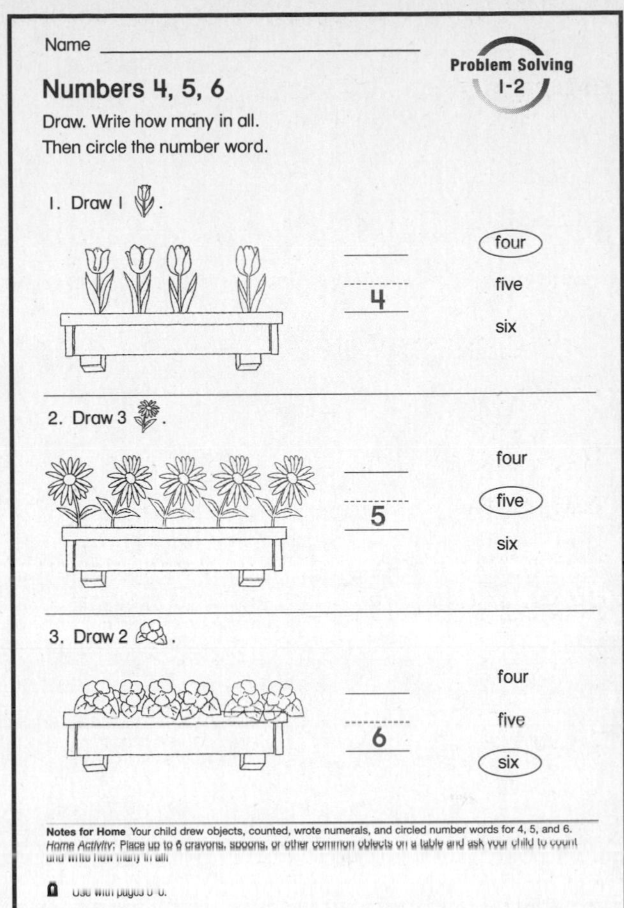

Name ______________________

Problem Solving 1-2

Numbers 4, 5, 6

Draw. Write how many in all.
Then circle the number word.

1. Draw 1 ( ). 4 — (four), five, six
2. Draw 3 ( ). 5 — four, (five), six
3. Draw 2 ( ). 6 — four, five, (six)

Notes for Home Your child drew objects, counted, wrote numerals, and circled number words for 4, 5, and 6. *Home Activity:* Place up to 6 crayons, spoons, or other common objects on a table and ask your child to count and write how many in all.

2 Use with pages 5–6.

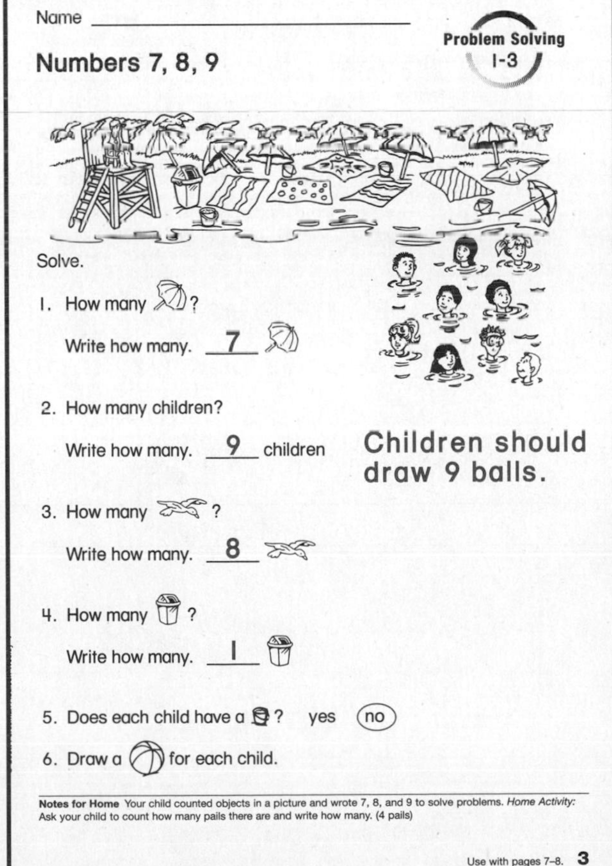

Name ______________________

Problem Solving 1-3

Numbers 7, 8, 9

Solve.

1. How many ( )?
   Write how many. 7 ( )
2. How many children?
   Write how many. 9 children
3. How many ( )?
   Write how many. 8 ( )
4. How many ( )?
   Write how many. 1 ( )
5. Does each child have a ( )? yes (no)
6. Draw a ( ) for each child.

Children should draw 9 balls.

Notes for Home Your child counted objects in a picture and wrote 7, 8, and 9 to solve problems. *Home Activity:* Ask your child to count how many pails there are and write how many. (4 pails)

Use with pages 7–8. 3

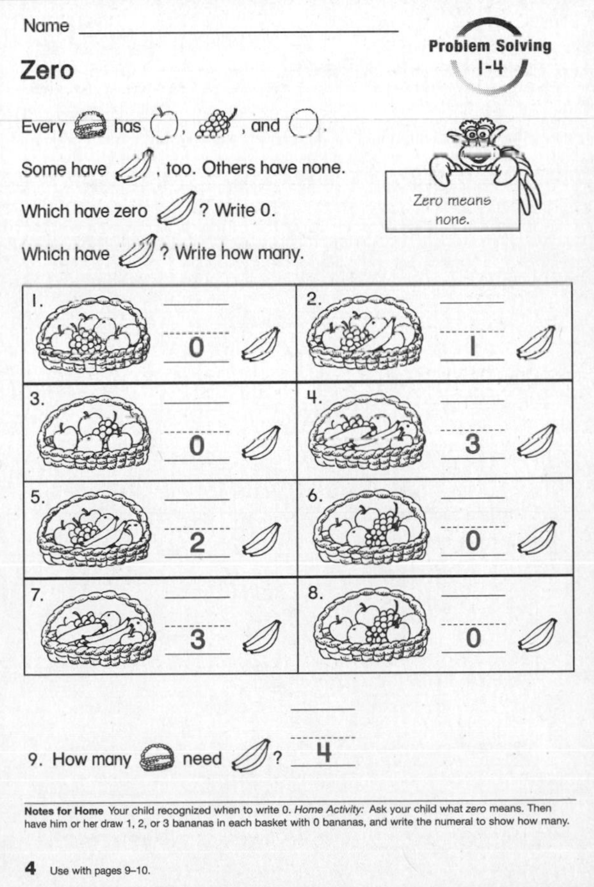

Name ______________________

Problem Solving 1-4

Zero

Every ( ) has ( ), ( ), and ( ).

Some have ( ), too. Others have none.

Which have zero ( )? Write 0.

Which have ( )? Write how many.

Zero means none.

1. 0	2. 1
3. 0	4. 3
5. 2	6. 0
7. 3	8. 0

9. How many ( ) need ( )? 4

Notes for Home Your child recognized when to write 0. *Home Activity:* Ask your child what *zero* means. Then have him or her draw 1, 2, or 3 bananas in each basket with 0 bananas, and write the numeral to show how many.

4 Use with pages 9–10.

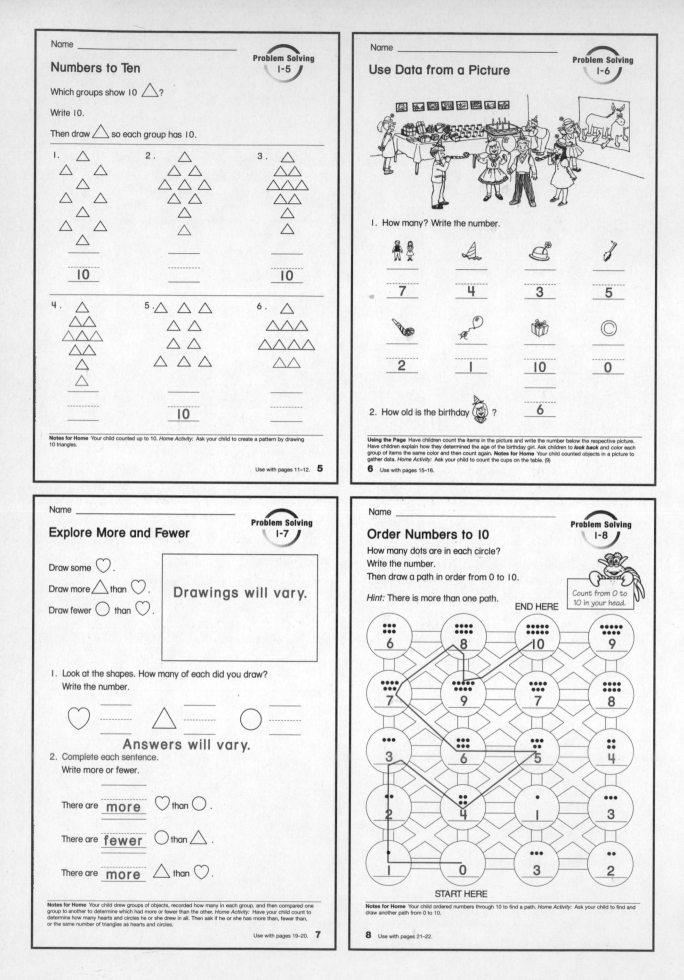

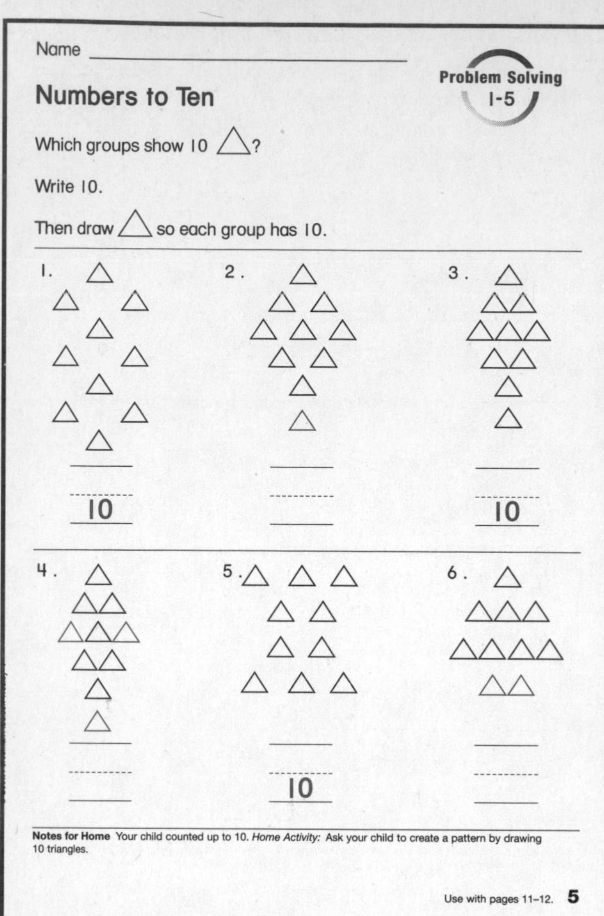

Name ______________________

Problem Solving 1-5

Numbers to Ten

Which groups show 10 △?

Write 10.

Then draw △ so each group has 10.

1. 10
2.
3. 10
4.
5. 10
6.

Notes for Home Your child counted up to 10. *Home Activity:* Ask your child to create a pattern by drawing 10 triangles.

Use with pages 11–12. **5**

Name ______________________

Problem Solving 1-6

Use Data from a Picture

1. How many? Write the number.

7 4 3 5

2 1 10 0

2. How old is the birthday ? 6

Using the Page Have children count the items in the picture and write the number below the respective picture. Have children explain how they determined the age of the birthday girl. Ask children to ***look back*** and color each group of items the same color and then count again. **Notes for Home** Your child counted objects in a picture to gather data. *Home Activity:* Ask your child to count the cups on the table. (9)

6 Use with pages 15–16.

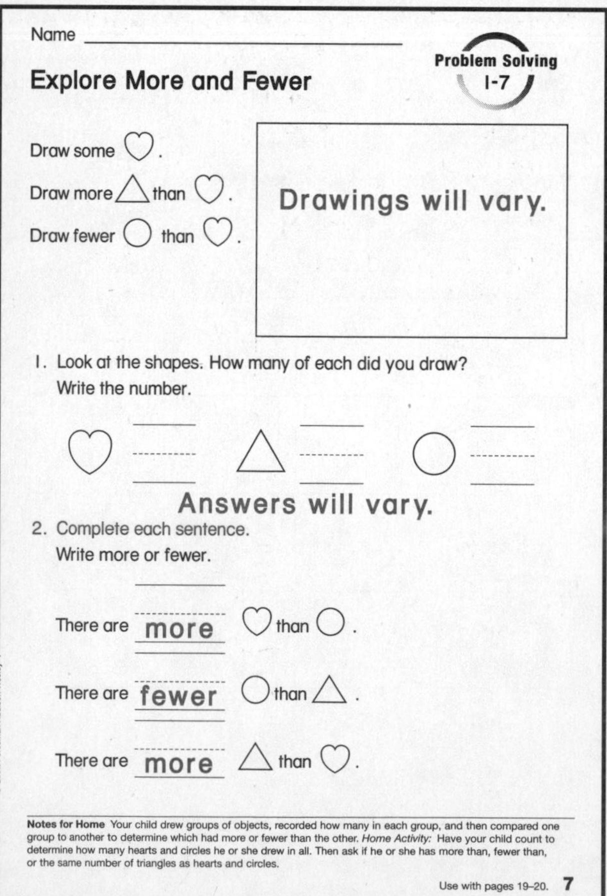

Name ______________________

Problem Solving 1-7

Explore More and Fewer

Draw some ♡.

Draw more △ than ♡.

Draw fewer ○ than ♡.

Drawings will vary.

1. Look at the shapes. How many of each did you draw? Write the number.

♡ ____ △ ____ ○ ____

Answers will vary.

2. Complete each sentence. Write more or fewer.

There are more ♡ than ○.

There are fewer ○ than △.

There are more △ than ♡.

Notes for Home Your child drew groups of objects, recorded how many in each group, and then compared one group to another to determine which had more or fewer than the other. *Home Activity:* Have your child count to determine how many hearts and circles he or she drew in all. Then ask if he or she has more than, fewer than, or the same number of triangles as hearts and circles.

Use with pages 19–20. **7**

Name ______________________

Problem Solving 1-8

Order Numbers to 10

How many dots are in each circle?

Write the number.

Then draw a path in order from 0 to 10.

Hint: There is more than one path.

Count from 0 to 10 in your head.

END HERE

6 8 10 9

7 9 7 8

3 6 5 4

2 4 1 3

1 0 3 2

START HERE

Notes for Home Your child ordered numbers through 10 to find a path. *Home Activity:* Ask your child to find and draw another path from 0 to 10.

8 Use with pages 21–22.

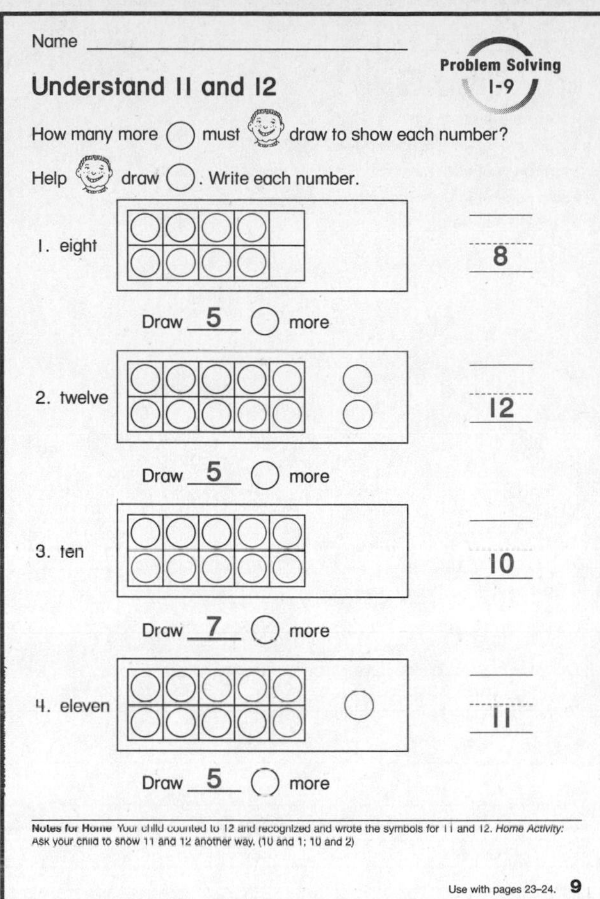

Name

Problem Solving 1-9

Understand 11 and 12

How many more ◯ must draw to show each number?

Help draw ◯. Write each number.

1. eight — 8 — Draw 5 ◯ more
2. twelve — 12 — Draw 5 ◯ more
3. ten — 10 — Draw 7 ◯ more
4. eleven — 11 — Draw 5 ◯ more

Notes for Home Your child counted to 12 and recognized and wrote the symbols for 11 and 12. *Home Activity:* Ask your child to show 11 and 12 another way. (10 and 1; 10 and 2)

Use with pages 23–24. **9**

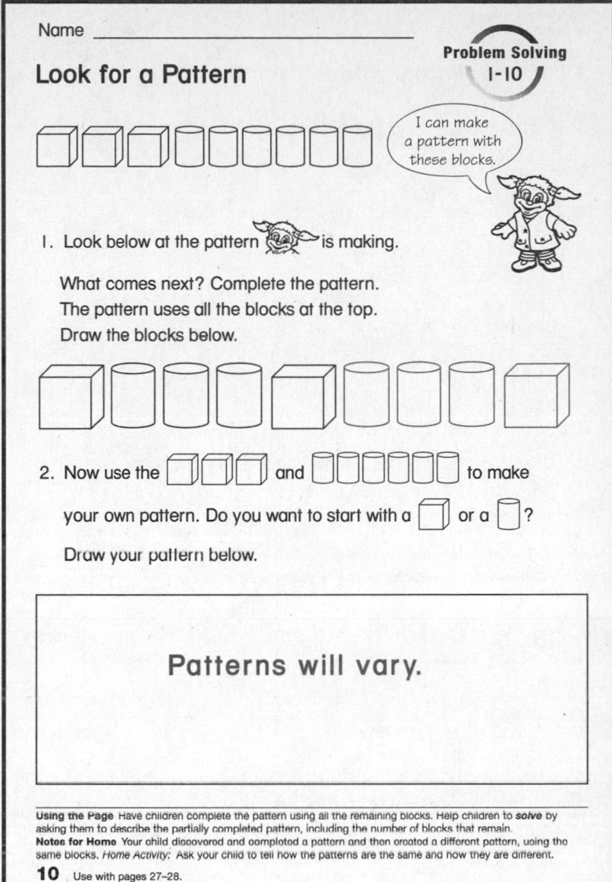

Name

Problem Solving 1-10

Look for a Pattern

I can make a pattern with these blocks.

1. Look below at the pattern is making.

   What comes next? Complete the pattern.
   The pattern uses all the blocks at the top.
   Draw the blocks below.

2. Now use the and to make your own pattern. Do you want to start with a or a ?

   Draw your pattern below.

Patterns will vary.

Using the Page Have children complete the pattern using all the remaining blocks. Help children to *solve* by asking them to describe the partially completed pattern, including the number of blocks that remain.
Notes for Home Your child discovered and completed a pattern and then created a different pattern, using the same blocks. *Home Activity:* Ask your child to tell how the patterns are the same and how they are different.

10 Use with pages 27–28.

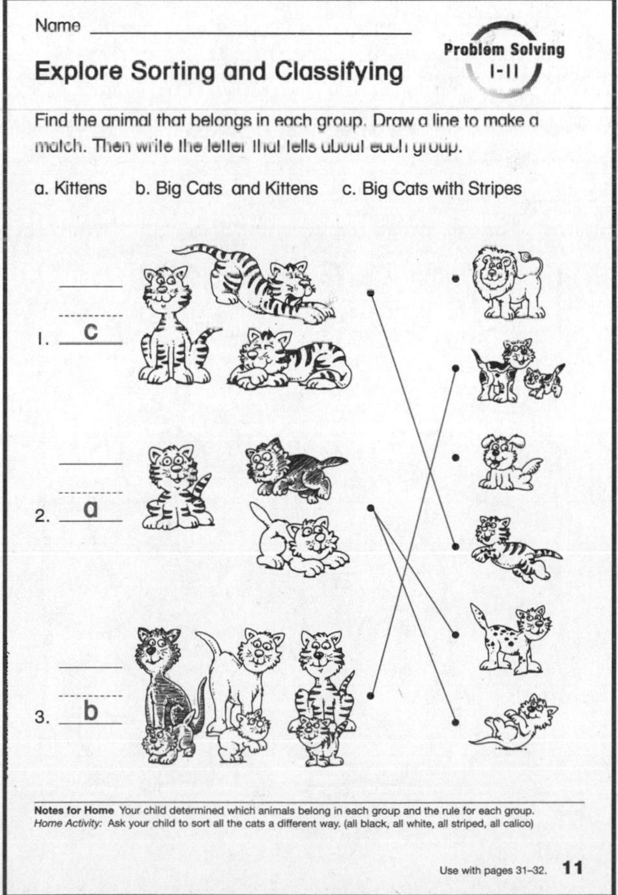

Name

Problem Solving 1-11

Explore Sorting and Classifying

Find the animal that belongs in each group. Draw a line to make a match. Then write the letter that tells about each group.

a. Kittens b. Big Cats and Kittens c. Big Cats with Stripes

1. c
2. a
3. b

Notes for Home Your child determined which animals belong in each group and the rule for each group. *Home Activity:* Ask your child to sort all the cats a different way. (all black, all white, all striped, all calico)

Use with pages 31–32. **11**

Name

Problem Solving 1-12

Create a Graph

Look at the picture.
Make a graph.
Then use the graph.
Which group has more?

1.
2.

Things in the Picture

3. Draw a picture. Choose 3 different things to count.
   Then make a graph.
   Ask a friend which group has more.

Drawings will vary.

Notes for Home Your child used items in a picture to make a graph and compared amounts. *Home Activity:* Ask your child to explain how he or she created the graph. Have him or her create another graph with other small objects, such as buttons and paper clips.

12 Use with pages 33–34.

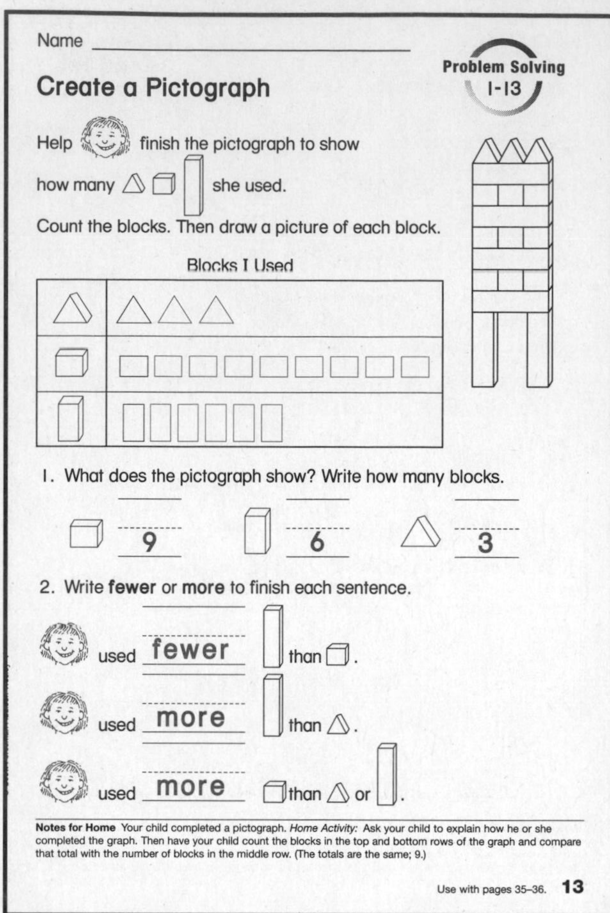
Name ______________________

Problem Solving 1-13

Create a Pictograph

Help [girl] finish the pictograph to show how many △ ▢ ▯ she used.

Count the blocks. Then draw a picture of each block.

Blocks I Used

△	△ △ △
▢	▢ ▢ ▢ ▢ ▢ ▢ ▢ ▢ ▢
▯	▯ ▯ ▯ ▯ ▯ ▯

1. What does the pictograph show? Write how many blocks.

▢ 9 ▯ 6 △ 3

2. Write **fewer** or **more** to finish each sentence.

[girl] used fewer ▯ than ▢.

[girl] used more ▯ than △.

[girl] used more ▢ than △ or ▯.

Notes for Home Your child completed a pictograph. *Home Activity:* Ask your child to explain how he or she completed the graph. Then have your child count the blocks in the top and bottom rows of the graph and compare that total with the number of blocks in the middle row. (The totals are the same; 9.)

Use with pages 35–36. **13**

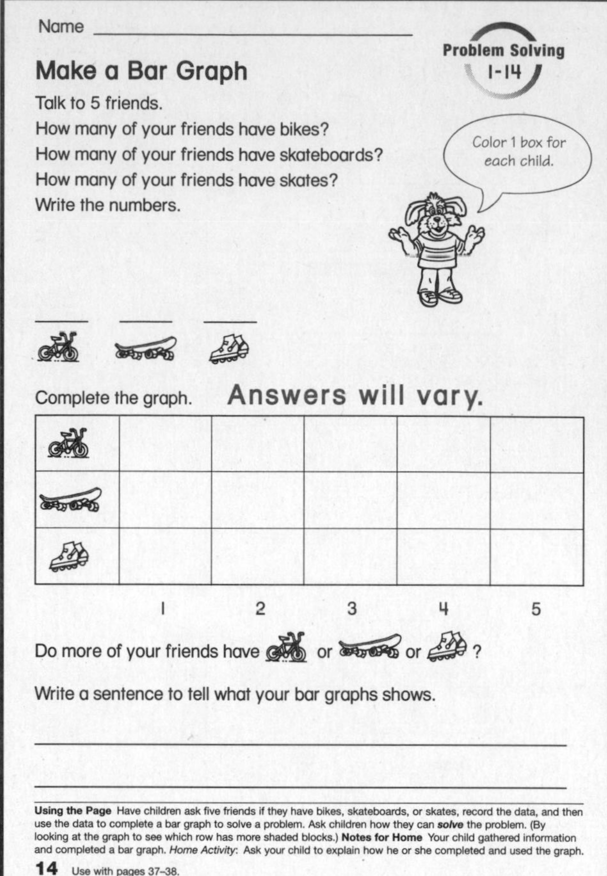
Name ______________________

Problem Solving 1-14

Make a Bar Graph

Talk to 5 friends.
How many of your friends have bikes?
How many of your friends have skateboards?
How many of your friends have skates?
Write the numbers.

___ [bike] ___ [skateboard] ___ [skates]

Complete the graph. **Answers will vary.**

[bike]					
[skateboard]					
[skates]					
	1	2	3	4	5

Do more of your friends have [bike] or [skateboard] or [skates]?

Write a sentence to tell what your bar graphs shows.

____

____

Using the Page Have children ask five friends if they have bikes, skateboards, or skates, record the data, and then use the data to complete a bar graph to solve a problem. Ask children how they can ***solve*** the problem. (By looking at the graph to see which row has more shaded blocks.) **Notes for Home** Your child gathered information and completed a bar graph. *Home Activity:* Ask your child to explain how he or she completed and used the graph.

14 Use with pages 37–38.

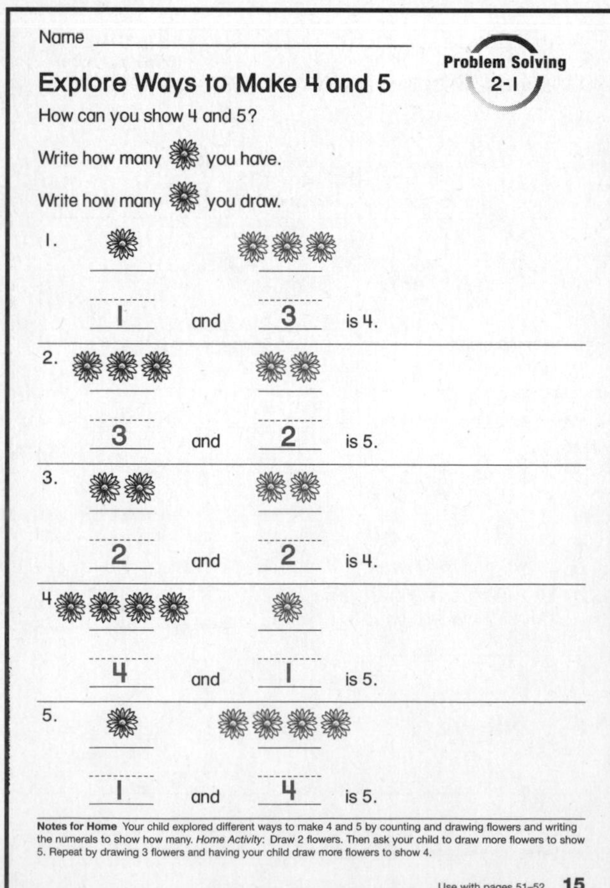
Name ______________________

Problem Solving 2-1

Explore Ways to Make 4 and 5

How can you show 4 and 5?

Write how many [flower] you have.

Write how many [flower] you draw.

1. 1 and 3 is 4.
2. 3 and 2 is 5.
3. 2 and 2 is 4.
4. 4 and 1 is 5.
5. 1 and 4 is 5.

Notes for Home Your child explored different ways to make 4 and 5 by counting and drawing flowers and writing the numerals to show how many. *Home Activity:* Draw 2 flowers. Then ask your child to draw more flowers to show 5. Repeat by drawing 3 flowers and having your child draw more flowers to show 4.

Use with pages 51–52. **15**

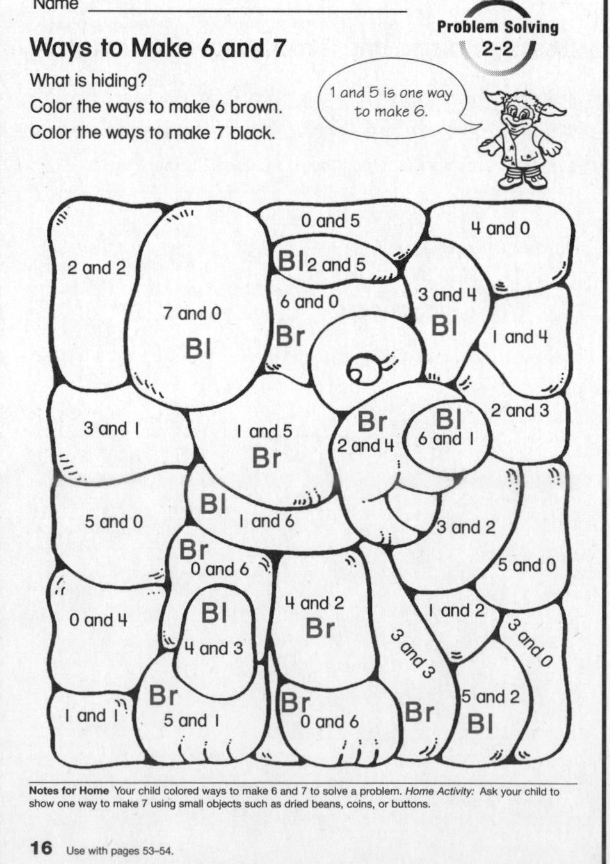
Name ______________________

Problem Solving 2-2

Ways to Make 6 and 7

What is hiding?
Color the ways to make 6 brown.
Color the ways to make 7 black.

Notes for Home Your child colored ways to make 6 and 7 to solve a problem. *Home Activity:* Ask your child to show one way to make 7 using small objects such as dried beans, coins, or buttons.

16 Use with pages 53–54.

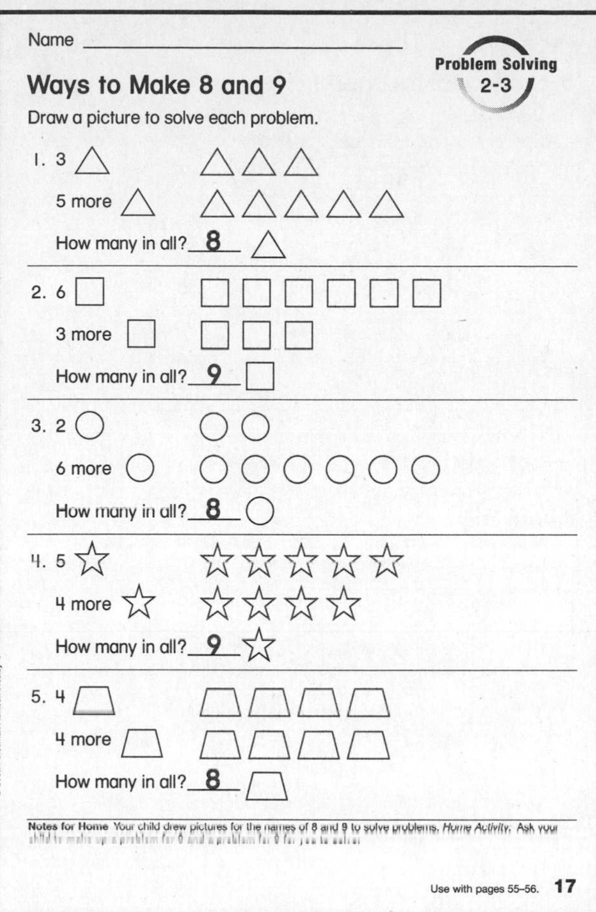

Name ______________________

Ways to Make 8 and 9

Problem Solving 2-3

Draw a picture to solve each problem.

1. 3 △ — △△△
   5 more △ — △△△△△
   How many in all? 8 △

2. 6 □ — □□□□□□
   3 more □ — □□□
   How many in all? 9 □

3. 2 ○ — ○○
   6 more ○ — ○○○○○○
   How many in all? 8 ○

4. 5 ☆ — ☆☆☆☆☆
   4 more ☆ — ☆☆☆☆
   How many in all? 9 ☆

5. 4 ⏢ — ⏢⏢⏢⏢
   4 more ⏢ — ⏢⏢⏢⏢
   How many in all? 8 ⏢

Notes for Home Your child drew pictures for the names of 8 and 9 to solve problems. *Home Activity:* Ask your [illegible]

Use with pages 55–56. **17**

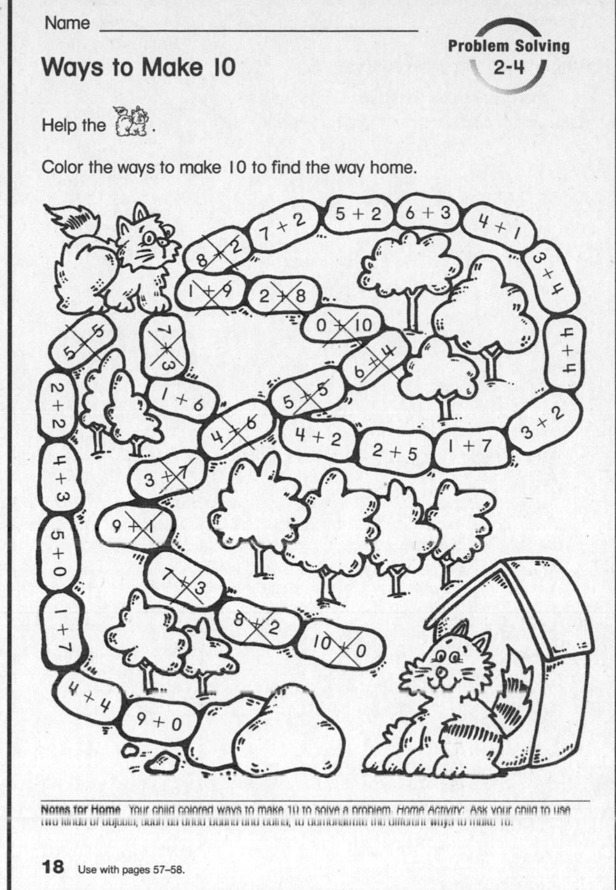

Name ______________________

Ways to Make 10

Problem Solving 2-4

Help the 🐱.

Color the ways to make 10 to find the way home.

Notes for Home Your child colored ways to make 10 to solve a problem. *Home Activity:* Ask your child to use [illegible]

18 Use with pages 57–58.

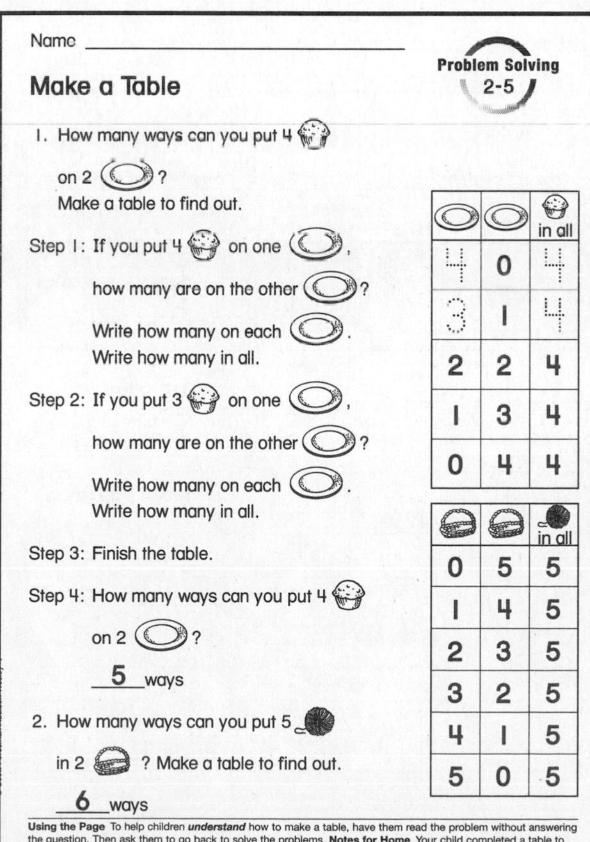

Name ______________________

Make a Table

Problem Solving 2-5

1. How many ways can you put 4 🧁 on 2 🍽? Make a table to find out.

Step 1: If you put 4 🧁 on one 🍽, how many are on the other 🍽? Write how many on each 🍽. Write how many in all.

Step 2: If you put 3 🧁 on one 🍽, how many are on the other 🍽? Write how many on each 🍽. Write how many in all.

Step 3: Finish the table.

Step 4: How many ways can you put 4 🧁 on 2 🍽?

5 ways

🍽	🍽	🧁 in all
4	0	4
3	1	4
2	2	4
1	3	4
0	4	4

2. How many ways can you put 5 🧶 in 2 🧺? Make a table to find out.

6 ways

🧺	🧺	🧶 in all
0	5	5
1	4	5
2	3	5
3	2	5
4	1	5
5	0	5

Using the Page To help children ***understand*** how to make a table, have them read the problem without answering the question. Then ask them to go back to solve the problems. **Notes for Home** Your child completed a table to solve problems. *Home Activity*: Ask your child to explain to you how to read a table.

Use with pages 61–62. **19**

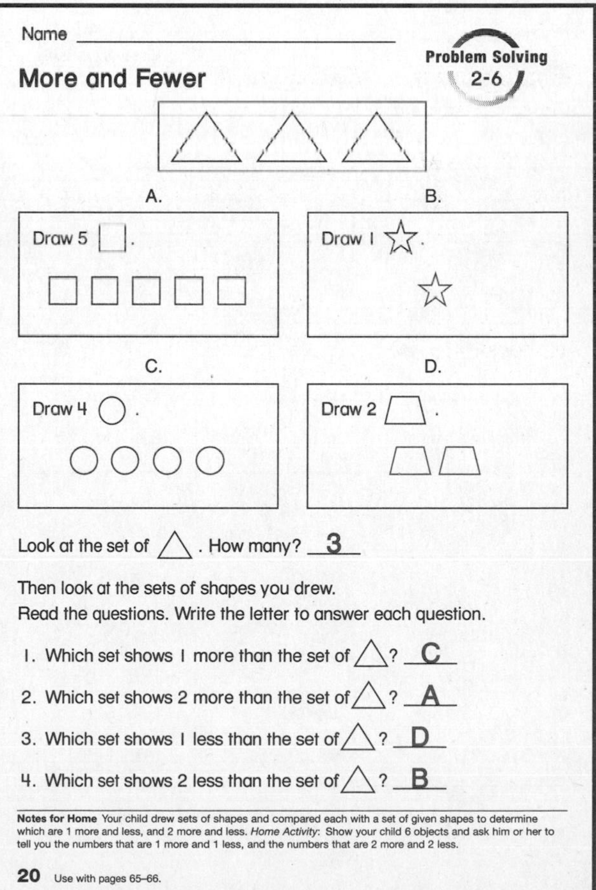

Name ______________________

More and Fewer

Problem Solving 2-6

△△△

A. Draw 5 □. — □□□□□

B. Draw 1 ☆. — ☆

C. Draw 4 ○. — ○○○○

D. Draw 2 ⏢. — ⏢⏢

Look at the set of △. How many? 3

Then look at the sets of shapes you drew.
Read the questions. Write the letter to answer each question.

1. Which set shows 1 more than the set of △? C
2. Which set shows 2 more than the set of △? A
3. Which set shows 1 less than the set of △? D
4. Which set shows 2 less than the set of △? B

Notes for Home Your child drew sets of shapes and compared each with a set of given shapes to determine which are 1 more and less, and 2 more and less. *Home Activity*: Show your child 6 objects and ask him or her to tell you the numbers that are 1 more and 1 less, and the numbers that are 2 more and 2 less.

20 Use with pages 65–66.

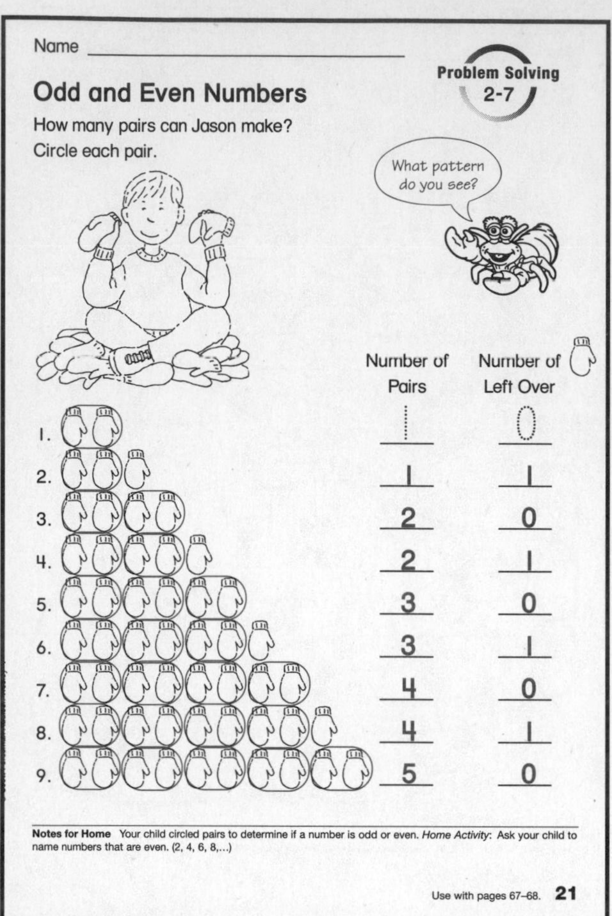

Name ____________________

Problem Solving 2-7

Odd and Even Numbers

How many pairs can Jason make?
Circle each pair.

	Number of Pairs	Number of Left Over
1.	1	0
2.	1	1
3.	2	0
4.	2	1
5.	3	0
6.	3	1
7.	4	0
8.	4	1
9.	5	0

Notes for Home Your child circled pairs to determine if a number is odd or even. *Home Activity:* Ask your child to name numbers that are even. (2, 4, 6, 8,...)

Use with pages 67–68. **21**

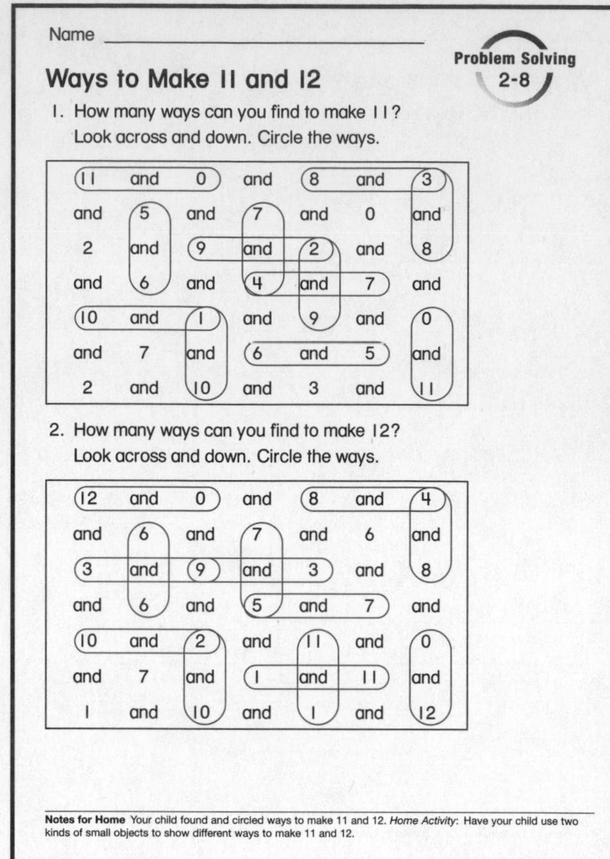

Name ____________________

Problem Solving 2-8

Ways to Make 11 and 12

1. How many ways can you find to make 11?
Look across and down. Circle the ways.

11	and	0	and	8	and	3
and	5	and	7	and	0	and
2	and	9	and	2	and	8
and	6	and	4	and	7	and
10	and	1	and	9	and	0
and	7	and	6	and	5	and
2	and	10	and	3	and	11

2. How many ways can you find to make 12?
Look across and down. Circle the ways.

12	and	0	and	8	and	4
and	6	and	7	and	6	and
3	and	9	and	3	and	8
and	6	and	5	and	7	and
10	and	2	and	11	and	0
and	7	and	1	and	11	and
1	and	10	and	1	and	12

Notes for Home Your child found and circled ways to make 11 and 12. *Home Activity:* Have your child use two kinds of small objects to show different ways to make 11 and 12.

22 Use with pages 69–70.

Name ____________________

Problem Solving 2-9

Find Missing Parts Through 7

Solve the problems.

1. 6 in all	2. 5 in all	3. 4 in all
How many are hiding? 4	How many are hiding? 3	How many are hiding? 1
4. 7 in all	5. 3 in all	6. 2 in all
How many are hiding? 5	How many are hiding? 2	How many are hiding? 1

Notes for Home Your child determined how many animals are hiding to solve problems. *Home Activity:* Use the problems as a model to create new problems for your child to solve.

Use with pages 71–72. **23**

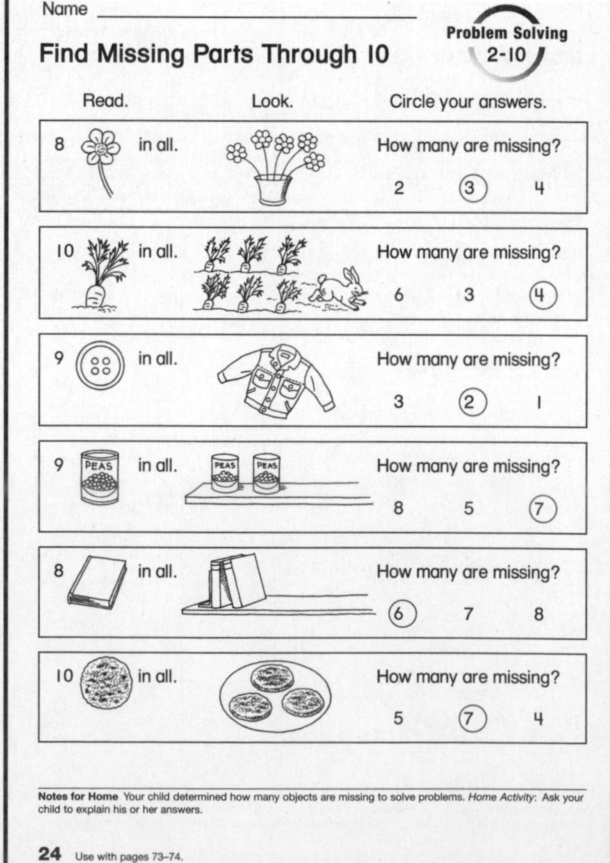

Name ____________________

Problem Solving 2-10

Find Missing Parts Through 10

Read.	Look.	Circle your answers.
8 in all.		How many are missing? 2 (3) 4
10 in all.		How many are missing? 6 3 (4)
9 in all.		How many are missing? 3 (2) 1
9 in all.		How many are missing? 8 5 (7)
8 in all.		How many are missing? (6) 7 8
10 in all.		How many are missing? 5 (7) 4

Notes for Home Your child determined how many objects are missing to solve problems. *Home Activity:* Ask your child to explain his or her answers.

24 Use with pages 73–74.

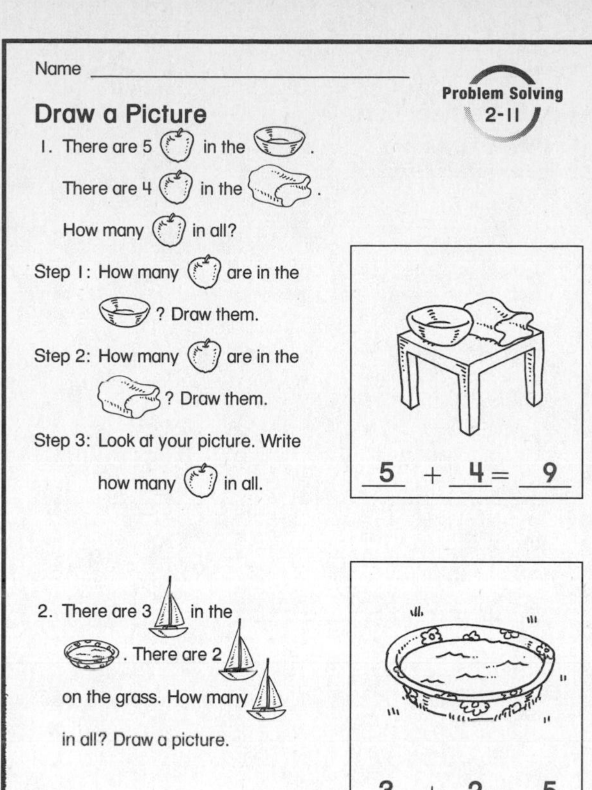

Name ______

Problem Solving 2-11

Draw a Picture

1. There are 5 in the . There are 4 in the . How many in all?

Step 1: How many are in the ? Draw them.

Step 2: How many are in the ? Draw them.

Step 3: Look at your picture. Write how many in all.

5 + 4 = 9

2. There are 3 in the . There are 2 on the grass. How many in all? Draw a picture.

3 + 2 = 5

Using the Page To help children ***plan***, have them read through the problem, and identify what they know and need to find out. Then have children follow the steps to solve the problem. **Notes for Home** Your child drew pictures to solve problems. *Home Activity*: Ask your child to explain how he or she solved Exercise 2.

Use with pages 77–78. **25**

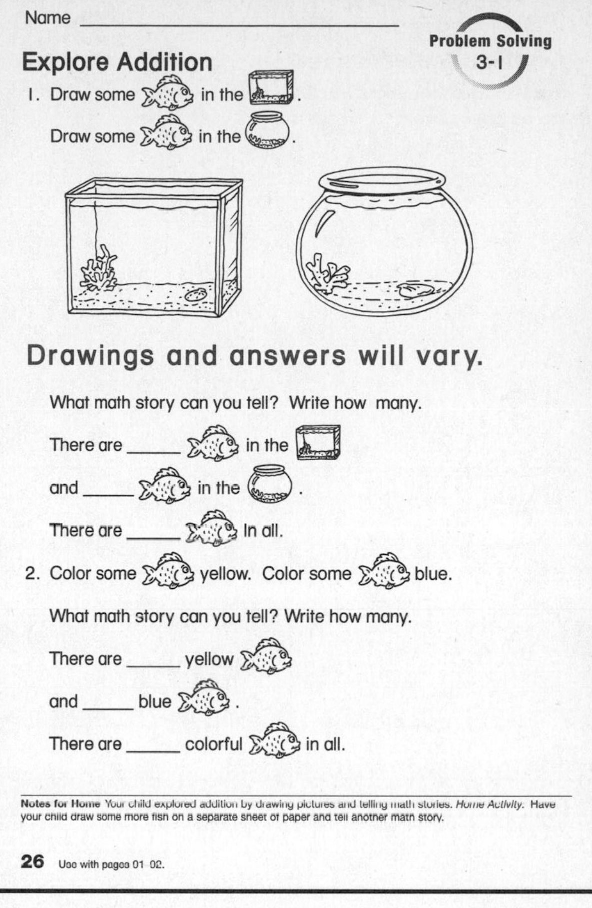

Name ______

Problem Solving 3-1

Explore Addition

1. Draw some in the . Draw some in the .

Drawings and answers will vary.

What math story can you tell? Write how many.

There are ______ in the

and ______ in the .

There are ______ in all.

2. Color some yellow. Color some blue.

What math story can you tell? Write how many.

There are ______ yellow

and ______ blue .

There are ______ colorful in all.

Notes for Home Your child explored addition by drawing pictures and telling math stories. *Home Activity.* Have your child draw some more fish on a separate sheet of paper and tell another math story.

26 Use with pages 91–92.

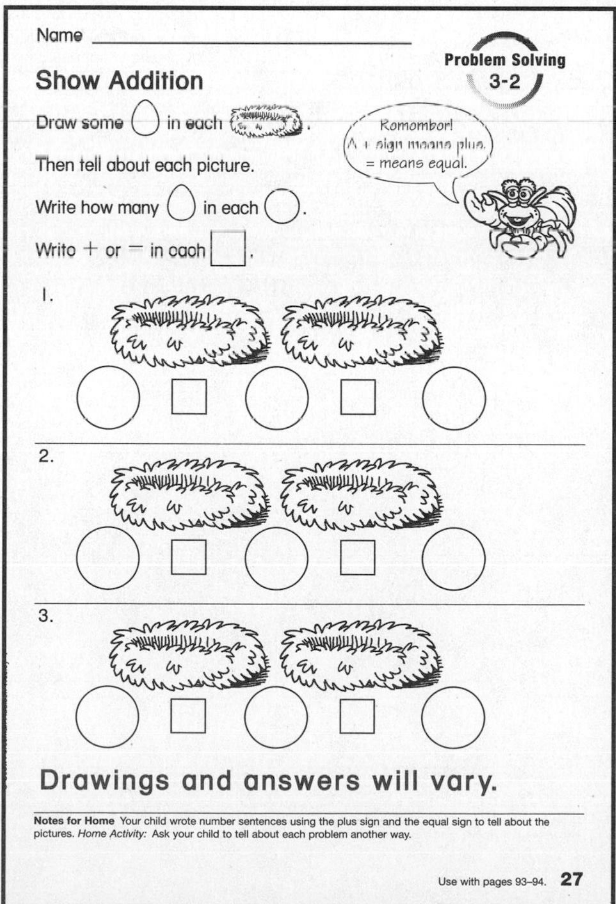

Name ______

Problem Solving 3-2

Show Addition

Draw some in each .

Then tell about each picture.

Write how many in each .

Write + or = in each .

Remember!
A + sign means plus.
= means equal.

1.

2.

3.

Drawings and answers will vary.

Notes for Home Your child wrote number sentences using the plus sign and the equal sign to tell about the pictures. *Home Activity:* Ask your child to tell about each problem another way.

Use with pages 93–94. **27**

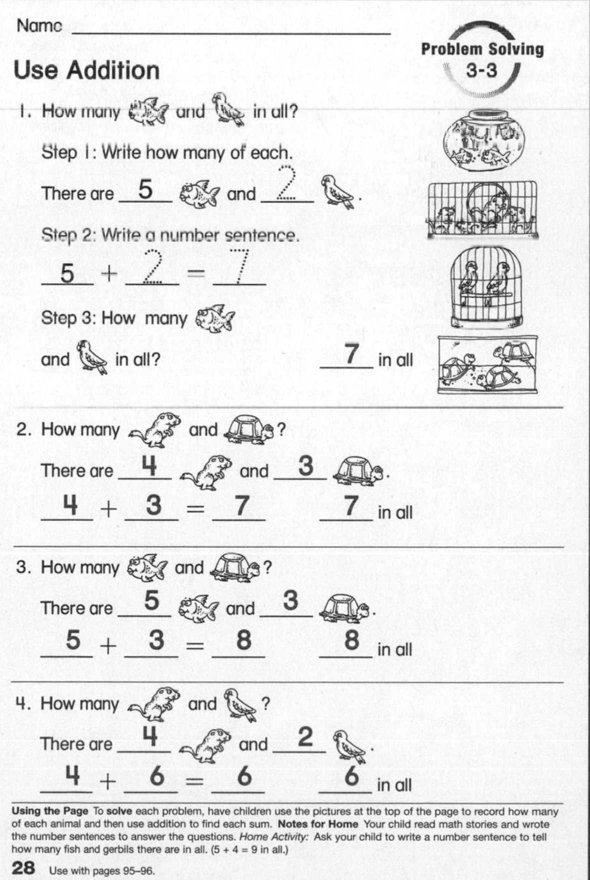

Name ______

Problem Solving 3-3

Use Addition

1. How many and in all?

Step 1: Write how many of each.

There are 5 and 2 .

Step 2: Write a number sentence.

5 + 2 = 7

Step 3: How many and in all? 7 in all

2. How many and ?

There are 4 and 3 .

4 + 3 = 7 7 in all

3. How many and ?

There are 5 and 3 .

5 + 3 = 8 8 in all

4. How many and ?

There are 4 and 2 .

4 + 6 = 6 6 in all

Using the Page To **solve** each problem, have children use the pictures at the top of the page to record how many of each animal and then use addition to find each sum. **Notes for Home** Your child read math stories and wrote the number sentences to answer the questions. *Home Activity:* Ask your child to write a number sentence to tell how many fish and gerbils there are in all. (5 + 4 = 9 in all.)

28 Use with pages 95–96.

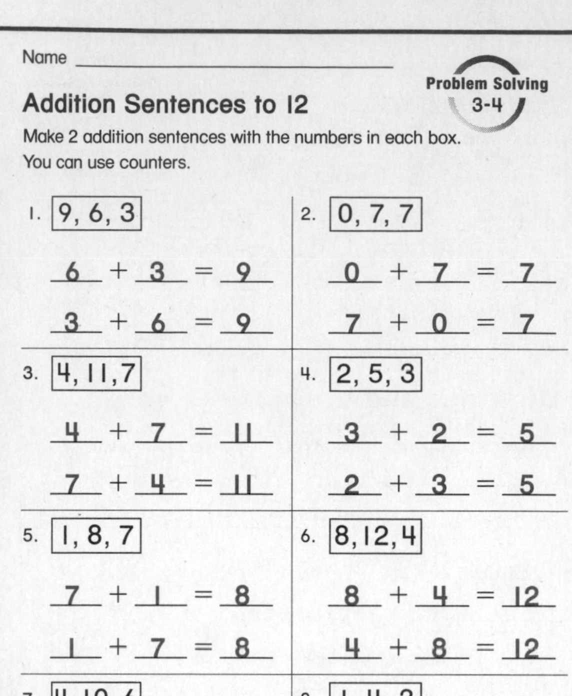
Name ____________________

Problem Solving 3-4

Addition Sentences to 12

Make 2 addition sentences with the numbers in each box.
You can use counters.

1. 9, 6, 3
6 + 3 = 9
3 + 6 = 9

2. 0, 7, 7
0 + 7 = 7
7 + 0 = 7

3. 4, 11, 7
4 + 7 = 11
7 + 4 = 11

4. 2, 5, 3
3 + 2 = 5
2 + 3 = 5

5. 1, 8, 7
7 + 1 = 8
1 + 7 = 8

6. 8, 12, 4
8 + 4 = 12
4 + 8 = 12

7. 4, 10, 6
6 + 4 = 10
4 + 6 = 10

8. 1, 4, 3
3 + 1 = 4
1 + 3 = 4

Notes for Home Your child wrote two number sentences for each set of numbers. *Home Activity:* Ask your child to choose a number from 6 to 12 and then write all the possible number sentences for that number. (Example: 0 + 6 = 6; 1 + 5 = 6; 2 + 4 = 6; 3 + 3 = 6; 4 + 2 = 6; 5 + 1 = 6; 6 + 0 = 6)

Use with pages 97–98. 29

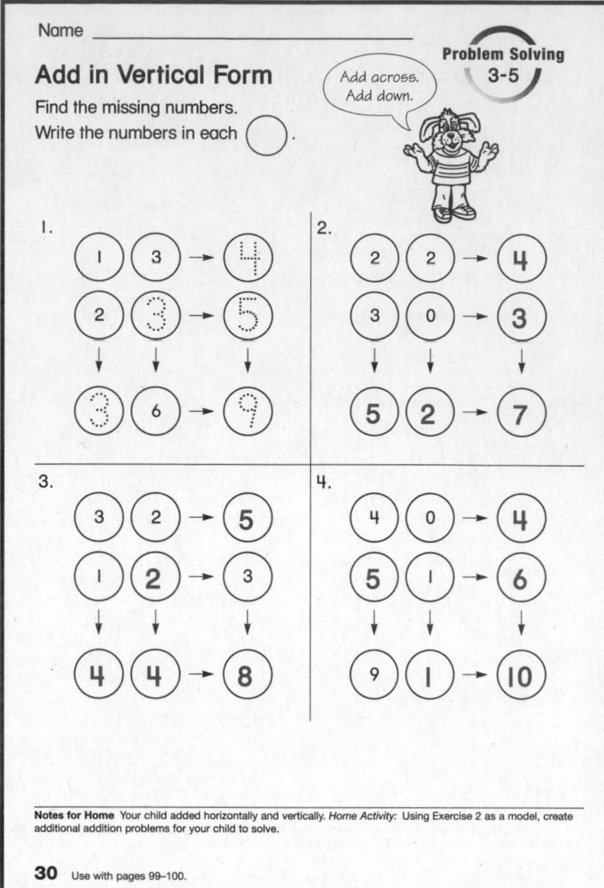
Name ____________________

Problem Solving 3-5

Add in Vertical Form

Find the missing numbers.
Write the numbers in each ◯.

1.
1 3 → 4
2 3 → 5
↓ ↓ ↓
3 6 → 9

2.
2 2 → 4
3 0 → 3
↓ ↓ ↓
5 2 → 7

3.
3 2 → 5
1 2 → 3
↓ ↓ ↓
4 4 → 8

4.
4 0 → 4
5 1 → 6
↓ ↓ ↓
9 1 → 10

Notes for Home Your child added horizontally and vertically. *Home Activity:* Using Exercise 2 as a model, create additional addition problems for your child to solve.

30 Use with pages 99–100.

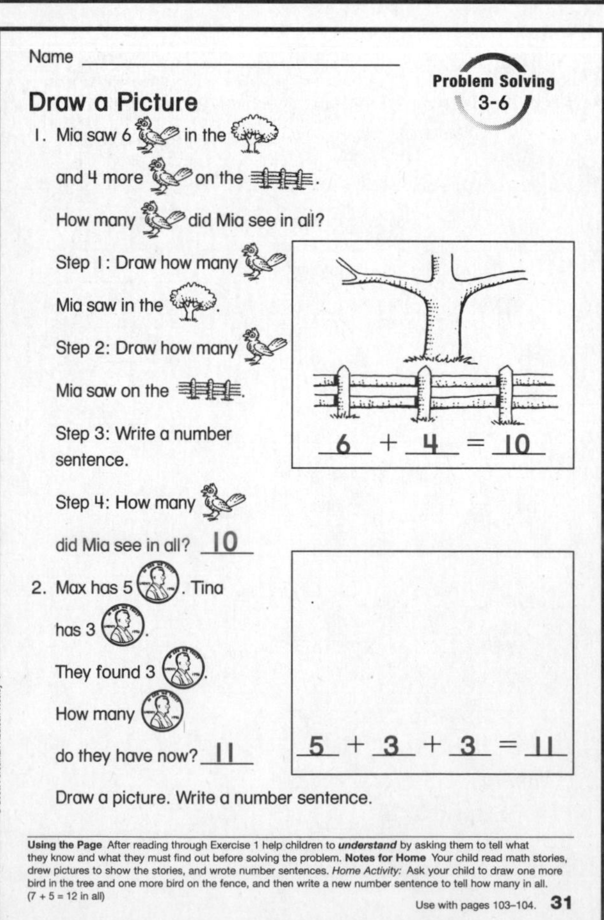
Name ____________________

Problem Solving 3-6

Draw a Picture

1. Mia saw 6 [bird] in the [tree]
and 4 more [bird] on the [fence].
How many [bird] did Mia see in all?
Step 1: Draw how many [bird] Mia saw in the [tree].
Step 2: Draw how many [bird] Mia saw on the [fence].
Step 3: Write a number sentence.
6 + 4 = 10
Step 4: How many [bird] did Mia see in all? 10

2. Max has 5 [penny]. Tina has 3 [penny].
They found 3 [penny].
How many [penny] do they have now? 11
5 + 3 + 3 = 11
Draw a picture. Write a number sentence.

Using the Page After reading through Exercise 1 help children to ***understand*** by asking them to tell what they know and what they must find out before solving the problem. **Notes for Home** Your child read math stories, drew pictures to show the stories, and wrote number sentences. *Home Activity:* Ask your child to draw one more bird in the tree and one more bird on the fence, and then write a new number sentence to tell how many in all. (7 + 5 = 12 in all)

Use with pages 103–104. 31

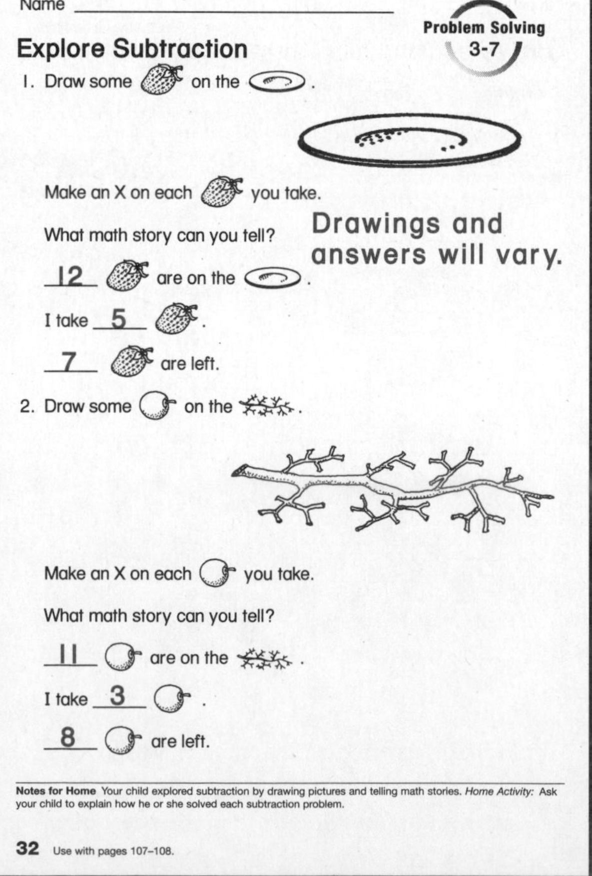
Name ____________________

Problem Solving 3-7

Explore Subtraction

1. Draw some [strawberry] on the [plate].
Make an X on each [strawberry] you take.
What math story can you tell?
12 [strawberry] are on the [plate].
I take 5 [strawberry].
7 [strawberry] are left.

Drawings and answers will vary.

2. Draw some [berry] on the [branch].
Make an X on each [berry] you take.
What math story can you tell?
11 [berry] are on the [branch].
I take 3 [berry].
8 [berry] are left.

Notes for Home Your child explored subtraction by drawing pictures and telling math stories. *Home Activity:* Ask your child to explain how he or she solved each subtraction problem.

32 Use with pages 107–108.

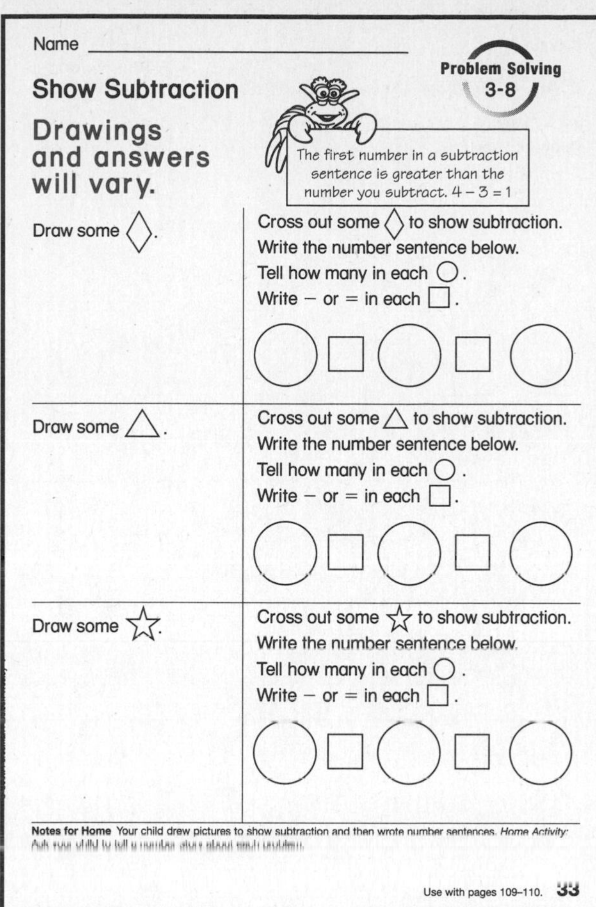

Name ____________________

Problem Solving 3-8

Show Subtraction

Drawings and answers will vary.

The first number in a subtraction sentence is greater than the number you subtract. 4 – 3 = 1

Draw some ◇.

Cross out some ◇ to show subtraction.
Write the number sentence below.
Tell how many in each ○.
Write – or = in each □.

○ □ ○ □ ○

Draw some △.

Cross out some △ to show subtraction.
Write the number sentence below.
Tell how many in each ○.
Write – or = in each □.

○ □ ○ □ ○

Draw some ☆.

Cross out some ☆ to show subtraction.
Write the number sentence below.
Tell how many in each ○.
Write – or = in each □.

○ □ ○ □ ○

Notes for Home Your child drew pictures to show subtraction and then wrote number sentences. *Home Activity:* Ask your child to tell a number story about each problem.

Use with pages 109–110. **33**

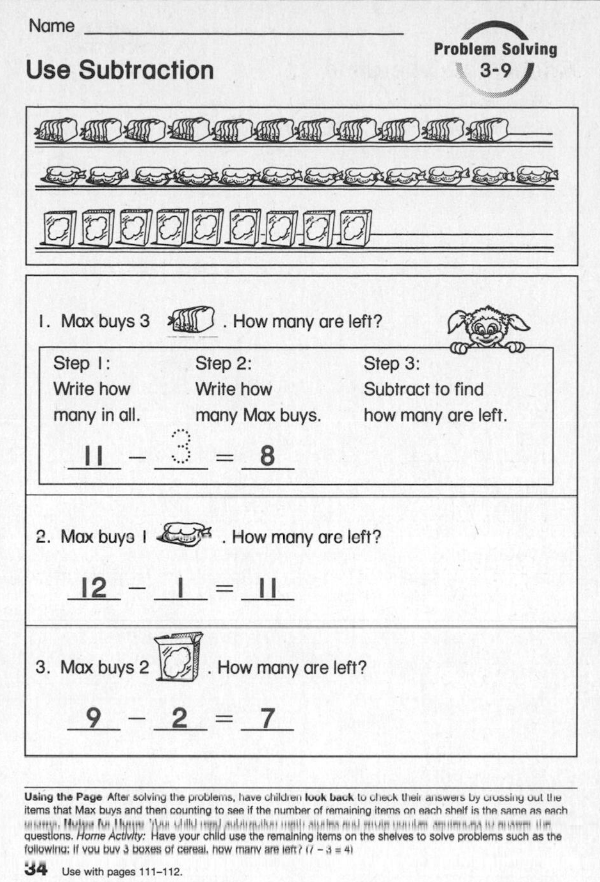

Name ____________________

Problem Solving 3-9

Use Subtraction

1. Max buys 3 [bread]. How many are left?

Step 1: Write how many in all.
Step 2: Write how many Max buys.
Step 3: Subtract to find how many are left.

11 – 3 = 8

2. Max buys 1 [sandwich]. How many are left?

12 – 1 = 11

3. Max buys 2 [cereal box]. How many are left?

9 – 2 = 7

Using the Page After solving the problems, have children **look back** to check their answers by crossing out the items that Max buys and then counting to see if the number of remaining items on each shelf is the same as each answer. **Notes for Home** Your child read subtraction math stories and wrote number sentences to answer the questions. *Home Activity:* Have your child use the remaining items on the shelves to solve problems such as the following: If you buy 3 boxes of cereal, how many are left? (7 – 3 = 4)

34 Use with pages 111–112.

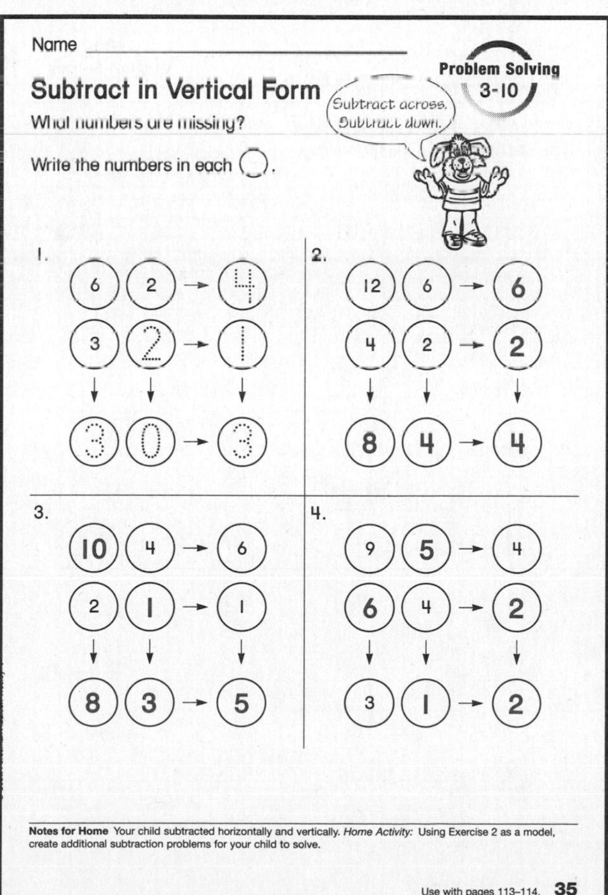

Name ____________________

Problem Solving 3-10

Subtract in Vertical Form

What numbers are missing?

Write the numbers in each ○.

Subtract across.
Subtract down.

1.
(6) (2) → (4)
(3) (2) → (1)
↓ ↓ ↓
(3) (0) → (3)

2.
(12) (6) → (6)
(4) (2) → (2)
↓ ↓ ↓
(8) (4) → (4)

3.
(10) (4) → (6)
(2) (1) → (1)
↓ ↓ ↓
(8) (3) → (5)

4.
(9) (5) → (4)
(6) (4) → (2)
↓ ↓ ↓
(3) (1) → (2)

Notes for Home Your child subtracted horizontally and vertically. *Home Activity:* Using Exercise 2 as a model, create additional subtraction problems for your child to solve.

Use with pages 113–114. **35**

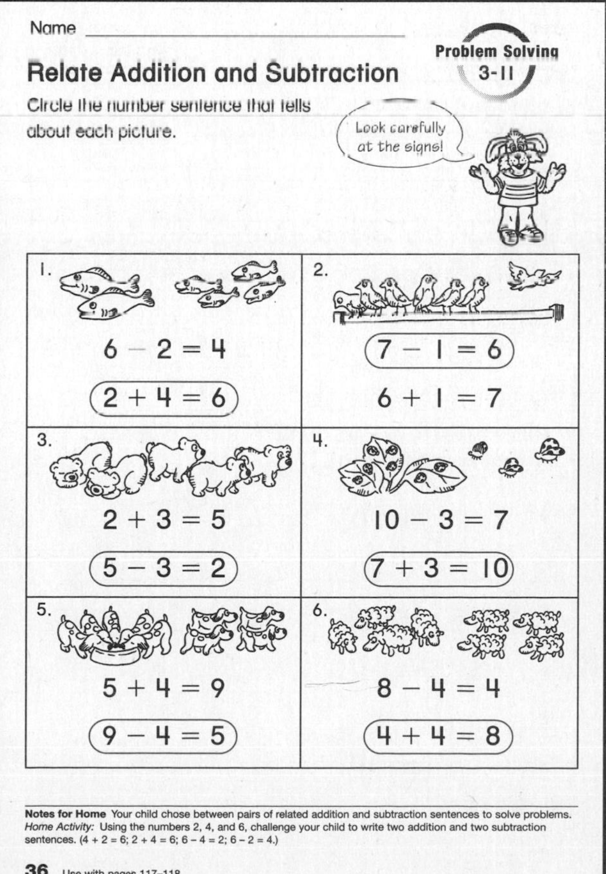

Name ____________________

Problem Solving 3-11

Relate Addition and Subtraction

Circle the number sentence that tells about each picture.

Look carefully at the signs!

1.
6 – 2 = 4
(2 + 4 = 6)

2.
(7 – 1 = 6)
6 + 1 = 7

3.
2 + 3 = 5
(5 – 3 = 2)

4.
10 – 3 = 7
(7 + 3 = 10)

5.
5 + 4 = 9
(9 – 4 = 5)

6.
8 – 4 = 4
(4 + 4 = 8)

Notes for Home Your child chose between pairs of related addition and subtraction sentences to solve problems. *Home Activity:* Using the numbers 2, 4, and 6, challenge your child to write two addition and two subtraction sentences. (4 + 2 = 6; 2 + 4 = 6; 6 – 4 = 2; 6 – 2 = 4.)

36 Use with pages 117–118.

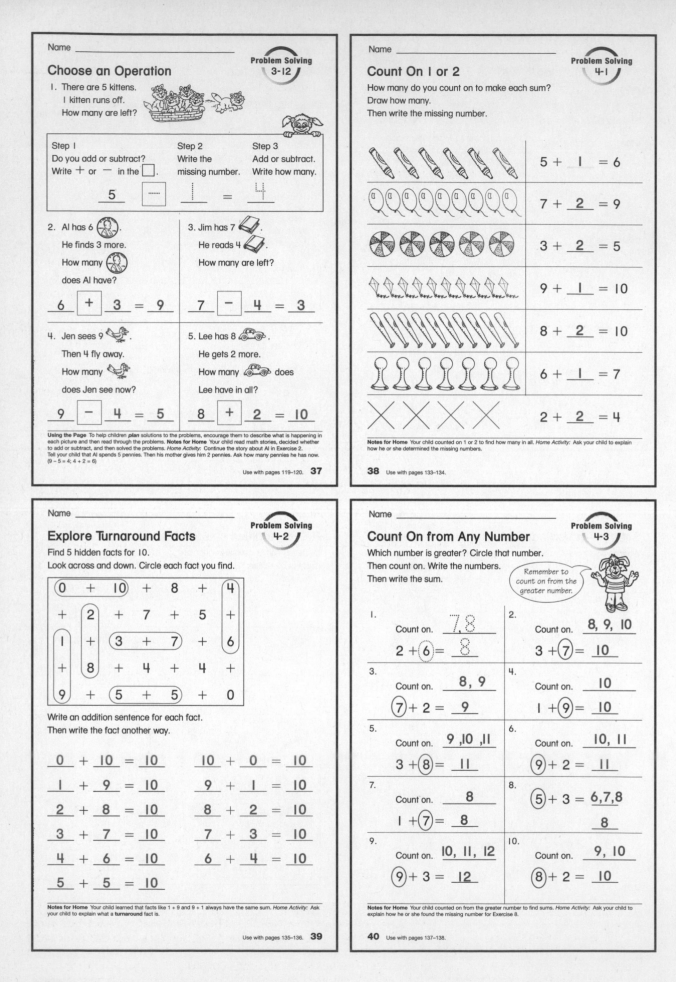

Name ______________________

Problem Solving 3-12

Choose an Operation

1. There are 5 kittens.
   1 kitten runs off.
   How many are left?

Step 1	Step 2	Step 3
Do you add or subtract? Write + or − in the □.	Write the missing number.	Add or subtract. Write how many.
5 [−]	1	= 4

2. Al has 6 pennies.
   He finds 3 more.
   How many pennies does Al have?
   6 [+] 3 = 9

3. Jim has 7 books.
   He reads 4 books.
   How many are left?
   7 [−] 4 = 3

4. Jen sees 9 birds.
   Then 4 fly away.
   How many birds does Jen see now?
   9 [−] 4 = 5

5. Lee has 8 cars.
   He gets 2 more.
   How many cars does Lee have in all?
   8 [+] 2 = 10

Using the Page To help children ***plan*** solutions to the problems, encourage them to describe what is happening in each picture and then read through the problems. **Notes for Home** Your child read math stories, decided whether to add or subtract, and then solved the problems. *Home Activity:* Continue the story about Al in Exercise 2. Tell your child that Al spends 5 pennies. Then his mother gives him 2 pennies. Ask how many pennies he has now. (9 − 5 = 4; 4 + 2 = 6)

Name ______________________

Problem Solving 4-1

Count On 1 or 2

How many do you count on to make each sum?
Draw how many.
Then write the missing number.

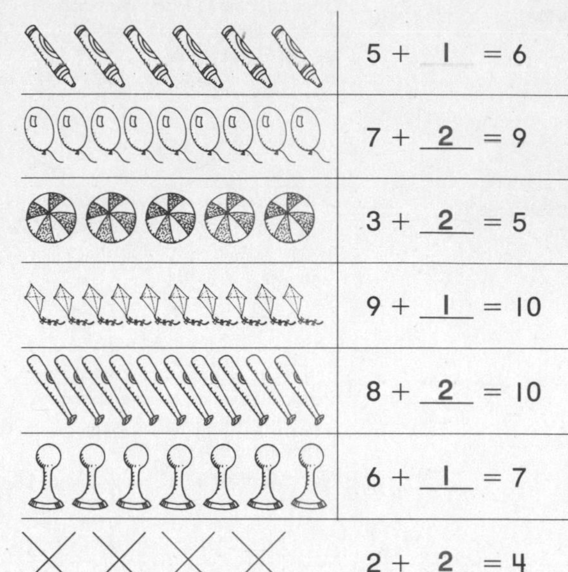

5 + 1 = 6

7 + 2 = 9

3 + 2 = 5

9 + 1 = 10

8 + 2 = 10

6 + 1 = 7

2 + 2 = 4

Notes for Home Your child counted on 1 or 2 to find how many in all. *Home Activity:* Ask your child to explain how he or she determined the missing numbers.

Name ______________________

Problem Solving 4-2

Explore Turnaround Facts

Find 5 hidden facts for 10.
Look across and down. Circle each fact you find.

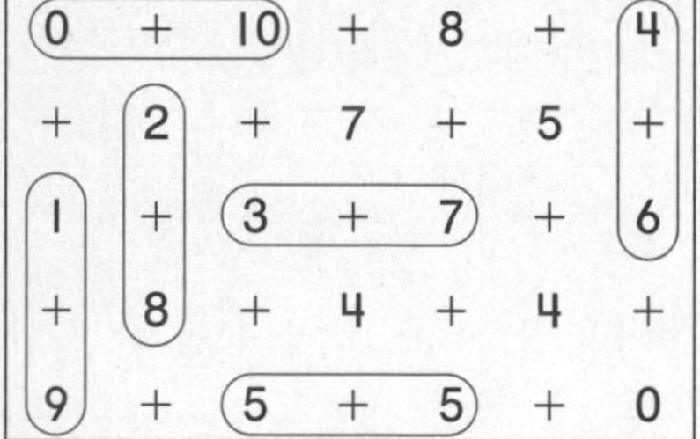

0	+	10	+	8	+	4
+	2	+	7	+	5	+
1	+	3	+	7	+	6
+	8	+	4	+	4	+
9	+	5	+	5	+	0

Write an addition sentence for each fact.
Then write the fact another way.

0 + 10 = 10	10 + 0 = 10
1 + 9 = 10	9 + 1 = 10
2 + 8 = 10	8 + 2 = 10
3 + 7 = 10	7 + 3 = 10
4 + 6 = 10	6 + 4 = 10
5 + 5 = 10	

Notes for Home Your child learned that facts like 1 + 9 and 9 + 1 always have the same sum. *Home Activity:* Ask your child to explain what a **turnaround** fact is.

Name ______________________

Problem Solving 4-3

Count On from Any Number

Which number is greater? Circle that number.
Then count on. Write the numbers.
Then write the sum.

Remember to count on from the greater number.

1. Count on. 7, 8
   2 + (6) = 8

2. Count on. 8, 9, 10
   3 + (7) = 10

3. Count on. 8, 9
   (7) + 2 = 9

4. Count on. 10
   1 + (9) = 10

5. Count on. 9, 10, 11
   3 + (8) = 11

6. Count on. 10, 11
   (9) + 2 = 11

7. Count on. 8
   1 + (7) = 8

8. (5) + 3 = 6, 7, 8
   8

9. Count on. 10, 11, 12
   (9) + 3 = 12

10. Count on. 9, 10
    (8) + 2 = 10

Notes for Home Your child counted on from the greater number to find sums. *Home Activity:* Ask your child to explain how he or she found the missing number for Exercise 8.

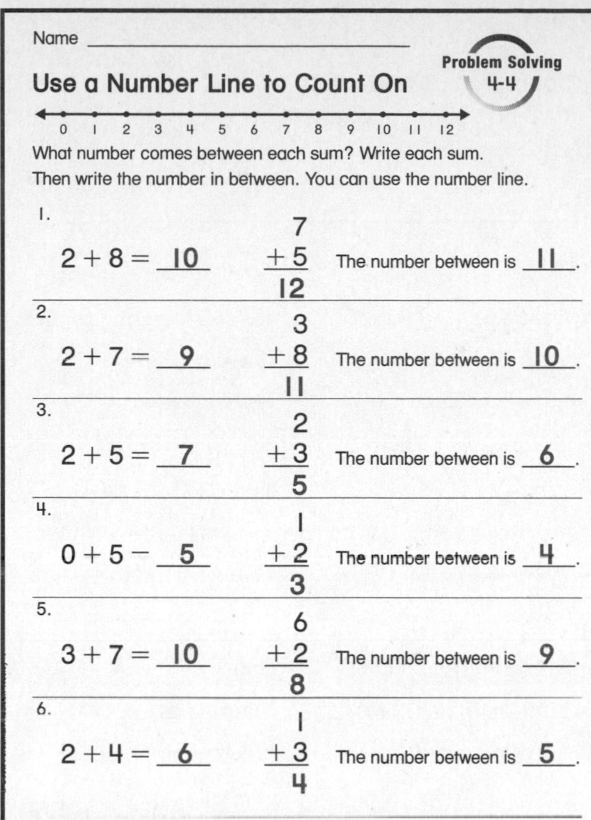

Name ____________________

Problem Solving 4-4

Use a Number Line to Count On

0 1 2 3 4 5 6 7 8 9 10 11 12

What number comes between each sum? Write each sum.
Then write the number in between. You can use the number line.

1. 2 + 8 = 10 | 7 + 5 = 12 | The number between is 11.
2. 2 + 7 = 9 | 3 + 8 = 11 | The number between is 10.
3. 2 + 5 = 7 | 2 + 3 = 5 | The number between is 6.
4. 0 + 5 = 5 | 1 + 2 = 3 | The number between is 4.
5. 3 + 7 = 10 | 6 + 2 = 8 | The number between is 9.
6. 2 + 4 = 6 | 1 + 3 = 4 | The number between is 5.

Notes for Home Your child used a number line to add 1, 2, or 3 to numbers. *Home Activity:* Ask your child to choose one exercise and draw the jumps to show how to use a number line to count on.

Use with pages 139–140. **41**

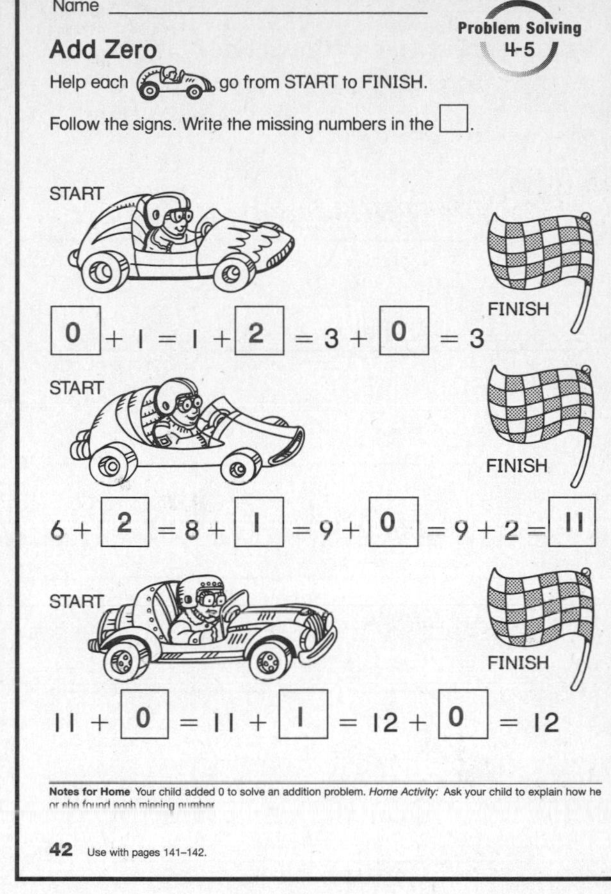

Name ____________________

Problem Solving 4-5

Add Zero

Help each car go from START to FINISH.

Follow the signs. Write the missing numbers in the □.

START — FINISH

[0] + 1 = 1 + [2] = 3 + [0] = 3

START — FINISH

6 + [2] = 8 + [1] = 9 + [0] = 9 + 2 = [11]

START — FINISH

11 + [0] = 11 + [1] = 12 + [0] = 12

Notes for Home Your child added 0 to solve an addition problem. *Home Activity:* Ask your child to explain how he or she found each missing number.

42 Use with pages 141–142.

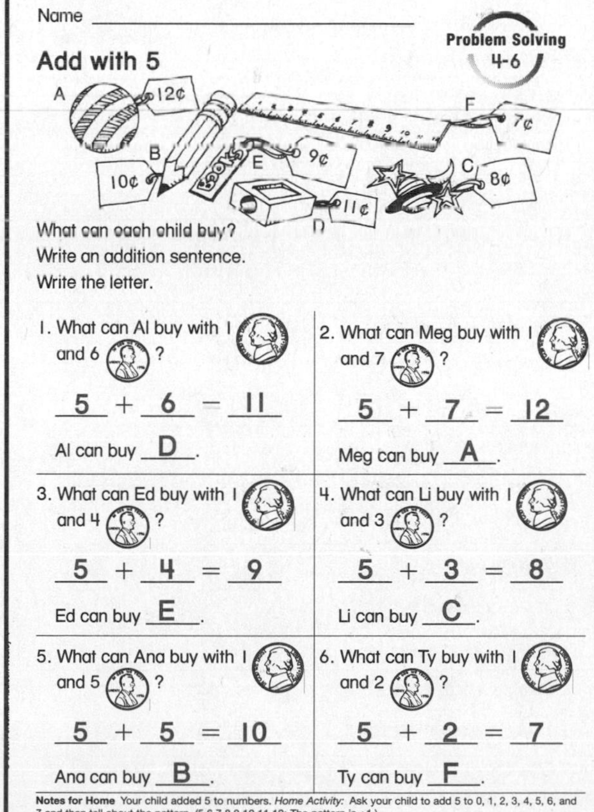

Name ____________________

Problem Solving 4-6

Add with 5

What can each child buy?
Write an addition sentence.
Write the letter.

1. What can Al buy with 1 nickel and 6 pennies?
   5 + 6 = 11
   Al can buy D.
2. What can Meg buy with 1 nickel and 7 pennies?
   5 + 7 = 12
   Meg can buy A.
3. What can Ed buy with 1 nickel and 4 pennies?
   5 + 4 = 9
   Ed can buy E.
4. What can Li buy with 1 nickel and 3 pennies?
   5 + 3 = 8
   Li can buy C.
5. What can Ana buy with 1 nickel and 5 pennies?
   5 + 5 = 10
   Ana can buy B.
6. What can Ty buy with 1 nickel and 2 pennies?
   5 + 2 = 7
   Ty can buy F.

Notes for Home Your child added 5 to numbers. *Home Activity:* Ask your child to add 5 to 0, 1, 2, 3, 4, 5, 6, and 7 and then tell about the pattern. (5,6,7,8,9,10,11,12; The pattern is +1.)

Use with pages 143–144. **43**

Name ____________________

Problem Solving 4-7

Make a List

How many ways can Mina buy 9 shells?

Step 1: Start a list. — 1 bag of 6 shells and 1 bag of 3 shells

Step 2: Look at the bags of shells. Find names for 9. Add each to the list.
- 1 bag of 5 shells and 1 bag of 4 shells
- 1 bag of 1 shells and 1 bag of 8 shells
- 1 bag of 2 shells and 1 bag of 7 shells

Step 3: Answer the question.

4 ways to buy 9 shells

How many ways can you buy exactly 11 shells?
Make a list.

1 bag of 6 and 1 bag of 5
1 bag of 7 and 1 bag of 4
1 bag of 3 and 1 bag of 8

Using the Page Ask children to *look back* at their lists by drawing pictures or using connecting cubes of two different colors to make sure each totals 9. **Notes for Home** Your child made a list to solve problems. *Home Activity:* Challenge your child to find and list two ways to combine three bags of shells to make 12. (6 + 3 + 2 = 11; 5 + 4 + 2 = 11; 7 + 1 + 3 = 11; 8 + 1 + 2 = 11)

44 Use with pages 145–146.

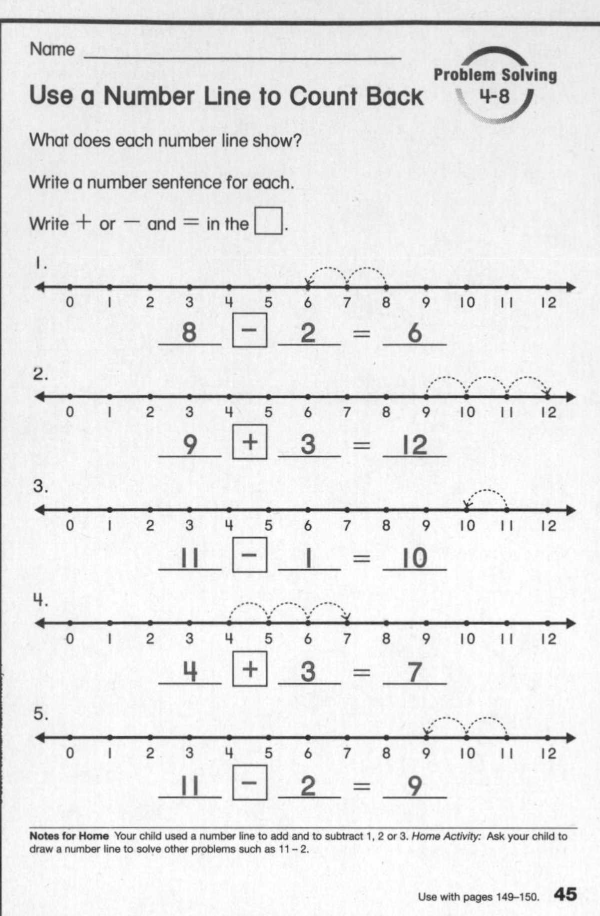

Name ______________________

Use a Number Line to Count Back

Problem Solving 4-8

What does each number line show?

Write a number sentence for each.

Write + or − and = in the □.

1. 0 1 2 3 4 5 6 7 8 9 10 11 12

8 [−] 2 = 6

2. 0 1 2 3 4 5 6 7 8 9 10 11 12

9 [+] 3 = 12

3. 0 1 2 3 4 5 6 7 8 9 10 11 12

11 [−] 1 = 10

4. 0 1 2 3 4 5 6 7 8 9 10 11 12

4 [+] 3 = 7

5. 0 1 2 3 4 5 6 7 8 9 10 11 12

11 [−] 2 = 9

Notes for Home Your child used a number line to add and to subtract 1, 2 or 3. *Home Activity:* Ask your child to draw a number line to solve other problems such as 11 − 2.

Use with pages 149–150. **45**

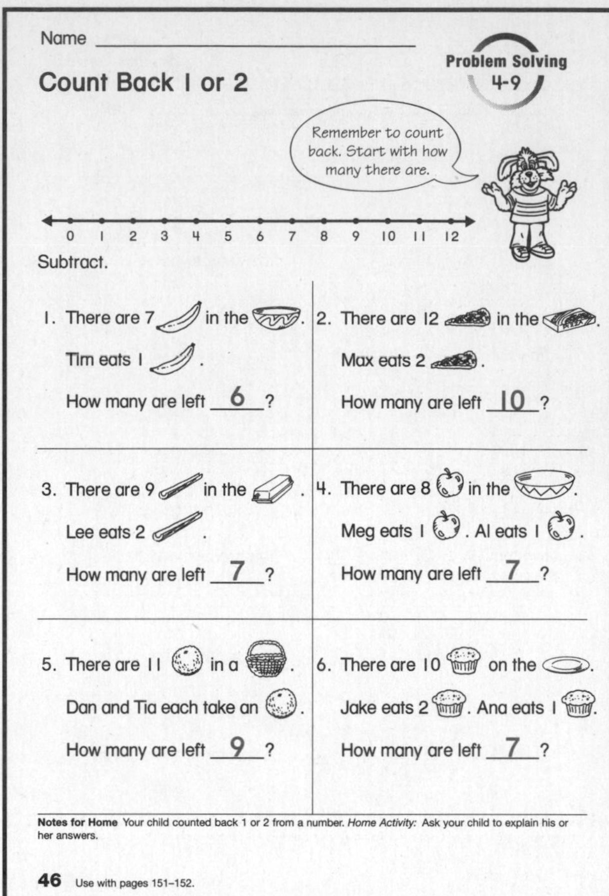

Name ______________________

Count Back 1 or 2

Problem Solving 4-9

Remember to count back. Start with how many there are.

0 1 2 3 4 5 6 7 8 9 10 11 12

Subtract.

1. There are 7 in the . Tim eats 1 . How many are left 6?
2. There are 12 in the . Max eats 2 . How many are left 10?
3. There are 9 in the . Lee eats 2 . How many are left 7?
4. There are 8 in the . Meg eats 1 . Al eats 1 . How many are left 7?
5. There are 11 in a . Dan and Tia each take an . How many are left 9?
6. There are 10 on the . Jake eats 2 . Ana eats 1 . How many are left 7?

Notes for Home Your child counted back 1 or 2 from a number. *Home Activity:* Ask your child to explain his or her answers.

46 Use with pages 151–152.

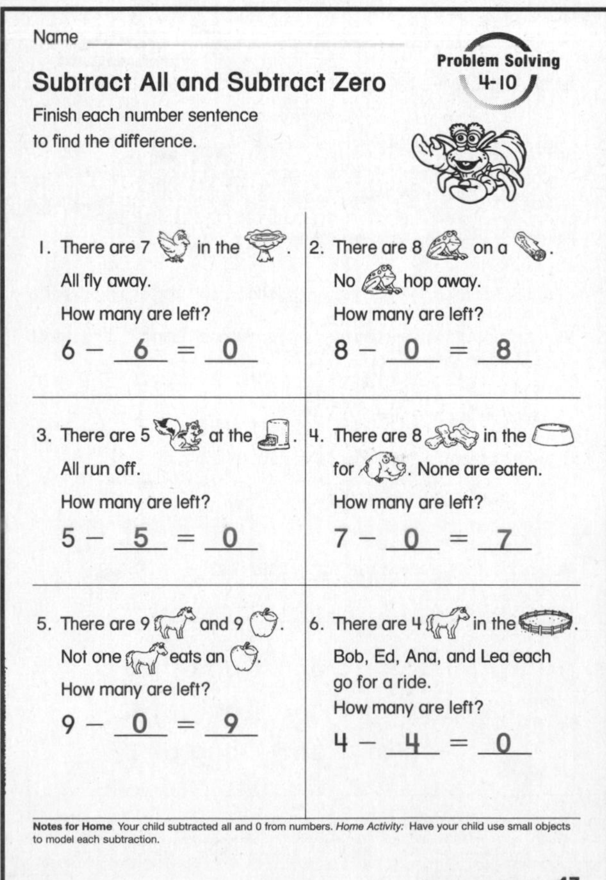

Name ______________________

Subtract All and Subtract Zero

Problem Solving 4-10

Finish each number sentence to find the difference.

1. There are 7 in the . All fly away. How many are left? 6 − 6 = 0
2. There are 8 on a . No hop away. How many are left? 8 − 0 = 8
3. There are 5 at the . All run off. How many are left? 5 − 5 = 0
4. There are 8 in the for . None are eaten. How many are left? 7 − 0 = 7
5. There are 9 and 9 . Not one eats an . How many are left? 9 − 0 = 9
6. There are 4 in the . Bob, Ed, Ana, and Lea each go for a ride. How many are left? 4 − 4 = 0

Notes for Home Your child subtracted all and 0 from numbers. *Home Activity:* Have your child use small objects to model each subtraction.

Use with pages 155–156. **47**

Name ______________________

Subtract with 5

Problem Solving 4-11

Read the problems.
Look at the pictures.
Finish the number sentences.

1. There are 6 in all. How many are in the ? 6 − 5 = 1
2. There were 9 in all. How many are in the ? 6 − 5 = 4
3. There are 10 in all. How many are in the ? 10 − 5 = 5
4. There are 8 in all. How many are in the ? 8 − 5 = 3
5. There are 7 in all. How many are in the ? 7 − 5 = 2

Notes for Home Your child subtracted 5 from numbers. *Home Activity:* Ask your child to make up a math story with 12 and 5.

48 Use with pages 157–158.

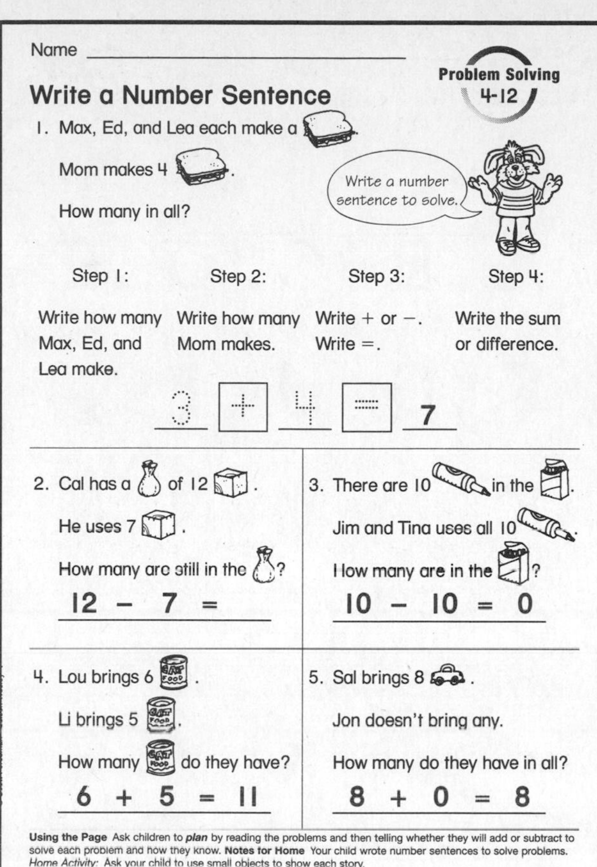

Name ______________________

Problem Solving 4-12

Write a Number Sentence

1. Max, Ed, and Lea each make a [sandwich].

Mom makes 4 [sandwich].

How many in all?

Write a number sentence to solve.

Step 1:	Step 2:	Step 3:	Step 4:
Write how many Max, Ed, and Lea make.	Write how many Mom makes.	Write + or −. Write =.	Write the sum or difference.

3 + 4 = 7

2. Cal has a [bag] of 12 [cubes].
He uses 7 [cubes].
How many are still in the [bag]?
12 − 7 =

3. There are 10 [markers] in the [box].
Jim and Tina uses all 10 [markers].
How many are in the [box]?
10 − 10 = 0

4. Lou brings 6 [cans].
Li brings 5 [cans].
How many [cans] do they have?
6 + 5 = 11

5. Sal brings 8 [cars].
Jon doesn't bring any.
How many do they have in all?
8 + 0 = 8

Using the Page Ask children to *plan* by reading the problems and then telling whether they will add or subtract to solve each problem and how they know. **Notes for Home** Your child wrote number sentences to solve problems. *Home Activity:* Ask your child to use small objects to show each story.

Use with pages 161–162. **49**

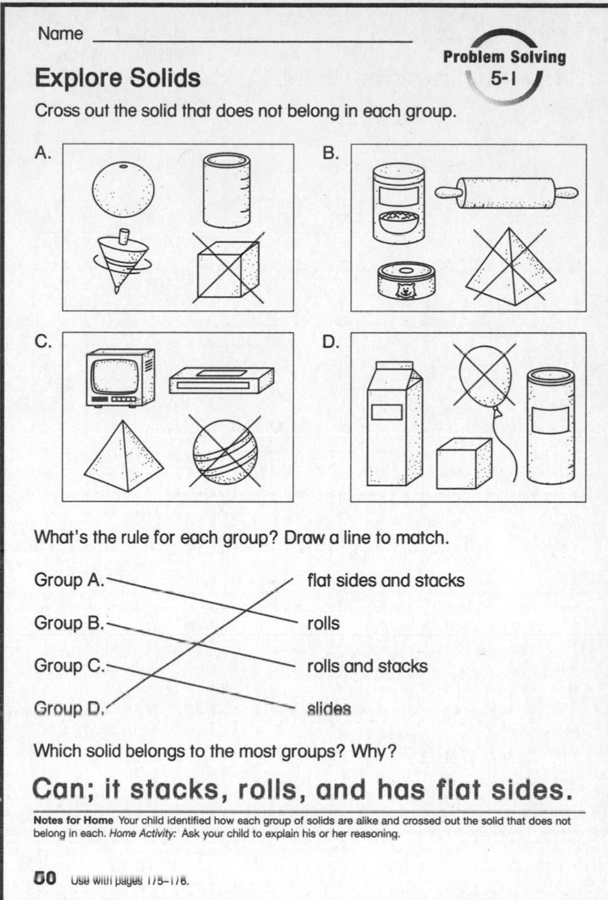

Name ______________________

Problem Solving 5-1

Explore Solids

Cross out the solid that does not belong in each group.

A. B. C. D.

What's the rule for each group? Draw a line to match.

Group A. — slides

Group B. — rolls

Group C. — rolls and stacks

Group D. — flat sides and stacks

Which solid belongs to the most groups? Why?

Can; it stacks, rolls, and has flat sides.

Notes for Home Your child identified how each group of solids are alike and crossed out the solid that does not belong in each. *Home Activity:* Ask your child to explain his or her reasoning.

50 Use with pages 175–176.

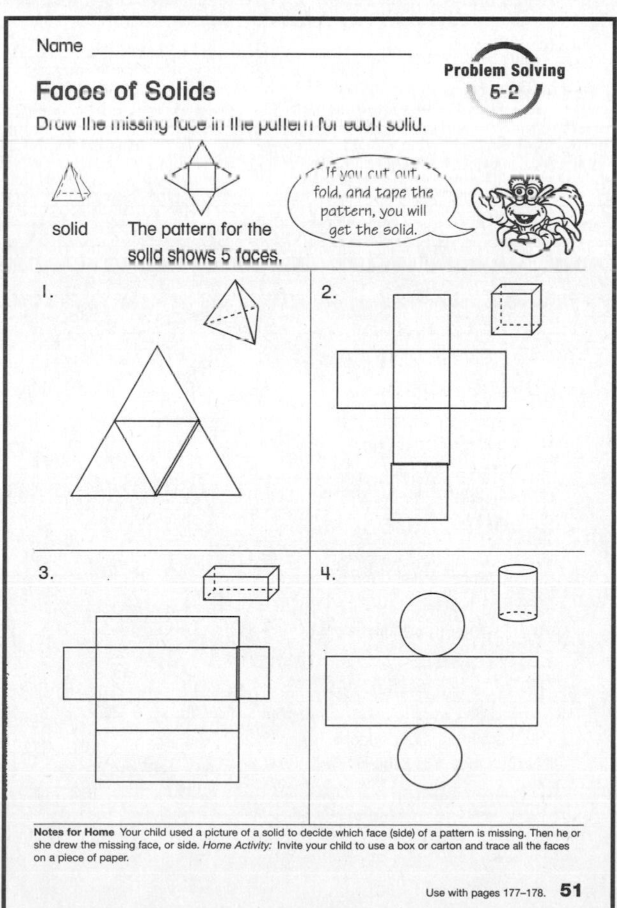

Name ______________________

Problem Solving 5-2

Faces of Solids

Draw the missing face in the pattern for each solid.

solid

The pattern for the solid shows 5 faces.

If you cut out, fold, and tape the pattern, you will get the solid.

1.

2.

3.

4.

Notes for Home Your child used a picture of a solid to decide which face (side) of a pattern is missing. Then he or she drew the missing face, or side. *Home Activity:* Invite your child to use a box or carton and trace all the faces on a piece of paper.

Use with pages 177–178. **51**

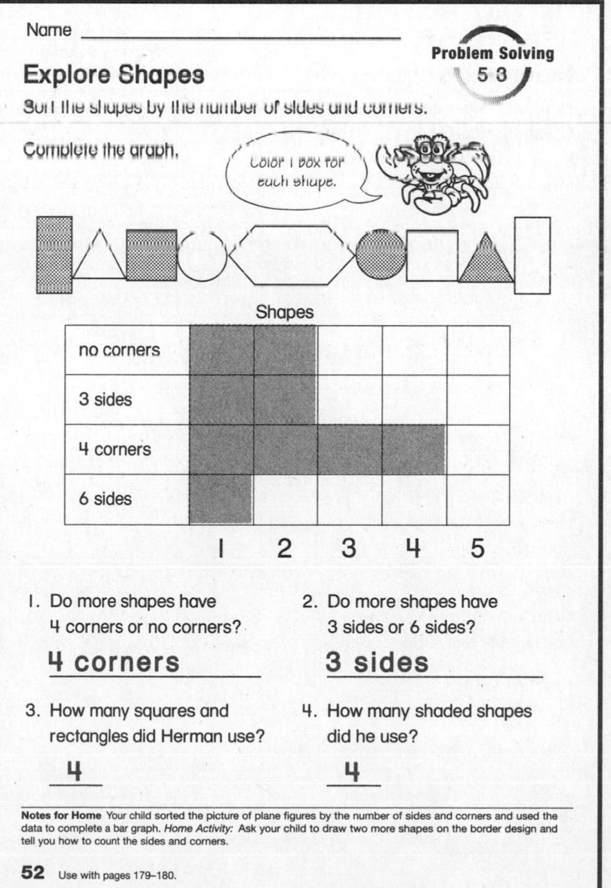

Name ______________________

Problem Solving 5-3

Explore Shapes

Sort the shapes by the number of sides and corners.

Complete the graph.

Color 1 box for each shape.

Shapes

no corners	■	■			
3 sides	■	■			
4 corners	■	■	■	■	
6 sides	■				
	1	2	3	4	5

1. Do more shapes have 4 corners or no corners?
4 corners

2. Do more shapes have 3 sides or 6 sides?
3 sides

3. How many squares and rectangles did Herman use?
4

4. How many shaded shapes did he use?
4

Notes for Home Your child sorted the picture of plane figures by the number of sides and corners and used the data to complete a bar graph. *Home Activity:* Ask your child to draw two more shapes on the border design and tell you how to count the sides and corners.

52 Use with pages 179–180.

Name ______________________

Problem Solving 5-4

Same Size and Shape

Draw a house the same size and shape.

Check children's drawings.

Notes for Home Your child used a dot grid to draw a house that is the same size and shape as the given house. *Home Activity:* Draw another window on the house that is given, and ask your child to draw the same size and shape on his or her house.

Use with pages 181–182. **53**

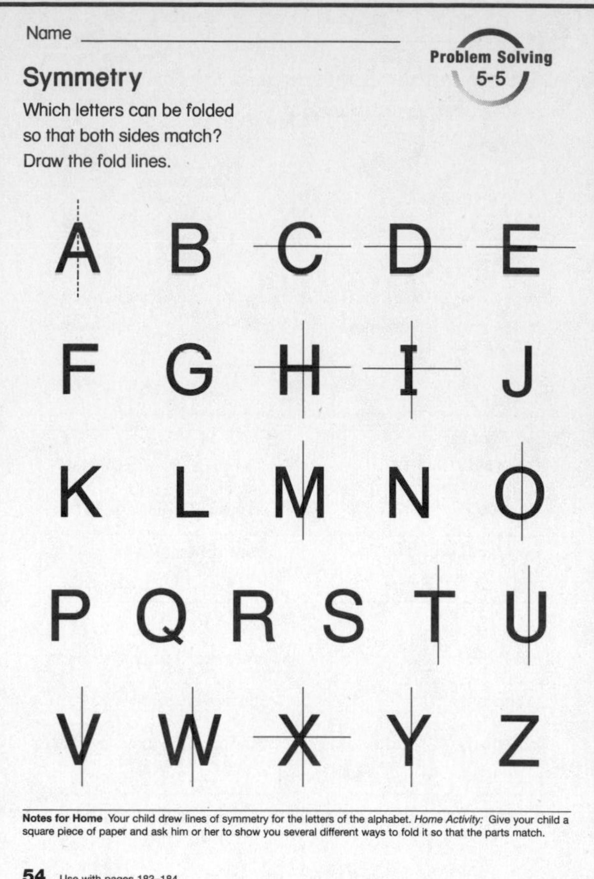

Name ______________________

Problem Solving 5-5

Symmetry

Which letters can be folded so that both sides match?
Draw the fold lines.

Notes for Home Your child drew lines of symmetry for the letters of the alphabet. *Home Activity:* Give your child a square piece of paper and ask him or her to show you several different ways to fold it so that the parts match.

54 Use with pages 183–184.

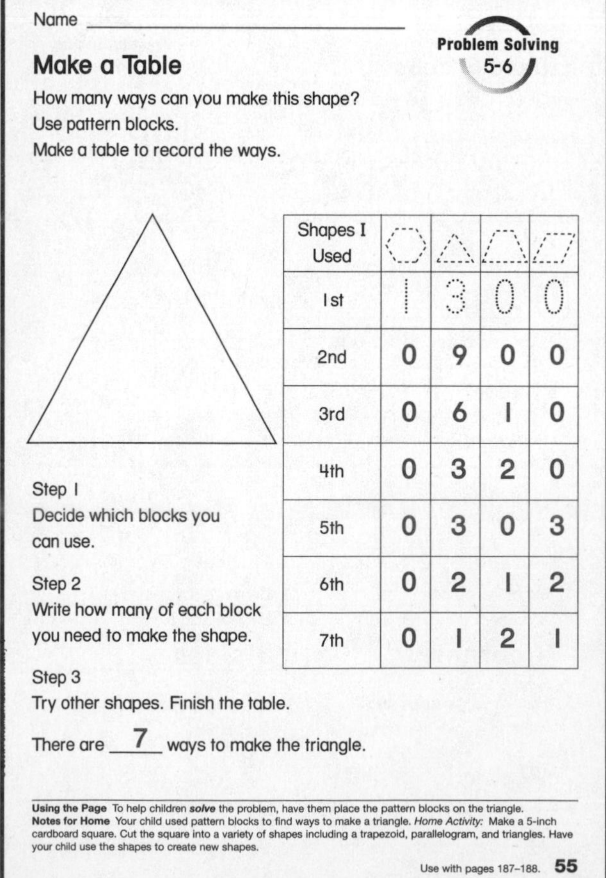

Name ______________________

Problem Solving 5-6

Make a Table

How many ways can you make this shape?
Use pattern blocks.
Make a table to record the ways.

Shapes I Used	hexagon	triangle	trapezoid	parallelogram
1st	1	3	0	0
2nd	0	9	0	0
3rd	0	6	1	0
4th	0	3	2	0
5th	0	3	0	3
6th	0	2	1	2
7th	0	1	2	1

Step 1
Decide which blocks you can use.

Step 2
Write how many of each block you need to make the shape.

Step 3
Try other shapes. Finish the table.

There are 7 ways to make the triangle.

Using the Page To help children *solve* the problem, have them place the pattern blocks on the triangle.
Notes for Home Your child used pattern blocks to find ways to make a triangle. *Home Activity:* Make a 5-inch cardboard square. Cut the square into a variety of shapes including a trapezoid, parallelogram, and triangles. Have your child use the shapes to create new shapes.

Use with pages 187–188. **55**

Name ______________________

Problem Solving 5-7

Fair Shares

Solve.

1. Jamal and Ann want to share some pens.
   There are 6 pens.
   How can they make fair shares?
   3 pens each
2. Four girls will share a berry pie.
   There are 4 slices of pie.
   How can they make fair shares?
   1 slice each.
3. Three boys want to share some balloons.
   There are 6 balloons.
   How can they make fair shares?
   2 balloons each
4. Bill and Amber will share a banana.
   There is 1 banana.
   How can they make fair shares?
   Cut in half.
5. Kira and Ben want to share some popcorn.
   There are 8 bags of popcorn.
   How can they make fair shares?
   4 bags each.

Notes for Home Your child solved word problems about how to make fair shares. *Home Activity:* Draw a circle and pretend it is a pizza. Ask your child to tell you some different ways that you and he or she could share a pizza to make fair shares.

56 Use with pages 191–192.

Name ______________________

Problem Solving 5-8

Halves

Draw a line and color to show what Kira ate each day.

1. On Monday, Kira drank half a glass of milk.
2. On Tuesday, she ate half a sandwich.
3. On Wednesday, she ate half a slice of pizza.
4. Kira ate half an apple on Thursday.
5. She ate half a muffin on Friday.

Notes for Home Your child drew a line and colored to show one half on each pictured item. *Home Activity:* Give your child an apple or orange, and ask him or her to show how to divide it into halves.

Use with pages 193–194. **57**

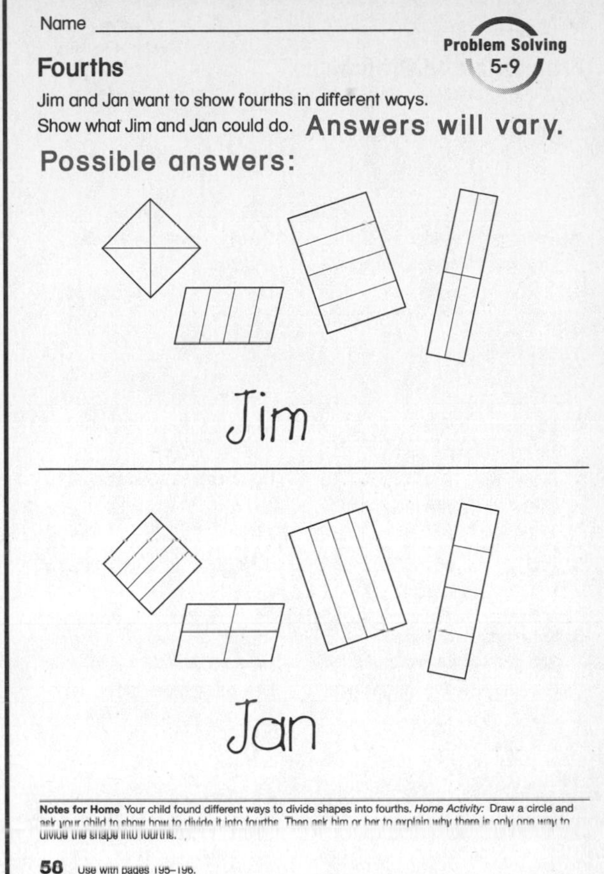

Name ______________________

Problem Solving 5-9

Fourths

Jim and Jan want to show fourths in different ways.
Show what Jim and Jan could do. **Answers will vary.**

Possible answers:

Notes for Home Your child found different ways to divide shapes into fourths. *Home Activity:* Draw a circle and ask your child to show how to divide it into fourths. Then ask him or her to explain why there is only one way to divide the shape into fourths.

58 Use with pages 195–196.

Name ______________________

Problem Solving 5-10

Thirds

Look at the picture.
Circle the correct word. Solve.

1. About $\frac{1}{3}$ of the children are girls. (boys.)
   Are there more boys or girls? (girls) boys
2. I boy and 2 girls go home.
   About $\frac{1}{3}$ of the children are girls. (boys.)
   Are there more boys or girls? (girls) boys
3. Draw a picture with many things. Circle about $\frac{1}{3}$ of your things.

Pictures and answers will vary.

Notes for Home Your child used a picture to estimate the fraction 1/3. *Home Activity:* Ask your child to fold a piece of paper into thirds.

Use with pages 197–198. **59**

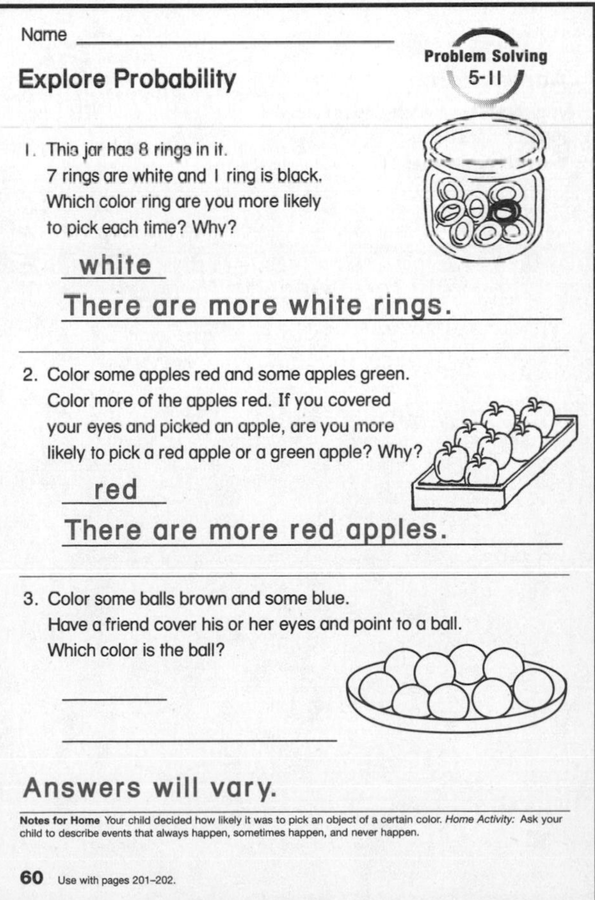

Name ______________________

Problem Solving 5-11

Explore Probability

1. This jar has 8 rings in it.
   7 rings are white and I ring is black.
   Which color ring are you more likely to pick each time? Why?

   white

   There are more white rings.

2. Color some apples red and some apples green. Color more of the apples red. If you covered your eyes and picked an apple, are you more likely to pick a red apple or a green apple? Why?

   red

   There are more red apples.

3. Color some balls brown and some blue. Have a friend cover his or her eyes and point to a ball. Which color is the ball?

   ______

   ____

Answers will vary.

Notes for Home Your child decided how likely it was to pick an object of a certain color. *Home Activity:* Ask your child to describe events that always happen, sometimes happen, and never happen.

60 Use with pages 201–202.

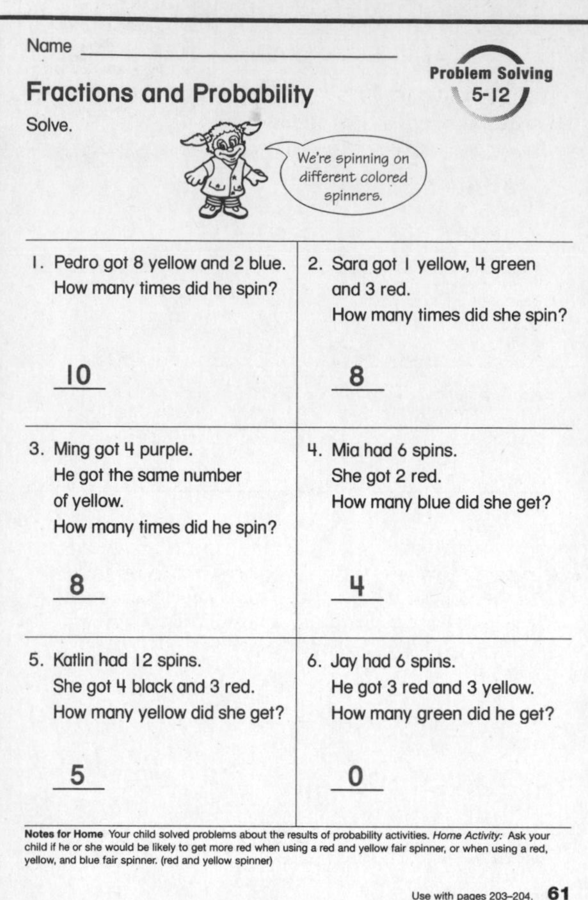

Name ____________________

Problem Solving 5-12

Fractions and Probability

Solve.

1. Pedro got 8 yellow and 2 blue. How many times did he spin? **10**	2. Sara got 1 yellow, 4 green and 3 red. How many times did she spin? **8**
3. Ming got 4 purple. He got the same number of yellow. How many times did he spin? **8**	4. Mia had 6 spins. She got 2 red. How many blue did she get? **4**
5. Katlin had 12 spins. She got 4 black and 3 red. How many yellow did she get? **5**	6. Jay had 6 spins. He got 3 red and 3 yellow. How many green did he get? **0**

Notes for Home Your child solved problems about the results of probability activities. *Home Activity:* Ask your child if he or she would be likely to get more red when using a red and yellow fair spinner, or when using a red, yellow, and blue fair spinner. (red and yellow spinner)

Use with pages 203–204. **61**

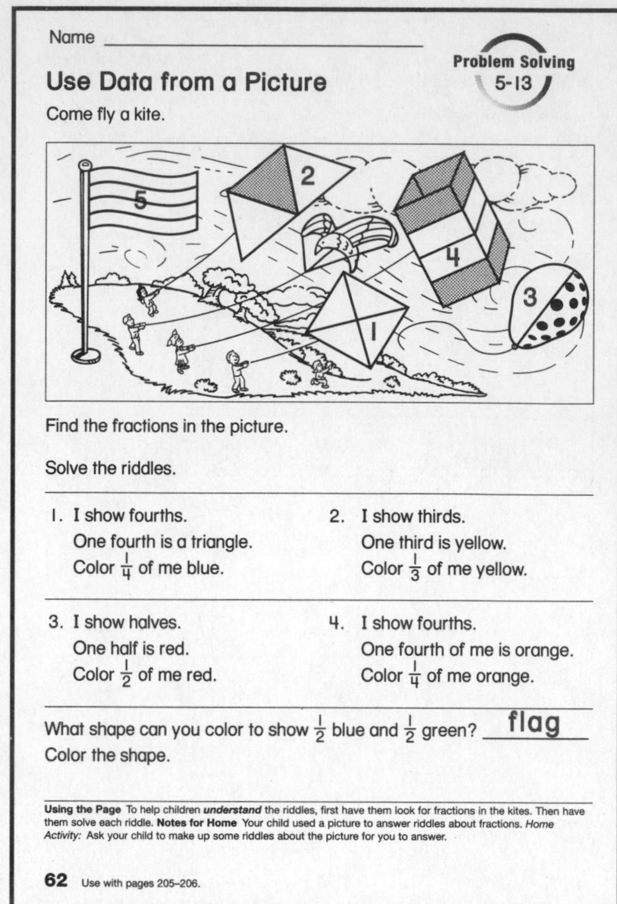

Name ____________________

Problem Solving 5-13

Use Data from a Picture

Come fly a kite.

Find the fractions in the picture.

Solve the riddles.

1. I show fourths. One fourth is a triangle. Color $\frac{1}{4}$ of me blue.	2. I show thirds. One third is yellow. Color $\frac{1}{3}$ of me yellow.
3. I show halves. One half is red. Color $\frac{1}{2}$ of me red.	4. I show fourths. One fourth of me is orange. Color $\frac{1}{4}$ of me orange.

What shape can you color to show $\frac{1}{2}$ blue and $\frac{1}{2}$ green? **flag**

Color the shape.

Using the Page To help children *understand* the riddles, first have them look for fractions in the kites. Then have them solve each riddle. **Notes for Home** Your child used a picture to answer riddles about fractions. *Home Activity:* Ask your child to make up some riddles about the picture for you to answer.

62 Use with pages 205–206.

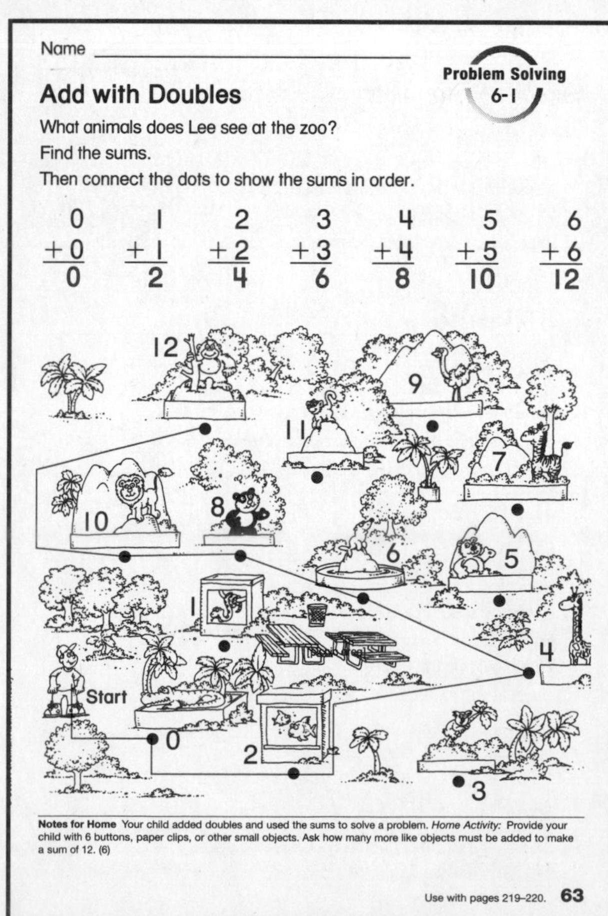

Name ____________________

Problem Solving 6-1

Add with Doubles

What animals does Lee see at the zoo?

Find the sums.

Then connect the dots to show the sums in order.

0	1	2	3	4	5	6
+0	+1	+2	+3	+4	+5	+6
0	**2**	**4**	**6**	**8**	**10**	**12**

Notes for Home Your child added doubles and used the sums to solve a problem. *Home Activity:* Provide your child with 6 buttons, paper clips, or other small objects. Ask how many more like objects must be added to make a sum of 12. (6)

Use with pages 219–220. **63**

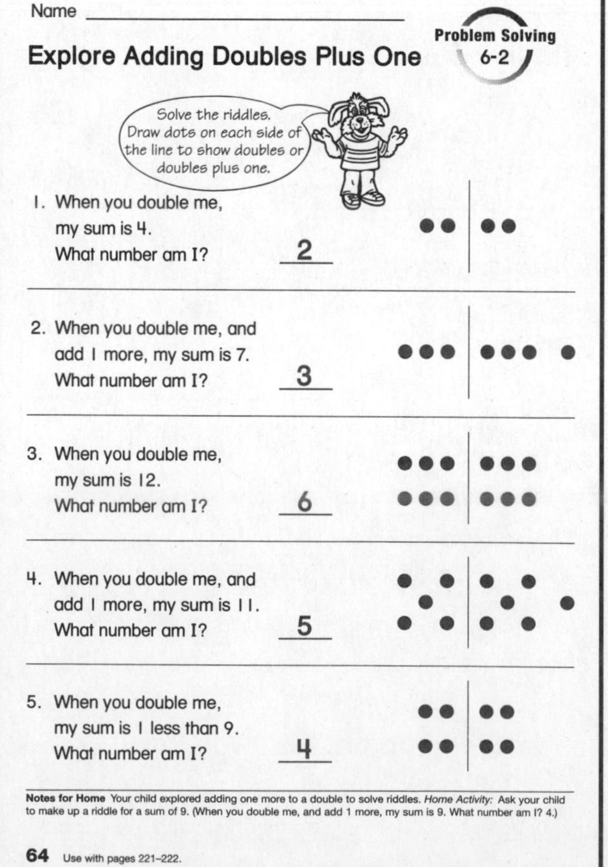

Name ____________________

Problem Solving 6-2

Explore Adding Doubles Plus One

1. When you double me, my sum is 4. What number am I? **2**
2. When you double me, and add 1 more, my sum is 7. What number am I? **3**
3. When you double me, my sum is 12. What number am I? **6**
4. When you double me, and add 1 more, my sum is 11. What number am I? **5**
5. When you double me, my sum is 1 less than 9. What number am I? **4**

Notes for Home Your child explored adding one more to a double to solve riddles. *Home Activity:* Ask your child to make up a riddle for a sum of 9. (When you double me, and add 1 more, my sum is 9. What number am I? 4.)

64 Use with pages 221–222.

Name ______________________

Add with Doubles Plus One

Problem Solving 6-3

What is the hidden picture?
Find each sum. Next, add 1 to each number in your head.
Then color the shape with the new sum.

$$0 + 0 = 0 \qquad 1 + 1 = 2 \qquad 2 + 2 = 4 \qquad 3 + 3 = 6 \qquad 4 + 4 = 8 \qquad 5 + 5 = 10$$

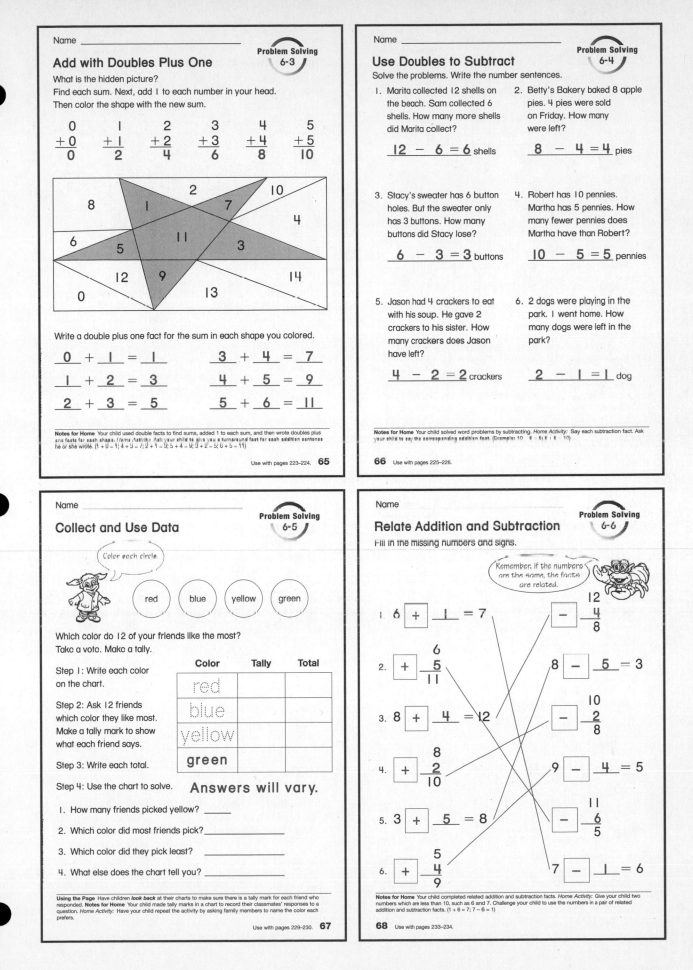

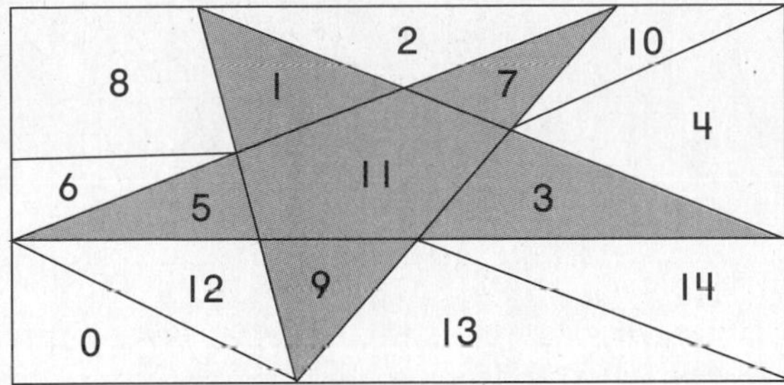

Write a double plus one fact for the sum in each shape you colored.

0 + 1 = 1   3 + 4 = 7
1 + 2 = 3   4 + 5 = 9
2 + 3 = 5   5 + 6 = 11

Notes for Home Your child used double facts to find sums, added 1 to each sum, and then wrote doubles plus one facts for each shape. *Home Activity:* Ask your child to give you a turnaround fact for each addition sentence he or she wrote. (1 + 0 = 1; 4 + 3 = 7; 2 + 1 = 3; 5 + 4 = 9; 3 + 2 = 5; 6 + 5 = 11)

Name ______________________

Use Doubles to Subtract

Problem Solving 6-4

Solve the problems. Write the number sentences.

1. Marita collected 12 shells on the beach. Sam collected 6 shells. How many more shells did Marita collect?
   12 − 6 = 6 shells
2. Betty's Bakery baked 8 apple pies. 4 pies were sold on Friday. How many were left?
   8 − 4 = 4 pies
3. Stacy's sweater has 6 button holes. But the sweater only has 3 buttons. How many buttons did Stacy lose?
   6 − 3 = 3 buttons
4. Robert has 10 pennies. Martha has 5 pennies. How many fewer pennies does Martha have than Robert?
   10 − 5 = 5 pennies
5. Jason had 4 crackers to eat with his soup. He gave 2 crackers to his sister. How many crackers does Jason have left?
   4 − 2 = 2 crackers
6. 2 dogs were playing in the park. 1 went home. How many dogs were left in the park?
   2 − 1 = 1 dog

Notes for Home Your child solved word problems by subtracting. *Home Activity:* Say each subtraction fact. Ask your child to say the corresponding addition fact. (Example: 10 − 5 = 5; 5 + 5 = 10)

Name ______________________

Collect and Use Data

Problem Solving 6-5

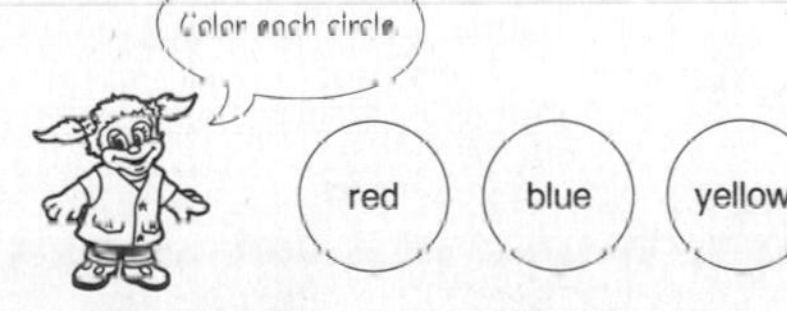

Which color do 12 of your friends like the most?
Take a vote. Make a tally.

Step 1: Write each color on the chart.

Step 2: Ask 12 friends which color they like most. Make a tally mark to show what each friend says.

Step 3: Write each total.

Step 4: Use the chart to solve.

Color	Tally	Total
red		
blue		
yellow		
green		

Answers will vary.

1. How many friends picked yellow? ____
2. Which color did most friends pick? ____________
3. Which color did they pick least? ____________
4. What else does the chart tell you? ____________

Using the Page Have children ***look back*** at their charts to make sure there is a tally mark for each friend who responded. **Notes for Home** Your child made tally marks in a chart to record their classmates' responses to a question. *Home Activity:* Have your child repeat the activity by asking family members to name the color each prefers.

Name ______________________

Relate Addition and Subtraction

Problem Solving 6-6

Fill in the missing numbers and signs.

Remember, if the numbers are the same, the facts are related.

	Addition	Subtraction
1.	6 + 1 = 7	12 − 4 = 8
2.	6 + 5 = 11	8 − 5 = 3
3.	8 + 4 = 12	10 − 2 = 8
4.	8 + 2 = 10	9 − 4 = 5
5.	3 + 5 = 8	11 − 6 = 5
6.	5 + 4 = 9	7 − 1 = 6

Notes for Home Your child completed related addition and subtraction facts. *Home Activity:* Give your child two numbers which are less than 10, such as 6 and 7. Challenge your child to use the numbers in a pair of related addition and subtraction facts. (1 + 6 = 7; 7 − 6 = 1)

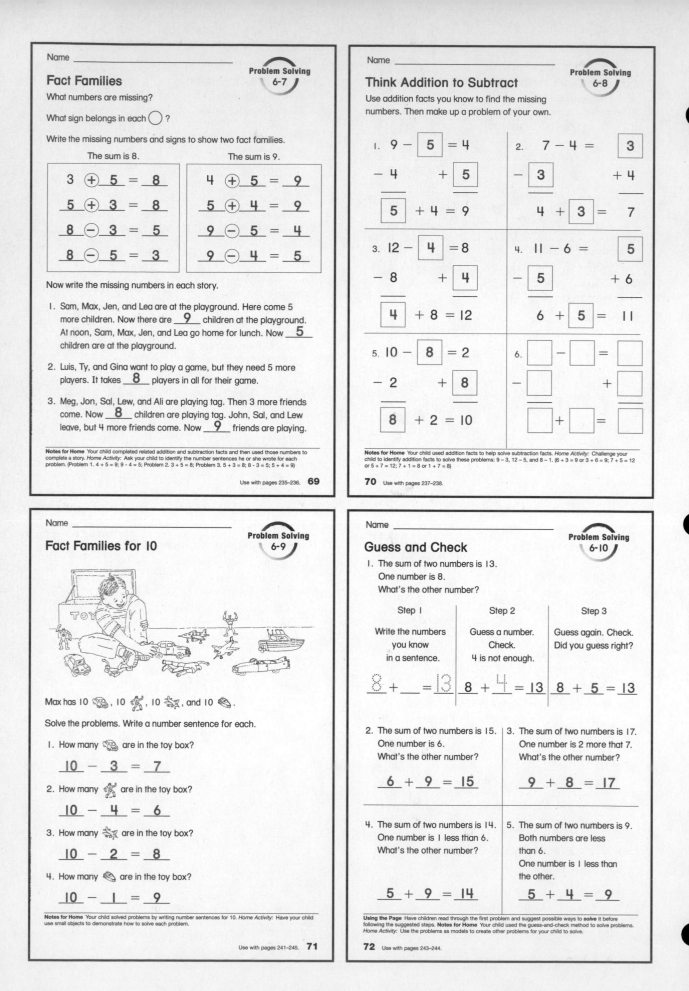

Name ______________________

Fact Families

Problem Solving 6-7

What numbers are missing?

What sign belongs in each ◯ ?

Write the missing numbers and signs to show two fact families.

The sum is 8.	The sum is 9.
3 (+) 5 = 8	4 (+) 5 = 9
5 (+) 3 = 8	5 (+) 4 = 9
8 (−) 3 = 5	9 (−) 5 = 4
8 (−) 5 = 3	9 (−) 4 = 5

Now write the missing numbers in each story.

1. Sam, Max, Jen, and Lea are at the playground. Here come 5 more children. Now there are __9__ children at the playground. At noon, Sam, Max, Jen, and Lea go home for lunch. Now __5__ children are at the playground.
2. Luis, Ty, and Gina want to play a game, but they need 5 more players. It takes __8__ players in all for their game.
3. Meg, Jon, Sal, Lew, and Ali are playing tag. Then 3 more friends come. Now __8__ children are playing tag. John, Sal, and Lew leave, but 4 more friends come. Now __9__ friends are playing.

Notes for Home Your child completed related addition and subtraction facts and then used those numbers to complete a story. *Home Activity:* Ask your child to identify the number sentences he or she wrote for each problem. (Problem 1. 4 + 5 = 9; 9 - 4 = 5; Problem 2. 3 + 5 = 8; Problem 3. 5 + 3 = 8; 8 - 3 = 5; 5 + 4 = 9)

Name ______________________

Think Addition to Subtract

Problem Solving 6-8

Use addition facts you know to find the missing numbers. Then make up a problem of your own.

1. 9 − [5] = 4
   − 4   + [5]
   [5] + 4 = 9

2. 7 − 4 = [3]
   − [3]   + 4
   4 + [3] = 7

3. 12 − [4] = 8
   − 8   + [4]
   [4] + 8 = 12

4. 11 − 6 = [5]
   − [5]   + 6
   6 + [5] = 11

5. 10 − [8] = 2
   − 2   + [8]
   [8] + 2 = 10

6. [ ] − [ ] = [ ]
   − [ ]   + [ ]
   [ ] + [ ] = [ ]

Notes for Home Your child used addition facts to help solve subtraction facts. *Home Activity:* Challenge your child to identify addition facts to solve these problems: 9 − 3, 12 − 5, and 8 − 1. (6 + 3 = 9 or 3 + 6 = 9; 7 + 5 = 12 or 5 + 7 = 12; 7 + 1 = 8 or 1 + 7 = 8)

Name ______________________

Fact Families for 10

Max has 10 cars, 10 robots, 10 planes, and 10 boats.

Solve the problems. Write a number sentence for each.

1. How many cars are in the toy box?
   10 − 3 = 7
2. How many robots are in the toy box?
   10 − 4 = 6
3. How many planes are in the toy box?
   10 − 2 = 8
4. How many boats are in the toy box?
   10 − 1 = 9

Notes for Home Your child solved problems by writing number sentences for 10. *Home Activity:* Have your child use small objects to demonstrate how to solve each problem.

Name ______________________

Guess and Check

Problem Solving 6-10

1. The sum of two numbers is 13.
   One number is 8.
   What's the other number?

Step 1	Step 2	Step 3
Write the numbers you know in a sentence.	Guess a number. Check. 4 is not enough.	Guess again. Check. Did you guess right?
8 + ___ = 13	8 + 4 = 13	8 + 5 = 13

2. The sum of two numbers is 15.
   One number is 6.
   What's the other number?
   6 + 9 = 15
3. The sum of two numbers is 17.
   One number is 2 more that 7.
   What's the other number?
   9 + 8 = 17
4. The sum of two numbers is 14.
   One number is 1 less than 6.
   What's the other number?
   5 + 9 = 14
5. The sum of two numbers is 9.
   Both numbers are less than 6.
   One number is 1 less than the other.
   5 + 4 = 9

Using the Page Have children read through the first problem and suggest possible ways to *solve* it before following the suggested steps. **Notes for Home** Your child used the guess-and-check method to solve problems. *Home Activity:* Use the problems as models to create other problems for your child to solve.

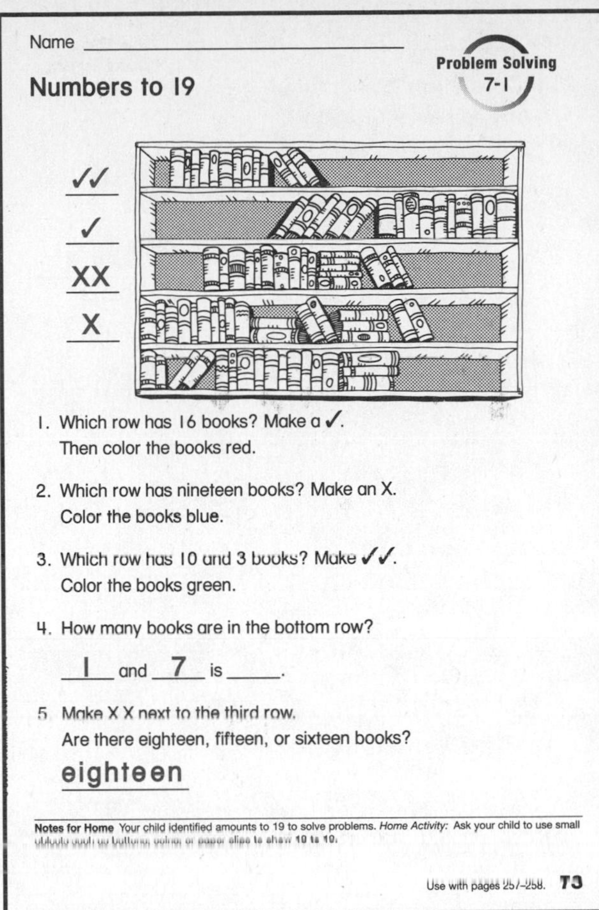

Name ______________________

Problem Solving 7-1

Numbers to 19

✓✓
✓
XX
X

1. Which row has 16 books? Make a ✓.
   Then color the books red.
2. Which row has nineteen books? Make an X.
   Color the books blue.
3. Which row has 10 and 3 books? Make ✓✓.
   Color the books green.
4. How many books are in the bottom row?
   __1__ and __7__ is _____.
5. Make X X next to the third row.
   Are there eighteen, fifteen, or sixteen books?
   eighteen

Notes for Home Your child identified amounts to 19 to solve problems. *Home Activity:* Ask your child to use small objects such as buttons, coins, or paper clips to show 10 to 19.

Use with pages 257–258. **T3**

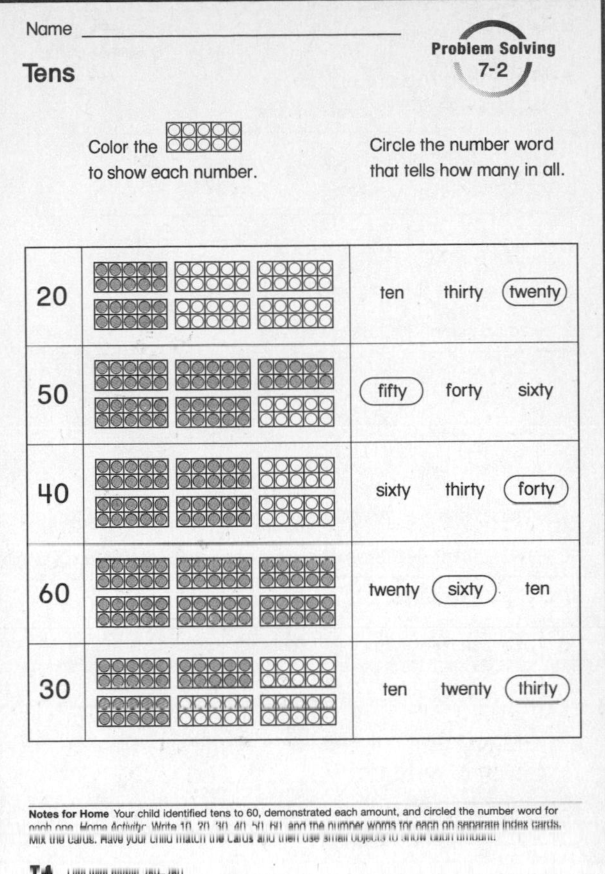

Name ______________________

Problem Solving 7-2

Tens

Color the [ten frame] to show each number.

Circle the number word that tells how many in all.

20		ten thirty (twenty)
50		(fifty) forty sixty
40		sixty thirty (forty)
60		twenty (sixty) ten
30		ten twenty (thirty)

Notes for Home Your child identified tens to 60, demonstrated each amount, and circled the number word for each one. *Home Activity:* Write 10, 20, 30, 40, 50, 60, and the number words for each on separate index cards. Mix the cards. Have your child match the cards and then use small objects to show each amount.

T4 Use with pages 259–260.

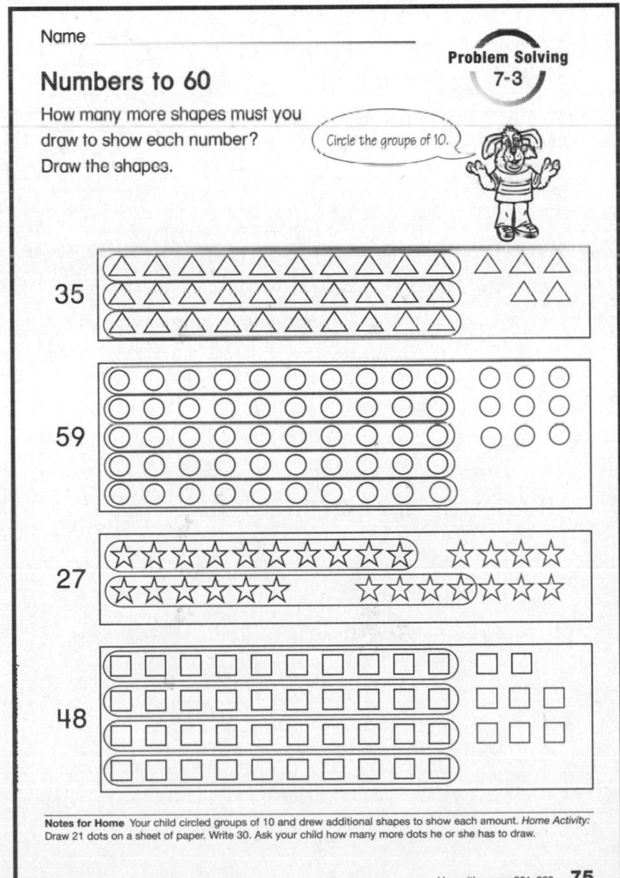

Name ______________________

Problem Solving 7-3

Numbers to 60

How many more shapes must you draw to show each number?
Draw the shapes.

35

59

27

48

Notes for Home Your child circled groups of 10 and drew additional shapes to show each amount. *Home Activity:* Draw 21 dots on a sheet of paper. Write 30. Ask your child how many more dots he or she has to draw.

Use with pages 261–262. **75**

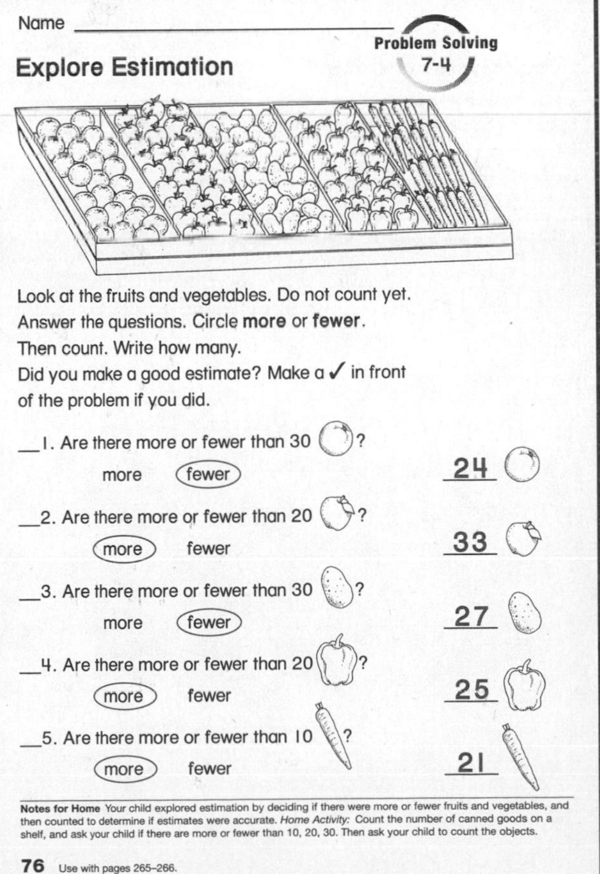

Name ______________________

Problem Solving 7-4

Explore Estimation

Look at the fruits and vegetables. Do not count yet.
Answer the questions. Circle **more** or **fewer**.
Then count. Write how many.
Did you make a good estimate? Make a ✓ in front of the problem if you did.

__1. Are there more or fewer than 30 ?
   more (fewer) __24__
__2. Are there more or fewer than 20 ?
   (more) fewer __33__
__3. Are there more or fewer than 30 ?
   more (fewer) __27__
__4. Are there more or fewer than 20 ?
   (more) fewer __25__
__5. Are there more or fewer than 10 ?
   (more) fewer __21__

Notes for Home Your child explored estimation by deciding if there were more or fewer fruits and vegetables, and then counted to determine if estimates were accurate. *Home Activity:* Count the number of canned goods on a shelf, and ask your child if there are more or fewer than 10, 20, 30. Then ask your child to count the objects.

76 Use with pages 265–266.

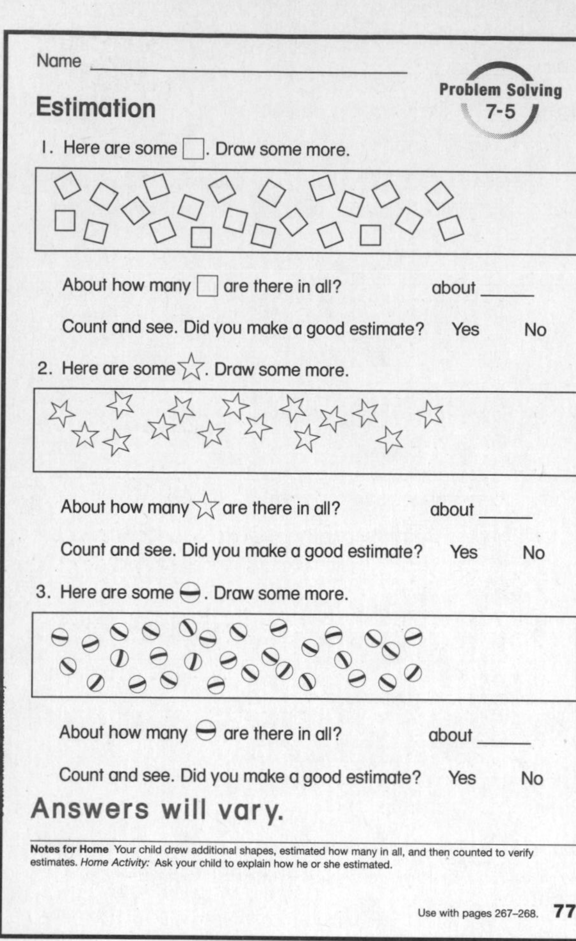

Name ______________________

Problem Solving 7-5

Estimation

1. Here are some □. Draw some more.

About how many □ are there in all? about _____

Count and see. Did you make a good estimate? Yes No

2. Here are some ☆. Draw some more.

About how many ☆ are there in all? about _____

Count and see. Did you make a good estimate? Yes No

3. Here are some ⊖. Draw some more.

About how many ⊖ are there in all? about _____

Count and see. Did you make a good estimate? Yes No

Answers will vary.

Notes for Home Your child drew additional shapes, estimated how many in all, and then counted to verify estimates. *Home Activity:* Ask your child to explain how he or she estimated.

Use with pages 267–268. **77**

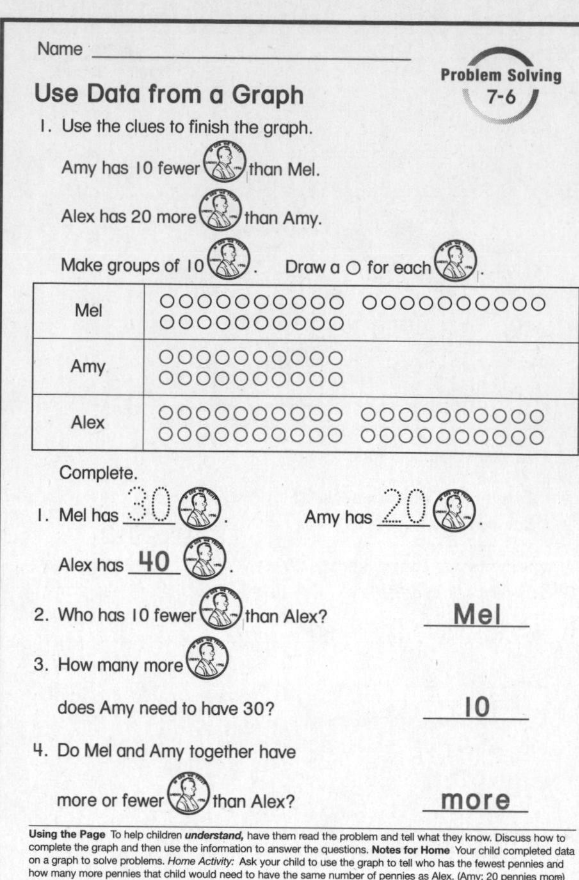

Name ______________________

Problem Solving 7-6

Use Data from a Graph

1. Use the clues to finish the graph.

Amy has 10 fewer (penny) than Mel.

Alex has 20 more (penny) than Amy.

Make groups of 10 (penny). Draw a ○ for each (penny).

Mel	○○○○○○○○○○ ○○○○○○○○○○ ○○○○○○○○○○
Amy	○○○○○○○○○○ ○○○○○○○○○○
Alex	○○○○○○○○○○ ○○○○○○○○○○ ○○○○○○○○○○ ○○○○○○○○○○

Complete.

1. Mel has 30 (penny). Amy has 20 (penny). Alex has 40 (penny).
2. Who has 10 fewer (penny) than Alex? **Mel**
3. How many more (penny) does Amy need to have 30? **10**
4. Do Mel and Amy together have more or fewer (penny) than Alex? **more**

Using the Page To help children ***understand,*** have them read the problem and tell what they know. Discuss how to complete the graph and then use the information to answer the questions. **Notes for Home** Your child completed data on a graph to solve problems. *Home Activity:* Ask your child to use the graph to tell who has the fewest pennies and how many more pennies that child would need to have the same number of pennies as Alex. (Amy; 20 pennies more)

78 Use with pages 269–270.

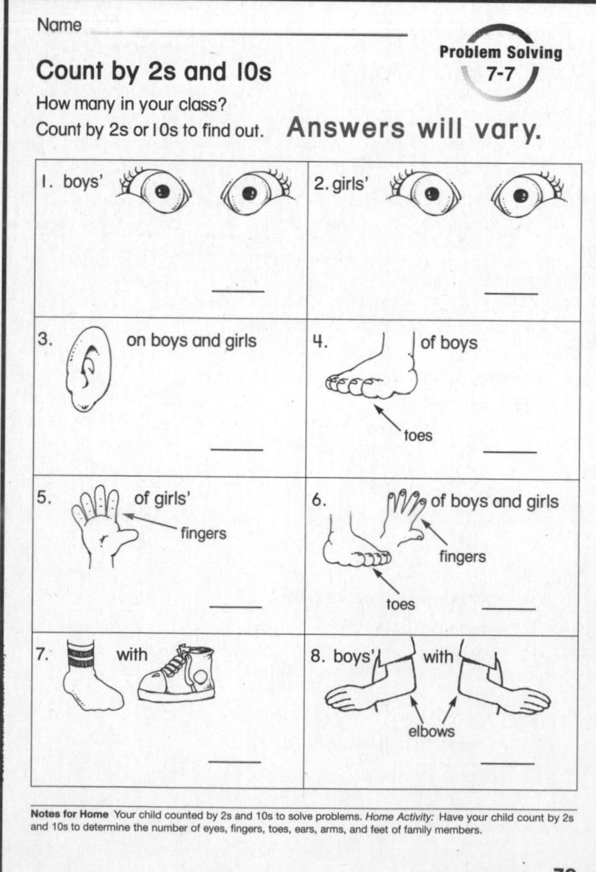

Name ______________________

Problem Solving 7-7

Count by 2s and 10s

How many in your class?

Count by 2s or 10s to find out. **Answers will vary.**

1. boys' (eyes) _____	2. girls' (eyes) _____
3. (ears) on boys and girls _____	4. (toes) of boys _____
5. (fingers) of girls' _____	6. (fingers and toes) of boys and girls _____
7. (sock) with (shoe) _____	8. boys' (elbows) with _____

Notes for Home Your child counted by 2s and 10s to solve problems. *Home Activity:* Have your child count by 2s and 10s to determine the number of eyes, fingers, toes, ears, arms, and feet of family members.

Use with pages 273–274. **79**

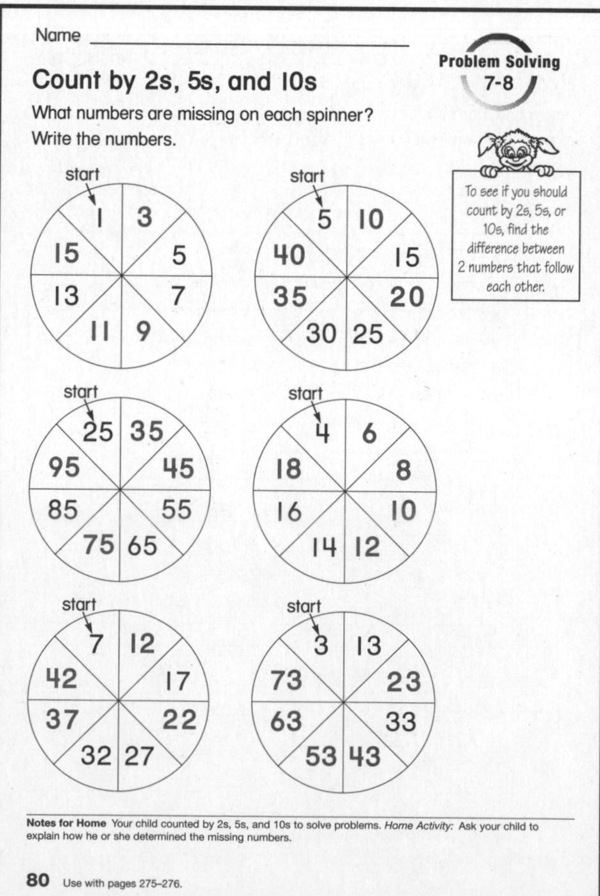

Name ______________________

Problem Solving 7-8

Count by 2s, 5s, and 10s

What numbers are missing on each spinner?

Write the numbers.

To see if you should count by 2s, 5s, or 10s, find the difference between 2 numbers that follow each other.

Notes for Home Your child counted by 2s, 5s, and 10s to solve problems. *Home Activity:* Ask your child to explain how he or she determined the missing numbers.

80 Use with pages 275–276.

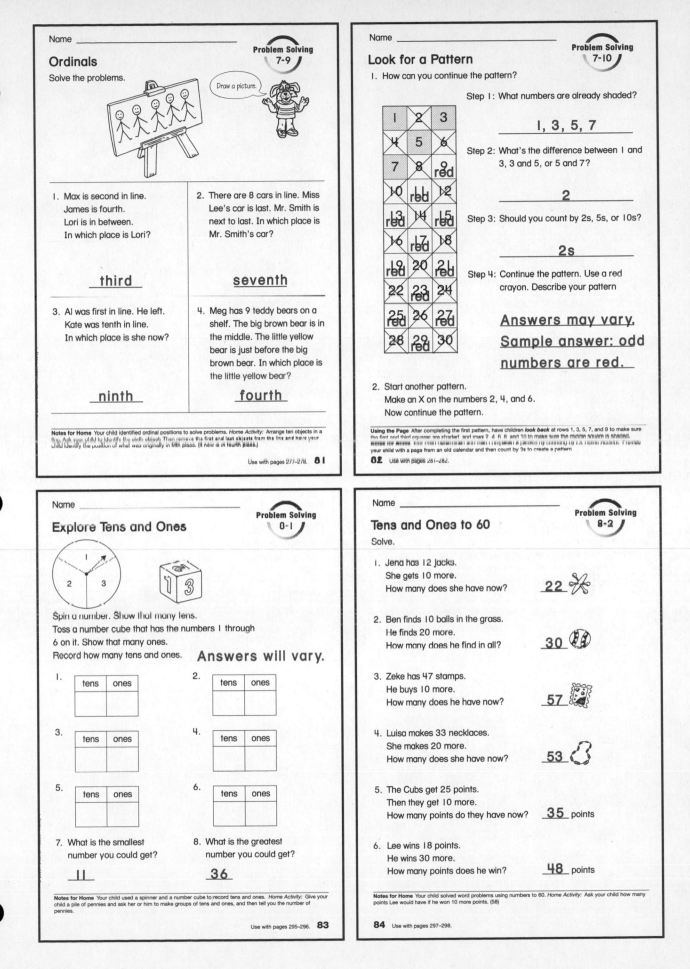

Name ______________________

Problem Solving 7-9

Ordinals

Solve the problems.

1. Max is second in line.
   James is fourth.
   Lori is in between.
   In which place is Lori?

   third

2. There are 8 cars in line. Miss Lee's car is last. Mr. Smith is next to last. In which place is Mr. Smith's car?

   seventh

3. Al was first in line. He left.
   Kate was tenth in line.
   In which place is she now?

   ninth

4. Meg has 9 teddy bears on a shelf. The big brown bear is in the middle. The little yellow bear is just before the big brown bear. In which place is the little yellow bear?

   fourth

Notes for Home Your child identified ordinal positions to solve problems. *Home Activity:* Arrange ten objects in a line. Ask your child to identify the sixth object. Then remove the first and last objects from the line and have your child identify the position of what was originally in fifth place. (It now is in fourth place.)

Name ______________________

Problem Solving 7-10

Look for a Pattern

1. How can you continue the pattern?

1	2	3
4	5	6
7	8	9 red
10	11 red	12
13 red	14	15 red
16	17 red	18
19 red	20	21 red
22	23 red	24
25 red	26	27 red
28	29 red	30

Step 1: What numbers are already shaded?

1, 3, 5, 7

Step 2: What's the difference between 1 and 3, 3 and 5, or 5 and 7?

2

Step 3: Should you count by 2s, 5s, or 10s?

2s

Step 4: Continue the pattern. Use a red crayon. Describe your pattern

Answers may vary. Sample answer: odd numbers are red.

2. Start another pattern.
   Make an X on the numbers 2, 4, and 6.
   Now continue the pattern.

Using the Page After completing the first pattern, have children ***look back*** at rows 1, 3, 5, 7, and 9 to make sure the first and third squares are shaded, and rows 2, 4, 6, 8, and 10 to make sure the middle square is shaded. **Notes for Home** [illegible] *Home Activity:* Provide your child with a page from an old calendar and then count by 3s to create a pattern

---

Name ______________________

Problem Solving 8-1

Explore Tens and Ones

1 2 3

Spin a number. Show that many tens.
Toss a number cube that has the numbers 1 through 6 on it. Show that many ones.
Record how many tens and ones.

Answers will vary.

1.

tens	ones

2.

tens	ones

3.

tens	ones

4.

tens	ones

5.

tens	ones

6.

tens	ones

7. What is the smallest number you could get?

   11

8. What is the greatest number you could get?

   36

Notes for Home Your child used a spinner and a number cube to record tens and ones. *Home Activity:* Give your child a pile of pennies and ask her or him to make groups of tens and ones, and then tell you the number of pennies.

Name ______________________

Problem Solving 8-2

Tens and Ones to 60

Solve.

1. Jena has 12 jacks.
   She gets 10 more.
   How many does she have now? 22

2. Ben finds 10 balls in the grass.
   He finds 20 more.
   How many does he find in all? 30

3. Zeke has 47 stamps.
   He buys 10 more.
   How many does he have now? 57

4. Luisa makes 33 necklaces.
   She makes 20 more.
   How many does she have now? 53

5. The Cubs get 25 points.
   Then they get 10 more.
   How many points do they have now? 35 points

6. Lee wins 18 points.
   He wins 30 more.
   How many points does he win? 48 points

Notes for Home Your child solved word problems using numbers to 60. *Home Activity:* Ask your child how many points Lee would have if he won 10 more points. (58)

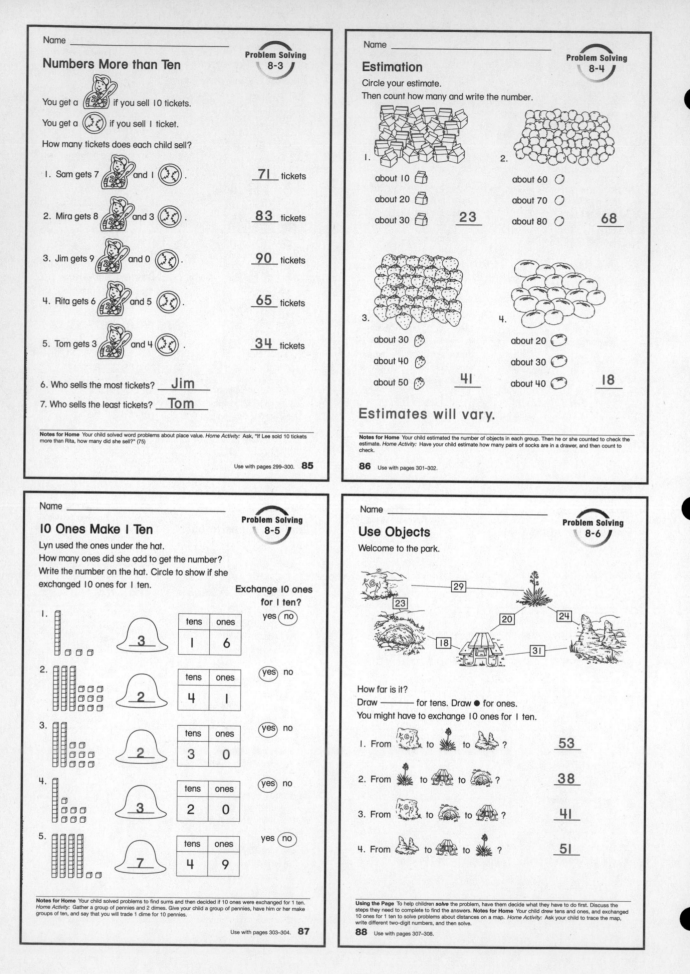

Name ______________________

Numbers More than Ten

Problem Solving 8-3

You get a (player card) if you sell 10 tickets.

You get a (ball) if you sell 1 ticket.

How many tickets does each child sell?

1. Sam gets 7 (player cards) and 1 (ball). 71 tickets
2. Mira gets 8 (player cards) and 3 (balls). 83 tickets
3. Jim gets 9 (player cards) and 0 (balls). 90 tickets
4. Rita gets 6 (player cards) and 5 (balls). 65 tickets
5. Tom gets 3 (player cards) and 4 (balls). 34 tickets
6. Who sells the most tickets? Jim
7. Who sells the least tickets? Tom

Notes for Home Your child solved word problems about place value. *Home Activity:* Ask, "If Lee sold 10 tickets more than Rita, how many did she sell?" (75)

Use with pages 299–300. **85**

Name ______________________

Estimation

Problem Solving 8-4

Circle your estimate.
Then count how many and write the number.

1.
about 10
about 20
about 30
23

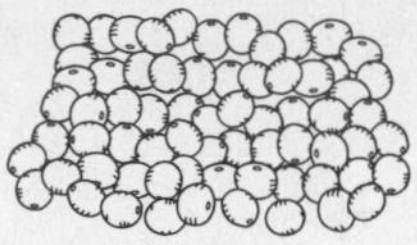

2.
about 60
about 70
about 80
68

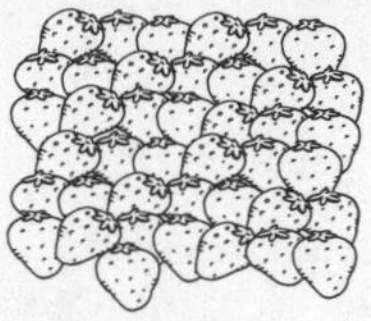

3.
about 30
about 40
about 50
41

4.
about 20
about 30
about 40
18

Estimates will vary.

Notes for Home Your child estimated the number of objects in each group. Then he or she counted to check the estimate. *Home Activity:* Have your child estimate how many pairs of socks are in a drawer, and then count to check.

86 Use with pages 301–302.

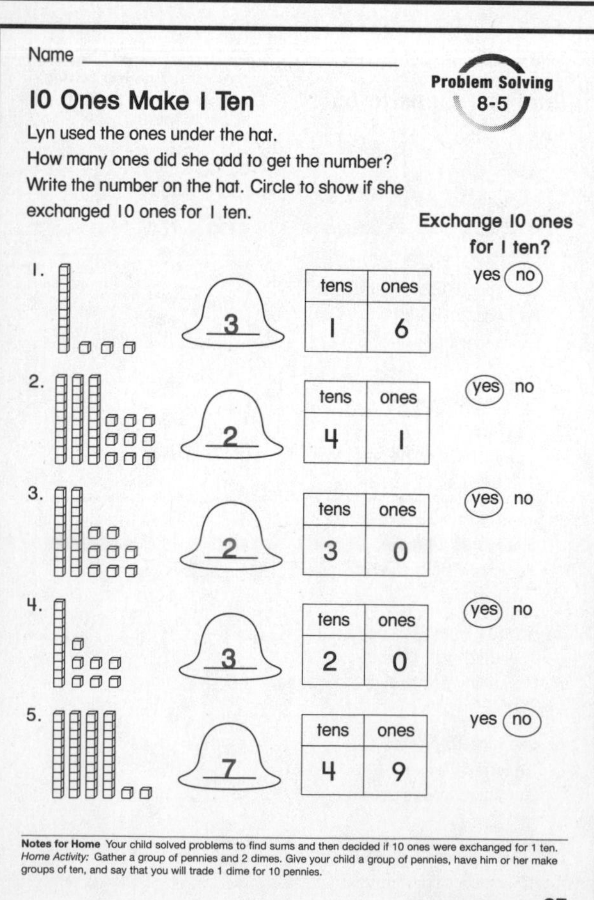

Name ______________________

10 Ones Make 1 Ten

Problem Solving 8-5

Lyn used the ones under the hat.
How many ones did she add to get the number?
Write the number on the hat. Circle to show if she exchanged 10 ones for 1 ten.

Exchange 10 ones for 1 ten?

1. 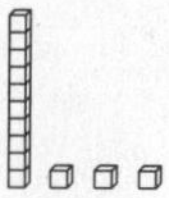 Hat: 3

tens	ones
1	6

yes (no)

2. 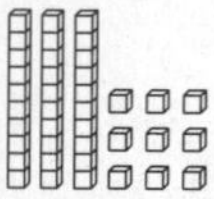 Hat: 2

tens	ones
4	1

(yes) no

3. 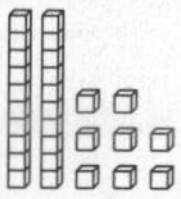 Hat: 2

tens	ones
3	0

(yes) no

4. 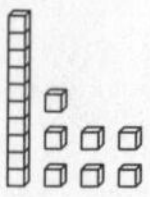 Hat: 3

tens	ones
2	0

(yes) no

5. 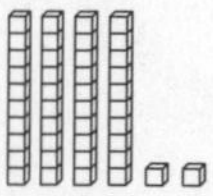 Hat: 7

tens	ones
4	9

yes (no)

Notes for Home Your child solved problems to find sums and then decided if 10 ones were exchanged for 1 ten. *Home Activity:* Gather a group of pennies and 2 dimes. Give your child a group of pennies, have him or her make groups of ten, and say that you will trade 1 dime for 10 pennies.

Use with pages 303–304. **87**

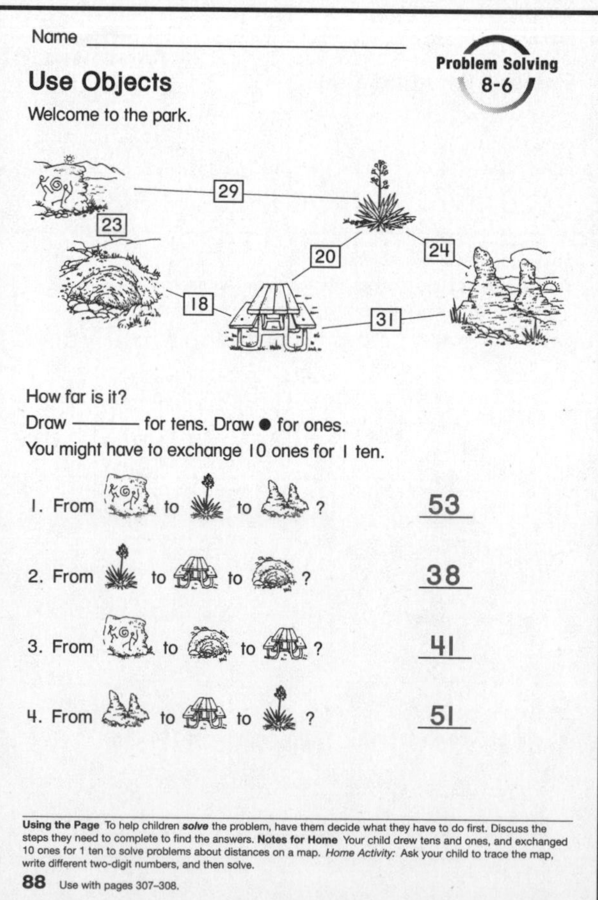

Name ______________________

Use Objects

Problem Solving 8-6

Welcome to the park.

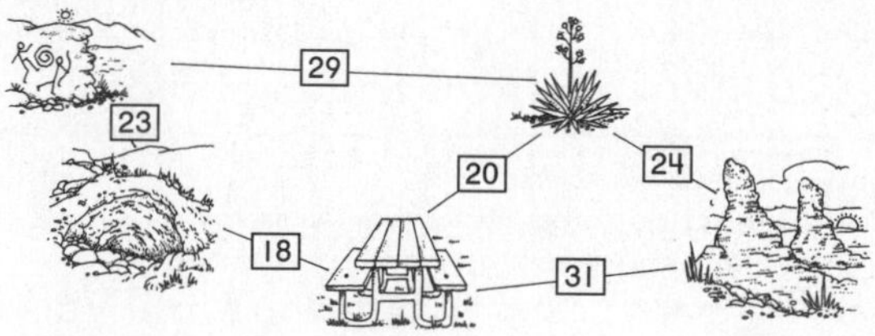

How far is it?
Draw ——— for tens. Draw ● for ones.
You might have to exchange 10 ones for 1 ten.

1. From (rock) to (plant) to (rocks)? 53
2. From (plant) to (table) to (cave)? 38
3. From (rock) to (cave) to (table)? 41
4. From (rocks) to (table) to (plant)? 51

Using the Page To help children *solve* the problem, have them decide what they have to do first. Discuss the steps they need to complete to find the answers. **Notes for Home** Your child drew tens and ones, and exchanged 10 ones for 1 ten to solve problems about distances on a map. *Home Activity:* Ask your child to trace the map, write different two-digit numbers, and then solve.

88 Use with pages 307–308.

Name ____________________

Problem Solving 8-7

Compare Numbers

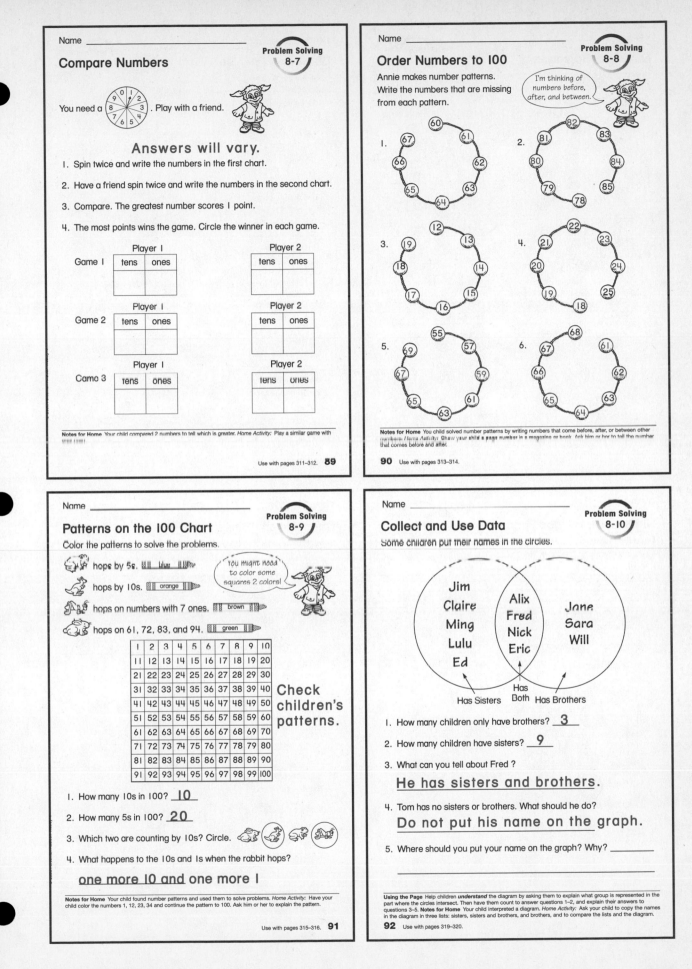

You need a [spinner]. Play with a friend.

Answers will vary.

1. Spin twice and write the numbers in the first chart.
2. Have a friend spin twice and write the numbers in the second chart.
3. Compare. The greatest number scores 1 point.
4. The most points wins the game. Circle the winner in each game.

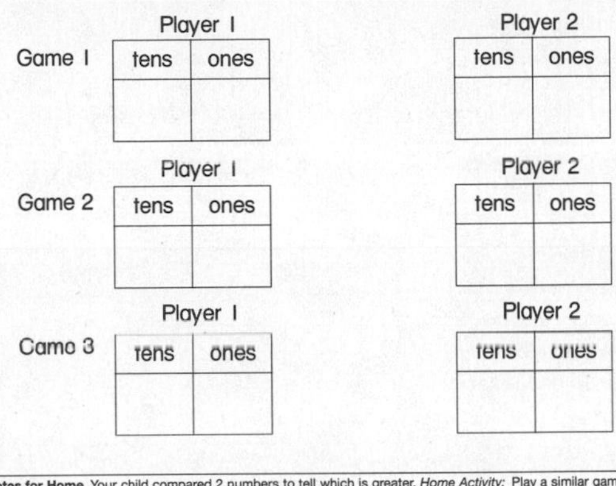

Game 1

Player 1	
tens	ones

Player 2	
tens	ones

Game 2

Player 1	
tens	ones

Player 2	
tens	ones

Game 3

Player 1	
tens	ones

Player 2	
tens	ones

Notes for Home Your child compared 2 numbers to tell which is greater. *Home Activity:* Play a similar game with [illegible]

Name ____________________

Problem Solving 8-8

Order Numbers to 100

Annie makes number patterns.
Write the numbers that are missing from each pattern.

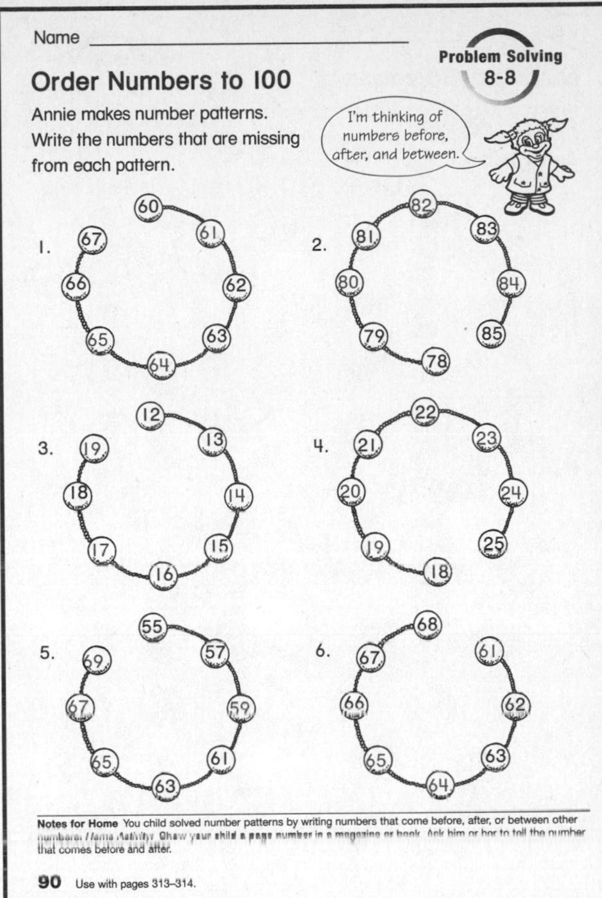

Notes for Home You child solved number patterns by writing numbers that come before, after, or between other numbers. *Home Activity:* Show your child a page number in a magazine or book. Ask him or her to tell the number that comes before and after.

Name ____________________

Problem Solving 8-9

Patterns on the 100 Chart

Color the patterns to solve the problems.

You might need to color some squares 2 colors!

[rabbit] hops by 5s. blue

[kangaroo] hops by 10s. orange

[grasshopper] hops on numbers with 7 ones. brown

[frog] hops on 61, 72, 83, and 94. green

1	2	3	4	5	6	7	8	9	10
11	12	13	14	15	16	17	18	19	20
21	22	23	24	25	26	27	28	29	30
31	32	33	34	35	36	37	38	39	40
41	42	43	44	45	46	47	48	49	50
51	52	53	54	55	56	57	58	59	60
61	62	63	64	65	66	67	68	69	70
71	72	73	74	75	76	77	78	79	80
81	82	83	84	85	86	87	88	89	90
91	92	93	94	95	96	97	98	99	100

Check children's patterns.

1. How many 10s in 100? **10**
2. How many 5s in 100? **20**
3. Which two are counting by 10s? Circle.
4. What happens to the 10s and 1s when the rabbit hops?

one more 10 and one more 1

Notes for Home Your child found number patterns and used them to solve problems. *Home Activity:* Have your child color the numbers 1, 12, 23, 34 and continue the pattern to 100. Ask him or her to explain the pattern.

Name ____________________

Problem Solving 8-10

Collect and Use Data

Some children put their names in the circles.

Jim
Claire
Ming
Lulu
Ed

Alix
Fred
Nick
Eric

Jane
Sara
Will

Has Sisters — Has Both — Has Brothers

1. How many children only have brothers? **3**
2. How many children have sisters? **9**
3. What can you tell about Fred?

He has sisters and brothers.

4. Tom has no sisters or brothers. What should he do?

Do not put his name on the graph.

5. Where should you put your name on the graph? Why? ____________________

____

Using the Page Help children ***understand*** the diagram by asking them to explain what group is represented in the part where the circles intersect. Then have them count to answer questions 1–2, and explain their answers to questions 3–5. **Notes for Home** Your child interpreted a diagram. *Home Activity:* Ask your child to copy the names in the diagram in three lists: sisters, sisters and brothers, and brothers, and to compare the lists and the diagram.

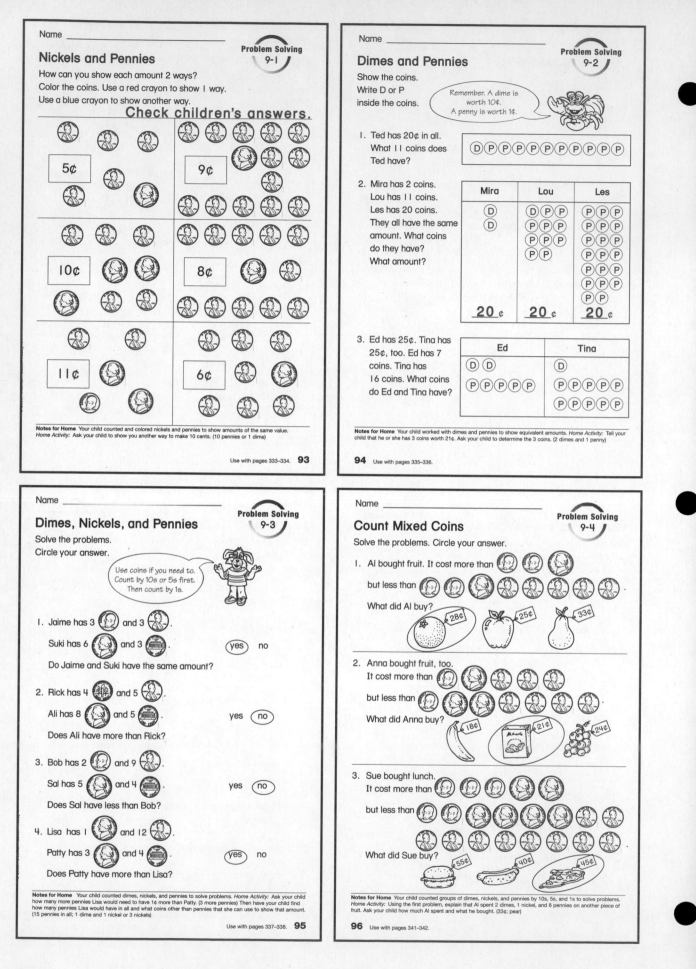

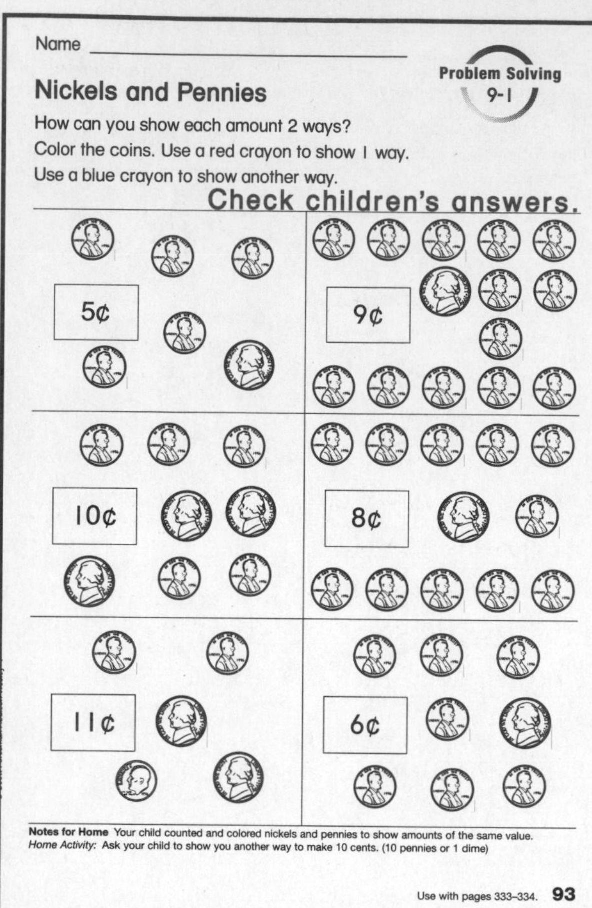

Name ______________________

Nickels and Pennies

Problem Solving 9-1

How can you show each amount 2 ways?
Color the coins. Use a red crayon to show 1 way.
Use a blue crayon to show another way.

Check children's answers.

5¢	9¢
10¢	8¢
11¢	6¢

Notes for Home Your child counted and colored nickels and pennies to show amounts of the same value. *Home Activity:* Ask your child to show you another way to make 10 cents. (10 pennies or 1 dime)

Use with pages 333–334. **93**

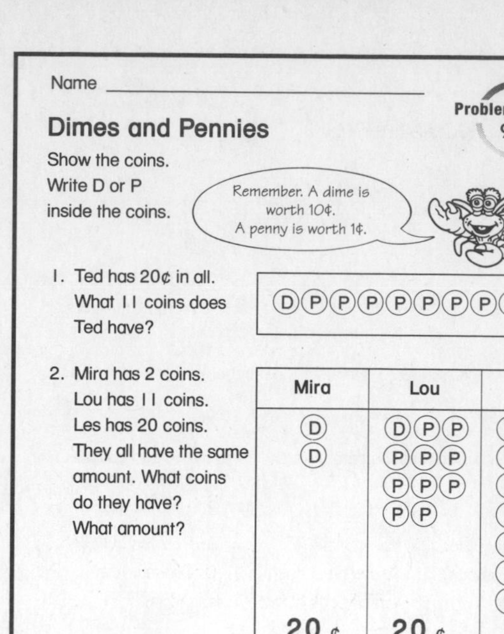

Name ______________________

Dimes and Pennies

Problem Solving 9-2

Show the coins.
Write D or P
inside the coins.

Remember. A dime is worth 10¢.
A penny is worth 1¢.

1. Ted has 20¢ in all. What 11 coins does Ted have?

   D P P P P P P P P P P

2. Mira has 2 coins. Lou has 11 coins. Les has 20 coins. They all have the same amount. What coins do they have? What amount?

Mira	Lou	Les
D D	D P P P P P P P P P P	P P P P P P P P P P P P P P P P P P P P
20 ¢	20 ¢	20 ¢

3. Ed has 25¢. Tina has 25¢, too. Ed has 7 coins. Tina has 16 coins. What coins do Ed and Tina have?

Ed	Tina
D D P P P P P	D P P P P P P P P P P P P P P P

Notes for Home Your child worked with dimes and pennies to show equivalent amounts. *Home Activity:* Tell your child that he or she has 3 coins worth 21¢. Ask your child to determine the 3 coins. (2 dimes and 1 penny)

94 Use with pages 335–336.

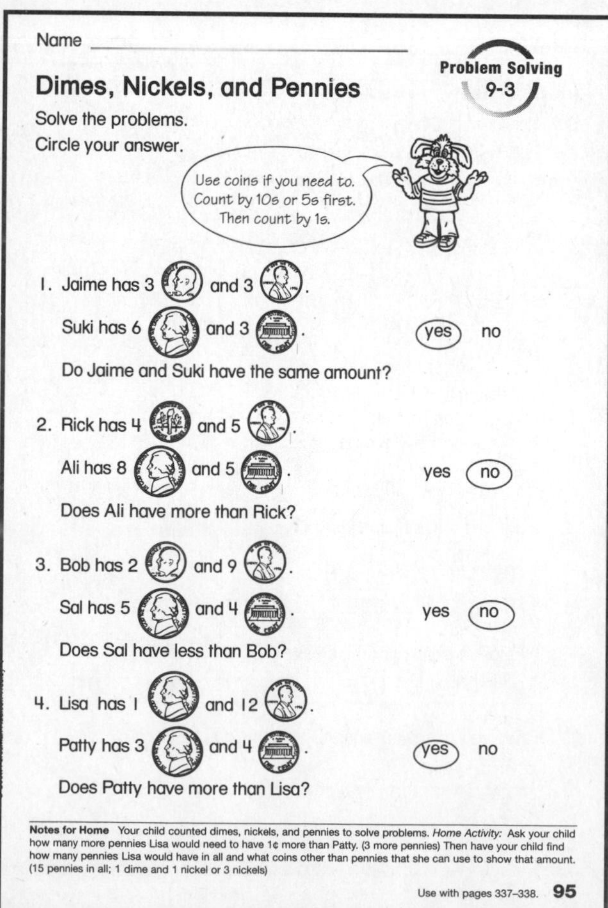

Name ______________________

Dimes, Nickels, and Pennies

Problem Solving 9-3

Solve the problems.
Circle your answer.

Use coins if you need to.
Count by 10s or 5s first.
Then count by 1s.

1. Jaime has 3 and 3 .
   Suki has 6 and 3 . (yes) no
   Do Jaime and Suki have the same amount?
2. Rick has 4 and 5 .
   Ali has 8 and 5 . yes (no)
   Does Ali have more than Rick?
3. Bob has 2 and 9 .
   Sal has 5 and 4 . yes (no)
   Does Sal have less than Bob?
4. Lisa has 1 and 12 .
   Patty has 3 and 4 . (yes) no
   Does Patty have more than Lisa?

Notes for Home Your child counted dimes, nickels, and pennies to solve problems. *Home Activity:* Ask your child how many more pennies Lisa would need to have 1¢ more than Patty. (3 more pennies) Then have your child find how many pennies Lisa would have in all and what coins other than pennies that she can use to show that amount. (15 pennies in all; 1 dime and 1 nickel or 3 nickels)

Use with pages 337–338. **95**

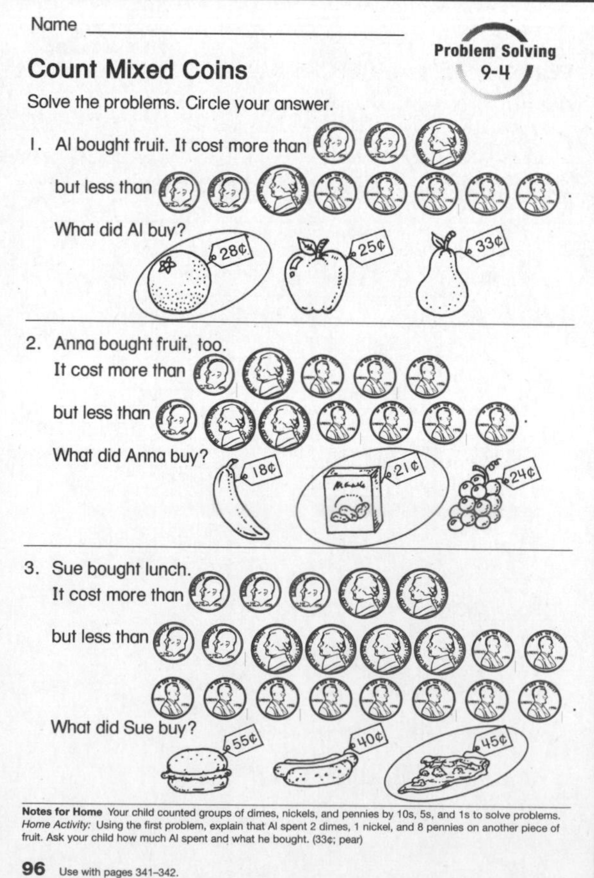

Name ______________________

Count Mixed Coins

Problem Solving 9-4

Solve the problems. Circle your answer.

1. Al bought fruit. It cost more than
   but less than .
   What did Al buy?
   28¢ 25¢ 33¢
2. Anna bought fruit, too.
   It cost more than
   but less than .
   What did Anna buy?
   18¢ 21¢ 24¢
3. Sue bought lunch.
   It cost more than
   but less than .
   What did Sue buy?
   55¢ 40¢ 45¢

Notes for Home Your child counted groups of dimes, nickels, and pennies by 10s, 5s, and 1s to solve problems. *Home Activity:* Using the first problem, explain that Al spent 2 dimes, 1 nickel, and 8 pennies on another piece of fruit. Ask your child how much Al spent and what he bought. (33¢; pear)

96 Use with pages 341–342.

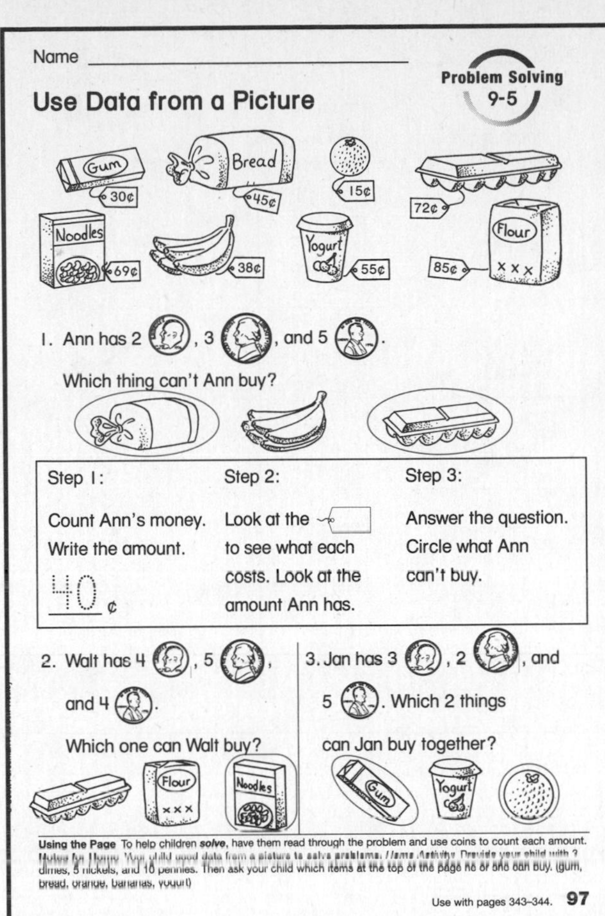

Name ______________________

Problem Solving 9-5

Use Data from a Picture

1. Ann has 2 , 3 , and 5 .

Which thing can't Ann buy?

Step 1:	Step 2:	Step 3:
Count Ann's money. Write the amount. 40 ¢	Look at the tag to see what each costs. Look at the amount Ann has.	Answer the question. Circle what Ann can't buy.

2. Walt has 4 , 5 , and 4 .

Which one can Walt buy?

3. Jan has 3 , 2 , and 5 . Which 2 things can Jan buy together?

Using the Page To help children *solve*, have them read through the problem and use coins to count each amount. Notes for Home Your child used data from a picture to solve problems. *Home Activity:* Provide your child with 2 dimes, 5 nickels, and 10 pennies. Then ask your child which items at the top of the page he or she can buy. (gum, bread, orange, bananas, yogurt)

Use with pages 343–344. 97

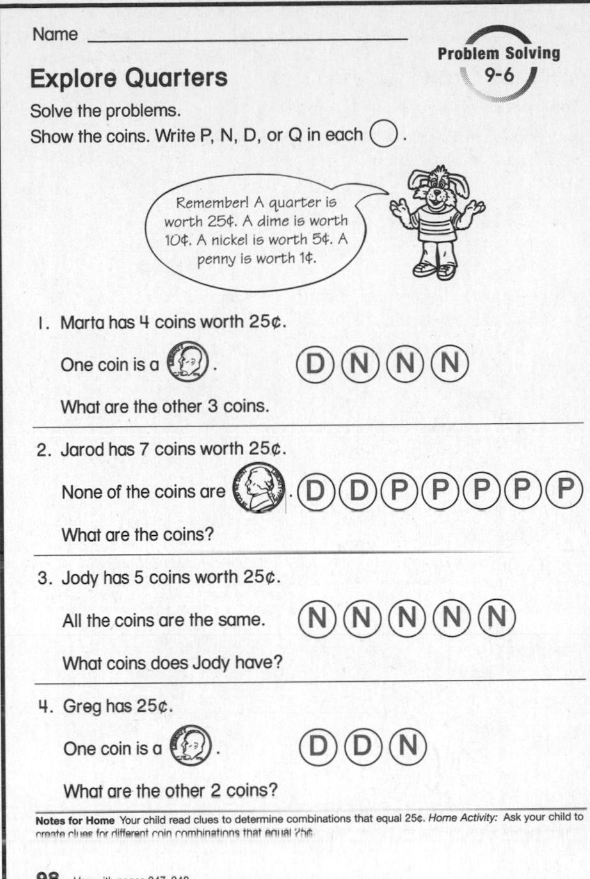

Name ______________________

Problem Solving 9-6

Explore Quarters

Solve the problems.

Show the coins. Write P, N, D, or Q in each ◯.

Remember! A quarter is worth 25¢. A dime is worth 10¢. A nickel is worth 5¢. A penny is worth 1¢.

1. Marta has 4 coins worth 25¢.

   One coin is a . (D) (N) (N) (N)

   What are the other 3 coins.

2. Jarod has 7 coins worth 25¢.

   None of the coins are . (D) (D) (P) (P) (P) (P) (P)

   What are the coins?

3. Jody has 5 coins worth 25¢.

   All the coins are the same. (N) (N) (N) (N) (N)

   What coins does Jody have?

4. Greg has 25¢.

   One coin is a . (D) (D) (N)

   What are the other 2 coins?

Notes for Home Your child read clues to determine combinations that equal 25¢. *Home Activity:* Ask your child to create clues for different coin combinations that equal 25¢.

98 Use with pages 347–348.

Name ______________________

Problem Solving 9-7

Quarters, Dimes, Nickels, and Pennies

What are the fewest number of coins that Herman can use to pay for each thing?

42¢

Q	D	N	P
1	1	1	2

49¢

Q	D	N	P
1	2		4

32¢

Q	D	N	P
1		1	2

26¢

Q	D	N	P
1			1

45¢

Q	D	N	P
1	2		

38¢

Q	D	N	P
1	1		3

Notes for Home Your child determined the fewest coins it would take to purchase each item. *Home Activity:* Ask your child to choose an item on the page and find another combination of coins to pay for it.

Use with pages 349–350. 99

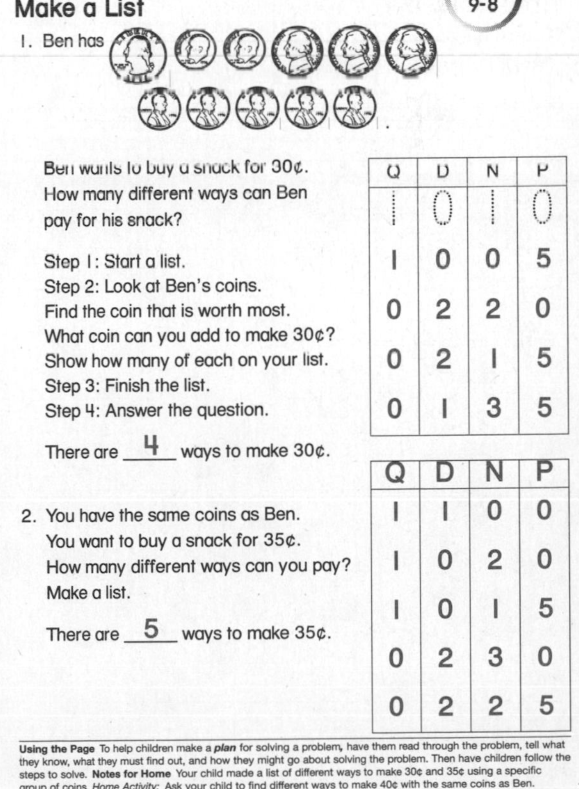

Name ______________________

Problem Solving 9-8

Make a List

1. Ben has .

Ben wants to buy a snack for 30¢.
How many different ways can Ben pay for his snack?

Step 1: Start a list.
Step 2: Look at Ben's coins.
Find the coin that is worth most.
What coin can you add to make 30¢?
Show how many of each on your list.
Step 3: Finish the list.
Step 4: Answer the question.

There are __4__ ways to make 30¢.

Q	D	N	P
1	0	1	0
1	0	0	5
0	2	2	0
0	2	1	5
0	1	3	5

2. You have the same coins as Ben.
You want to buy a snack for 35¢.
How many different ways can you pay?
Make a list.

There are __5__ ways to make 35¢.

Q	D	N	P
1	1	0	0
1	0	2	0
1	0	1	5
0	2	3	0
0	2	2	5

Using the Page To help children make a ***plan*** for solving a problem, have them read through the problem, tell what they know, what they must find out, and how they might go about solving the problem. Then have children follow the steps to solve. **Notes for Home** Your child made a list of different ways to make 30¢ and 35¢ using a specific group of coins. *Home Activity:* Ask your child to find different ways to make 40¢ with the same coins as Ben.

100 Use with pages 353–354.

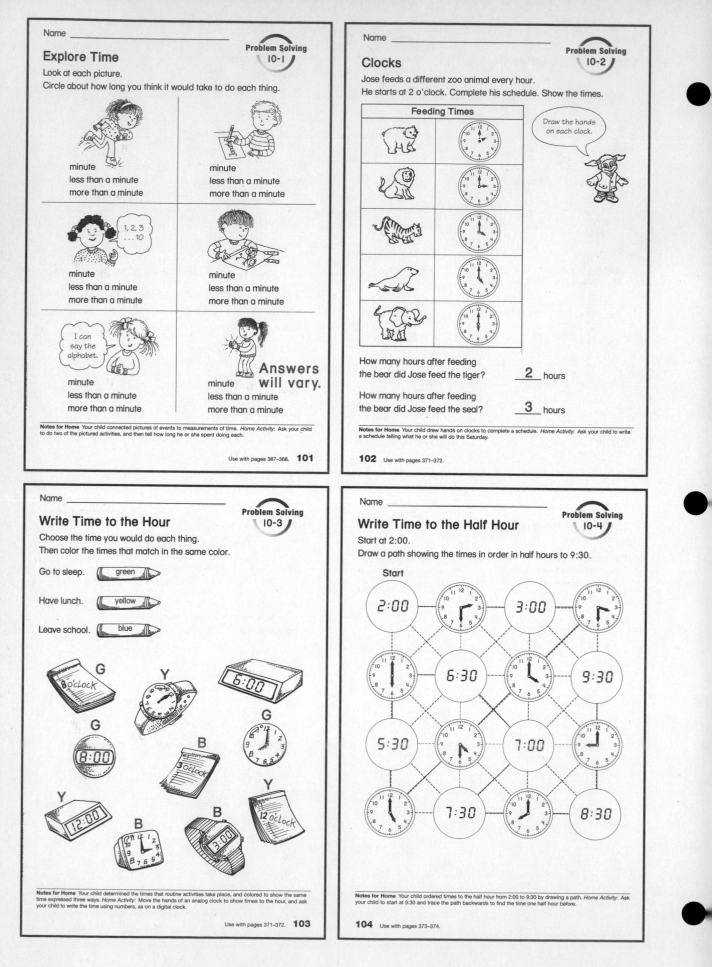

Name ____________________

Problem Solving 10-1

Explore Time

Look at each picture.

Circle about how long you think it would take to do each thing.

minute less than a minute more than a minute	minute less than a minute more than a minute
minute less than a minute more than a minute	minute less than a minute more than a minute
minute less than a minute more than a minute	minute less than a minute more than a minute

Answers will vary.

Notes for Home Your child connected pictures of events to measurements of time. *Home Activity:* Ask your child to do two of the pictured activities, and then tell how long he or she spent doing each.

Use with pages 367–368. **101**

Name ____________________

Problem Solving 10-2

Clocks

Jose feeds a different zoo animal every hour.

He starts at 2 o'clock. Complete his schedule. Show the times.

Feeding Times	

Draw the hands on each clock.

How many hours after feeding the bear did Jose feed the tiger? __2__ hours

How many hours after feeding the bear did Jose feed the seal? __3__ hours

Notes for Home Your child drew hands on clocks to complete a schedule. *Home Activity:* Ask your child to write a schedule telling what he or she will do this Saturday.

102 Use with pages 371–372.

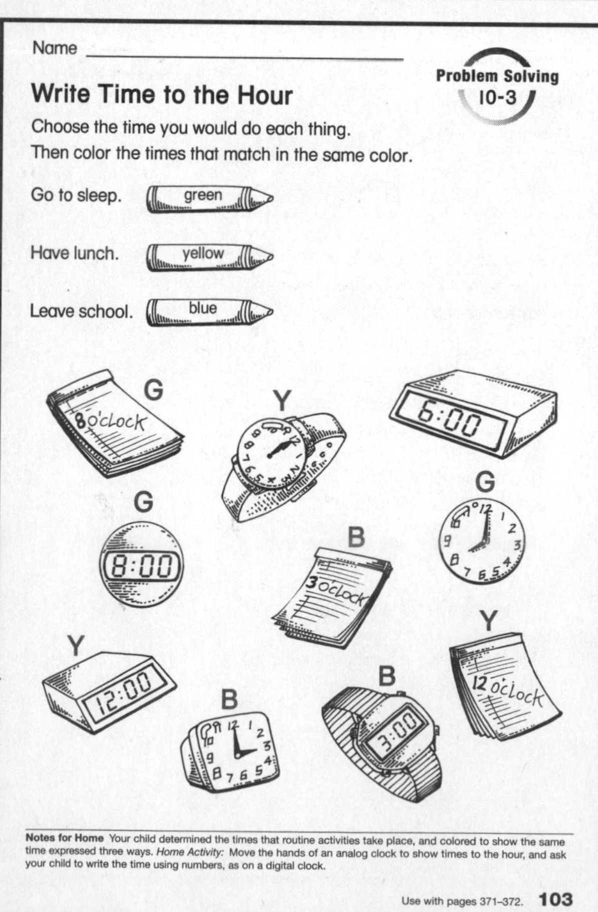
Name ____________________

Problem Solving 10-3

Write Time to the Hour

Choose the time you would do each thing.

Then color the times that match in the same color.

Go to sleep. green

Have lunch. yellow

Leave school. blue

Notes for Home Your child determined the times that routine activities take place, and colored to show the same time expressed three ways. *Home Activity:* Move the hands of an analog clock to show times to the hour, and ask your child to write the time using numbers, as on a digital clock.

Use with pages 371–372. **103**

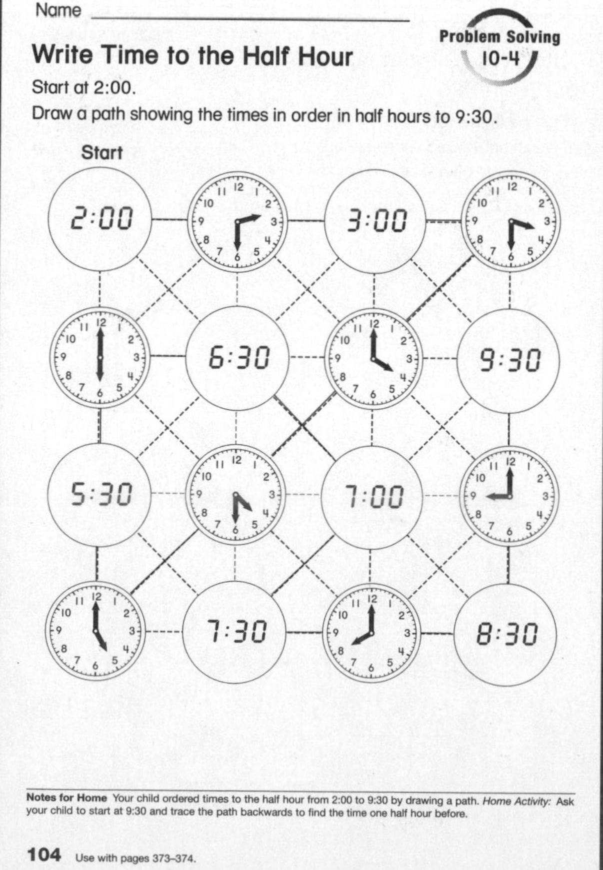
Name ____________________

Problem Solving 10-4

Write Time to the Half Hour

Start at 2:00.

Draw a path showing the times in order in half hours to 9:30.

Notes for Home Your child ordered times to the half hour from 2:00 to 9:30 by drawing a path. *Home Activity:* Ask your child to start at 9:30 and trace the path backwards to find the time one half hour before.

104 Use with pages 373–374.

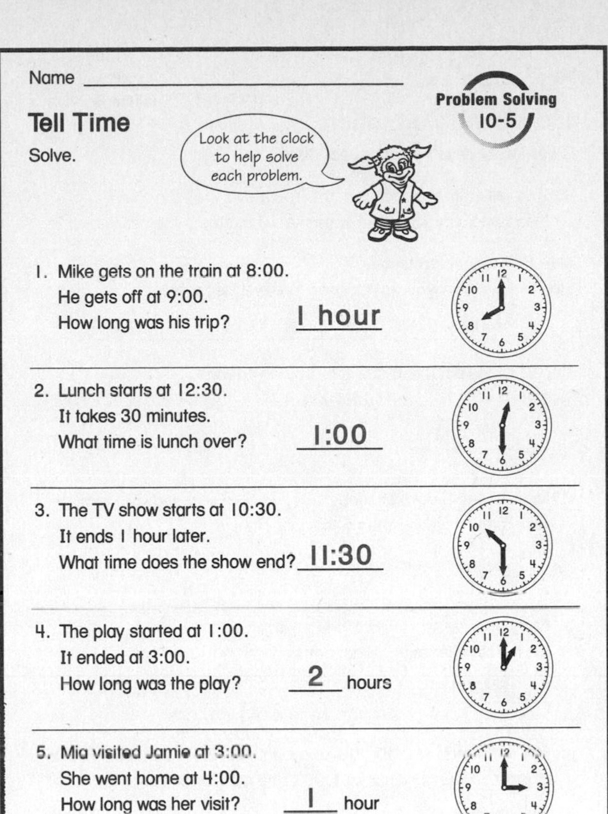

Name ______________________

Problem Solving 10-5

Tell Time

Solve.

Look at the clock to help solve each problem.

1. Mike gets on the train at 8:00.
   He gets off at 9:00.
   How long was his trip? I hour

2. Lunch starts at 12:30.
   It takes 30 minutes.
   What time is lunch over? 1:00

3. The TV show starts at 10:30.
   It ends 1 hour later.
   What time does the show end? 11:30

4. The play started at 1:00.
   It ended at 3:00.
   How long was the play? 2 hours

5. Mia visited Jamie at 3:00.
   She went home at 4:00.
   How long was her visit? I hour

Notes for Home Your child solved problems about time. *Home Activity:* With your child, note the times at which you begin activities such as eating dinner or watching a special television program. When you have finished the activity, note how much time has passed to the nearest hour or half hour.

Use with pages 375–376. **105**

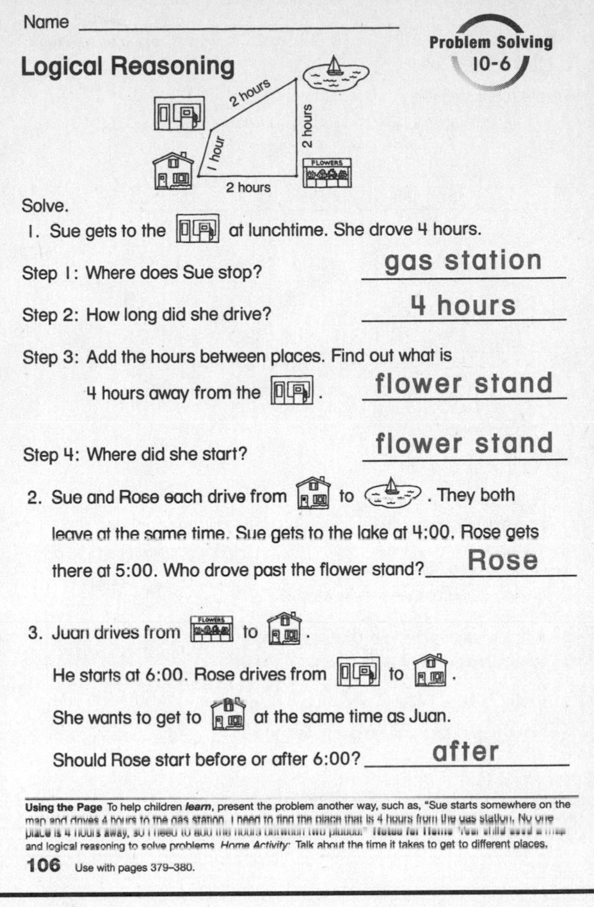

Name ______________________

Problem Solving 10-6

Logical Reasoning

Solve.

1. Sue gets to the [gas station] at lunchtime. She drove 4 hours.

   Step 1: Where does Sue stop? gas station

   Step 2: How long did she drive? 4 hours

   Step 3: Add the hours between places. Find out what is 4 hours away from the [gas station]. flower stand

   Step 4: Where did she start? flower stand

2. Sue and Rose each drive from [house] to [lake]. They both leave at the same time. Sue gets to the lake at 4:00. Rose gets there at 5:00. Who drove past the flower stand? Rose

3. Juan drives from [flower stand] to [house].
   He starts at 6:00. Rose drives from [gas station] to [house].
   She wants to get to [house] at the same time as Juan.
   Should Rose start before or after 6:00? after

Using the Page To help children ***learn***, present the problem another way, such as, "Sue starts somewhere on the map and drives 4 hours to the gas station. I need to find the place that is 4 hours from the gas station. No one place is 4 hours away, so I need to add the hours between two places." **Notes for Home** Your child used a map and logical reasoning to solve problems. *Home Activity:* Talk about the time it takes to get to different places.

106 Use with pages 379–380.

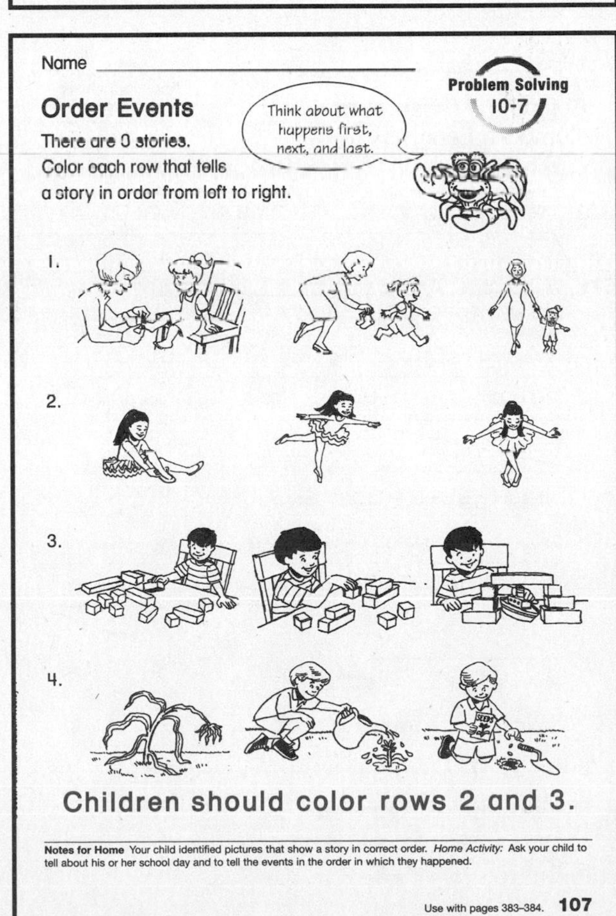

Name ______________________

Problem Solving 10-7

Order Events

There are 0 stories.
Color each row that tells a story in order from left to right.

Think about what happens first, next, and last.

1.

2.

3.

4.

Children should color rows 2 and 3.

Notes for Home Your child identified pictures that show a story in correct order. *Home Activity:* Ask your child to tell about his or her school day and to tell the events in the order in which they happened.

Use with pages 383–384. **107**

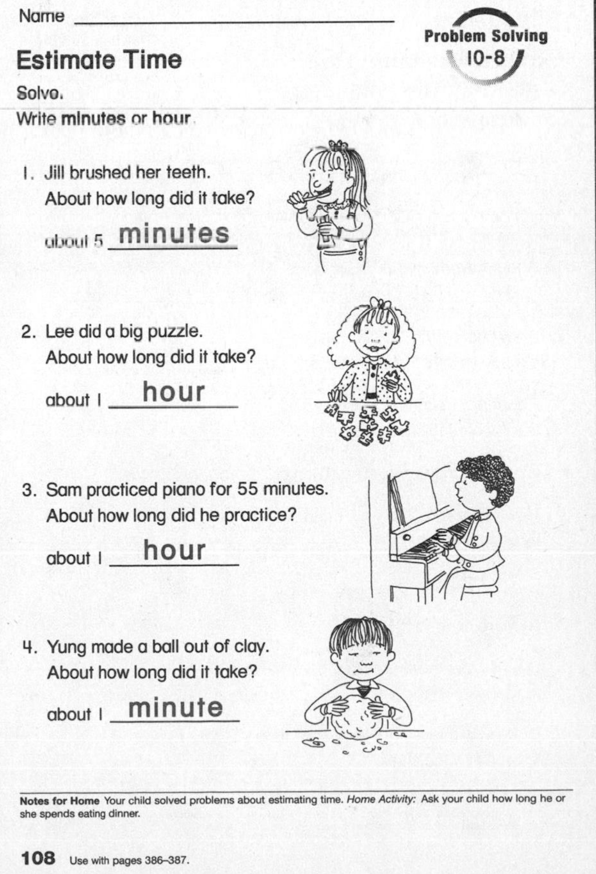

Name ______________________

Problem Solving 10-8

Estimate Time

Solve.
Write **minutes** or **hour**.

1. Jill brushed her teeth.
   About how long did it take?
   about 5 minutes

2. Lee did a big puzzle.
   About how long did it take?
   about 1 hour

3. Sam practiced piano for 55 minutes.
   About how long did he practice?
   about 1 hour

4. Yung made a ball out of clay.
   About how long did it take?
   about 1 minute

Notes for Home Your child solved problems about estimating time. *Home Activity:* Ask your child how long he or she spends eating dinner.

108 Use with pages 386–387.

Name ____________________

Calendar

Problem Solving 10-9

This is Al's calendar.

May						
S	M	T	W	T	F	S
			1	2	3	4
5	6	7	8	9	10	11
12	13	14	15	16	17	18
19	20	21	22	23	24	25
26	27	28	29	30	31	

Use the calendar.
Solve.

1. Al swims every Saturday.
How many times will he swim this month? 4 times

2. Al goes on a trip May 15th.
On what day of the week is May 15th? Wednesday

3. Al's birthday is the last Thursday in May.
What is the date of his birthday? May 30

4. Al gets a star each day he cleans his room.
How many stars can he get in May? 31 stars

Notes for Home Your child used a calendar to solve problems. *Home Activity:* Have your child use a calendar to find the month, date, and day of the week on which his or her birthday falls this year. Then look together for the birthdays of friends and family members.

Use with pages 387–388. **109**

Name ____________________

Too Much Information

Cross out what you do not need. Solve.

1. Ned will go the movies at 1:00. The movie lasts 2 hours.
Ned takes a bus for 30 minutes. At what time is the movie over?

Step 1: Read the problem.
Step 2: Find what you do not need to solve the problem.

Ned takes the bus for 30 minutes.

Step 3: Cross out the information you do not need.
Step 4: At what time is the movie over?

3:00

2. Mira missed 3 days of school. ~~She went to school on Monday.~~
How many days did she go to school that week?
2 days

3. ~~Story hour begins at 10:00.~~ Math is after story hour.
Art time is after math. What comes last?
art

4. Ray eats lunch at 1:30. Alix eats lunch at 12:30. ~~Pam eats dinner at 5:00.~~ Sam eats lunch at 1:00. Who eats lunch second?
Sam

Using the page To help children ***understand*** how to identify unnecessary information, ask them to read through the first problem to find the question being asked. Then have them read each sentence to see if they need the information to answer the question. **Notes for Home** Your child identified unnecessary information in order to solve problems. *Home Activity:* Ask your child to explain his or her answers.

110 Use with pages 391–392.

Name ____________________

Explore Measuring with Nonstandard Units

Problem Solving 11-1

Look at the snake.

Answers will vary.

1. About how many
long do you think the snake is? about _____ long

2. About how many
long do you think the snake is? about _____ long

3. About how many
long do you think the snake is? about _____ long

Now, use a string to measure. Then check your estimates.

4. How many , , and
long is the snake?

9   15   3

Circle more or fewer.

5. Did you use more or fewer than
to measure the snake? more (fewer)

6. Did you use more or fewer than
to measure the snake? (more) fewer

Notes for Home Your child explored measurement using crayons, snap cubes, and paper clips. *Home Activity:* On a sheet of paper, draw a line to show the distance from your wrist to your elbow. Ask your child to estimate the length in pennies placed end to end and then measure to check.

Use with pages 405–406. **111**

Name ____________________

Estimate, Measure, and Compare Lengths

Problem Solving 11-2

Circle your estimates. All estimates may vary.

1. This is Lou's piece of string. This is Ali's piece of string.

Ali's string is 3 long.

About how long is Lou's string? 3 (7) 9 12

2. This is Jim's piece of string. This is Meg's piece of string.

Jim's string is about 6 long.

About how long is Meg's piece of string? 2 (4) 10 12

3. This is Jen's piece of string. This is Mark's piece of string.

Mark's string is about 4 long.

About how long is Jen's string? 2 (5) 8 10

Now use a to measure and check your estimates.

Draw a line under each correct length.

Notes for Home Your child estimated and measured lengths of string. *Home Activity:* Cut two pieces of string into varying lengths. Have your child use a paper clip to measure the length of one piece of string and then estimate the length of the other before measuring to check.

112 Use with pages 407–408.

Name ______________________

Problem Solving 11-3

Estimate and Measure with Inches

1. Look at line A.

A ______________________

All estimates may vary.

About how many inches long is it?
Estimate. Then measure it to check. Use an inch ruler.

about _____ inches   __4__ inches

2. Look at line B. Then look at line A.

B ______________________________

About how many inches longer is line B than line A?
Estimate. Then measure to check.

about _____ inches longer   __2__ inches longer

3. Look at line C. Then look at line B.

C __________

About how many inches shorter is line C than line B?
Estimate. Then measure to check.

about _____ inches shorter   __4__ inches shorter

4. Look at line C. Then look at line A.
About how many inches shorter is line C than line A?
Estimate. Then measure to check.

about _____ inches shorter   __2__ inches shorter

Notes for Home Your child estimated, compared, and then measured line lengths with an inch ruler. [illegible]
Ask your child to estimate how much longer and shorter each line is before measuring to check.

Name ______________________

Problem Solving 11-4

Compare to One Foot

Remember! There are 12 inches in a foot.

1. Carl has a big [robot]. It is 1 foot and 1 inch tall. About how many inches tall is it?

__13__ inches tall

2. [dog] Boots' tail is 1 foot long. Spot's tail is 3 inches shorter. About how many inches long is Spot's tail?

__9__ inches long

3. Max has a toy [truck]. It is 2 inches shorter than 1 foot. How long is it?

__10__ inches long

4. Sam's [table] is 1 foot and 6 inches across. How wide is it?

__18__ inches wide

5. Gina's [bear] is 1 foot tall. Lea's [bear] is 4 inches taller. How tall is Lea's [bear]?

__16__ inches tall

6. Patty's [doll] is 1 foot tall. Meg's [doll] is 8 inches. How much shorter is Meg's doll?

__4__ inches shorter

Notes for Home Your child solved problems involving measurements of 1 foot. *Home Activity:* Have your child measure household items that are longer and shorter than 1 foot, and then find the difference.

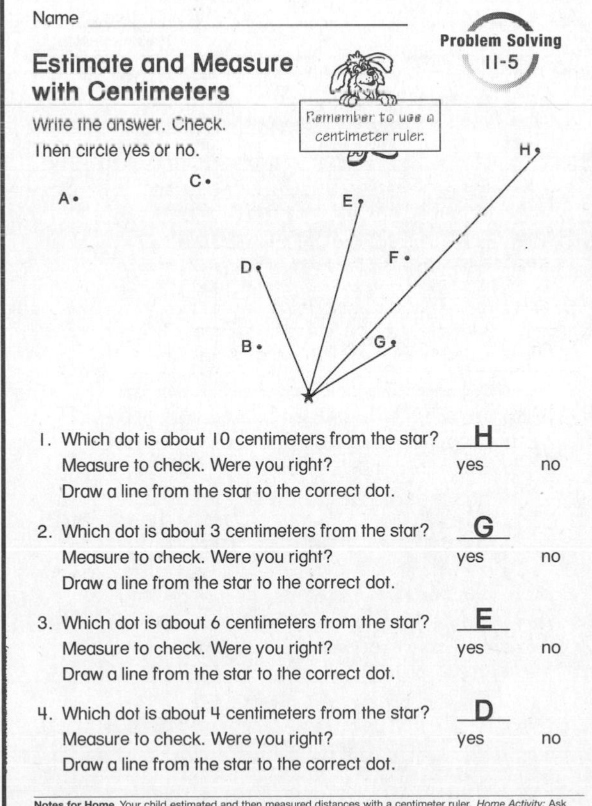

Name ______________________

Problem Solving 11-5

Estimate and Measure with Centimeters

Write the answer. Check.
Then circle yes or no.

Remember to use a centimeter ruler.

1. Which dot is about 10 centimeters from the star? __H__
Measure to check. Were you right? yes no
Draw a line from the star to the correct dot.

2. Which dot is about 3 centimeters from the star? __G__
Measure to check. Were you right? yes no
Draw a line from the star to the correct dot.

3. Which dot is about 6 centimeters from the star? __E__
Measure to check. Were you right? yes no
Draw a line from the star to the correct dot.

4. Which dot is about 4 centimeters from the star? __D__
Measure to check. Were you right? yes no
Draw a line from the star to the correct dot.

Notes for Home Your child estimated and then measured distances with a centimeter ruler. *Home Activity:* Ask your child to draw a dot that is 1 centimter from the star.

Name ______________________

Problem Solving 11-6

Group Decision Making

Work in a small group.

1. Ed, Ted, and Fred want to measure something.
Choose an object for them. Then follow the steps below.

Step 1 Decide what to measure. Draw it.	**Step 2** Decide what tools to use to measure. Draw what to do.	**Step 3** Estimate how big it is.	**Step 4** Measure to find how big it is.
Answers will vary.		about ____ inches	____ inches

2. As a group, choose something else to measure.
Follow the steps. Find how big around it is.

		about ____ inches	____ inches

Using the Page To help children *plan*, have them suggest the most effective way to measure the rim of the wastebasket and to explain the reason for their choices. **Notes for Home** Your child worked with a group to solve measurement problems. *Home Activity:* Have your child use a tape measure, a string and ruler, or a string and a yardstick to measure around an object in your home.

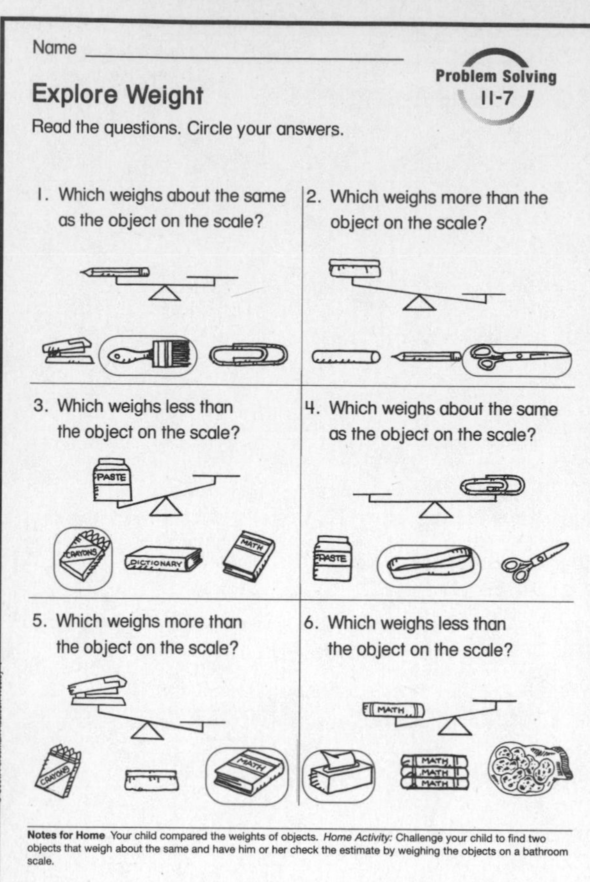
Name
Problem Solving 11-7
Explore Weight
Read the questions. Circle your answers.
1. Which weighs about the same as the object on the scale?
2. Which weighs more than the object on the scale?
3. Which weighs less than the object on the scale?
4. Which weighs about the same as the object on the scale?
5. Which weighs more than the object on the scale?
6. Which weighs less than the object on the scale?
Notes for Home Your child compared the weights of objects. Home Activity: Challenge your child to find two objects that weigh about the same and have him or her check the estimate by weighing the objects on a bathroom scale.
Use with pages 421–422. 117

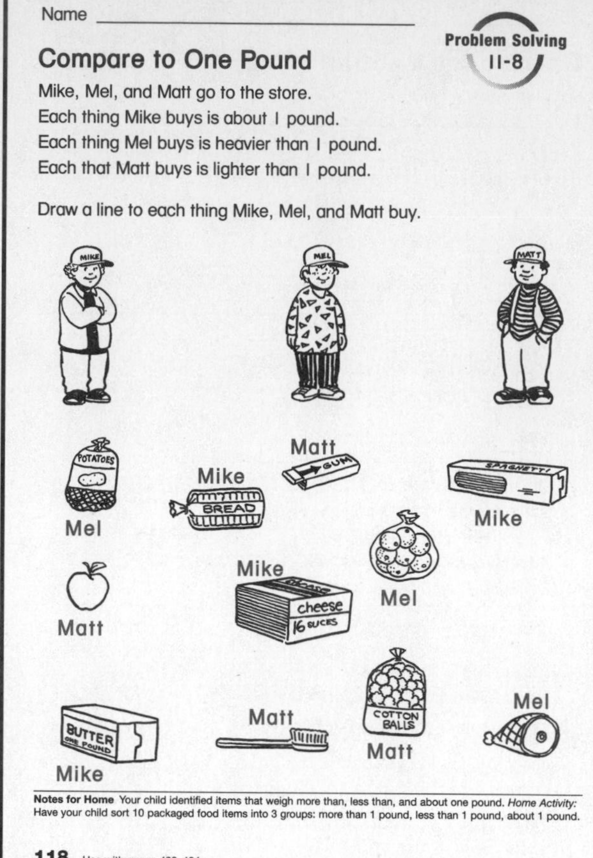
Name
Problem Solving 11-8
Compare to One Pound
Mike, Mel, and Matt go to the store.
Each thing Mike buys is about 1 pound.
Each thing Mel buys is heavier than 1 pound.
Each that Matt buys is lighter than 1 pound.
Draw a line to each thing Mike, Mel, and Matt buy.
Notes for Home Your child identified items that weigh more than, less than, and about one pound. Home Activity: Have your child sort 10 packaged food items into 3 groups: more than 1 pound, less than 1 pound, about 1 pound.
118 Use with pages 423–424.

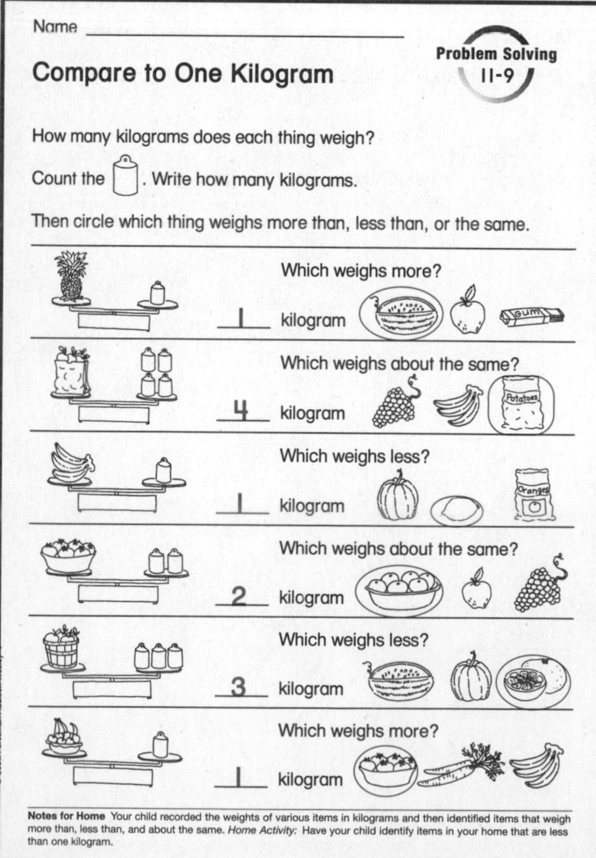
Name
Problem Solving 11-9
Compare to One Kilogram
How many kilograms does each thing weigh?
Count the . Write how many kilograms.
Then circle which thing weighs more than, less than, or the same.
Which weighs more?
kilogram
Which weighs about the same?
kilogram
Which weighs less?
kilogram
Which weighs about the same?
kilogram
Which weighs less?
kilogram
Which weighs more?
kilogram
Notes for Home Your child recorded the weights of various items in kilograms and then identified items that weigh more than, less than, and about the same. Home Activity: Have your child identify items in your home that are less than one kilogram.
Use with pages 425–426. 119

Name
Problem Solving 11-10
Compare Cups, Pints, and Quarts
Remember. One pint is the same as 2 cups.
One quart equals 2 pints or 4 cups.
1. Jack has 2 pints of water. Jill has 1 quart of water. Does Jack have more than, less than, or the same amount of water as Jill? Color the cups to see.
Jack
Jill
2. Jack and Jill each made juice. Jack made 2 pints of juice. Jill made a quart of juice. Then she made another pint. Did Jack make more than, less than, or the same amount of juice as Jill? Color the cups to see.
Jack
Jill
3. Jack bought 1 quart of green paint and 1 quart of yellow paint. Jill bought 2 pints of blue paint and 1 pint of red paint. Did Jack buy more than, less than, or the same amount of paint as Jill? Color the cups to see.
Jack
Jill
Notes for Home Your child solved problems by comparing quarts and pints with cups. Home Activity: Fill various containers with water. Ask your child if the container holds about 1 cup, 1 pint, or 1 quart. Then help your child to measure to check.
120 Use with pages 427–428.

Name ______________________

Problem Solving 11-11

Compare to One Liter

Draw a picture to solve each problem.

1. Ben went to the store. He bought 1 bottle of apple juice, 2 bottles of grape juice, and 3 bottles of orange juice. Each bottle holds 1 liter. How many liters of juice did he buy?

   6 liters **Sample drawings are shown.**

2. Mrs. Lee made 1 pot of vegetable soup and 1 pot of chicken soup. Each pot holds 2 liters. How many liters of soup did she make?

   4 liters

3. Mr. James' class made 3 bowls of punch for the party. Each bowl holds 5 liters. How many liters of punch did the class make?

   15 liters

4. There are 4 first grade classes. Each class drank 10 liters of juice in 1 week. How many liters did the first grade classes drink in all?

   40 liters

Notes for Home Your child determined how many liters in all by drawing pictures and counting by ones, twos, [illegible] his or her own problem.

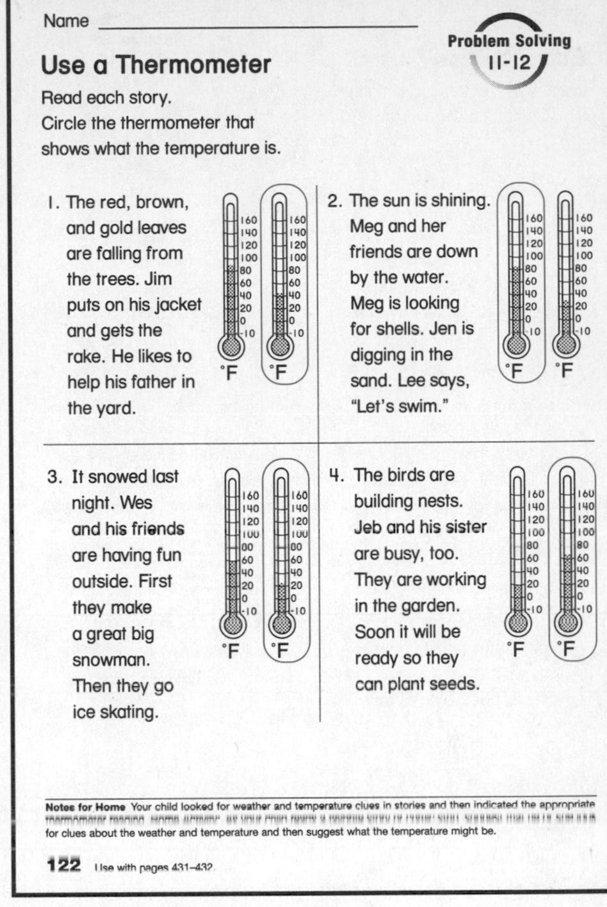

Name ______________________

Problem Solving 11-12

Use a Thermometer

Read each story.
Circle the thermometer that shows what the temperature is.

1. The red, brown, and gold leaves are falling from the trees. Jim puts on his jacket and gets the rake. He likes to help his father in the yard.

2. The sun is shining. Meg and her friends are down by the water. Meg is looking for shells. Jen is digging in the sand. Lee says, "Let's swim."

3. It snowed last night. Wes and his friends are having fun outside. First they make a great big snowman. Then they go ice skating.

4. The birds are building nests. Jeb and his sister are busy, too. They are working in the garden. Soon it will be ready so they can plant seeds.

Notes for Home Your child looked for weather and temperature clues in stories and then indicated the appropriate [illegible] for clues about the weather and temperature and then suggest what the temperature might be.

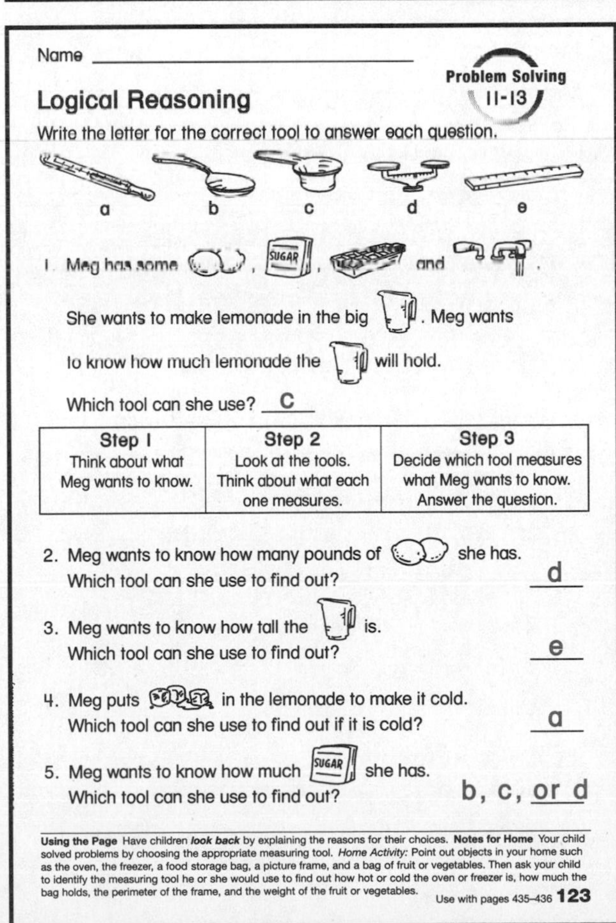

Name ______________________

Problem Solving 11-13

Logical Reasoning

Write the letter for the correct tool to answer each question.

a b c d e

1. Meg has some [lemons], [sugar], [ice], and [water]. She wants to make lemonade in the big [pitcher]. Meg wants to know how much lemonade the [pitcher] will hold.

   Which tool can she use? c

Step 1	Step 2	Step 3
Think about what Meg wants to know.	Look at the tools. Think about what each one measures.	Decide which tool measures what Meg wants to know. Answer the question.

2. Meg wants to know how many pounds of [lemons] she has. Which tool can she use to find out? d

3. Meg wants to know how tall the [pitcher] is. Which tool can she use to find out? e

4. Meg puts [ice] in the lemonade to make it cold. Which tool can she use to find out if it is cold? a

5. Meg wants to know how much SUGAR she has. Which tool can she use to find out? b, c, or d

Using the Page Have children ***look back*** by explaining the reasons for their choices. **Notes for Home** Your child solved problems by choosing the appropriate measuring tool. *Home Activity:* Point out objects in your home such as the oven, the freezer, a food storage bag, a picture frame, and a bag of fruit or vegetables. Then ask your child to identify the measuring tool he or she would use to find out how hot or cold the oven or freezer is, how much the bag holds, the perimeter of the frame, and the weight of the fruit or vegetables.

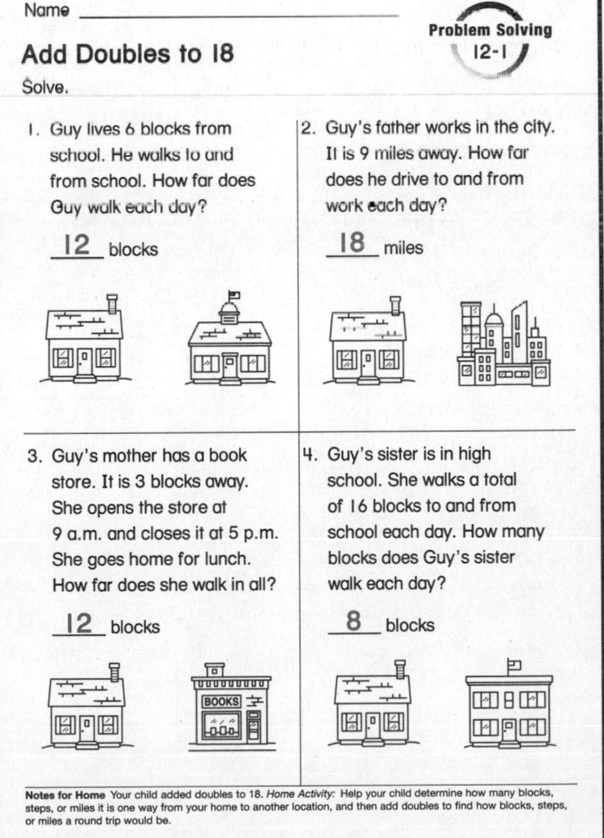

Name ______________________

Problem Solving 12-1

Add Doubles to 18

Solve.

1. Guy lives 6 blocks from school. He walks to and from school. How far does Guy walk each day?

   12 blocks

2. Guy's father works in the city. It is 9 miles away. How far does he drive to and from work each day?

   18 miles

3. Guy's mother has a book store. It is 3 blocks away. She opens the store at 9 a.m. and closes it at 5 p.m. She goes home for lunch. How far does she walk in all?

   12 blocks

4. Guy's sister is in high school. She walks a total of 16 blocks to and from school each day. How many blocks does Guy's sister walk each day?

   8 blocks

Notes for Home Your child added doubles to 18. *Home Activity:* Help your child determine how many blocks, steps, or miles it is one way from your home to another location, and then add doubles to find how blocks, steps, or miles a round trip would be.

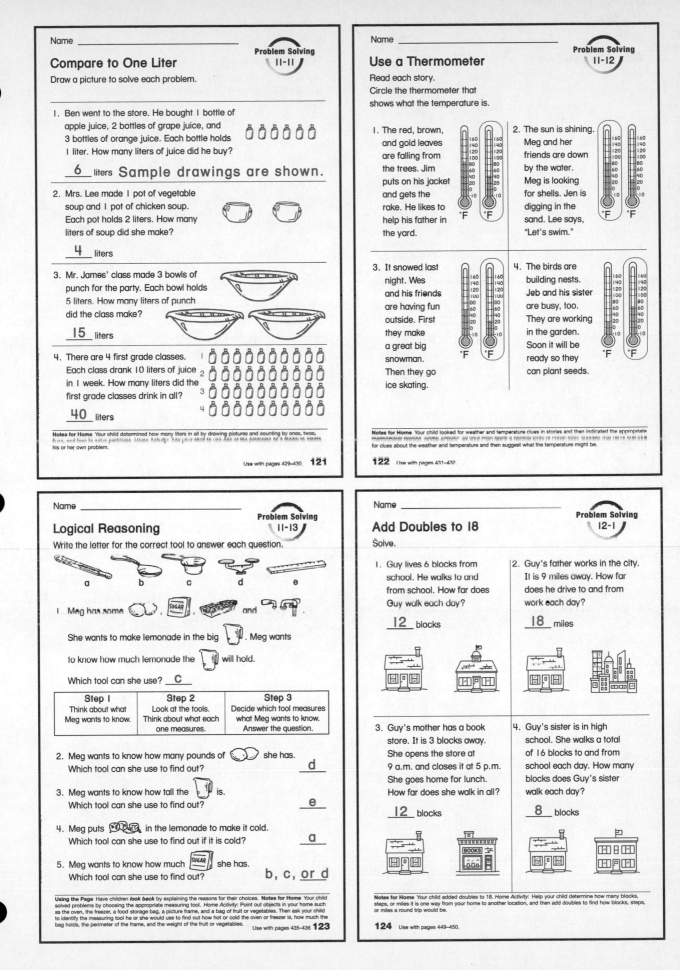

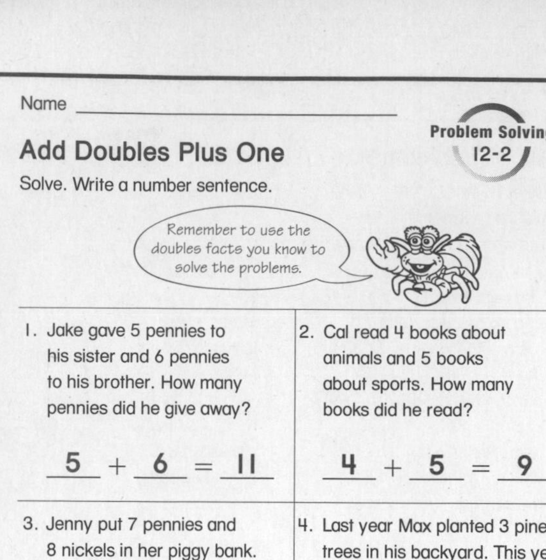

Name ______________________

Problem Solving 12-2

Add Doubles Plus One

Solve. Write a number sentence.

Remember to use the doubles facts you know to solve the problems.

1. Jake gave 5 pennies to his sister and 6 pennies to his brother. How many pennies did he give away?

   5 + 6 = 11

2. Cal read 4 books about animals and 5 books about sports. How many books did he read?

   4 + 5 = 9

3. Jenny put 7 pennies and 8 nickels in her piggy bank. How many coins did she put in her piggy bank?

   7 + 8 = 15

4. Last year Max planted 3 pine trees in his backyard. This year he planted 4 more trees. How many trees did he plant in all?

   3 + 4 = 7

5. Ben made 2 peanut butter sandwiches and 3 cheese sandwiches. How many sandwiches did he make?

   2 + 3 = 5

6. Alex peeled 6 red apples and 7 green apples. How many apples did he peel?

   6 + 7 = 13

Notes for Home Your child added doubles plus one facts. *Home Activity:* Ask your child to write the doubles fact for each problem. (1. 5 + 5 = 10, 2. 4 + 4 = 8, 3. 7 + 7 = 14, 4. 3 + 3 = 6, 5. 2 + 2 = 4, 6. 6 + 6 = 12).

Use with pages 451–452. **125**

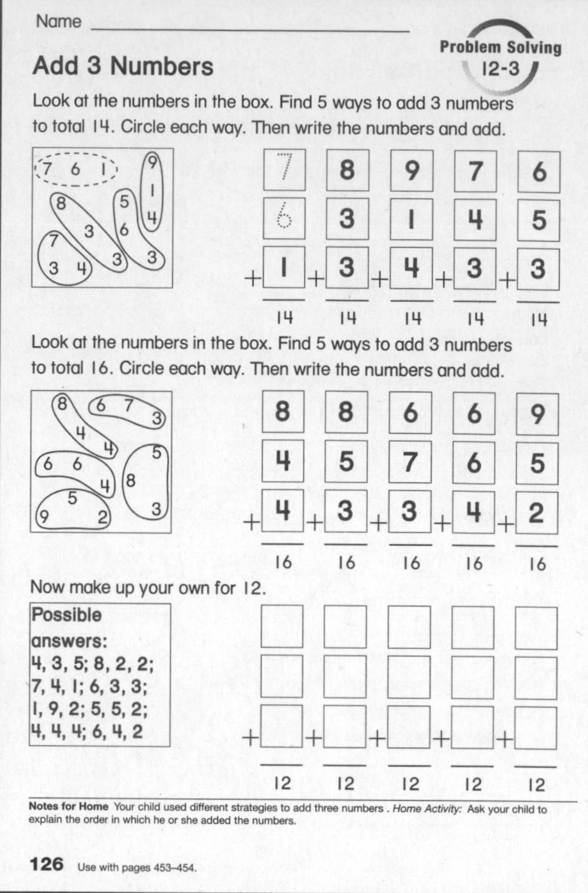

Name ______________________

Problem Solving 12-3

Add 3 Numbers

Look at the numbers in the box. Find 5 ways to add 3 numbers to total 14. Circle each way. Then write the numbers and add.

7	8	9	7	6
6	3	1	4	5
+ 1	+ 3	+ 4	+ 3	+ 3
14	14	14	14	14

Look at the numbers in the box. Find 5 ways to add 3 numbers to total 16. Circle each way. Then write the numbers and add.

8	8	6	6	9
4	5	7	6	5
+ 4	+ 3	+ 3	+ 4	+ 2
16	16	16	16	16

Now make up your own for 12.

Possible answers:
4, 3, 5; 8, 2, 2; 7, 4, 1; 6, 3, 3; 1, 9, 2; 5, 5, 2; 4, 4, 4; 6, 4, 2

+	+	+	+	+
12	12	12	12	12

Notes for Home Your child used different strategies to add three numbers . *Home Activity:* Ask your child to explain the order in which he or she added the numbers.

126 Use with pages 453–454.

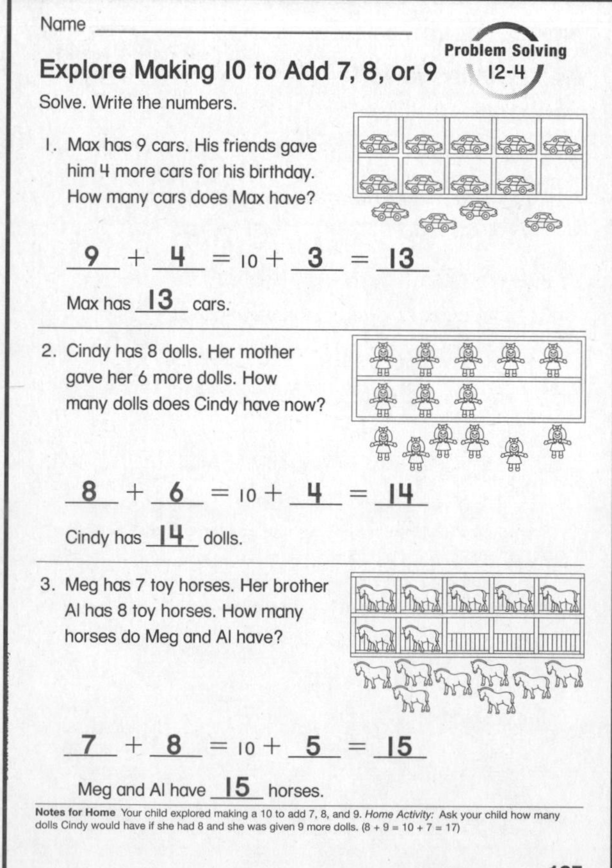

Name ______________________

Problem Solving 12-4

Explore Making 10 to Add 7, 8, or 9

Solve. Write the numbers.

1. Max has 9 cars. His friends gave him 4 more cars for his birthday. How many cars does Max have?

   9 + 4 = 10 + 3 = 13

   Max has 13 cars.

2. Cindy has 8 dolls. Her mother gave her 6 more dolls. How many dolls does Cindy have now?

   8 + 6 = 10 + 4 = 14

   Cindy has 14 dolls.

3. Meg has 7 toy horses. Her brother Al has 8 toy horses. How many horses do Meg and Al have?

   7 + 8 = 10 + 5 = 15

   Meg and Al have 15 horses.

Notes for Home Your child explored making a 10 to add 7, 8, and 9. *Home Activity:* Ask your child how many dolls Cindy would have if she had 8 and she was given 9 more dolls. (8 + 9 = 10 + 7 = 17)

Use with pages 457–458. **127**

Name ______________________

Problem Solving 12-5

Make 10 When Adding 7, 8, or 9

Lisa is having a party. There will be 14 children in all. Use the picture to answer the questions.

1. How many [party hats] does Lisa have? 6
   How many more [party hats] does she need? 8 more
2. How many [balloons] does Lisa have? 0
   How many more [balloons] does she need? 14 more
3. How many [cups] does Lisa have? 9
   How many more [cups] does she need? 5 more
4. How many [noisemakers] does Lisa have? 14
   How many more [noisemakers] does she need? 0 more
5. How many [napkins] does Lisa have? 5
   How many more [napkins] does she need? 9 more

Notes for Home Your child added numbers including 7, 8, 9. *Home Activity:* Ask your child how many more balloons Lisa would need if she had only 10. (4 more balloons)

128 Use with pages 459–460.

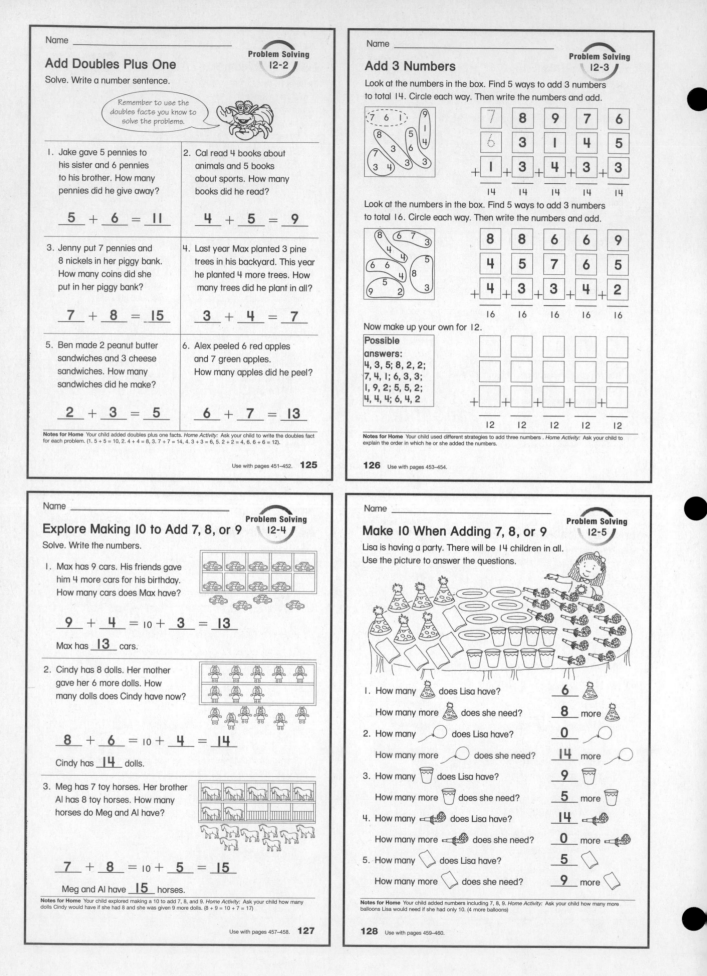

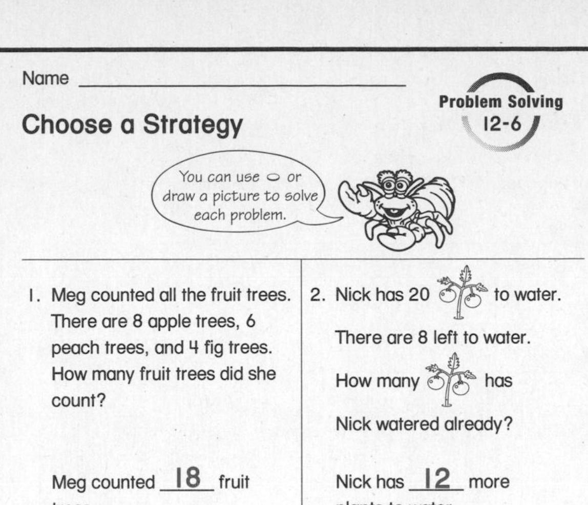

Name ______________________

Choose a Strategy

Problem Solving 12-6

You can use ⊂⊃ or draw a picture to solve each problem.

1. Meg counted all the fruit trees. There are 8 apple trees, 6 peach trees, and 4 fig trees. How many fruit trees did she count?

   Meg counted __18__ fruit trees.

2. Nick has 20 [plants] to water. There are 8 left to water. How many [plants] has Nick watered already?

   Nick has __12__ more plants to water.

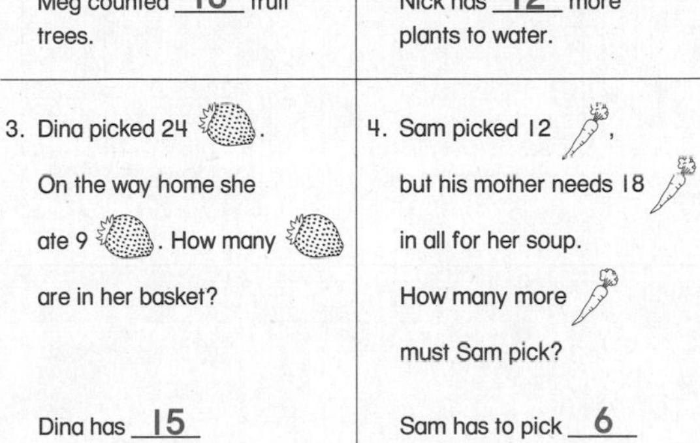

3. Dina picked 24 [strawberries]. On the way home she ate 9 [strawberries]. How many are in her basket?

   Dina has __15__ berries in her basket.

4. Sam picked 12 [carrots], but his mother needs 18 [carrots] in all for her soup. How many more [carrots] must Sam pick?

   Sam has to pick __6__ more carrots.

Using the Page Have children *look back* to check their answers by using a different strategy. **Notes for Home** Your child solved problems by drawing a picture or by using counters and ten frames. *Home Activity:* Ask your child to demonstrate how drawing a picture or using counters and ten frames can help to solve one of the problems.

Use with pages 461–462. **129**

Name ______________________

Relate Addition and Subtraction

Problem Solving 12-7

What signs and numbers are missing?

Write +, −, or = in each ◯.

Write the correct number in each □.

Here's a hint. These numbers are related.

1. 7 (+) [5] = 12 (−) [7] = 5
2. [11] (−) 3 = 8 (+) [3] = 11
3. 3 + 7 (=) [10] (−) 3 (=) 7
4. [11] (−) 7 = 4 (+) [7] = 11
5. 12 (−) 3 (=) 9 (+) 3 (=) 12
6. [9] (−) 4 (=) 5 + [4] = 9
7. 2 (+) [6] = 8 (−) [2] = 6
8. 6 + 7 (=) [13] (−) 6 (=) 7
9. 8 (+) [7] = 15 (−) [8] = 7
10. 10 (+) [0] = 10 (−) [10] = 0

Notes for Home Your child completed related addition and subtraction facts. *Home Activity:* Ask your child how he or she identified the missing signs and numbers.

130 Use with pages 465–466.

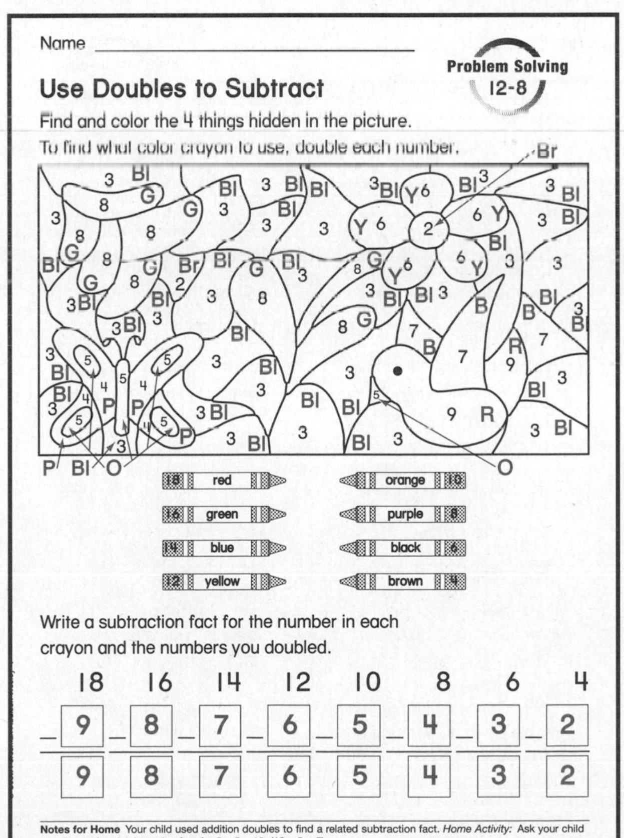

Name ______________________

Use Doubles to Subtract

Problem Solving 12-8

Find and color the 4 things hidden in the picture.

To find what color crayon to use, double each number.

18 red	orange 10
16 green	purple 8
14 blue	black 6
12 yellow	brown 4

Write a subtraction fact for the number in each crayon and the numbers you doubled.

18	16	14	12	10	8	6	4
− 9	− 8	− 7	− 6	− 5	− 4	− 3	− 2
9	8	7	6	5	4	3	2

Notes for Home Your child used addition doubles to find a related subtraction fact. *Home Activity:* Ask your child to write a related subtraction fact for 5 + 5 = 10. (10 − 5 = 5)

Use with pages 467–468. **131**

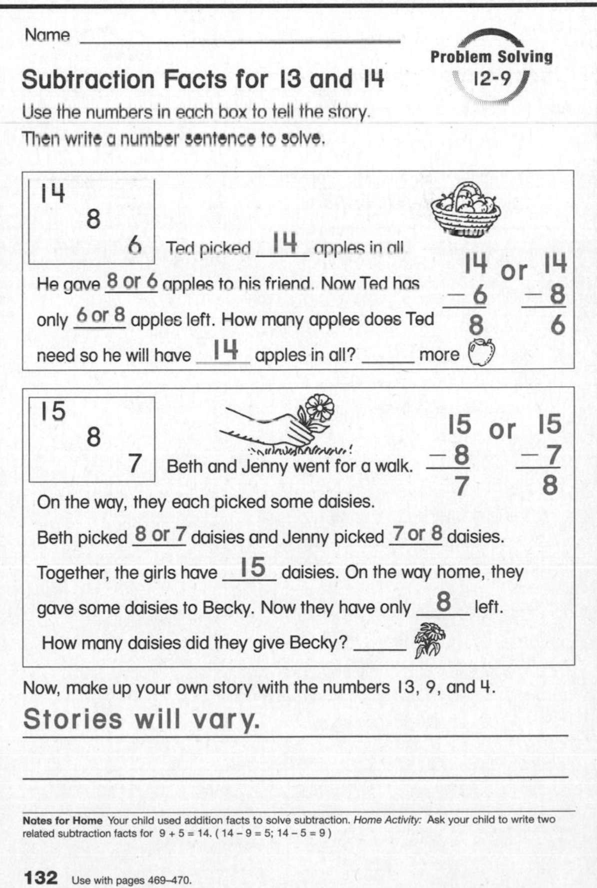

Name ______________________

Subtraction Facts for 13 and 14

Problem Solving 12-9

Use the numbers in each box to tell the story.

Then write a number sentence to solve.

14 8 6

Ted picked __14__ apples in all. He gave __8 or 6__ apples to his friend. Now Ted has only __6 or 8__ apples left. How many apples does Ted need so he will have __14__ apples in all? _____ more

14 − 6 = 8 or 14 − 8 = 6

15 8 7

Beth and Jenny went for a walk. On the way, they each picked some daisies. Beth picked __8 or 7__ daisies and Jenny picked __7 or 8__ daisies. Together, the girls have __15__ daisies. On the way home, they gave some daisies to Becky. Now they have only __8__ left. How many daisies did they give Becky? _____

15 − 8 = 7 or 15 − 7 = 8

Now, make up your own story with the numbers 13, 9, and 4.

Stories will vary.

Notes for Home Your child used addition facts to solve subtraction. *Home Activity:* Ask your child to write two related subtraction facts for 9 + 5 = 14. (14 − 9 = 5; 14 − 5 = 9)

132 Use with pages 469–470.

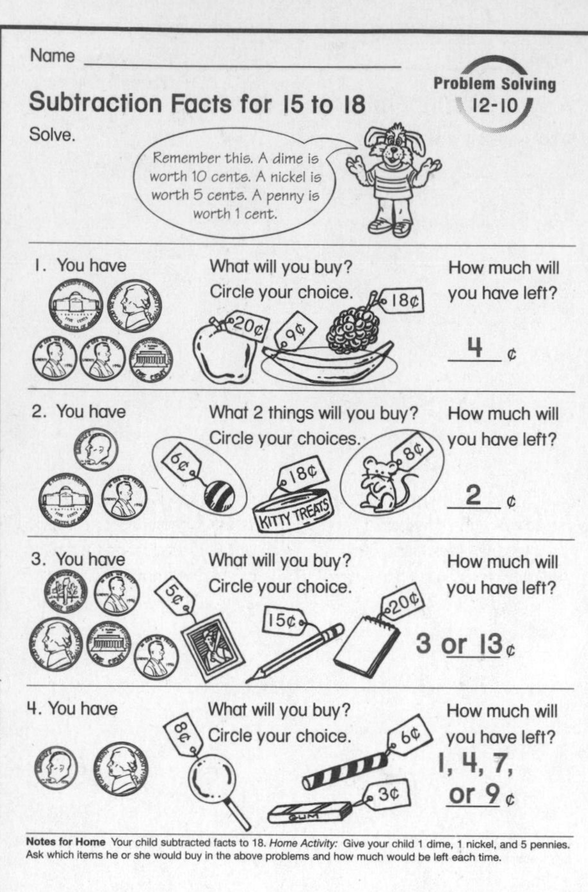
Name ______________________

Problem Solving 12-10

Subtraction Facts for 15 to 18

Solve.

Remember this. A dime is worth 10 cents. A nickel is worth 5 cents. A penny is worth 1 cent.

1. You have — What will you buy? Circle your choice. — How much will you have left? 4 ¢

2. You have — What 2 things will you buy? Circle your choices. — How much will you have left? 2 ¢

3. You have — What will you buy? Circle your choice. — How much will you have left? 3 or 13 ¢

4. You have — What will you buy? Circle your choice. — How much will you have left? 1, 4, 7, or 9 ¢

Notes for Home Your child subtracted facts to 18. *Home Activity:* Give your child 1 dime, 1 nickel, and 5 pennies. Ask which items he or she would buy in the above problems and how much would be left each time.

Use with pages 471–472. **133**

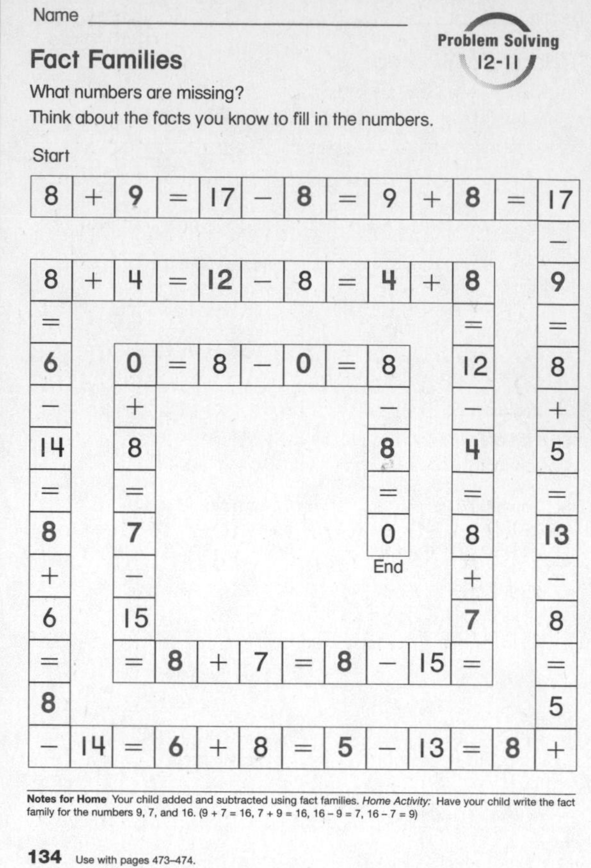
Name ______________________

Problem Solving 12-11

Fact Families

What numbers are missing?

Think about the facts you know to fill in the numbers.

Start

8	+	9	=	17	−	8	=	9	+	8	=	17
												−
8	+	4	=	12	−	8	=	4	+	8		9
=										=		=
6		0	=	8	−	0	=	8		12		8
−		+						−		−		+
14		8						8		4		5
=		=						=		=		=
8		7						0		8		13
+		−						End		+		−
6		15								7		8
=		=	8	+	7	=	8	−	15	=		=
8												5
−	14	=	6	+	8	=	5	−	13	=	8	+

Notes for Home Your child added and subtracted using fact families. *Home Activity:* Have your child write the fact family for the numbers 9, 7, and 16. (9 + 7 = 16, 7 + 9 = 16, 16 − 9 = 7, 16 − 7 = 9)

134 Use with pages 473–474.

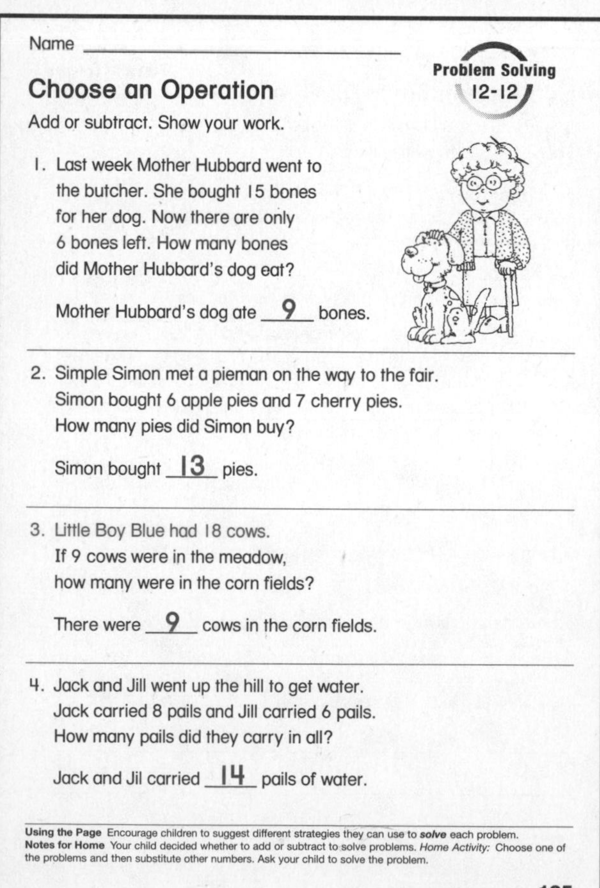
Name ______________________

Problem Solving 12-12

Choose an Operation

Add or subtract. Show your work.

1. Last week Mother Hubbard went to the butcher. She bought 15 bones for her dog. Now there are only 6 bones left. How many bones did Mother Hubbard's dog eat?

   Mother Hubbard's dog ate 9 bones.

2. Simple Simon met a pieman on the way to the fair. Simon bought 6 apple pies and 7 cherry pies. How many pies did Simon buy?

   Simon bought 13 pies.

3. Little Boy Blue had 18 cows. If 9 cows were in the meadow, how many were in the corn fields?

   There were 9 cows in the corn fields.

4. Jack and Jill went up the hill to get water. Jack carried 8 pails and Jill carried 6 pails. How many pails did they carry in all?

   Jack and Jil carried 14 pails of water.

Using the Page Encourage children to suggest different strategies they can use to *solve* each problem.
Notes for Home Your child decided whether to add or subtract to solve problems. *Home Activity:* Choose one of the problems and then substitute other numbers. Ask your child to solve the problem.

Use with pages 477–478. **135**

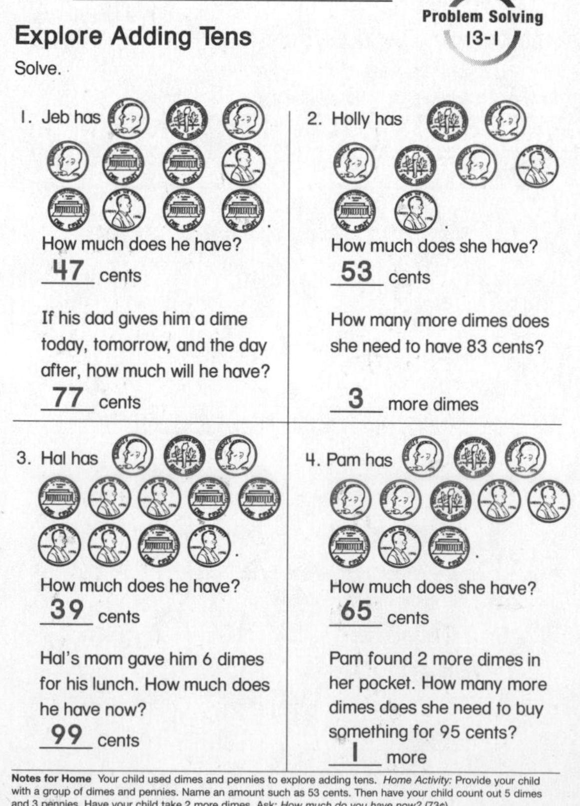
Name ______________________

Problem Solving 13-1

Explore Adding Tens

Solve.

1. Jeb has

   How much does he have? 47 cents

   If his dad gives him a dime today, tomorrow, and the day after, how much will he have? 77 cents

2. Holly has

   How much does she have? 53 cents

   How many more dimes does she need to have 83 cents? 3 more dimes

3. Hal has

   How much does he have? 39 cents

   Hal's mom gave him 6 dimes for his lunch. How much does he have now? 99 cents

4. Pam has

   How much does she have? 65 cents

   Pam found 2 more dimes in her pocket. How many more dimes does she need to buy something for 95 cents? 1 more

Notes for Home Your child used dimes and pennies to explore adding tens. *Home Activity:* Provide your child with a group of dimes and pennies. Name an amount such as 53 cents. Then have your child count out 5 dimes and 3 pennies. Have your child take 2 more dimes. Ask: *How much do you have now?* (73¢)

136 Use with pages 491–492.

Name ____________________

Problem Solving 13-2

Add Tens

1. Here are two ways to make the sum of 60.
   How many more ways can you make a sum of 60?

10	30	20	40	50
+ 50	+ 30	+ 40	+ 20	+ 10
60	60	60	60	60

2. Here are two ways to make the sum of 90.
   How many more ways can you make a sum of 90?

10	20	30	40	50	60	70	80
+ 80	+ 70	+ 60	+ 50	+ 40	+ 30	+ 20	+ 10
90	90	90	90	90	90	90	90

3. Here are two ways to make a sum of 56.
   How many more ways can you make a sum of 56?

16	36	26	46	56
+ 40	+ 20	+ 30	+ 10	+ 0
56	56	56	56	56

4. Here are two ways to make a sum of 71.
   How many more ways can you make the sum of 71?

11	41	21	31	51	61	71
+ 60	+ 30	+ 50	+ 40	+ 20	+ 10	+ 0
71	71	71	71	71	71	71

Notes for Home Your child added tens to two-digit numbers. *Home Activity:* Ask your child to count by tens from [illegible]

Name ____________________

Problem Solving 13-3

Add Tens and Ones

Solve.

1. I am a number between 50 and 65. If you add 3 tens and 2 ones, and 2 tens and 7 ones, you'll find out what I am.

	3	2
+	2	7
	5	9

2. I am an even number. I am less than 68 but greater than 51. Just add 4 tens and 3 ones and 23 to see what I am.

	4	3
+	2	3
	6	6

3. I am an odd number. I am greater than the double of 3 tens but less than 7 tens. Add 5 tens and 3 ones, and 1 ten and 4 ones, to find out what I am.

	5	3
+	1	4
	6	7

4. I am a number between 7 tens and 2 ones, and 9 tens and 9 ones. Just add 2 tens and 5 ones, and 5 tens and 2 ones, to find out what I am.

	2	5
+	5	2
	7	7

Notes for Home Your child solved riddles by adding two-digit numbers. *Home Activity:* Have your child use one [illegible]

Name ____________________

Problem Solving 13-4

Regroup with Addition

What has fifty heads and fifty tails?
To solve this riddle, first write the missing number to solve each problem.

t	e	n	f
79	87	89	29
+ 2	+ 8	+ 1	+ 0
81	95	90	29

p	i	s	i
60	11	56	28
+ 10	+ 11	+ 4	+ 5
70	22	60	33

e	n	f	y
48	56	29	43
+ 3	+ 6	+ 7	+ 9
51	62	36	52

Now write the letter for each problem above its answer.

f	i	f	t	y		p	e	n	n	i	e	s
0	5	7	2	9		10	8	1	6	11	3	4

Notes for Home Your child found the missing addend and used regrouping to solve problems. *Home Activity:* Ask your child to explain how he or she determined the missing numbers.

Name ____________________

Problem Solving 13-5

Use Objects

1. Beth and Jeff played ring toss.
   Beth scored 18 points in Game 1 and 7 points in Game 2.
   Jeff scored 16 points in Game 1 and 8 points in Game 2.
   How many points did Beth score?
   How many points did Jeff score?
   Who had more points?

Step 1

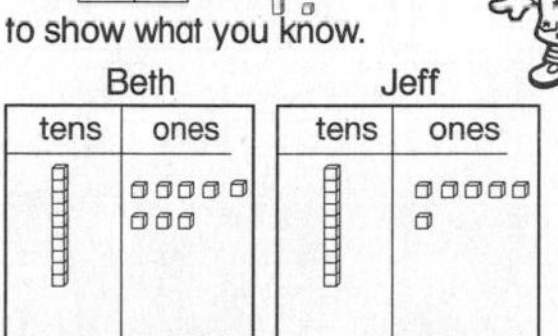

Use [tens/ones mat] and [blocks] to show what you know.

Beth		Jeff	
tens	ones	tens	ones

Step 2

Add to solve. Remember to regroup if there are more than 10 ones.

Beth	Jeff
18	16
+ 7	+ 8
25	24

Beth had more points.

2. Miss Lee asked 50 first graders what they like to do most after school. 15 children like to watch TV. 9 like to skate. 8 like to read. 17 like to play video games.

How many children in all like to watch TV and read?
15 + 8 = 23

How many children like to play video games and skate?
17 + 9 = 26

Using the Page As children read through each problem, help them to ***plan*** by asking how they know whether to add or subtract. **Notes for Home** Your child solved problems involving addition by using objects. *Home Activity:* Ask your child to use pennies or dry beans to demonstrate how he or she solved one of the problems.

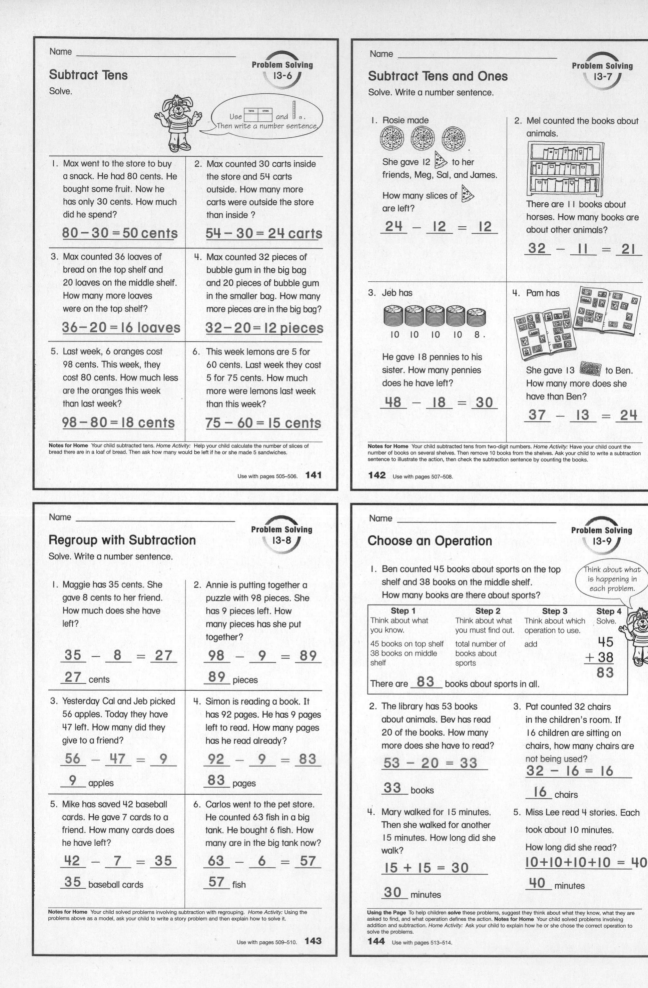

Name ______________________

Use tens ones and .
Then write a number sentence.

Problem Solving 13-6

Subtract Tens

Solve.

1. Max went to the store to buy a snack. He had 80 cents. He bought some fruit. Now he has only 30 cents. How much did he spend?

   80 – 30 = 50 cents

2. Max counted 30 carts inside the store and 54 carts outside. How many more carts were outside the store than inside ?

   54 – 30 = 24 carts

3. Max counted 36 loaves of bread on the top shelf and 20 loaves on the middle shelf. How many more loaves were on the top shelf?

   36 – 20 = 16 loaves

4. Max counted 32 pieces of bubble gum in the big bag and 20 pieces of bubble gum in the smaller bag. How many more pieces are in the big bag?

   32 – 20 = 12 pieces

5. Last week, 6 oranges cost 98 cents. This week, they cost 80 cents. How much less are the oranges this week than last week?

   98 – 80 = 18 cents

6. This week lemons are 5 for 60 cents. Last week they cost 5 for 75 cents. How much more were lemons last week than this week?

   75 – 60 = 15 cents

Notes for Home Your child subtracted tens. *Home Activity:* Help your child calculate the number of slices of bread there are in a loaf of bread. Then ask how many would be left if he or she made 5 sandwiches.

Name ______________________

Problem Solving 13-7

Subtract Tens and Ones

Solve. Write a number sentence.

1. Rosie made

   She gave 12 to her friends, Meg, Sal, and James.

   How many slices of are left?

   24 – 12 = 12

2. Mel counted the books about animals.

   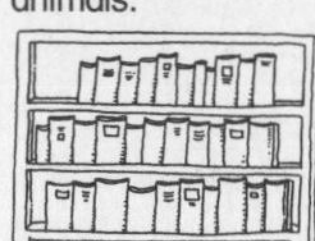

   There are 11 books about horses. How many books are about other animals?

   32 – 11 = 21

3. Jeb has

   10 10 10 10 8.

   He gave 18 pennies to his sister. How many pennies does he have left?

   48 – 18 = 30

4. Pam has

   She gave 13 to Ben. How many more does she have than Ben?

   37 – 13 = 24

Notes for Home Your child subtracted tens from two-digit numbers. *Home Activity:* Have your child count the number of books on several shelves. Then remove 10 books from the shelves. Ask your child to write a subtraction sentence to illustrate the action, then check the subtraction sentence by counting the books.

Name ______________________

Problem Solving 13-8

Regroup with Subtraction

Solve. Write a number sentence.

1. Maggie has 35 cents. She gave 8 cents to her friend. How much does she have left?

   35 – 8 = 27

   27 cents

2. Annie is putting together a puzzle with 98 pieces. She has 9 pieces left. How many pieces has she put together?

   98 – 9 = 89

   89 pieces

3. Yesterday Cal and Jeb picked 56 apples. Today they have 47 left. How many did they give to a friend?

   56 – 47 = 9

   9 apples

4. Simon is reading a book. It has 92 pages. He has 9 pages left to read. How many pages has he read already?

   92 – 9 = 83

   83 pages

5. Mike has saved 42 baseball cards. He gave 7 cards to a friend. How many cards does he have left?

   42 – 7 = 35

   35 baseball cards

6. Carlos went to the pet store. He counted 63 fish in a big tank. He bought 6 fish. How many are in the big tank now?

   63 – 6 = 57

   57 fish

Notes for Home Your child solved problems involving subtraction with regrouping. *Home Activity:* Using the problems above as a model, ask your child to write a story problem and then explain how to solve it.

Name ______________________

Problem Solving 13-9

Choose an Operation

Think about what is happening in each problem.

1. Ben counted 45 books about sports on the top shelf and 38 books on the middle shelf. How many books are there about sports?

Step 1 Think about what you know.	Step 2 Think about what you must find out.	Step 3 Think about which operation to use.	Step 4 Solve.
45 books on top shelf 38 books on middle shelf	total number of books about sports	add	45 + 38 83

There are 83 books about sports in all.

2. The library has 53 books about animals. Bev has read 20 of the books. How many more does she have to read?

   53 – 20 = 33

   33 books

3. Pat counted 32 chairs in the children's room. If 16 children are sitting on chairs, how many chairs are not being used?

   32 – 16 = 16

   16 chairs

4. Mary walked for 15 minutes. Then she walked for another 15 minutes. How long did she walk?

   15 + 15 = 30

   30 minutes

5. Miss Lee read 4 stories. Each took about 10 minutes. How long did she read?

   10+10+10+10 = 40

   40 minutes

Using the Page To help children *solve* these problems, suggest they think about what they know, what they are asked to find, and what operation defines the action. **Notes for Home** Your child solved problems involving addition and subtraction. *Home Activity:* Ask your child to explain how he or she chose the correct operation to solve the problems.